CONTRACTUAL EMPLOYMENT IN INDIAN LABOUR MARKET

About The Editors

N.M.P. Verma is a Professor of Economics at Babasaheb Bhimrao Ambedkar University, Lucknow. He specialises as a development economist with the focus on labour, marginalised groups and environment. He has authored many books and extensively contributed papers in professional journals of national and international repute. He has discharged administrative duties as the Head, Department of Economics, Dean, School for Ambedkar Studies, Dean of Students' Welfare, and also officiated as Registrar and Vice Chancellor of the University. He is also the recipient of "Rajiv Gandhi Excellence Award", 'Bharat Jyoti' Award and 'Best Citizens of India' Award.

I.C. Awasthi, a Ph.D from the Jawaharlal Nehru University, is presently a senior faculty at the Institute of Applied Manpower Research, Delhi. He received specialised training on manpower planning from the Institute of Employment Studies, University of Sussex, United Kingdom. His areas of specialisation are labour, employment, decentralised planning and human resource development. He has contributed over three dozen papers in professional journals and co-authored two books and three edited volumes. He is also an alumnus of Indian Institute of Management, Ahmedabad.

CONTRACTUAL EMPLOYMENT in INDIAN LABOUR MARKET

Emergence and Expansion

Edited by
N.M.P. Verma
I.C. Awasthi

CONCEPT PUBLISHING COMPANY, PVT. LTD.,
NEW DELHI-110059

ISBN : 13-978-81-8069-698-5

First Published 2010

Published and Printed by

Concept Publishing Company Pvt. Ltd.
Regd. Office:
A/15-16, Commercial Block, Mohan Garden
New Delhi-110059 (India)
Phones : 25351460, 25351794, *Fax* : 091-11-25357109
Email : publishing@conceptpub.com,
Website: www.conceptpub.com

Editorial Office:
H-13, Bali Nagar, New Delhi-110 015, India.

Cataloging in Publication Data-- *Courtesy:* D.K. Agencies (P) Ltd. <docinfo@dkagencies.com>

National Seminar on "Emerging Patterns of Contractual Employment" (2008 : Lucknow, India)
Contractual employment in Indian labour market : emergence and expansion / edited by N.M.P. Verma, I.C. Awasthi.
p. cm.
Papers presented at the National Seminar on "Emerging Patterns of Contractual Employment", held at Lucknow during 28-29 February 2008.
Includes bibliographical references.
Includes index.
ISBN 13: 9788180696985
ISBN 10: 8180696987

1. Contract labor--India--Congresses. 2. Contract labor--India--Regional disparities-Congresses. 3. Labor contract--India--Congresses. I. Verma, N. M. P. (Neel Mani Prasad), 1959- II. Awasthi, I. C. (Ishwar Chandra), 1955- III. Title.

DDC 331.5420954 22

Dedicated

to

the Fond Memory of

Late Professor Ashok Mathur

PREFACE

It is well known that employment has been a central issue of development planning that has profound implications on the well-being of the people. This is more so in a globalised regime where nature, pattern and form of employment are changing very fast primarily due to close links across countries.

Growth is indeed an important aspect without which resources cannot be generated for investment, but growth has to be inclusive with shared benefits. In order to ensure that growth be broad-based and inclusive, there is a need to implement effective public policies and strategies that bring more people into mainstream, promote an increased participation of poor men and women in economic decision-making, reduce poverty and disparities, and enhance equitable access to benefits of growth. It is now increasingly realised that development goals need to be expressed in explicit and real terms so that the fruits of development are widely shared. This ought to be an important policy objective, and rightly so where a large segment of population is marginalised, and socially and economically excluded. Where social security is an integral part of the governance, it becomes an effective strategy in carrying out both protective and promotional security measures. It would, therefore, be imperative to empower them through a protective social security. Indeed, the provision of employment is the most powerful instrument to provide social security to the people of any country.

It is well known that the quality of employment in the informal sector is poor with low level of wages and precarious working conditions. It is important from the policy point of view to make the employment productive through specific interventions that could help develop more dynamic and better protected informal sector and its progressive integration into society. This calls for an improvement in the productive capacity through advanced training and modern technology, and establishing a proper regulatory framework with appropriate forms of protection and regulation.

It has been observed that forms of employment are changing fast and contractorisation of employment is emerging in various segments of economy, which is largely unprotective with abysmally low wages and precarious working and living conditions. A large part of such employment is occurring in the unorganised or informal sector.

Regularly paid employment is generally considered secure, and self-employment as fairly secure, even though incomes from certain types of self-employment activities might be highly irregular, inadequate and even uncertain. But for typical casual workers, neither the duration of employment nor the income is certain.

There are many issues involved in the forms or status of employment, and it has been observed that contractorisation of employment needs to be construed in the wider framework of labour market.

Presently, Indian labour market is facing three major challenges:

(i) Growing unemployment among skilled and unskilled youth

(ii) Mass labour migration from rural to urban area and undeveloped to developed area – nationally and internationally

(iii) Frequent job changes especially because of liberalisation, privatisation and globalisation (LPG), i.e. liberal economic reform, privatisation and disinvestments in public sector units (PSUs), and better opportunities available globally especially in multinational corporations (MNCs)

Because of the above three reasons there have been sudden changes in the mode of recruitments and labour placement.

Labour market segmentation is increasingly discernible in Indian and International labour markets. In the organised sector wage is high, work environment is better, flexible wage components exist and promotional opportunities are always available. The second type of labour market is one, which is still based on conventional engagements through two types of contractors and labour suppliers. One is through licensed contractors and the other through non-licensed contractors. This is largely observed in traditional sectors and real estate, domestic and international migration of illiterates and semi-literates. In this sector, wage is lower and is not paid in accordance with the labour input involved. Labour broker takes advantage of illiteracy and lack of job opportunities in such labour market that is highly discriminatory and exploitative in nature.

Thus, identification of a contractual labour market as a distinct analytical category is somewhat difficult owing to conceptual ambiguities, though it is pervasive in the labour market. There is also a lack of secondary data-based studies for developing a framework for comprehending this segment. Of course, some case studies are available, but they can hardly help either in policy formulation or understanding the complexities and diversities of labour market owing to limited scope and small sample sizes.

Since early 1980s, large parts of the world have undergone a process of economic restructuring, commonly called as economic liberalisation and economic reforms. The key elements associated with this process happen to be a stabilisation and structural adjustment programme (SAP). Actually, stabilisation stands for a sharp reduction, preferably, elimination of a government fiscal deficit and the SAP advocates a wholesale privatisation and rapid marketisation of an economy. Thus, the main agenda of economic liberalisation has been (a) to facilitate a free play of the market forces in different product and factor markets including financial markets, both within a country and internationally; and (b) drastic reduction in the economic functions of the state, not only as a producer and promoter but also as a regulator.

In the first couple of years of the so-called New Economic Policy, 1991 (NEP), there was substantial liberalisation of the government control ranging from the delicensing of investment and production, to removal of export subsidies and financial liberalisation measures – for both residents and external investors. However, it seems eminently clear that the period of NEP in India has brought several changes in economic structure. The structure of workforce is affected. The growth of workforce has increased in all sectors. There is significant increase in employment in the private sector rather than the government sector. But, the nature of employment has changed. The regular salaried workforce has fallen 13.8 to 13 per cent during the last decade. Self-employed workforce has also fallen, but casualisation of labour has increased. The casual or contractual wage workforce has increased from 28.6 to 32.4 per cent in the same period. The rise in the number of casual labourers is mainly due to the fact that most of the government and private organisations are indulging in the practice of appointing contractual workers rather than permanent salaried workers.

At present, contractual labour is becoming an increasingly prominent feature of the labour market in India. A large portion of the workforce is engaged in a typical work and is spending long hours on poorly-paid activities. There is no scope for bargaining for a reasonable wage. The labourers have neither any job security nor income security. They are working at the mercy of the employer who is often a labour broker.

Contractual workers are constituents of the informal labour force as the terms and conditions of employment are outside the purview of any regulatory body. The casual labourers get lower wages and face less satisfying work conditions than their co-workers engaged in regular jobs. The representation of casual labour is high, but they have limited access to education and training and other facilities. They are also unable to claim any accident or injury allowances. Particularly, migrant casual workers are more vulnerable. The contractual labourers do not have the protection of labour legislations, wage levels and social welfare. Moreover, a large portion of them confront with the problems of unemployment and underemployment, and resultant poverty in all the States in India. Further, the issue of contractualisation becomes important in the context of the ongoing process of liberalisation of the Indian economy, which has an inherent tendency towards greater casualisation also. Hence, there is a need to understand the trends and various dimensions of contractual labour in the context of liberalised market regime.

Some of the issues identified for discussion in the National Seminar on "Emerging Patterns of Contractual Employment in Indian Labour Market" held on February 28-29, 2008 were as follows:

(1) To deliberate on the conceptualisation of contractual employment;

(2) To discuss the problems and consequences of contractual labour relating to wage, industrial relations and other aspects;

(3) To discuss the existing legal safety measures as well as required socio-economic changes for contractual labour; and

(4) To recommend necessary changes as an aid towards policy.

Often casualisation is also considered as a short-term contractual employment in the labour market. Casual workers are defined as those who work on others' farm and non-farm, and government and private organisations and paid wages on daily or periodic basis. Casual workers include those who appear to be long-term workers of an employer but are bound by a daily or periodic renewal of the contract work. The National Sample Survey (NSS) classifies the casual wage labour into two types – in public works and in other types of work.

The rate of growth in casual employment has witnessed a varying degree of increase in all sectors in the post-reforms period. In trade, storage, communication, finance, insurance, real estate, construction and community & social and educational & personal services, the growth of casual labour has increased since the inception of new economic policy. The incidence of casualisation is likely to intensify in the future, as after the initiation of free market economy, multinational companies have come up which have higher capital intensity and low potential for employment generation. Most of the organisations are employing labour on the basis of contract or casual daily wage. Therefore, industrially developed States like Karnataka, Maharashtra, Andhra Pradesh and Tamil Nadu, which received a major share of direct foreign investment, have been witnessing a higher rate of growth in contractual-cum-casual employment.

The increased use of contractual workers has adverse effects on both workers themselves and the society. Hence, the problem of contractual employment is to be carefully studied in the context of direction and magnitude of the changes in wages for different occupations and activities as well as the working condition and satisfaction or the level of the utilization of skills of the workers. Thus, it is worthwhile to discuss the following emerging issues relating to contractual labour market:

(1) Conceptualisation;

(2) Various trends and dimensions;

(3) Regional and socio-economic deprivations and discrimination;

(4) Wage pattern in different sectors and sub-sectors;

(5) Social security – promotional and protective measures;

(6) Recent changes in industrial/organisational relations;

(7) Gender dimension of contractual labour market; and

(8) Indian contractual labour market, migration and global competition.

The above issues have been discussed in six technical sessions in two days. More than 40 papers were presented followed by discussions and observations made by the respective technical-session chairpersons and co-chairpersons. About 100 participants attended the seminar and actively participated in the discussions. Participants of the seminar were drawn from diverse fields including leading experts from educational institutions, policy makers, non-government organisations (NGOs), representatives from the industry, trade unions and implementation agencies. The outcome of these deliberations is expected to aid the policy that has wider ramification to the labour market in the context of emerging labour market scenario. The collection of this volume is expected to substantiate the existing knowledge-base, and the policy recommendations thereof would be of immense value for academics, planners and policy makers.

This volume consists of twenty-five chapters presented in the National Seminar and broadly grouped into four themes covering some of the important aspects of the contract labour in the emerging labour market situations. The four themes under which various chapters have been grouped are: (I) Contract Labour: Conceptual Issues, (II) Contract Labour in the Emerging Labour Market, (III) Social Security in the Contract Labour Market; and (IV) Diversities in Contract Labour: Regional Perspective.

Under the first theme, five chapters deal with different aspects of conceptual issues of contract labour. The chapter by P. K. Chaubey "Contractual Employment in Formal Sector : Concepts and Contemporary Structure in India" argues that except engagement for one's own pleasure and self-employment, all employment is contractual and more so voluntary one, which is the characteristics of the modern system – capitalistic or socialistic – because it is the labour power of a person which is sold in such systems. The labour under slavery, serfdom and indenture systems may perhaps be not rated as employment, but they were sort of contracts in a sense, as slaves, serfs and indentured persons were human beings. But, the contract was neither voluntary in legal terms nor for a specific set of duties in the case of slavery, nor were they paid in a regular manner; though they were treated as a little better or worse than cattle.

N. M. P. Verma's paper "Conceptualisation of Indian Labour Market" describes the contractual employment that traces its link to economic history during the British regime. It was controlled through labour brokers popularly called as muqaddams. The argument that the institution of contractors could become costly for the employer, especially because, it could potentially compromise skills, training, quality, and incentives, faces objections from both economic theory and economic history and, therefore, needs to be qualified and contextualised. He discusses the issues such as quality concern, contemporary perspectives, comparative cost, unfair competition, labour regime, workers' unions, fixed wage factor, efficiency agenda, etc.

A. B. Deogirikar and Yugandhara S. Topare in their chapter "Conceptualisation of Contract Labour" argue that contractual labour acquired prominence due to cost minimising attempt by companies. By highlighting different perceptions on the theme, they discuss legal aspects of contractual labour. They suggest that contractual labour should be slowly discouraged and direct employment should be encouraged.

Prasoon Kumar Roy and Meera Kumari in their chapter "The Gloomy Picture of Contract Labour in India" analyse and assess the contract labour in India. The chapter has been divided into six sections. Section I analyses the factors influencing the emergence of contract labour. Section II discusses the concept of contract labour. Section III highlights the relevance of the contract labour. Section IV explains the oppositions of the concept. Section V discusses the regulations made regarding contract labour in India. Section VI analyses the suggestions to make contract labour more lucrative for labourers.

J. V. Vaishampayan and Nagendra Kumar Maurya in their paper "Evaluation of Contract Labour Employment in India" describe that in the changing structure of employment, contract labour is emerging as a potential system for employment generation. While economic factors such as cost-effectiveness and flexibility may justify the system of contract labour, considerations of protection of labourer and prevention of exploitation of labourer call for its proper regulation. This chapter seeks an evaluation of contract labour system in India and its future prospects.

There are five chapters in the second theme that covers broad contours of contract labour in the emerging labour market.

Ashok Mathur's chapter "The Status and Prospects of Contract Labour in the Era of Economic Reforms", depicts the distinctive characteristics of contract labourers which sets it apart from those in regular employment is that, in their case the principal employer for whom contract labourers work is different from the person or the agency which engages them as contract labourers. Contract labourers are by and large non-unionised, which makes it difficult for them to act as a pressure group and reduces their bargaining strength. Thus, from a producer's point of view, contract labour system provides him certain advantages that save his costs. Although from labourer's point of view, it is exploitative. There are the advantages conferred by the system to the producer, which led to its evolution in the early phases of industrialisation in India, initially in the form of jobbers employed by English technicians who were not conversant with the lingua franca.

C. S. Verma's chapter on "Contractual Labour Market in the Era of Globalisation" points to the corporate and public policy nexus in undermining the profitable public sector industries. By taking case studies and empirical studies from IDPL and contractual farming, he demonstrates that labour conditions are worsening because of globalisation.

L. S. Singh's chapter on "Earning Patterns of Contractual Employment in Indian Labour Market" discusses that in the post-liberation period, the Indian industry is more opened to global competition despite no significant changes brought in the labour laws. However, the general weakening of bargaining powers of the workers coupled with relaxed enforcement of mechanism and increased use of informal labour in the form of contract labour is making the degree of casualisation and feminisation of workforce more vulnerable. The regulatory provisions of the contract labour are diluted in practice and non–unionised employment with more labour flexibility norms are being witnessed in the organised sector of the economy.

Rashmi Tripathi's chapter on "Emerging Pattern of Contractual Employment in Indian Labour Market" describes that recently the organisations are struggling with staffing challenges aroused from the increased knowledge work, labour market shortages, increasing competition for applicants and workforce diversity, technological developments, applicants' perceptions of selection procedures, and construct-driven approaches. Solving these challenges requires the staffing scholars to expand their focus from individual-level recruitment, and selection research to multi-level research demonstrating the business unit/organisational level impact of staffing.

Vinod Kumar Srivastava's chapter on "Indian Contractual Labour Market, Migration and Global Competition" focuses on the reasons for migration and its social implications. He concludes that migrants are insecure and needs serious attention of the government.

The third theme "Social Security in the Contract Labour Market" discusses some of the broad issues of social security in the unorganized sector and recent initiatives undertaken by the government through a Bill introduced in the Parliament. This section also critically examines various social security measures for contract labour.

Rajesh Kumar's chapter on "Social Security on Contractual Workers" raises concern regarding the lack of social security provisions for contractual workers. He compares and contrasts the regular and contractual workers and emphasise that there is a major difference between the two. While the former enjoys multiple benefits for being regular, the latter suffers multiple depreciations. The chapter deals with several other aspects such as the Social Security Bill-2007, and the impact of globalisation on the same. He appreciates the role played by Employees' State Insurance (ESI) for social security. He wants the benefits to be enjoyed by the workers.

Preeti Mishra and Pradeep Kumar Pandey in their chapter "The Contract Labour (Regulation and Abolition) Act, 1970 : A Critical Evaluation" reveal that by taking advantage of labourers' poverty, illiteracy, ignorance and helplessness, the contractors offer standard form of contract to the labourers with unreasonable terms and conditions. In contractual labour system, the employer is in the most gainful position as they are under no obligation regarding the worker's bonus, provident fund, housing facilities and leave with wages, etc. The chapter looks into the provisions of the Act and critically examines whether Contract Labour (Regulation and Abolition) Act, 1970 has been successful in achieving its objectives.

I.C. Awasthi and A.P. William Wordsworth examines "The Unorganised Sector Workers' Social Security Bill, 2007: Implementation Challenges", which has been tabled in the parliament for ratification. This Bill is indeed a landmark towards empowering the unorganised labour, however, it poses enormous implementation challenges. The authors raise certain conceptual issues of social security that need to be understood in a wider framework rather than through a piecemeal approach.

Shakti Kumar's chapter on "Magnitude and Constitutional Protection of Informal Contract Child Labour in India" starts with the economic and social problems associated with the child labour in India. The chapter discusses the multiple factors responsible for rapid increase in child labour in the context of industrial society. It suggests certain measures such as population control, increase in income of household, rigorous implementation of programmes to curb child labour etc.

P. K. Sinha and Rashi Krishna Sinha describe in their chapter "Child Labour and Development Paradigm in India" the constitutional safeguards provided for the protection of child rights, and how these are important for the eradication of child labour in India. They link the growth of child labour with poverty, and demonstrated the connection between them. They suggest certain measures to deal with the problem of child labour in India.

The fourth section deals with the diversities of contract labour in the regional perspective, which captures some of the regional diversities and helps in understanding the region and sector-specific complexities and nuances.

V. M. Ravi Kumar's chapter on "Contractual Labour and Deprivation of Tribal Rights: An Assessment of Community Forest Management in Visakhapatnam District of Andhra Pradesh" conceptualises the contractual labour in community development programmes and brought about the different dynamics of it. Further, he projects the problems associated with the contractual labour in the context of absence of adequate safeguards. He suggests certain safety mechanisms for contractual labourers in participatory forest management.

Bhaskar Majumdar's chapter on "Wage Employment Pattern of Contractual Labours in UP's Rural Economy: Some Facts and Possibilities" demonstrates the problems associated with the implementation of the 'food for work programme' and suggests certain measures such as increase in the role of state in providing social security, creation of vocational training institutes and various other measures.

D. M. Diwakar's chapter on "Dimensions of Interlocking Labour Market in Backward Indian Agriculture" links contractual labour with agriculture, and argued that the present paradigm of contractual labour is basically exploitative. He suggests new paradigm to understand the problem and to make policy on contractual labour.

Alok Chantia's chapter on "Various Trends and Dimensions of Contractual Labour with Special Reference to Teaching on Contractual Basis in Uttar Pradesh" refers empirical evidences. He has widely studied this problem from the perspective of stress and psychology. He also says that the wage of the contractual teacher goes against the basic human rights of teachers. The study being a theoretical one opens many issues of teaching in higher education sector for further probe.

S. S. A. Jafri's chapter on "Chikan Craft as a Subsistence Occupation in Lucknow" brings out historical, economic and sociological dimension of chikan production in Lucknow. He shows the exploitation of *dalits* and women in the chikan production and urges for government intervention in the form of loan and other financial help for the workers.

Nirankar Srivastav's chapter on "Patterns of Emerging Labour Force and Growing Unemployment in North-East India: Some Issues" states with statistical corroboration that the nature of unemployment in North-Eastern India is different from the rest of the country. He puts forward that the growth in educational opportunities/education attainments are directly proportional to unemployment. According to him, youth unemployment is more in Assam and Tripura. He advocates job-oriented economic growth and opening of trade links with neighbouring countries.

Ashutosh N. Sinha in his chapter on "Contractual Employment in Indian Labour Market : A Study of Faizabad District" describes that in the present era of liberalisation and globalisation, firms are desperately trying to cut production costs so as to face competition from other domestic and foreign firms; and in the process substituting contract workers for regular workers. This has increased the woes of the contract workforce in India. However, the problems faced by the contract workers at a backward place are a little different. The employers are finding the provisions of the existing law too stringent for pursuing their business activities, but the labour unions hold the opposite view.

Sunit Kumar's chapter on "Effect of Outsourcing on Manpower Requirements" observes that the Indian call centre sector has been experiencing an unprecedented growth in the past few years. It is an industry which has been at the forefront of global attention. It has raised more debates and outcry than any other industry. It is an industry that has been on democrat candidate John Kerry's agenda in his presidential campaign in the last US Presidential election.

Mukul Srivastava's chapter on "Trends in Banking Industry in India" tries to study the trends in the growth of banking sector in India, especially related to employment issues, effect of increased business on the productivity, business per employee, challenges the industry has to face, and training and human resource development required to face the upcoming challenges.

Shalini Tiwari and Ankita Gupta in their chapter on "Women Empowerment and its Reflection on Society" attempts to deal with the socio-economic aspects of women empowerment. Women empowerment has several dimensions – the process involves both social and economic forces, and political will-power.

We are immensely grateful to the Planning Commission, ICSSR, New Delhi for their financial support in organising the National Seminar. We also take the opportunity to place in records our sincere thanks to the contributors for submitting the full-length papers for publication. Thanks are also due to Ms. Pratibha Raj and Miss Madhu Patel for extending their assistance during the compilation and editing of papers.

We are grateful to Shri Ashok K. Mittal of Concept Publishing Company Pvt. Ltd., for taking personal interest in bringing out this volume in a record time.

However, the onus of all the omissions and errors lies with us.

New Delhi
June, 2009

N.M.P. Verma
I.C. Awasthi

THE CONTRIBUTORS

A. B. Deogirikar, Professor, Department of Economics, Dr. B.A. M. University, Aurangabad (M.S).

Alok Chantia, Lecturer, Department of Anthropology, Sri J.N.P.G. (K.K.C.) College, Lucknow (U.P.).

Ankita Gupta, Lecturer, Department of Economics, M.G.Kashi Vidyapith, Varanasi (U. P.).

Ashok Mathur, Distinguished Professor, Centre for Study of Regional Development, Jawaharlal Nehru University and Visiting Professor, Institute of Human Development, New Delhi.

Ashutosh N. Sinha, Reader, Department of Economics & Rural Development, Dr. R.M.L. Avadh University, Faizabad (U. P.).

A.P. William Wordsworth, Faculty, Institute of Applied Manpower Research, Delhi.

Bhaskar Majumder, G.B. Pant Social Science Institute, Allahabad (U. P.).

C.S. Verma, Reader, Department of Economics, M.B.P. Government Degree College, Lucknow, (U.P.).

D.M. Diwakar, Professor of Economics, Giri Institute of Development Studies, Lucknow (U.P.).

I.C. Awasthi, Senior Faculty, Institute of Applied Manpower Research, Delhi.

J.V. Vaishampayan, Professor, Department of Applied Economics, University of Lucknow, Lucknow (U.P.).

L.S. Singh, Department of Economics, Magadh University, Bodh Gaya (Bihar).

Meera Kumari, Reader, L. N. T. College, B. R. A. Bihar University, Muzaffarpur (Bihar).

Mukul Srivastava, Economist, United Commercial Bank, Kolkata (W.B.).

Nagendra Kumar Maurya, Junior Research Fellow, Department of Applied Economics, University of Lucknow, Lucknow (U. P.).

N.M.P. Verma, Professor and Head, Department of Economics and Dean, School for Ambedkar Studies, Babasaheb Bhimrao Ambedkar University, Lucknow (U. P.).

Nirankar Srivastav, North-Eastern Hill University, Shillong (Meghalaya).

P.K. Chaubey, Professor of Economics, Indian Institute of Public Administration, New Delhi.

P. K. Sinha, Professor of Economics, Dr. R.M.L. Avadh University, Faizabad (U.P.).

Pradeep Kumar Pandey, Research Scholar, Department of Human Rights, School for Legal Studies, Babasaheb Bhimrao Ambedkar University, Lucknow (U.P.).

Prasoon Kumar Roy, Professor, Department of Economics, B. R. A. Bihar University, Muzaffarpur (Bihar).

Preeti Misra, Senior Lecturer, Department of Human Rights, School for Legal Studies, Babasaheb Bhimrao Ambedkar University, Lucknow (U. P.).

Rajesh Kumar, Deputy Director, ESI Corporation, Jawaharlal Nehru Marg, Patna (Bihar).

Rashi Krishna Sinha, Research Officer, Ambedkar Chair, Department of Economics & Rural Development, Dr. R.M.L. Avadh University, Faizabad (U.P.).

Rashmi Tripathi, AZAD Institute of Engineering and Technology, Lucknow (U.P.).

S.S.A. Jafri, Professor, Giri Institute of Development Studies, Lucknow (U. P.).

Shakti Kumar, Senior Lecturer, Department of Economics and Rural Development, Dr. R.M.L. Avadh University, Faizabad (U.P.).

Shalini Tiwari, Research Scholar, Department of Economics, University of Allahabad, Allahabad (U.P.).

Sunit Kumar, Research Scholar, Lucknow University, Lucknow (U.P.).

V. M. Ravi Kumar, Lecturer, Babasaheb Bhimrao Ambedkar University, Lucknow (U.P.).

Vinod Kumar Srivastava, Senior Lecturer, Department of Economics and Rural Development, Dr. R.M.L. Avadh University, Faizabad (U.P.).

Yugandhara S. Topare, Lecturer, Department of Economics, Government College of Arts & Science, Aurangabad (M.S).

CONTENTS

PART–III
SOCIAL SECURITY IN THE CONTRACT LABOUR MARKET

PART–IV
DIVERSITIES IN CONTRACT LABOUR : REGIONAL PERSPECTIVE

PART - I

Contractual Labour

Conceptual Issues

1

CONTRACTUAL EMPLOYMENT IN FORMAL SECTOR

Concepts and Contemporary Structure in India

P.K. CHAUBEY

INTRODUCTION

In this chapter, I propose to deal with two separate but interconnected aspects of contractual employment in modern times. I wish to differentiate in this piece between contractual employment, which is employment of a natural person under a legal person—often an organization, and contractual labour, which has assumed a particular meaning—a legal connotation—so far as India is concerned. I transit to discuss the emerging pattern of employment in Indian labour market, with particular reference to formal sector though boundary between formal and informal is somewhat blurring in the times of what has come to be known as outsourcing. I deal with chief characteristics of different segments within the formal sector and the tendencies of movement across segments within the formal sector.

I have avoided historical anecdotes from discussion, which at times, through prism of helplessness of labourers in difficult times, suggest superiority of pre-capitalist non-wage unfree labour in preference to capitalist free wage labour. I have also avoided reference to the idea of serfdom under socialist regime of the erstwhile USSR, where it is understood, it survived till mid-seventies of the past century.

I have taken advantage of the observations made by friend-scholars after the presentation of this chapter in the seminar. While I have discussed the issues, which is more important matter, I have avoided mentioning particular names for the fear of being controverted.

This chapter is divided in six sections. The first section dwells on some of the definitional issues about employment, systems of employments, contract, and employment as a contract. The second section discusses types of employment—major and minor and contractual labour and the way it is metamorphosing. After defining terms like employer, employee, hierarchy and their stakes in risk bearing in Section 3, employment relationship is delineated in Section 4 in terms of levels from worker to manager. Section 5 is about the present day labour market in formal sector, particular chief contrasting characteristics of the wage structure two segments known as private and public sectors and the kind of tendencies they generate in the movement in labour market from one segment to the other within and between generations. The concluding section points towards the implications of globalization through improvement in the growth rate of the economy and increase in foreign investment through multinational corporations. There is need to recognize these facts so that certain sectors, sections and services do not suffer for want of new talent.

I. DEFINITIONAL SQUIBS

Employment

If one starts with saying that all employment is contractual employment, one may not be far away from the fact. Except one's engagement for one's own pleasure and working for one's kith and kin, which prevails in the phase of community production, and self-employment, which may obtain in the phase of commodity production, all employment is contractual. Here we are assuming that we are talking of systems in which labour enjoys freedom from any kind of bondage and chooses his occupation voluntarily, which is a chief characteristic of the modern system, capitalistic or socialistic, because it is labour power of the person which is sold in such systems.

Systems of Employment

Employment of a natural person can be broadly divided between two systems : one under coercion and the other under freedom. Labour under slavery, serfdom and indenture systems may perhaps not be rated as employment but they were sort of contract in a sense as slaves, serfs and indentured persons were all human beings but contract was neither voluntary in legal terms nor was it for a specific set of duties— particularly in the case of slavery, nor were they paid in any regular manner. Though, some scholars maintain that the slaves were maintained a little better, not worse, than the cattle as both were properties owned by the master and could be sold. Conscription is also a system of coercion though it was sought by modern states to deal with war situations and still it is on the statues of some countries.

Contracts

A contract needs two parties. Any transaction between any two parties is a contract, a legal binding, an exchange of promises, legally enforceable. Be it a sale-purchase transaction, whether of goods, services, financial papers or IPRs; be it a borrowing-lending transaction involving a variety of debt instruments detailing rate of interest, mode of servicing, and termination before or extension beyond the period; or be it that of employment of human agents with elaborate terms and conditions. Mortgage, lease and release are all contractual transactions, creating usufruct or proprietary rights. These are instances of economic variety. But one can extend it to social phenomena, like marriage, with ease.

A contract is usually seen as concurrence of wills or meeting of minds and it includes an agreement on offer and acceptance, consideration/compensation, and intention to create legal relations. It can take shape of warranty and guarantee in the case of durable goods for free and paid services, repair and replacement and in case of services, compensation for deficiency. It takes the shape of types of usufruct in the case of lease of physical assets like land or intellectual product like patent and copyright. There exist several kinds of terms and conditions in transaction of financial papers in terms of price-band, entry/exit loads, and premium/penalty, etc. Similarly there is a huge variety of terms in the case of employment, sometimes making difficult for many a social scientist to differentiate between categories of employment for the fact that distinguishing characteristics are getting slimmer and thinner.

Employment as Contract

Employment can thus be seen as a contractual relationship between two parties known as employee (usually a real person) and employers (usually a legal person), which is voluntarily entered under a custom or a law. It often includes clauses regarding joining time, duration, and other contingency conditions like leave and vacations and holidays, etc, besides those of acceptance and monetary consideration (pay, salary or wages). But the contract can be oral or verbal rather than written one. In fact there can be an employment contract implied by the acts of the parties rather than explicitly made in writing, verbally or orally. Based on the terms of contract the employees are known as casually employed or regularly employed. Employment on contract, however, is the term/phrase used in India for a fixed duration employment, usually for a few years, in contrast to regular employment or permanent employment, though regular is contrasted with casual and permanent is contrasted with temporary. Temporary appointment has been accepted as a case of one's employment in place of someone else who is on some kind of long leave—sometimes from a lower cadre to a higher one.

II. TYPES OF EMPLOYMENT

Self-employment and Wage-employment

Employment may basically be of two types in a monetised market economy : self-employment and wage-employment. Under self-employment the person serves the customer or client while under wage-employment(s) he serves the employer who in turn serves the customers or clients. Though at times, may be now very often, the employee and customer/client of the employer may be more in contact, say in hospitals or hotels, but the employee is working on behalf of the employer, which is the crux of the matter. Wage employment for short may be called just employment.

Wage-employment: Casual and Regular

As indicated above, one can be employed on regular basis or on casual basis. Besides employment for an indefinite period, there is often an element of social security in the case of regular employment. A regular employee often enjoys both job security and social security. Casual employee on the other hand enjoys neither. He can be hired at his will but fired at employer's will.

There is a subtle theoretical point here. Voluntary employment is for a set of specified duties. But howsoever duties of a category of employees are specified, in most cases complete specification is difficult. For example, a security man has to be put on security duty but timings, places/points, and manner may not be completely specified. Let us take an example of hiring a teacher for mathematics tuition for a given syllabus and another of hiring a teacher of economics who would develop courses, will do specific duties for part of the time and switch over other courses and may have to handle some administrative assignment. Or let us take case of a surgeon who is invited for a particular operation or a teacher for a particular course on IPR and another case of a resident doctor or nurse or a permanent faculty in economics. The former is likely to be casually employed (say as a visiting faculty) whereas the other is employed as a regular faculty (say as Professor of Economics). It may be observed that in most of the service contract there is at least one open clause, which is to say that, in general, all duties cannot be completely specified.

It is held that if duties can be perfectly defined, the employer will usually go for casual employment and if there is left some scope for delineation of duties of the employee, the employer is likely to go for regular employment. In the former case much control is not needed whereas in the latter it is very much needed. In theory, the former has been accepted as sale contract (like sitting in an interview board as an expert) and the latter as the employment contract.

AN INTERESTING CASE

An issue could be raised, and was indeed raised in the seminar, about the plight of rickshaw-walas who often get the rickshaw on rental from the owner for a specified number of hours in a day. In my view rickshaw plier is in self-employment whether he owns the rickshaw or leases it in on rental. There is a lease contract between the owner and the plier. The rider/passenger in this case is a customer rather the employer. Thus, neither the owner nor the riders are employer of the ricksaw puller; the rickshaw puller self-employs. The two contracts involved in the case are not employment contracts.

A good point was raised during the discussion that the primary characteristic of self-employment is ownership of means of production, which is largely true in an empirical sense. But there is a subtle difference between an empirical characteristic and a defining condition. From a pure analytical angle, even if one does not own the means of production and has taken it on lease or loan, one may still be in self-employment. Let us take the case of a sharecropper who leases in land with a complex contract of sharing risks, costs and produce, yet he is self-employed even though he may himself hire labour for some of the operations of farming. It will be interesting to analyse the put-out system in which raw material is given to the worker and payment is made according to piece rate and the worker may not need to use much of tools and equipments, say in the case of beedi rolling.

EMPLOYMENT CONTRACT

To reiterate, employment is a contract entered into at the commencement of employment between two parties, as said earlier, one being the employer and the other being the employee. It usually contains a statement about the nature of employment relationship like job, compensation package and duration of employ. The contract may be for casual employment or regular employment, for short period or long term, part-time or full time, of temporary or permanent nature. Consideration may be in terms of time spent or work performed or a combination of the two. There may be conditions attached with social security or termination of contract or even breach of contract. However, if the employee and employer both are legal persons, the relationship could be called only outsourcing or sale contract, not employment. Since the term legal person includes natural person, there may be a case of overlap.

CONTRACTUAL LABOUR

However, there is a curious case. Employment of labour can be a direct one or indirect one. Indirect employment of labour is often known, at least in India, as contractual labour. In such a case there is a contract between the employer and the contractor and there is another between the contractor and the employee. There is a go-between contractor, and employment of the primary employees is contingent upon the contract between the contractor and the final employer. This contractor normally has contact with labour say in villages and is often found to pay some advance wages (and may be in the form of loan) and bring labour in hordes to the factory gate or on construction site for the final employer with whom he had procured a contract of supplying labour. The final employer could be a business house or at times government department. This employment is often portrayed as an intersection set of three stakeholders: sets of employees, employers and contractors of supply of labour for a fee.

III. METAMORPHOSIS OF CONTRACTUAL LABOUR

This variety of employment is now changing in many subtle ways. There is one-on-one employment. Almost as a broker or an agent, rather than as a usual contractor, there is a person who sends the primary employee(s) to the final employer and stands guarantee for the conduct of employee and take the commission, much like real estate broker. Many companies these days are depending quite a bit on placement agencies for recruiting their employees, which is again a kind of outsourcing.

Employee and Employer

Let us formally define these terms for better delineation and clarity so as to apply the tests for determination of a relationship if it could be called employment or not. If one or the other test fails to apply then one may try to analyse as to what is the real relationship.

Employee

An employee may legally be defined as : A real person in the service of another person, real or legal, for a set of duties under any contract of hire, express or implied, oral or written, where the employer has the power or right to control and direct the employee in the material details of how the work is to be performed within the specified set of duties. He is called in modern parlance as teammate or associate while in earlier dispensation he was dismissed as worker. Sense of dignity or level of motivation might be changing with change in nomenclature but the essence of the relationship remains the same. Manager and supervisor for this purpose fall in the category of the employee, though he may be employing employees on behalf of the employer.

Employer

An employer is a person or institution, which means a legal person that hires employees—each for a set of duties—and exercises the control and gives the direction within the scope provided by the contract. Though the person known as employer recruits the employees through one or the other employees except in case of proprietorship or partnership firms where employers are real persons even though firms are legal persons.

Hierarchy

Employees are stacked in a kind of hierarchy. Those workers are usually at the lower end of the ladder with supervisors in the middle and managers at the top, with increasing power to control the functioning of the subordinates. While workers are there to do the job, as it colloquially put, managers have job to get the jobs done.

Para-employees

Now, employees on contract are many a time designated as consultants and advisors. They have also started appearing in literature as in organisations. They are a kind of para-employees and they are of both in-sourced and out-sourced varieties.

Risk Bearing

A basic distinction which is often made between the employer and the employee is that the former bears the risk, not the latter. This is largely true but not entirely. In many employment relationships, like *jajmani*, both float together. In modern capitalist structure also the employees also face the risk of being fired if things go pretty wrong and of losing generally assured extra-wage entitlements like bonus.

Risk is, therefore, shared by both the parties in many situations of contract, including that of employment contract, for it is about a venture in business. Yet from a pure analytical angle there is a great deal of substance in saying that capital (ists) suffers the risk, as they are the last recipients of the share in the contribution of the economic activity the organisation undertakes.

IV. EMPLOYMENT RELATIONSHIP

Employee and Worker

An employee is there for a set of defined duties—of a jobman/worker, foreman/supervisor or manager. Employers offer wages or a salary to the workers in exchange for the worker's labour power, depending upon whether the employee is paid by the hour or at a set rate per pay period. A salaried employee is typically not paid more for more hours worked than the minimum, whereas wages are paid for all hours worked, including overtime, though of late various other incentive schemes have been devised. The employer includes everything from individuals hiring a domestic help to governments and businesses, which may hire thousands of employees. In most modern societies governments are the largest single employers, but most of the workforce of a country is employed in small and medium businesses in the private sector in any usual economy.

Contribution of an Employee

An employee contributes labour and expertise to an endeavour. We may note that though employees may contribute to the evolution of an enterprise, organisation or institution, the employer maintains autonomous control over the productive base of land and capital. The employer typically also maintains ownership of intellectual property created by an employee within the scope of employment and as a function thereof. An employer's relative level of power over employees is dependent upon numerous factors, the most influential being the nature of the employment relationship.

Relationship between Employer and Employees

The relationship the employer shares with the employees is affected by three significant factors—interests, control and motivation. It is up to employers to effectively manage and balance these factors to ensure a harmonious and productive working relationship. Interests can be best described as economic pressures placed on organizations in their pursuit of profits. It covers facets such as labour productivity, wages and the effect of financial markets on businesses. Control can be either output focused, focusing on desired targets with managers defining and using their own methods for reaching targets, or process focused, which specify the manner in which tasks will be achieved.

Manager

Who is this manager? He is an employee too ! Employee can have several levels : worker, supervisor and manager—with sub-levels within each category—with increasing level of power to control. The owner/employer cannot manage, control and supervise on his own. In modern world where ownership is widely disperesed through holding and cross-holding of shares, the control has also to be diversified and it is often exercised through or rather by management. Small owners can be shown doors. Usually it is found that promoters themselves take up managerial positions.

Managerial Control

Managerial control within an organization rests at many levels and has important implications for staff and productivity alike, with control forming the fundamental link between desired outcomes and actual processes. Thus employers must balance interests such as softening wage constraints with maximization of labour productivity in order to achieve a prolific employment relationship. Motivation is the third and most difficult of the factors in the employment relationship for employers to effectively manage. Employee's motivation can often be in direct conflict with control mechanisms of employers, and can be broadly defined as that which energizes, directs and sustains human behaviour or, as differently put, something that moves a person to action, and continues him in the course of action already initiated.

The employment relationship is thus a difficult challenge for employers to manage, as all three facets are often in direct competition with each other, with interests, control and motivation often clashing in the equally important quest for autonomy of individual employee, command of employer and ultimately profits.

Modern Recruitment Methods

Specifically, an employee is any person hired by an employer to do a specific "job". In most modern economies the term employee refers to a specific defined relationship between an individual employee and an employer (organisation/institution/corporation), which differs from those of customer or client. Most individuals attain the status of employee after a thorough process of recruitment through examinations, group discussions and interviews—technical and personality. If the individual is found to be a satisfactory fit for the position, he is given an official offer of employment within that organisation for a defined starting salary and position. An offer of employment, however, does not guarantee employment for any length of time and each party may terminate the relationship at any time before joining. Once he joins then he has all the rights and privileges of an employee, which may include medical benefits and vacation days. The relationship between a corporation and its employees is usually handled through the human resource department, which handles the incorporation of new recruits, and the disbursement of any benefits which the employee may be entitled, or any grievances that employees may have.

V. PRESENT DAY FORMAL LABOUR MARKET IN INDIA

Formal and Informal Sectors

There are two dichotomies prevalent in the present context: organised and unorganised and formal and informal. Some distinction is made between two overlapping informal and unorganised sectors in terms of the fact that unorganised sectors includes, besides unincorporated proprietary/household enterprises, cooperative societies, trusts, private and public limited companies— which may not maintain any regular accounts. We can treat the formal and organised sectors as equivalent from the angle of organisational set up. But from the angle of employees, one notices that formal sector may increasingly be employing people in an informal style as daily wage worker or outsource employees or tasks. Some of the recent reports submitted to the Government of India have noted the rampart practice of informal employment, as daily wager or contractual labour, in the organised sector of corporate business as in government outfits.

Employment in Formal Sector

Changing Scenario

There are two major categories of employers : government and private corporate business in the formal set-up. Government, including armed forces, and their outfits, corporations, boards, authorities, councils, agencies, as well as establishments of manufacturing and utilities, used to attract, not long ago, employees in all the departments and at all levels. Private business used to be the second choice for a majority of people. Today the scene is changing. At higher level young boys and girls are attracted towards private corporate sector jobs where along with indigenous capital, foreign capital has made a headway in practically all sectors through a multitude of multinational corporations be it manufacturing, retail, insurance, hospitality industry or hospitals. Some of these boys and girls, young as they are, are not so much bothered about job security and social security—which they may be seeking through various insurance schemes rather through employers or government set-up. These are high salary jobs. Children well educated and belonging to well-off parents choose this sector.

There is the other end of spectrum where people are still seeking jobs in government with preference for job security. In the hope that some day they will be regularised, many seek daily wage or casual work employment. Peons and drivers make the queue here.

Contrasting Wage Structure in Private and Public Sectors

The reason is not far to seek why. The wage spread in the public sector is very narrow while that in the private sector is very wide even if the average is just about the same. Worker/manager ratio among the employees is pretty high in public sector while that is pretty low in private corporate sector. Low work pressure and disguised unemployment characterised by low productivity but high income in government attracts people with low managerial skills though often with high manual skills. On the other hand high pressured employment accompanied by high productivity in private sector can still get plenty of low grade workers at pretty low wages; as the people at lower end of the society suffering from low levels of income and poverty still queue up. As the higher end of the wage ladder in the private corporate sector is higher than the higher end of the wage ladder in the public sector, what one notices is that people in higher echelons prefer private sector jobs and/or try to get government salaries pushed up. As the lower end of the wage ladder in the private corporate sector is considerably lower than the lower end of the wage ladder in the public sector, we notice that people in at lower levels prefer public sector jobs and try to move to get government jobs, relinquishing their private sector jobs.

VI. BY WAY OF CONCLUSION

An offshoot of this dichotomy is that employees in public sector at higher end would seek parity with their counterparts in the private corporate sector and will try to influence the pay commissions which are set up to revise the pay scales at an interval of say ten years during which productivity of the society rises beyond a certain level. Wage structure is so distorted that highly skilled in fields like surgery, information technology, biotechnology, or management, prefer private corporate sector as pay package is 100 per cent to 400 per cent higher than its counterpart public sector. So new talent may not be forthcoming to public sector and fields like education. In cases where it is difficult to measure performance of organisations, leave alone individual employees, it becomes too difficult to assert for a particular level of hike in pay except by pressure or at most by competitive employability. However, it is incumbent upon the political masters to see that government and non-profit organisations, especially educational institutions, do attract best brains so as to better serve the young generation—the parents of the next generation, as Mrshall called them.

At the same it is only through the massive government intervention in terms of job creation, rather than fixing minimum wages, that the lot of low paid workers can improve. Productivity gains have to be more widely shared. What about the self-employed in activities that do not fetch prices remunerative enough to sustain life beyond poverty ditch? No attempt is made to answer it in this chapter.

2

CONTRACTUALISATION OF INDIAN LABOUR MARKET

N. M. P. Verma

Composition of Contract

Although a debate is on for defining various dimensions of contractual labour market, however, simple symptoms of contractual labour market are as follows:

Historically, the contract labour market is a place where principal employer for whom labour works is different from the person or agency, which engages them as labour on wage or non-wage contracts. The agency may be a labour broker's organization. The agent hiring such labour is known as labour broker or a contractor. Sometimes, he is also known as intermediary or middleman between the capitalist and labour. This is not the case in regular recruitments and workers where principal employer does not operate through agent. Exceptions are formal sector and firms where workers are directly employed with an agreement (i.e. contract paper duly signed), which are normally in favour of firm owner or the capitalist producer. This situation is observed in case of skilled and highly skilled workers.

The indirect employer or the so-called principal employer, makes a payment to the contractor as per the terms and conditions for completion of the said works including for supplying labour according to its needs. The terms and conditions for supply of labour to the production unit are settled by the contractor with the principal employer and the workers. The wages paid tend to be much lower than those in regular employment in majority of cases and especially in the case of unskilled workers. The labour laws are ignored knowingly by contractors. Implications of contract employment are that since the principal employer is not the direct employer, therefore, they have no responsibility to follow labour laws and pay benefits. The labour employed is not given any form of social security protection such as provident fund, medical reimbursement and so on.

A worker can be hired and fired at the will of the contractor. He does not have any liability to pay any separation costs in case he is fired without any notice. Further, since contract labour is very poorly paid, workers often have to take loans in the form of advances, particularly to meet any exigencies like cost of treatment in case of illness, social expenditure like marriage of dependents within the family, etc. They find it difficult to repay these loans, which often put them in almost perpetual bondage to the contractor. In case of migrant labour, it cannot run away from its liability to the contractor since the contractor himself generally belongs to the area from which labour is obtained and has close contacts at the root level in that area.

Finally, contract labour is by and large non-unionised, which makes it difficult for it to act as a pressure group and reduces its bargaining strength. It is for all these reasons that contract labour is taken to be a highly exploited segment of labour. Thus, from a producer's point of view the contract labour system provides it with certain advantages that save his costs although from labour's point of view it is exploitative (Mathur, 2009).

The casual and contractual labourers have an unfair deal in the process of economic liberalization and reforms over the preceding decade. There is no evidence of an improved labour status in terms of employment, wages, other benefits, hours of work, job security or the ability to save. There is no positive impact of industrial growth, trade intensity or technological upgradings on the socio-economic status of industrial workers. The young entrants are stressed because of long hours of work, and mode of casual/contractual status recruitments. Those with job skills as well as those who are young as compared to other workers seem to be subject to the changed work atmosphere of contractual and casualised recruitments which offers very little to non-wage benefits (PF, bonus) or opportunities to participate in union activities (Sen and Dasgupta, 2008). Thus given the recent trends in India and elsewhere in Asia, Africa and industrialized countries the theme and key words such as emerging patterns, contractual employment, and Indian Labour Market are well justified. Starting from the last word it has been observed that contractual employment has its base in economic history; during British regime also it was very popular. It was controlled through labour brokers popularly called as *muqaddams*. After independence in every Five Year Plan thrust has been given on growth of employment in different sectors either through CWS, CDS or UPS. Given the nature of mixed Indian economy private sector has always employed skilled and non-skilled person on contractual basis. Even in some of the public sector units works were done through contractual basis especially in real estate sector, manufacturing sector, formal and informal sector. Nevertheless, the cotractualisation has been less legalized in informal sector than formal sector. This has further generated a sense of insecurity and lack of governmental protection in informal sector contractual employment in comparison to formal sector employment. Further, economic reform initiatives taken after 1990s, labour sector liberalization, disinvestments in public sector units and growth of private investment resulted in tremendous fall in permanent and regular employment and increase in casual and contractual employment. If we analyse the sector-wise scenario then again it is being observed that contractualisation has gone up in recent years in sectors such as business processing, information technology, real estate, manufacturing health and hygiene sector, service sector like banks, private post offices and couriers, insurance, railways, transport and to some extent in rural sector developmental programmes and even further to a lesser extent in agricultural sector in a few States and regions. In addition, because of privatization contractual recruitments have also gone up in social sectors such as primary, secondary, higher, technical and professional educational institutions and health sector like private nursing homes, specialized and non-specialized private hospitals. Even some of the public institutions have of late started appointing consultants on contractual basis and also on very high wage rates like in sports such as ICC and BCCI and other national and international public institutions.

Data Limitations

There is acute dearth of secondary data on contractual labour. The National Sample Survey (NSS) classifies employment in terms of self employed, casual worker and regular worker by sex and by agriculture and non-agriculture sector. In NSS reports reference of classification of workers on the basis of education, sex and region like rural and urban are recorded. But there is no reference of mode of appointment on the basis of short term or long-term contract. This is also true for migrant contractual workers overseas. Thus there is lack of published secondary data on contractual employment. Primary data based studies are available but their focus is hardly on the issues linked directly to contractual jobs in various sectors and sub-sectors.

NSS Classifications of Workers and Employments

1. Self-employed workers are defined as those who work on their own farm or non-farm based enterprise, or those who are engaged independently in a profession or trade on own account with one or more partners. The essential feature of the self-employed worker is that sale or profits from goods and services produced determine remuneration. The self-employed are further sub-classified as own account workers, employers and helpers.

   (a) *Own account workers:* Self-employed workers who operate on their own account or with partners but do not hire external labour are own-account workers. They may, however, take help from unpaid family members in running the enterprise.

   (b) *Employers:* Self-employed workers who run their household enterprise on their own or in association with one or more partners and in addition hire paid labour, either family members or external labour, are classified as self-employed employers.

(c) *Helpers :* Workers in household enterprise who work full-or part-time and do not receive a regular wage or salary in return are called helpers. They comprise mainly family members. In the last quinquennial survey on employment and unemployment (50th round for 1993-94), family members who worked for a share in the household earnings were classified as helpers. In earlier rounds, this group of family workers had been termed as 'self-employed on workers' if they shared the family earning in some way. Thus there was a change in the definition of helpers in the 50th round of the NSS, with a fraction of the workforce earlier identified as self-employed own account workers being reclassified as helpers.

2. Regular workers are defined as those who work on others' farm or non-farm enterprises, either household or non-household, and are paid regular wages or salaries. Regular workers are not bound by daily or periodic 'renewal of work contracts'. Their salaries or wages can be piece-rated or time-rated and the work can be full-time or part-time.

3. Casual workers are defined as those who work for others' farm or non-farm enterprise and are paid wages that are daily or periodic in nature. Casual workers include those who appear to be long-term workers of an employer but are bound by daily or periodic renewal of the work contract. The NSS classifies casual workers into two types: workers at public works sponsored by government agencies or local bodies are categoriesd as 'casual workers in public works', and other workers are termed 'casual workers in other type of works'.

The self-employed own-account worker category includes owners in registered partnership firms and professionals like doctors, lawyers and charter accountants. The work and incomes of such persons comes under the purview of various regulatory authorities, and they are not strictly informal sector workers. The NSS defines 'regular workers' on the basis of the regularity of their work and the payment of wages and salaries to them (Pais, 2002). This does not mean that regular workers are necessarily formal sector workers. Workers with a regular monthly wage (including domestic help) and who are not entitled to any other employment-related benefits or social security are also termed regular workers. Thus, a section of regular workers could well be characterized as part of the informal labour force.

Casual workers, of course, are constituents of the informal labour force as the terms and conditions of employment are outside the purview of any regulatory body. It is also of note that the definition of casual labour has remained consistent over the different rounds of the NSS. Therefore, as a starting point in understanding the structure of informal employment in urban India, we focus on the category of casualisation of the labour force is important in itself, argue Mukhopadhyay. It reflects changes in 'contractual conditions and the status of labour' (Mukhopadhyay, 1992).

Table 2.1: Share of Workers by Employment Status, India, 1983 to 1996-97

(in per cent)

Year	Round	Self-employed	Regular	Casual
1983	38	57.3	13.8	28.6
1987-88	43	56.0	14.4	29.6
1989-90	45*	57.1	13.4	29.8
1990-91	46*	50.3	23.4	26.3
1992-93	48*	56.5	12.7	30.8
1993-94	50	54.8	13.2	32.0
1994-95	51*	55.6	12.2	32.2
1995-96	52*	54.6	13.0	32.4
1996-97	53*	54.6	12.9	32.5

Note : (1) All figures are for combined rural and urban workforce.
(2) An (*) indicates that data are from annual rounds. Rests of the data are from quinquennial rounds.

Source: Gupta (1999).

Table 2.2 : Employment Status Categories in the National Sample Surveys on Employment and Unemployment

NSS code	Description
11	Self-employed own account workers
12	Self-employed employers
21	Helpers in household enterprise
31	Regular workers
41	Casual workers in public works
51	Casual workers in other type of works

Contractual Recruitment of Professionals

The first filtering mechanism that comes into play here is the fact that all the major IT companies visit only selected institutions each year to recruit students, based on their ranking of engineering colleges. The large companies usually visit 50-60 campuses, while multi-national corporations (MNCs) and the medium-sized Indian products or services companies may visit about 10 select campuses. The ranking of the top 50 colleges are more or less the same for all the companies, and the majority of engineering colleges are not even ranked by the major companies. This means that for the major companies (which are the largest employers), the pool of candidates is limited at the outset to students of the best engineering colleges in India.

Second, only those students with a certain cut-off percentage throughout their course (usually 70 per cent aggregate marks) are allowed to apply for placement. In fact, many IT companies require candidate to have had a consistent average of 70 to 75 per cent marks from standard 10 onwards. This requirement tends to exclude engineering students who have gotten seats on government quotas (SC/ST or OBC) with lower cut-off marks and who were not able to score well in previous examinations because of their educational and social background.

The third level of filtering occurs during the interview process, which follows a written test (usually of logical, analytical, and problem-solving skills, as well as English and Maths). First, there is a group discussion to evaluate communication skills, personality and spontaneous thinking abilities. The candidates who are short-listed in this round are then individually interviewed. There are two types of interview—technical and human resource (HR). The HR interview is designed to assess non-technical attributes of candidates, such as attitudes and values, personality, career aspirations, and "soft skills" and to determine whether he/she will "fit" into the company's culture. The most important "soft skill" that is assessed during the HR interview is communication skill. Since many software jobs, especially in services companies, are "client-facing", good communication skills are considered to be essential, and a candidate who is otherwise well qualified may be rejected purely on this basis. The requirement for good spoken English, which is assessed during the interview, tends to exclude those from lower caste, rural, and less privileged backgrounds. While fluency in English is a basic requirement, the term "communication skills" refers more broadly to the ability to converse and interact easily in different social and cultural situations. The assessment of the candidate's general appearance, demeanour, and "ability to mingle" during the HR interview acts effectively as an exclusionary mechanism, in that it is weighted against those who are not from middle class, cosmopolitan and English-speaking backgrounds. Good communication and social skills, confidence, and the right kind of personality are elements of cultural capital that students from urban middle class (and usually high caste) families are most likely to possess (Fuller and Narasimhan, 2006). With the increasing emphasis that is placed on soft skills by the IT industry, candidates from non-metropolitan, non-middle class, and lower caste background are even more likely to be passed over. Thus, students who have entered engineering colleges through government quotas, who have the requisite marks in their engineering course, and who have passed the initial written tests, are still likely to be "weeded out" in the subsequent rounds.

Thus, the sharp disparities in the higher education system together with the industry's recruitment practices tend to skim off only the cream among engineering graduates as well as privileged students with the right kind of cultural capital- social skills, communication style, deportment, and so on. In addition, these filtering mechanisms have created a system of stratification within the IT workforce, in that a software engineer's position and career prospects in the industry are largely determine by his or her educational background. While graduates from the IITs and other premier institutions land the best jobs (in MNCs and the more challenging technical jobs in reputed companies), those from tier two and three colleges tend to be slotted into the more routine and low – end jobs. For instance, several of the large Indian software services companies prefer to hire students from tier three campuses rather than from the top ranking colleges, because the best students are not suitable for the kind of routinised work that is on offer. As an HR manager put it, they require "guys who can just sit and code and not ask questions". This remark suggests that hiring practices tend to reproduce within the industry the social hierarchy or class fractions that characterise the middle class in general: the best "high-end" and top management jobs are likely to be monopolized by the people from more privileged social backgrounds (i.e., middle to upper class and caste, from the best institutions), while greater "diversity" may be found at the lower end of the job market.

Job Contracts (Permanent or Casual)

Table 2.3 indicates the casual and permanent worker divide. As expected, casual workers are more hard pressed than the permanent and regular workers in every respect, in terms of wages, hours of work, PF and gratuity. They are naturally insecure about their jobs and have less to do with union membership.

Social Background

Workers in our sample can further be grouped in terms of their social background. We observe that the "general category" workers (which include all workers except the SCs, STs, and minorities) are relatively better placed. However, we did not find caste playing an important role at the time of recruitment in the private sector. But SCs, STs, and minorities come with a background, which adversely affects their education and skill. Hence, at a time when the demand for skilled labour is rising, it is quite plausible that the "others category" of workers are losing out.

Labour in SEZS or Other Industries

As we have mentioned earlier, of the 16 areas selected for interviewing

Table 2.3 : Labour in Industries producing Importables

		Number	Mean hourly wage (Rs)	Mean hours of work	Saving (%)	Union membership (%)	Fear of losing job (%)	Provident fund	Gratuity (%)	Bonus (%)
Importable	**Mean**	15.41	9.79	0.3	0.07	0.43	0.13	0.07	0.34	15.41
	Variance	65.93	1.90	0.21	0.06	0.25	0.12	0.07	0.22	65.93
Others	**Mean**	14.26	8.92	0.25	0.47	0.52	0.51	0.23	0.63	14.26
	Variance	63.04	1.74	0.18	0.25	0.25	0.5	0.18	0.23	63.04

industrial labour, three were SEZs. These included Falta in West Bengal, NOIDA in the international capital region of Delhi (which is actually located within the administrative jurisdiction of Uttar Pradesh) and the Santacruze SEEPZ at Mumbai in Maharashtra. Of the 615 workers in our sample, only 60 belonged to these three SEZ areas. Industrial units set up within a SEZ need not play the minimum wages as prevail in industries located in the neighbourhood of the SEZs. In SEZs, labour laws as well as taxation norms of the land are not applicable. Flexible hire and fire practices, therefore, are even easier to implement. The above further deprives labour its due share of production in terms of both wage and non-wage benefits as well as with other amenities as normally available elsewhere in the country, which is self-evident in delineating this disparity between SEZ and non-SEZ workers. The gap between average hourly wage between non-SEZ and SEZ workers is Rs. 5.08, which is significant at the 1 per cent level. SEZ workers work on an average 0.48 hours more a day than their non-SEZ counterparts. Besides, the variance for the mean hours of work is more in the case of SEZ workers indicating flexible working time and very long daily working hours in the case of few workers in the sample.

As for unionization, those outside SEZs are relatively more organized as members of trade unions with a higher percentage of SEZs workers (almost three-fourth of SEZ workers in our sample) fear losing jobs and thus live with uncertain job prospects as compared to their non-SEZ counterparts. Similarly, a lower percentage of SEZ workers do receive retirement benefits in the form of PF and gratuity and earn yearly bonus. As expected under this kind of situation, only 2 per cent of SEZ workers in our sample have a savings as against 28 per cent in the case of non-SEZ workers. Thus the SEZs, which are supposed to be the leading enclaves of export-oriented growth, derive their comparative advantage by offering labour at a level, which is even lower than what is available outside these zones. Labour processes in both SEZ and non-SEZ areas are exploitative, the degree of which varies as case studies of Falta, SEEPZ and NOIDA indicate.

Labour in SEZs is exploited to an extent, which is only comparable to the experiences of industrial labour in England in the beginning of industrial revolution in the eighteenth century. Growth as takes place on account of export initiatives of these SEZs is thus asymmetric. Thus, welfare loss in terms of labour deprivation is not compensated by adequate welfare gain through redistribution of social surplus from the process. The plight of labour in the SEZs thus requires immediate attention of the policy-makers to build up a strong social safety network as has been argued in several studies and is being currently debated. In an era where labour efficiency is the buzzword of reform and development, the real test will lie in combining efficiency with safeguarding the legitimate demand and authentic interest of labour.

Contractualisation : Recalling History

Labour contractors are found during British India and may be before that. Establishment of new economic activities, ports and transportation of goods and services and also opposition of slavery gave birth to growth of middlemen for supply of labour not only within India but also in many other countries for doing menial works like loaders, coolie, farm workers etc. This was possible because India was a country enriched in natural resources and population. The growth of Industrial revolution also required huge demand of workers in many countries including UK and Mauritius. China has also same situations where these labour brokers were called as Ketou (head of guests), Shuike (guest coming by water), Baotou (labour contractor) or Renkou fanzi (traders of labourers). Broadly, these contractors are of two types in China (Minghuan, 2004) and also in India. One who settled abroad and wanted continuous flow of their natives, relative and friends, partly for providing jobs to jobless and partly because of better wages abroad. Some of the poor people even sold their sons, daughters and wives for this purpose. Within India also this situation was observed during peak agricultural season, labour demand during mining and loading/unloading of ships.

Most large scale enterprises in ninteenth century India did not recruit workers directly, but recruited through labour contractors. During this period onwards large scale employers such as factories plantations and ports left a great deal of supervision and training to these contractors. For this, the contractors received most important privileges i.e. hire and as and when required with bare minimum consent of management. The managers gave the work to intermediaries but they later got that job done by work team of workers.

The argument that the institution of the contractor could become costly for the employer, especially because it could potentially compromise skills, training, quality, and incentives, faces objections from both economic theory and economic history, and therefore, needs to be qualified and contextualized. Economic theory and economic history recognize that hiring a labour contractor can be a rational employment decision in certain contexts. For example, when a labour market is undeveloped, or the employers do not know the prospective workers well enough, or the market is too risky or too seasonal for continuous direct employment, or labour regulations make direct employment contracts too costly for the employer, engaging a labour contractor may be rational. Consistent with this insight, early or late industrialisation relied heavily on an agent for recruitment and for retaining rural labour in urban and unfamiliar workplaces. The agent was ubiquitous in the early ninteenth century cotton textile mills in England and North America, and in Japan and India in the late ninteenth century. I explore the significance of the worker-intermediary to the study of industrialisation in India more fully in 'Sardars, Jobbers, Kanganies: Historically, the drives behind such decisions included a lack of information on labour markets, and sometimes communication gap between the workers and employers.' Seasonality and risks were at work too. Regulatory law was rarely an important factor in the early history of contracting. On the other hand, there were two additional drivers behind the importance of the contractor in the early history of the mechanized factory, which have not drawn sufficient attention from labour economists. One of these was the scarcity of managerial talents and specialized managers, which led employers to share some managerial functions with skilled foremen. And the other was the scarcity of technical schools, and in turn the need to rely on the skilled foremen as a master or provider of training. This is the context in which the phrase "inside contractor" was often used in the early ninteenth century New England mills (Roy, 2008)".

The Jobber and Contract Labour

The person in charge of communication with the workers, and who was by default in charge of training, was not the owner, nor the manager, but the "jobber". The jobber was a senior worker who began as a labour contractor, evolved into a supervisor or head of work-teams, and throughout, was given over significant powers to hire casual labourers and fire them as well, on a token permission from the immediate superior. Unlike the manager, the jobber was "one of the workers", a counterpart of the headman of worker gangs or a master artisan. They belonged in a segment of the hierarchy that was distinct from that segment represented by the Parsi or European foremen and technical supervisors. But the latter could neither do without nor replace the former. In one view, the jobber became necessary because of a class cultural distance between the technical men and the raw labourers (Morris, 1960). However, the Mumbai jobber was only one instance of a whole variety of labour contractors who supplied workers to the modern large-scale enterprises since the mid-ninteenth century, suggesting that search costs and supervision costs were also important factors behind the universal need for the agent. The much discussed and sometimes misunderstood jobber clearly had played a very positive role in looking after the interests of the ordinary workers. Pioneering figures in labour mobilization and organization emerged from the jobber background. Many workers had good reasons to look up to them for welfare, fair treatment from the employers, and moral support. Jobbers were also far from a homogeneous class. All that said, in the 1920s, the jobber had acquired a largely negative connotation. Sections of capital felt that the jobber-undermined quality of effort, and sections of labour felt that the jobber exploited the privilege to hire and fire workers. Where did these complaints come from? Whatever their origins, in the 1920s the jobbers conducted much more than recruitment. They were effectively workers entrusted with the duties of a personnel manager, they were in charge of full utilisation of the machines, and in the absence of a well-developed apprenticeship, in charge of supplying and shaping skill levels as well. The managers and the owners could wash their hands off training and education precisely because the jobber was by default, but rarely in practice, in charge of these functions. "People speak of the inefficiency of labour" in Mumbai mills, a Tariff board member, pointed out to G.W. Burley, head of the largest technical training institute in India at that time. Is it possible for the mill managers "to organize some instruction for them"? No, Burley answered. "The matter is entirely in the hands of the jobber. He is a jobber because he can bring labour into the mill...they bring in people who know nothing at all about textile work, and instruction appears to be largely in the hands of the jobber". Note the phrase "appears to be ", suggesting that this function was not deliberately contracted out, but was an unintended consequence of decentralizing the employers' responsibilities. Many jobbers themselves were poorly trained, but even when they were in full command of the machinery, they preferred not to teach too much (Roy, 2008).

Fixed and Variable Wage Component

In the fully legalised long duration contractual employment in corporate sector it has been observed that workers are being paid both fixed and variable wages. While fixed wage is just as per the terms of contract and paid monthly, the variable wage component is estimated quarterly on the basis of performance of the firm. For example, Infosys paid 100 per cent variable salary to its 88,000 employees in over 44 offices worldwide during the third quarter of 2007. The Company further appreciated the contract labourer for better depth and breadth of talent availability. The percentage of variable pay at Infosys, India's second biggest software exporter, ranges from nearly 10 per cent of total compensation at the entry level to 50 per cent of total compensation at senior level roles. The variable pay outs are done on a quarterly basis, some part of the variable pay is paid on a monthly basis too. Only for the very senior roles, the variable payouts take place on a half yearly basis. In contrast to Infosys, Tata Consultancy Services (TCS), Asia's largest software services firm and India's largest Private sector employer has cut salary packages of its employees in order to control cost and counter balance value of rising rupee. The company informed recently to its employees about an imminent cut in the variable cut in the pay on the basis of its third quarter October–December performance. Though the company has made its revenue target for third quarter, it fell short of meeting its Economic Value Added (EVA) target due to a combination of internal and external factors. Thus the EVA target forms the basis of the variable pay computation. The variable component, linked to the performance of the company and that of an individual, consists of 30 per cent of the compensation structure for most TCS workers, while the senior management, from vice president to higher levels; the variable portion is 40–50 per cent. This component is paid monthly, based on the company's expected performance for the quarter and is now being slashed by 20 per cent.

TCS has reassessed compensation based on various factors and hence decided to make adjustments in the variable component, the impact on the annual compensation of an employee is 1.5 per cent, he added. TCS said no changes have been to perquisites. The rupee has appreciated by 12 per cent over the last year compared to dollar and sign of a slowdown in US economy has become a concern for IT companies. In Q3, TCS' revenues increased 5.04 per cent to Rs. 5,924 crores and net profit rose 6.72 per cent to Rs. 1,331 crore. The third quarter for the first time saw its revenues from the North American region drop below 50 per cent. Thus the important issues involved with the contractual workers are related to the following factors:

Quality Concern

Contemporary Perspectives

Comparative Cost

Unfair Competition

Labour Regime

Worker Unions

Fixed Wage Factor

The Efficiency Agenda

Migrant Contractual Workers

Overseas employment for all workers, male and female, is a high risk proposition. It involves workers to face adjustment problems in an alien country; worry about the contractual nature of their overseas employment; and cope with a social, economic and political set up different than their own. The problem is much aggravated for women workers both domestic workers and entertainers or entertaining workers migrated in Asia, Gulf countries. In several countries like those of west Asia and East Asia with booming economies increases in levels of income and standard of living has made hiring contractual workers on domestic services a status of symbol. Historically also these countries have long tradition of having domestic help like slavery and feudal set-up despite westernization and urbanisation. A strong demand for overseas domestic contractual workers emerged because of low status and low wage. Migrant contractual women workers preferred entertainment industries because of higher status, more wage and less arduous employment. The Asian countries having major exporters of women contractual workers to West Asia are the Philippines, Thailand, Indonesia and Sri Lanka. In recent years Bangladeshi migrants are also working in Indian Contractual Labour market especially in metro cities. The workers may have migrated illegally overseas through unauthorized channels or even staying without the authorization of host country. Informally it is believed that for every two legal migrant workers in west Asia there is one illegal worker from India. Both employers and agents take full advantage of their vulnerability as illegal workers and are exploited in terms of less wage, more working hours and sexual abuse. This need diplomatic protection (Gulati, 1997).

Contractual Employment in Indian PSUs

The employment in banking sector has been mainly regular and full time. All the jobs of the banking are bound by the 'terms of contract', where it is clearly defined about the job conditions and 'notice under which job can be terminated'. Since, the employment in banking sector in India was dominated by Public Sector Banks, whose 'terms of contract' are bound by negotiations with unions and bi-partite treaties; the job insecurity for bank personnel are very less. Apart from this, there is 'Indian Banks Association', the apex organization to look into the co-ordination issues of the Banking Industry in India, it caters to the requirements of Banks, and it negotiates with other organizations' for and on behalf of the Banks.

The jobs on 'contract basis for a fixed term' in Banking were predominantly low-paid jobs related to data-entry, cyclostyle and menial jobs, but off late the trend has changed and high end jobs like advocates, economist, chartered accountants and marketing professionals are also being offered on 'contract basis for a short term'. With India providing Business Process Outsourcing solutions to the Global Banking giants, the contractual employment in the Indian Industry has increased. The plight remains same for the personnel employed on contract for a term, whether for high end job or low end job, there are no unions who can give a good deal by bi-lateral negotiations. Although, the job market for high end job in this category is supply driven, but the working conditions are more or less same, due to lack of group buying power. As the private sector Banks have more operational freedom, they employ a number of staff for a fixed term with fixed salary for a specified work. Once that particular work is done, the services of the worker are terminated, ofcourse with a notice. Due to specific jobs and industry-specific skills that cannot be transferred in the short to medium term, the plight of Contractual employees is weak. With Indian Banking going Global, the trend in employment will change and more employees will be recruited 'on contract basis for a fixed term'. It has also been observed for scheduled commercial banks that there is declining trend in volume of employment in the last decade, nevertheless, the amount handled per employee shows a strong rising trend. Further, in the public sector banks there has a tremendous decline in employment whereas in private banks there has been a rise in employment. As a result, there is hardly any disparity in per branch employment in public and private sector bank in 2007. This is hovering around 19 persons per branch. Earlier this gap was larger in 1995. Such situation has taken place because of VRS in PSB and change in competitive work environment (Srivastava, 2009).

Railway is also a large employer of contractual labours in public sector undertakings. More than a decade ago except hiring of labours through contractors railway board used to recruit all types of persons and staff along with UPSC which appoints engineers and bureaucrats.

But after reforms, contractual employment has gone up in areas like construction, catering, cleaning and office maintenance. Perhaps that is one of the reasons of bringing railways in a profitable zone. Further in railways the labour brokers supply labourers to big construction contractors. Thus there is a linkage between various types of contractors here. These labour brokers are also having command over specialized, skilled and non-skilled labours such as plumber, civil works, electrical, mechanical and various other types of works.

All the development authorities of urban areas at district and State level also take up construction and maintenance works on contract basis. Of late, maintenance works have been privatized by these authorities and private contractors employ labourers on contract basis as per the contract agreements.

NOTES

1. "*The Labour Contractor in Indian Economic History*", Modern Asian Studies, forthcoming.
2. On "Inside Contractors in Pre-1850 New England Mills", Andrew Dawson, A New Framework for Workshop Contracting: Philadelphia Machine Building, 1870-1914, *Labour History*, 47(3), 2006, pp 343-59.
3. Based on a primary survey conducted during 2004-06 in pockets of Delhi, Gujarat, Haryana, Maharashtra and West Bengal.

REFERENCES

Abraham, Katharine G. and Susan K. Taylor (1996), "Firms Use of Outside Contractors; Theory and Evidence" *Journal of Labour Economics*, Vol. 14, No. 3.

Fuller, C.J. and Haripriya Narsimhan (2006), "Engineering Colleges Exposure and Information Technology Profesionals in Tamil Nadu", *Economic and Political Weekly*, Vol. XLI, No. 3, January 21.

Gulati, Leela (1997), "Asian Women in International Migration; With Special Reference to Domestic Work and Entertainment", *Economic and Political Weekly*, Vol. XXXII, No. 47, November, 1997.

Kannappan, Subbih (1985), "Urban Employment the Labour Market in Developing Nations", *Economic Development and Cultural Change*, Vol. 33, No. 4.

Mathur, Ashok (2009), The Status and Prospects of Contract labour in the Era of Economic Reforms in Verma and Awasthi (eds.) 2009.

Minghuan, Li (2004), "Re-emergence of Labour Brokers in China Today: The Xiamen Example", *Indian Journal of Labour Economics*, Vol.47, No.3, 20.

Morris, D. Moris (1960), *Growth of Large Scale Industries*, as quoted in Roy, Tirthankar (2005).

Mukhopadhyoy, Swapna (1992), "Casualisation of Labour in India : Concept, Incidence and Policy Options", *Indian Journal of Labour Economics*, Vol. XXXV, No. 3.

Pais, Jesim, (2002), "Casualisation of Urban Labour Force", *Economic and Political Weekly*, Vol.XXXVII, No. 7.

Roy, Tirthankar (2005), *Economic History of India*, Oxford University Press, New Delhi.

Roy, Tirthankar, (2008) "Labour Institutions, Japanese Competition, and the Crisis of Cotton Mills in Interwar Mumbai", *Economic and Political Weekly*, January 5, 2008.

Sen, Sunanda Dasgupta, Byasdeb (2008), "Labour Under Stress: Findings from a Survey", *Economic and Political Weekly*, Vol.XLIII, No.3.

Srivastava, Mukul (2009), *Trends in Banking Industry in India (1969-2006 and onwards)* in Verma and Awasthi (eds.) (2009).

Standing, G. (1999), *Global Labour Flexibility: Seeking Distributive Justice*, Macmillan Press.

Upadhya, Carol (2007), "Employment, Exclusion and Merit in the Indian IT Industry", *Economic and Political Weekly*, Vol. XLII, No. 20, May 19.

Unni, Jeemol and Raveedran, G. (2007), "Growth of Employment 1993-94 to 2004-05: Illusion of Inclusiveness", *Economic and Political Weekly*, Vol. XLII, No. 3, January 20.

Verma, N.M.P. and I.C. Awasthi (eds.) (2009), *Contractual Employment in Indian Labour Market : Emergence and Expansion*, Concept Publishing Company, New Delhi.

3

CONCEPTUALISATION OF CONTRACT LABOUR

A. B. Deogirikar and Yugandhara S.Topare

Introduction

Contract labour in Indian Industries has engaged the attention of policy makers for the last 100 years. Government actions in this area have begun as early as 1861. Now, in this globalised era, the competitive forces resulting from the removal of barriers to entry, leading to rapid growth, which requires cheap labour.

Contract labour has contributed to reduction in costs, streamline administrative and accounting procedure, a greater utilization of technological changes, outside expertise and superior technical know-how, stabilization of labour force, elimination of wastage, labour turnover, labour troubles etc.

Technological developments, faster and different form of globalization, rise of demand for specialized products, uncertainty about market growth are the major factors which support firms to adopt flexible labour practices. This has created informalization of labour. Contract labour is one of the forms of it.

Contract Labour : Meaning and Significance

The Contract labour is applied to labour which is employed to perform same work through a contractor and hence no direct employment relationship between the final employer and employee. They have contractual relationship employers prefer to use contract labour for many reasons. Employing a permanent labour imposes heavy costs.

The type of skilled employee is in demand for a specific duration.

The contract labour need not necessarily mean unskilled labour but it may involve variety of skills.

When employer concentrates on basic or core activities, he may use contract labour by outsourcing. There are two different views about the regulation and essentiality of contract labour. Judicial view explains that contract labour has to be employed for work, which is specific, and for definite duration. On the other side economic factors like cost effectiveness may justify system of contract labour.

This chapter focuses on the conceptual framework of contract labour in non-farm sector in India. It exists in formal as well as informal sector, which is known as an unorganized sector in India. Following are the key objectives of this chapter :

1. To study the Contract Labour Act, 1970 in the context of changing concepts of contract labour.
2. To find out new dimensions of contractual employment in the globalized era.
3. To study the extent of employment of contract labour in some non-farm sector in India.

Contract Labour Act, 1970

According to this act, an employment contract is an agreement entered into between an employer and employee of the commencement of the period of employment. The contract labour (Regulation and Abolition) act was passed in the 1970 to regulate the employment of contract labour in certain establishments and to provide its abolition in certain circumstances. It is applicable to the establishments employing 20 or more contract workers and to contractors employing 20 or more workers.

Section 10 of the act empowers the State government to prohibit after consultation with the board employment of contract labour in any process, operation or other work in any establishments.

The Act also seeks to promote the health and welfare of contract labour. One thing is important that contract labourers are covered under the Minimum Wages Act, employees provident fund act and employees state insurance act. They however cannot claim bonus or gratuity, as wages under the act does not consider bonus or gratuity as a part of wages.

Economic Survey 2000-01 observed that the contract labour law as it is exists today, makes it impossible for genuine small scale entrepreneurs to provide service to industry. Reforms are important in respect of contract labour.

In case of Industrial labour the judicial decisions under the labour laws also define the legal framework. If the contract is not genuine, then the contract workers can themselves raise an industrial dispute demanding regularization of their services and claiming benefits available for regular workers and the industrial tribunal can give the award on the dispute. The regular workers and not the contract workers can raise industrial dispute in this case for abolition of contract labour because there exists no employer–employee relationship between contract labourer and the principal employer. The situation is not different in other non-farm sectors.

Non-Farm Sector and Contract Labour

Various studies on labour shows that globalization has created contractualization and casualisation of workers. That is why many services are not exception to it.

In hospitals and healthcare services, contract labour in management is common. Staffing and management practices may differ among hospitals according to ownership or type of control. Study by Paul Shoemaker in USA regarding Contract Labour in hospitals shows that contract labour is more costly than permanent labour in USA's hospital sector.

In case of many other developed countries, they have separate medical directory showing the size and nature of contract workers for teaching activities. In case of India outsourcing for other administrative and management practices is a common thing in the leading states like Maharashtra, Gujarat and Andhra Pradesh in India.

According to the various amendments in the contract law in some core sectors, contract labour was prohibited but now the Government is planning to exempt certain industries such as information technology, transport, construction and maintenance of building, roads and bridges etc.

Views of Employers on Contract Labour

There is a sea change in economic activity. Economy has transformed from protectionism to liberalism. According to employers association

1. Contract labour system offers tremendous opportunities to employees. This helps to improve productivity and Services.
2. The act should be made applicable only to the main and core activities of the establishments.
3. Supportive or allied activities of an establishments like maintenance, housekeeping should be out sourced and the act should only provide for regulating the working conditions.
4. If the Contract Labour system is cost effective, is not allowed to continue industries may go in for technological restructuring with less number of workers leading to reduction of employment.

Trade unions are opposed to the idea of outsourcing of services in jobs. According to them :

1. Outsourcing will lead to a type of employment, which is exploitative.
2. Second Labour Commission has also specified that contract labour shall not be engaged for core production/services activities. However for sporadic seasonal demand the employer may engage temporary labour for core production/service activity.

Economic Reforms and Labour Policy

The number of contract workers is high in informal sector. According to the ILO Report, 1999 (International Labour Organization) on

"Decent Work" the primary goal at the ILO today is to promote opportunities for women and men to obtain decent and productive work, in conditions of freedom, equity, security and human dignity.

Here ILO's Four strategic objectives are :

"The promotion of rights at work, employment, social protection and social dialogue" Means, here we have to consider the unorganized sector also. This is neglected regarding implementation of labour laws even today. There is a need of separate law for unorganized sector.

The data and statistics regarding contract labour other than manufacturing sector are not available. This will be helpful for study as well as for policy formulation.

Statistics regarding outsourcing in healthcare, education, construction, engineering and information technology is important for the study. It should be maintained. Finally we can conclude that:

Conclusion

1. Changes and amendments are important in Contract Act, 1970 on the background of changing economic conditions.
2. Unorganized sector should be considered as an integral part in the labour policy formulation.
3. According to the ILO reports, creation of jobs will not create human dignity but acceptable quality of job is also important

4

THE GLOOMY PICTURE OF CONTRACT LABOUR IN INDIA

PRASOON KUMAR ROY AND MEERA KUMARI

The aim of this chapter is to analyse and assess contract labour in India. For this purpose, the chapter is divided into six sections. Section-I analyses the factors influencing the emergence of contract labour. Section-II discusses the concept of contract labour. Section-III highlights the relevance of the contract labour. Section-IV explains the oppositions of the concept. Section-V discusses the regulation made regarding contract labour in India. Section VI analyses the suggestions to make contract labour more lucrative to labourers.

I. Factors Influencing the Emergence of Contract Labour

Contract labour is one of the modes of recruiting labour in any firm or an establishment or by an individual. It is more prevalent in big size industries. Simultaneously different jobs (skilled or unskilled) have also adopted this in their workings. In other words, contract labour has got deep roots in many industries of India. The important industries may be named as engineering, cotton textile, dock yards, paper, coir matting, mining, central and states public welfare department etc. It shows that these industries are big industries which do not seek only works to be done perfectly and timely but would also like to get free from the responsibilities of labourers such as leave, pension, dearness allowance, gratuity, promotions etc. So this concept makes work easy not only to be done under the existing conditions but also makes possible to achieve the targeted result. In this way contract labour is very common and result oriented in the mines of India, particularly of West Bengal, Bihar, Jharkhand, Madhya Pradesh, Orissa and Andhra Pradesh. Besides these, at present the prospect of job has brightened in the sphere of medical, engineering, teaching, banking, consultancy etc. That is why engineers, doctors, lecturers, bankers, consultants are recruited on contract. These factors have influenced the emergence of contract labour in India.

II. The Concept of Contract Labour

So far the concept of contract labour is concerned we may say that a labour who is hired, supervised and remunerated by the firm or by an establishment or by an individual on a contract is called a contract labour. In other words, a workman is supposed to be employed as contract labour when he is hired in connection with work of an establishment by or through a contractor (Datt, 2003). According to the contract labour (Regulation and Abolition Act 1970), a person is said to be employed as a contract labour, in or in connection with the work of an establishment when he is hired for such work by or through a contractor, with or without the knowledge of the principal employer (Garg, 1999). Dr. Shakuntala Mahawal says that a contract labour is a person who is hired, supervised, contracted and remunerated by a contractor, who in turn, is compensated by the user enterprises (Mahawal, 2004). From the above mentioned views it seems that a labour who possesses the criteria of having indirect relationship with the firm or an establishment and wage payment, is a contract labour. So contract labour becomes an indirect employee of the firm or an establishment. They do not involve themselves in any direct responsibility with regard to the labour. Saxena (1986) has rightly said about the causes of non-involvement of the firm or industry regarding the contract labour. A contract labour is neither on pay roll nor is paid directly. This is the essence of the concept of contract labour. So contract labour implies the conditions like an agreement, lack of responsibilities like leave, medical, fringe benefits and no further considerations for works etc.

The contract labour is of different types. It is normally of three types: First labour contract workers, second out workers and third sub-contract workers.

First, labour contract workers are such type of workers who are dependent on contractors or agents. These workers are hired for the employers. In other words, these workers totally depend upon the contractors for their works to the employers.

Second type is outworkers. By outworkers we mean casual labour who works on contract basis. The employers prefer to recruit this type of labour whenever they need labour for works.

Third, Sub-contract workers are those workers who do the works indirectly. In other words they are the workers who are deprived of the benefits of labour laws.

After the discussion of the types of contract labour we may say that it is the contract labour who bears the real burden or target of production in the establishment or an organisation with result.

III. The Relevance of Contract Labour

Now the question arises regarding the relevance of the contract labour in the industries. Its relevance is evident by its uses in different industries and in different jobs. It would be worthwhile to point out the statement of the Labour Investigation Committee 1946. The Committee states that immediate employment of a large force at short notice to facilitate speedy execution of work, the want of adequate supervisory staff, and the absence of adequate machinery of employment exchanges which would supply the required number of workers when needed have been one of the reasons advanced in favour of the employment of contract labour (G.O.I., 1969). They do not bother to maintain establishment and make efforts to invest capital and to instal plants. Secondly, employers are free from the worries of labour because they do not engage labour directly. The labour comes through the contractor, which may be a firm or an establishment or an individual. So they have not to provide any benefit or welfare measures to the workers. Employers do not pay even fringe benefit like leave, provident fund, sickness benefit and minimum wages etc. Thirdly, contract labour is beneficial particularly for those types of works which have vast dimensions. Public works department and construction works are important examples of it. It is very convenient for these works. Fourthly, contract labour gives result in production without proper supervision. In other words, it comprises supervision and look after. It reduces the working cost of the firm or an organisation. In this way, this concept makes efforts to get the employers benefited in many ways.

IV. The Oppositions of the Contract Labour

This section comprises the oppositions of the concept. Contract labour is considered as the most exploited form of labour. The Second Five Year Plan also supports the fact of extreme exploitation of the contract labour (Datt, 2003). The Royal Commission on labour also recommended the legal abolition of contract labour because it enables the employer to escape most of the provisions of the Labour Acts. The employers become free from making available the Acts, like Factories Act, the Payment of Wages Act and the Maternity Benefit Act. The workmen Compensation Act provides protection to workers only in a few areas. Secondly, the contract system lacks the sense of obligation towards labour, which the employers should keep. They exploit the weak position of the labour as far as they can do. The Bihar Labour Enquiry Committee has rightly said that ordinarily it lacks the sense of moral obligation towards labour which the employers or their managers are expected to have and, therefore, do not often hesitate to exploit the helpers position of labour in their charge (Tyagi, 2004). Thirdly, contract system depends upon the bid of the contract. Normally contract is given to the lowest bidder. So he tries to give low wages as far as possible to their employees or he would be in loss. This spreads the messages of exploitation through wages in the society. One of the important defects of the Contract system or labour is the financial gain, which the employer gets by escaping the responsibility for any welfare measures. From the above discussion it reveals that contract system gives an illusory views of contract labour but it is a great exploitation of the labour in the society.

V. Regulation Made Regarding Contract Labour in India

This section discusses the regulation made by the Government regarding the Contract Labour in India. Before this regulation many efforts were done to remove the defects of the contract system but it remained the same for a long period. A bill for regulation and abolition of employment of contract labour was presented in the Lok Sabha on July 31, 1967 to get it passed. The Contract Labour (Regulation and Abolition) Bill was passed by the Parliament in 1970 and became the Act on 5th September, 1970 after getting the consent of the President of India. It came into force with effect from 10th February, 1971. Following are the main provisions of the contract labour (Regulation and Abolition) Act 1970.

The first and foremost provision of the contract Labour (Regulation and Abolition) Act 1970 is the application of the Act. The Act applies in all parts of the country since its inception. It covers such type of establishment or an organisation where twenty or more than twenty labourers are engaged in permanent nature of works. It means that the act does not apply to those organisations or an establishment where casual nature of work is performed.

Another provision of the Contract Labour Act is the definition of a contractor. The Act defines such a person as a contractor who does the works of job contract with a given result. This Act has also defined a sub-contractor as a contractor because he performs the works of supplying contract labour for any work of an organisation and establishment. The act makes it clear that if a work s done by a person on a contract basis then he may be called a contractor.

One of the features of contract Labour Act is licensing of contractors. It reveals that a contractor can do work as the provision are made in a license. Hours of work, fixation of wages and other conditions are laid down in the license issued to them by the licensing officer. In no case they can go beyond the arrangements of the license.

The Act provides certain facilities such as canteen, restrooms, safe drinking water, latrines, urinals, first aid facilities etc to the contract labourers. These facilities enhance the spirit of the contract labourers to the managements.

The Act provides ways to determine the wages to be paid by the contractor to the contract labourers. The contractor follows the following two methods while he determines the rate of wage payment. Firstly, the contractor has to fix the wage as it is given in the minimum wages Act 1948. The question does not arise how the rate is fixed? How has it been fixed by an agreement or settlement or award? In other words, it can be said that wage is always fixed according to the Minimum Wage Payment Act 1948.

Secondly, the contractor considers the issues such as wage rate, holidays, hours of work and other facilities etc. for the similar works to the contractor as is given to the directly employed labourers. In other words the contractor keeps in his mind the facilities directly provided to the employed labourers.

The act lays down the responsibility regarding the payment of wages to the labourers. The contractor is solely responsible for making wage payment to the contract labour as the period is fixed in the Agreement of Contract. The act is supervised by the nominated person of the main employers. Its aim is to restrict exploitation of the contractor and to perform works smoothly and peacefully in the industries or an organisation.

The above mentioned are the provisions of Contract Labour (Regulation and Abolition) Act 1970. The aim of this act is to restrict exploitation of the contract labour by keeping them at par with the permanent labour through ensuring payment of wages and to perform the contract works smoothly and peacefully by providing facilities to the contract labour by the contractor (G.O.I., 2002).

So far the enforcement of this act is concerned it may be said that the Central and State governments are empowered for its working. They can prohibit employment of contract labour in any activity or in establishment and can grant exemption of the provision of the Act to establishments/ contractors in the case of emergency (Mahawal, 2004). The Central Industrial Relation Machinery has the power of enforcing the provisions and rules of the Act in the case of central issues. In this way, it acts at the Central and State levels in the country (G.O.I., 2006).

VI. Suggestions to make Contract Labour more Lucrative to Labourers

This section consists of suggestions, which are made to make the contract labour more effective and lucrative. We may suggest certain measures for removing the evils of contract labour.

Firstly, to solve the problem of contract labour efforts should be made to know about the nature and prospects of its problems. So it examines the possibilities of its end. It thinks to save the exploitation of labourers with the help of acceptable measures.

Secondly, efforts should be made to decide the types of works where the responsibility of wage payment and good working conditions can be put over the shoulders of both contractor as well as the employer. The situation turns automatically in favour of the contract labour when both share the responsibility. The labourers start gaining the benefits of contract labour.

Thirdly, measure should be taken to remove the contract system gradually, while doing so they should be watchful for the labourers. If the labourers become unemployed they should quickly be engaged in other works also. It means that measures should be taken in view of the labourers' position and their future in their action plans.

Fourthly, contract labour should get all types of protection and working conditions what do other labourers get in industries. In other words, contract labour deserves the same type of behaviour and treatment what other labourers do get there. It removes not only the evil of discrimination but also injects the feelings of dedication to work more for their establishments.

And lastly, the system of contract labour should be replaced by the direct system of employment. Direct system consists of transparency and security and Certainty of works which help the labourers to perform works sincerely and dedicatedly.

At last, we may conclude that the contract labour gives a gloomy picture for the labourers but it should be handled with care for a country like India where the problem of labour force prevails.

REFERENCES

Datt, Ruddar (2003), *Economic Reforms, Labour and Employment*, Deep and Deep Publications, New Delhi, p. 291.

Garg, Ajay (1999), *Labour Laws One Should Know*, A Noble Publication, New Delhi, p. 25.

Government of India, *Economic Survey 2005-2006*, Ministry of Finance, Economic Division, New Delhi, 2006, p. 218.

Government of India, *Report of the National Commission on Labour*, Ministry of Labour, New Delhi, 1969, p. 69.

Government of India (2002), *Report of the National Commission on Labour*, Ministry of Labour, New Delhi, 2002, Vol. II, pp. 38-39.

Mahawal, Shakuntala (2004), *India—A Reference Annual, Publication Division, Ministry of Information and Broadcasting*, Government of India, New Delhi, 2004, p. 503.

Saxena, R. C. (1986), *Labour Problems and Social Welfare*, K. Nath & Co., Meerut, p. 46.

Tyagi, B. P. (2004), *Labour Economics and Social Welfare*, Jai Prakash Nath and Co. Meerut, 2004, p. 37.

5

EVALUATION OF CONTRACT LABOUR EMPLOYMENT IN INDIA

J. V. VAISHAMPAYAN AND NAGENDRA KUMAR MAURYA

Introduction

As different countries of the world embark on the path of economic reforms for faster economic growth and development, many new challenges are forthcoming. On the one hand, there is a challenge of faster economic growth and on the other there is the challenge of ensuring distributive justice and inclusive growth. Similarly, due to increasing population, on the one hand, we want employment opportunities to grow fast, and on the other, we want labour to be protected. The system of contract labour is perceived to be a mechanism of improving employment opportunities. But there are serious implications for protecting the interest of labour. In this chapter we seek to address this issue in the context of our country.

India is a country of the largest labour market in the world. With globalisation, the employment structure in the Indian economy has been undergoing changes. In order to adapt to the fast changing world and compete effectively in a globalised market, firms need flexibility relating to labour, capital, or bureaucracy. In this regard, stringent labour regulations not only put domestic producers at a disadvantage but also deter foreign direct investment and eventually impact adversely on investments, output and employment. Over the last two decades, number of countries has attempted to liberalise their respective labour markets and have also amended their labour laws so as to make them more investment and employment friendly, a process that has weakened job security and collective bargaining.

Indian labour market is characterized by a sharp dichotomy, a large number of establishments in the unorganized sector remain outside any regulation, while the organised sector has been regulated fairly stringently. It can be reasonable to argue that the unorganized sector has provided too little to too many. In unorganized sector we have been witnessing increasing share of non-permanent employment over time, that is casualisation of employment.

Table 5.1 : Distributions of Workers (usual status) by Category of Employment (per cent)

Year	Self- employed	Regular salaried	Casual
1977-78	59.9	13.9	27.2
1987-88	56.0	14.4	29.6
1993-94	54.8	13.2	32.0
1999-2000	52.9	13.9	33.2

Source: Deshpande *et al.*, 2004.

The system of employing contract labour is prevalent in most industries in different occupations including skilled and semiskilled job. It is also prevalent in agricultural and allied operations and to some extent in the services sector.

A workman shall deemed to be employed as a 'contract labour' in or in connection with the work of an establishment when he is hired in or in connection with such work by or without the knowledge of the principal employer. 'Contractor' in relation to an establishment, means a person who undertakes to produce a given result for the establishment other than a mere supply of goods of articles of manufacture to such establishments, through contract labour or who supplies contract labour for any work of the establishment and includes a sub-contractors. Contract workmen are indirect employees, persons who are hired, supervised and remunerated by a contractor who, in turn, is compensated by the establishment. Contract labour has to be employed for a period, which is specific, and for definite duration. Inferior labour status, casual nature of employment lack of job security and poor economic conditions is the major characteristics of contract labour. While economic factors like cost effectiveness may justify system of contract labour, considerations of social justice call for its abolition or regulation.

The Contract Labour (Regulation and Abolition) Act, 1970

In the Constitution of India, 'industrial relations' is a concurrent subject. This implied that Central and State governments have joint jurisdiction over labour regulation legislation. The key piece of central legislation is the Industrial Dispute Act of 1947, which sets out the conciliation, arbitration and adjudication procedures to be followed in the case of an industrial dispute. The regulation that is relevant for the contract labour class is the Contract Labour (Regulation and Abolition) Act, 1970. Contract labour act makes certain provisions for the welfare of the contract labour class. They include payment of minimum wage, certain health and sanitation facilities in the work premise, provident fund benefits and so on. In order to ascertain that such norms are complied with, labour inspectors are engaged for supervision.

The Contract Labour (Regulation and Abolition) Act, 1970 and the Contract Labour (Regulation and Abolition) Central Rules, 1971 came into force on 10-02-1971. The constitutional validity of the Act and the Central Rules were challenged before the Supreme Court but the Supreme Court upheld the constitutional validity of the Act and Rules and held that there is no unreasonableness in the measure. The Act and Rules were enforced with effect from 21-03-1974.

The Act is applicable to every establishment in which 20 or more workmen are employed or were employed on any day in the preceding 12 months as contract labour and to every contractor who employs or who has employed on any day of the preceding 12 months 20 or more workmen. It does not apply to establishments where the work performed is of intermittent or seasonal nature. An establishment wherein work is of intermittent and seasonal nature will be covered by the Act if the work performed is more than 120 days and 60 days in a year respectively. The Act also applies to establishments of the Government and local authorities as well.

The jurisdiction of the Central and State governments has been laid down by the definition of the 'Appropriate Government' in Section 2(1)(a) of the Act, as amended in 1986. The Appropriate Government in relation to an establishment would be the Central Government if, the concerned Central government company/ undertaking or any undertaking is included by name in clause (a) of Section 2 of the Industrial Disputes Act, or any industry carried on by or under the authority company, or any such controlled industry as may be specified in this behalf by the Central government, otherwise in relation to any other establishment, the government of the State in which that other establishment is situated will be the appropriate government.

The Central government and State governments are required to set up Central and State Advisory Contract Labour Boards to advise the respective Governments on matters arising out of the administration of the Act as are referred to them. The Boards are authorized to constitute committees as deemed proper.

Licensing of Contractors

The establishment covered under the Act is required to be registered as principal employers with the appropriate authorities. Every contractor is required to obtain a license and not to undertake or execute any work through contract labour except under and in accordance with the license issued in that behalf by the licensing officer. The license is granted subject to such conditions as to hours of work, fixation of wages and other essential amenities in respect of contract labour as laid down in the rules. In the central sphere, the Central Industrial Relations Machinery (CIRM) have been entrusted with the responsibility of enforcing the provisions of the Act and the rules made thereunder, through Inspectors, Licensing Officers, Registering Officers and Appellate Authorities appointed under the Act. The Field Officers of the CIRM are conducting regular inspections and prosecutions are launched against the establishment, whenever violations of the Act/Rules/Notifications of contract labour are detected.

But the contractors are not so honest. They are continuously playing with rules and regulations. This has evidenced by following Table 5.2.

Table 5.2 : Enforcement of Contract Labour (Regulation and Abolition) Act, 1970

Year	Registration certificates issued to principal employers (A)	Registration certificates revoked (B)	Licences issued to contractors (C)	Licences revoked/ cancelled (D)	(D/C*100)
1996-97	375	23	3613	757	20.95
1997-98	425	NIL	4660	1371	29.42
1998-99	639	NIL	5471	1669	30.50
1999-00	670	NIL	6632	1099	16.57
2000-01	658	2	7734	3562	46.06
2001-02	516	NIL	6827	3904	57.18
2002-03	796	NIL	7081	6552	92.53
2003-04	720	52	6788	4014	59.13
2004-05	590	08	7277	6601	90.71
2005-06	747	211	7317	7632	104.3

Source: Annual Reports, Ministry of Labour, and Government of India—Various Issues.

In Table 5.2 we see that number of Registration Certificates issued to principal employers is increasing, and the cancellations are few or nil. However, in recent years the cancellation rates are very high. This can be due to non-compliance of various rules of the act by the principal employers. Similarly, this increasing tendency of non-compliance is also evidenced by increasing number of licenses cancelled of contractors. For example, number of licenses cancelled in 1996 was 20.09 per cent of issued licenses, which increased to 57.18 per cent in 2001 and 90.71 per cent in 2004. Even in the year 2005, total numbers of cancelled licenses were more than issued. These trends question the effectiveness of the provisions of the Contract Labour Act.

Table 5.3 : Enforcement of Contract Labour (Regulation and Abolition) Act, 1970

Year	Contract labour covered by licences (1)	Licences issued to contractors (2)	Licences revoked/ cancelled (3)	Contract labour per licence (1/2)	Contract labour per licence (adjusted) [1/(2—3)]
1996-97	489776	3613	757	135.56	171.44
1997-98	588678	4660	1371	126.33	178.98
1998-99	664216	5471	1669	121.41	174.74
1999-00	762425	6632	1099	114.96	137.79
2000-01	773849	7734	3562	100.06	185.49
2001-02	709030	6827	3904	103.86	242.57
2002-03	1327298	7081	6552	187.44	2509.06
2003-04	853690	6788	4014	125.76	307.75
2004-05	968792	7277	6601	133.13	1433.12
2005-06	983707	7317	7632	134.44	-

Source: Annual Reports, Ministry of Labour, Government of India—Various Issues.

If we talk about the number of contract labour per licensed contractor, then there is not any clear trend and it is around 125 per licensed contractor. But if we take into account cancellation of licenses then, there is sudden increase in number of contract labour per licensed contractor. For example, in 1996, it increases from 135.56 to 171.41, in 2000 from 100.06 to 185.49 and in 2004 form 133.13 to 1453.12. This increasing number poses a challenge to the government for their commitment to provide safety cover to contract labour.

Contract Labour and Wages

The contractor is required to pay wages and a duty is cast on him to ensure disbursement of wages in the presence of the authorized representative of the principal employer. In case of failure on the part of the contractor to pay wages either in part or in full, the principal employer is liable to pay the same. The contract labour, who performs same or similar kind of work as regular workmen, will be entitled to the same wages and service conditions as regular workmen as per the Contract Labour (Regular and Abolition) Rules, 1971. But the reality is somewhat different. A number of complaints have been received by the Deputy Chief Labour Commissioner (Central) from the contract workers or their unions, claiming that the

Table 5.4 : Number of Cases Received and Disposed of under the Contract Labour (Regulation and Abolition) Central Rules, 1971 relating to Wages

Year	Number of cases received under rule 25 (2)(v)(a) and (b)	Order issued
1996-97	04	01
1997-98	06	04
1998-99	15	03
1999-00	35	05
2000-01	23	20
2001-02	46	22
2002-03	23	06

Source: Annual Report, Ministry of Labour, Government of India, various issues.

Table 5.5 : Wages per Man-day Worked (Rs.)

Year	2001-02	2002-03	2003-04
All Workers	152.38	158.75	165.55
Contract Workers	90.95	96.68	100.96

Source: Annual Report, Ministry of Labour, Government of India, 2006-07.

contract workers are performing the same or similar work as performed by the workmen employed by the principal employer but they are not getting payment and other service benefits.

In Table 5.4 we see that number of complaints is increasing which shows irregularities in payments of wages and non-compliance of rules regarding payment of wages. These irregularities also show the fact that bargaining power of the contract labour is very weak. Table 5.5 also supports this fact. Table 5.5 shows that the gap between wages of contract labourers and other workers is increasing.

Welfare and Health of Contract Labour

The Act has laid down certain amenities to be provided by the contractor to the contract labour of establishment of canteens and rest rooms and arrangements for sufficient supply of drinking water, latrines, urinals, washing facilities have been made obligatory. In cases of failure on the part of the contractor to provide these facilities, the principal employer is liable to provide the same.

Prospects of Contract Labour Employment

Since, the enactment of the law in 1970, the economy has undergone a sea change, from an era of protectionism to liberalization, from restricted domestic competition to international competitiveness. This increasing contractualisation of employment has both types of effects on the economy.

The system of contract labour offers tremendous opportunities for employment and allows the employers flexibility to choose what is best for them. This helps improve efficiency, productivity and service competitiveness. Contract Labour is more suited to supportive or allied activities of an establishment like maintenance, house keeping etc. If the contract labour system, which is cost effective, is not allowed to continue, industries may go in for technological restructuring with lesser number of workers leading to reduction in employment opportunities or they may lose their international competitiveness which would have serious implications for both growth and employment generation. That is why it is often pointed out that economic reforms are not complete without labour reforms.

On the other hand there are several limitations also. The contract labour generally belongs to weaker section and is generally unskilled or semi-skilled, which puts them in a disadvantageous position as compared to regular employees. The contract labour is not always suitable for employers also. They do not have any affinity or loyalty for the establishment where they are working. There is high turnover in contract employment because the contract labour is always in search of a more suitable employment. Efficiency levels will, therefore, decrease in an establishment, as the establishment will be deprived of experienced staff. Similarly, coordination of activities with large number of contractors and sub-contractors well prove to be more time consuming and costly.

We can, therefore, say that the system of contract labour is of mixed blessings. While it can create high level of employment opportunities, exploitation of labour is also to be avoided. Only the laws and rules relating to the contract labour are not sufficient to improve their socio-economic conditions, some other complementary measures should also be taken in this regard. Abolition of the contract labour is not the solution; there is need for more proper and strict vigilance of activities of contractors and principal employers. The Contract Labour (Regulation and Abolition) Central Rules, 1971, should try to cover each and every contract labour under its periphery. In this regard, the principal employers should ensure payment of wages to contract labour as laid down under the law in force as also other basic amenities and social security benefits.

They should be provided training for works requiring specialized skills within the establishment and there should be in-house improvements and restructuring. By doing this we can provide them more opportunities that would help them in raising their economic status and bargaining power.

REFERENCES

Contract Labour (Regulation and Abolition) Act, 1970.

"Contract Labour (Regulation and Abolition) Central Rules", 1971.

Meenakshi, Rajeev (2005), *Contract Labour Act in India: A Pragmatic View*, Institute for Social and Economic Change, Bangalore.

Ministry of Finance, *Economic Survey*, Government of India, 2006-07.

Ministry of Labour, Annual Report, Government of India, Various Issues.

Part - II

Contract Labour in the Emerging Labour Market

6

THE STATUS AND PROSPECTS OF CONTRACT LABOUR IN THE ERA OF ECONOMIC REFORMS

ASHOK MATHUR

ATTRIBUTES OF CONTRACT LABOUR

The distinctive characteristic of contract labour which sets it apart from those in regular employment is that in their case the principal employer for whom contract labour works is different from the person or agency which engages them as contract labour. Actual production takes place in the production unit (or corporation) where contract labour works while it is the contractor or the agency, which pays it the wages. Ensuring work performance on the floor of a factory or construction site is responsibility of the principal employer. But the term on which remuneration is to be made is settled by the contractor or the agency. The indirect employer, or the so-called principal employer, makes a payment to the contractor, which may be a lump sum, for supplying it labour according to its needs. Labour supplied may vary over different seasons, depending upon the needs of the production unit at different times. Thus the use of contract labour frees a production unit from the hassles of finding suitable labour in desired numbers, verifying its antecedents, settling its wages, etc. The producer can concentrate his energies more efficiently on the task of undertaking production and marketing the product that enables him to reap certain economies of scale.

This system of procuring labour through a contractor carries with it certain implications. First, the terms and conditions for supply of labour to the production unit are settled by the contractor with the principal employer who owns the unit, often without any binding about the wages which the contractor may pay to labour involved in production process. It is, therefore, in the interest of the contractor to pay as little as possible by way of monetary wages to the workers. The wages paid, therefore, tend to be much lower than those in regular employment. This is the ground reality despite labour laws which contractors bypass in view of weak law implementation machinery.

Secondly, since the principal employer is not the actual hirer of labour, the employer bears no responsibility for conforming to any requirements under labour laws. He does not have to pay any fringe benefits. The labour employed is not given any form of social security either by way of provident fund, entitlement to any health expenditure in case of illness, etc. Thus remuneration received by labour for its services tends to be extremely poor.

Thirdly, there is no security of tenure. A worker can be hired and fired at the will of the contractor. He does not have any liability to pay any separation costs in case he is fired without any notice. Further, since contract labour is very poorly paid, workers often have to take loans in the form of advances, particularly to meet any exigencies like cost of treatment in case of illness, social expenditure like marriage of dependents within the family, etc. They find it difficult to repay these loans, which often put them in almost perpetual bondage to the contractor. In case of migrant labour, it cannot run away from its liability to the contractor since the contractor himself generally belongs to the area from which labour is obtained and has close contacts at the root level in that area.

Finally, contract labour is by and large non-unionized, which makes it difficult for it to act as a pressure group and reduces its bargaining strength. It is for all these reasons that contract labour is taken to be a highly exploited segment of labour. Thus remuneration received by labour for its services tends to be extremely poor.

Thus, from a producer's point of view the contract labour system provides it with certain advantages that save his costs although from labour's point of view it is exploitative. It is these advantages to the producer conferred by the system, which led to its evolution in the early phases of industrialization in India, initially in the form of jobbers employed by English technicians who were not conversant with the *lingua franca.*

IMPERATIVES OF DEALING WITH CONTRACT LABOUR ISSUES

In any approach to the issue of contract labour, particularly in the context of present economic environment, three considerations need to be kept in mind. First, labour is one of the three basic factors of production, viz., land, labour and capital. But labour, and by that taken contract labour, stands on a very different plane from the other two, at least in one respect. Labour is a 'living entity', but land and capital are 'non-living' factors of production, although owners of these two factors are also living beings. Being a living entity, consideration of human welfare become very important in the context of labour and cannot be set aside while formulating policy.

The second consideration has acquired a centre stage position since the advent of economic reforms of nineteen-nineties and the widening impact of globalization. This refers of the Structural Adjustment component of economic reforms of nineteen nineties and the widening impact of globalization. The Structural Adjustment component of economic reform package emphasizes that free-play of competitive market forces is essential for achieving a fast pace of economic growth. This is considered to be necessary to achieve higher levels of productive efficiency at lower level of costs, particularly in the context of globalization where lower costs are crucial for promoting exports and attracting direct foreign investment. Lower level of costs in the context of labour market implies that wage and other payments to workers should be kept as low as possible. From this perspective and from employers' point of view, contract labour becomes more suited than labour in regular employment where remuneration to labour tends to be higher for reasons that have been outlined earlier. However, the spirit of this formulation runs counter to the first imperative outlined in the previous paragraph. It is, therefore, important to examine the manner in which the area of conflict between social considerations and the pace of growth inherent in a Structural Adjustment programme can be minimized. It is not inevitable that the two must run counter to each other. This is an issue that shall be addressed later in this chapter .

The third consideration one has to bear in mind is the fact that contract labour is only one segment of the labour which is in non-regular employment and is not covered by legislation providing essential requirements for decent employment in the form of norms regarding hours of work, wages, minimum social security requirements, etc. Those employed in the informal or so-called unorganized sector or even casual workers working in the organized sector are not covered by labour legislation ensuring minimum requirements for decent working conditions. Some of these categories overlap one another. They are no better than contract labour in terms of human welfare. That is one of the reasons why ILO has not postulated an international standard dealing with contract labour despite a lot of discussion and debates concerning contract labour. ILO has relied on a broader approach concerning all forms of labour needing protection in order to ensure norms for decent working conditions.

Moreover, contract labour itself is characterized by more than one form. There are at least two major forms, that of 'labour contract' and 'job contract'. In the former case only the services of labour are provided by an intermediary known as contractor or an agency supplying labour. Only the remuneration paid to workers and provision of the requisite number of persons needed by the producer at any point of time fall within the domain of contractor's duties. Management of labour on the shop floor, extracting work out of labour supplied timings of work and how proficiently labour works, are the responsibility of the producer. On the other hand, in case of 'job contract', which is akin to what earlier used to be called the 'putting out' system, the contractor is responsible for ensuring work performance of labour and delivering the finished product. Raw materials required, other processed inputs and equipment or specialized tools/instruments needed in the production process are generally provided by the producer, who is considered to be the principal employer. But here also the contractor has very little responsibility to ensure 'decent work' conditions. Provision of crèches, social security to workers or any health facilities, are not the responsibility of the contractor or sub-contractors, which are many a time engaged by the contractor.

There is also a third variant of contracting-out system in which the entire responsibility for producing and supplying the desired product becomes that of the contracting party. The equipment and raw materials are also purchased directly by the contracting party, whose main responsibility is to produce and supply the desired goods as and when needed. This type of product supply relationship is akin to that of ancillary production. Here, although the labour required is engaged by the producer, but strictly speaking it cannot be designated as that of contract system since there is a direct employer-employee relationship of the ancillary producer with labour engaged in producing the ancillary output. The responsibility for conforming to labour laws becomes that of the ancillary producer. But in practice this responsibility is mostly non-operative since the ancillary producers are generally — but not always — informal sector units. The second variant outlined above is also similar to ancillary production in many respects but falls short of it since certain obligations are still the responsibility of principal employer, viz., provision of raw materials, equipment, space for production, etc.

QUANTITATIVE MAGNITUDE OF CONTRACT LABOUR

In the background of what has been outlined above, it is imperative to bear in mind as to how significant is the size of contract labour within the total unprotected category of labour and, secondly, to examine its growth in relation to that of other types of employment. There are two difficulties, which arise in this context when one tries to assess the quantitative magnitudes. First, data are available only in respect of labour employed by licensed contractors, which are collected by the Director General of Employment and Training (DGET). But even within the category of contract labour, licensed contractors form only one category. They cover those contractors who employ more than 20 workers. Those providing labour on contract to small producers, and employ less than 20 workers, do not generally obtain license and would mostly fail to get enumerated.

However, if we confine our attention only to licensed contractors, their number increased from 4.90 lakh in 1996 to 7.62 lakh in 1999 and 9.5 lakh in 2005 as shown by Table 6.1, which is reproduced from M.S. Ramanujam (2004). One has, however to bear in mind that licensed contract labour does not cover those working on job contract, home based workers working on individual contracts, etc. If one includes all such categories, the size of contract labour would go up manifold.

Table 6.1 : Organised and Unorganised Sector Workers and Contract Labour Engaged by Licenced Contractor (in lakh)

Year	Organised Sector	Contract Workers engaged by licenced contractor
1996	279.41	4.90
1997	282.45	5.89
1998	281.45	6.64
1999	283.91	7.62

Source : M.S. Ramanujam (2004).

In order to gauge the relative magnitude of licensed contract labour in relation to unorganized workers, one may turn to recent estimates prepared by the National Commission for Enterprise in the Unorganized Sector (NCEUS, 2007). According to NCEUS, number of workers engaged in the Unorganized Sector, which it defines as enterprises employing less than ten workers, was 342.6 million in 1999-2000 and 394.9 million in 2004-05. However, NCEUS has estimated, on the one hand, that 1.4 million of these are formal workers having social security cover, etc. Thus, out of 342.6m workers in 1999-00 in unorganized sector (393.5 million in 2004-05),

341.3 million were unprotected workers. On the other hand, in addition to these unprotected workers in the unorganized sector, all workers in the organized sector are not protected. As high as 20.5 million workers among the organized sector workers in 1999-00 (29.1 million in 2004-05) were also unprotected thus qualifying only as informal workers. If one adds these informal workers in the formal sector, the total magnitude of informal (unorganized) workers emerges to be 361.7 million in 1999-00 (422.6 million in 2004-05) and not 342.6 million in 1999-00 (394.9 million in 2004-05), which is the size of unorganized sector workforce. Thus total number of unorganized workers is slightly higher than the unorganized sector workforce of 361.7 million in 1999-00 (422.6 million in 2004-05). It one uses total unprotected workforce of 361.7 million in 1999-00 (422.6 million in 2004-05), the proportion of licensed contract labour (7.62 lakh in 1999-00) works out to be only 0.21 per cent in 1999-00 and 2.2 per cent in 2004-05. However, this proportion would be much higher if one were to include non-licensed contract labour, whose exact magnitude is not captured by the existing data.

Another form of classification, which also throws some light, though from a different angle, on the relative magnitude of unprotected worker is in terms of National Sample Survey's categorization of labour into the three types of employment status, viz., regular wage employed, self employed and casual workers. Out of these, the last category would be almost entirely unprotected. Contract labour would, by and large, belong to the third category, namely, that of casual workers since there are no restrictions on hire and fire conditions applicable to them. Only a very small proportion may qualify for the regular employment status. A look at Table 6.2. reveals that the largest segment of labour belongs to the self-employed category. This obviously does not include any contract labour. But it consists of dualism within itself. There are those belonging to a fairly high level of income like these engaged as practising lawyers, medical consultants architects, chartered accountants, technicians, prosperous businessmen, etc. At the other end are those engaged as street hawkers, shoe-shiners, rickshaw pullers, etc. A good many of these would fall in the category of those who are already in need of some sort of protection and support to enhance

Table 6.2 : Trend of Employment Status (per cent of Total Workforce)

Year	Overall			Rural			Urban		
	S.E.	**W.E**	**C.L**	**S.E.**	**W.E**	**C.L**	**S.E.**	**W.E**	**C.L**
1978	57.0	14.6	28.4	60.4	8.6	31.0	40.3	44.2	15.5
1983	54.1	15.3	30.6	57.8	8.5	33.7	39.7	42.2	18.1
1988	53.6	15.2	31.2	56.7	8.6	34.7	40.5	42.7	16.8
1994	51.9	14.7	33.5	55.1	7.2	37.7	40.3	41.5	18.2
1996	52.4	15.9	32.8	56.3	6.4	37.3	39.9	42.0	18.2
1997	52.6	14.5	32.9	57.0	6.1	36.9	38.7	40.9	20.4
1998	50.7	12.3	37.0	53.0	6.0	41.0	40.8	39.3	19.9
2000	49.8	21.6	28.6	55.8	67.5	37.4	42.3	39.9	17.8
2005	53.5	21.7	24.7	60.2	70.2	32.8	45.5	39.4	15.1

Note : S.E. stand for self-employed; W.E. is wage employed; C.L. is casual labour

Source: Ashok Mathur, (2002); and various issues of NSS Reports on Employment and Unemployment.

their level of living, as do the workers in categories of casual and regular workers.

APPROACH OF GOVERNMENT TO CONTRACT AND OTHER LABOUR CATEGORIES

The focus of Government's approach towards labour issues after the dawn of independence has been much more on those employed in the organized sector than on those engaged in informal activities. It is only for the last few years after the setting up of the National Commission for Enterprises in the Unorganized Sector that some change has been initiated in the approach to informal sector workers. In case of organized sector workers, Government's approach has taken the form of measures based on legislative Acts. These can be classified into four distinct categories, which are outlined below :

(i) Social Security and Labour Welfare Legislation

The basic aim of this type of legislation is to provide decent working conditions, adequate safeguards against disease/affliction and some support beyond the working life span. This category includes a large number of legislative measures in areas covering compensation to workers in case of disability or death of worker; provision of Provident Fund/Pension to employees, maternity benefits in case of women workers; health insurance and medical benefits; regulation of working conditions like hours of work and minimum age of workers, etc. (Sasikumar, 1998). A good many of these fall within the area of labour standards enunciated by ILO and India has progressively moved in the direction of enlarging the scope of legislation in this area.

(ii) Minimum Wage Legislation

Keeping in view the absymally low levels of earning in many of the occupations, Minimum Wages Act was passed shortly after attaining independence in 1948 and is applicable to about a dozen categories of employment, in addition to that for agricultural workers. Minimum wages fall within the jurisdiction of State governments and some of the progressive ones have extended its application beyond those scheduled types of employment enumerated in the original Act. The stipulated level of minimum wage is fixed on the basis of subsistence level requirements and as such does not ensure anything beyond a bare minimum.

This point is of some relevance in the context of current debates about Structural Adjustment Policy and we shall revert to it subsequently. However, the main shortcoming in respect of Minimum Wage Legislation is not so much its level but gaps and difficulties in its effective implementation, which means that substantial segments of labour continue to subsist on sub-minimal level of earnings despite the protection of minimum wages being ensured by law (See Das, 1998).

(iii) Job Security Legislation

The third prop to support legislative measures for improving the working lives of labour basically stems from the objective of providing not only avenues of employment but also some degree of stability in employment. In many of the advanced economies, particularly those which had subscribed to the concept of welfare state, the objective of some stability in income was sought to be achieved through provision of unemployment insurance. In India, although this has at times been discussed, it has not been found practicable. Unemployment insurance, therefore, does not exist in the country. However, lately Ministry for Rural Development (2005) formulated the National Rural Employment Guarantee Act, which was one way of addressing the problem of unemployment.

In lieu of unemployment insurance, the measure, which had tried to provide some sort of stability of employment to those already in employment, was a set of two legislations undertaken during the seventies and eighties. The 1976 legislation made it mandatory for enterprises employing 300 workers or more to seek government's permission before any enterprise could be shut down. Presenting a case before the government, outlining reasons for shut down and obtaining the necessary permission for closing down an enterprise is a time-consuming process. In addition, in the event of a shut down being permitted, the enactment provides for compensation to retrenched employees at a specified rate. The scope of this job security legislation was sought to be widened and according to the 1984 amendment, these provisions were to apply also to enterprises relatively smaller than those covered earlier. The size of enterprises covered by this legislation was reduced to enterprises employing at least 100 workers instead of the earlier limit of 300 workers.

These are the two pieces of labour legislation, which have lately aroused maximum controversy. It is being increasingly argued that existence of job security regulations in their present form does not permit production and employment to respond to changes in market conditions and shelters production in inefficient enterprises (*cf.* Lucas and Fallon, 1991; Isher Ahluwalia, 1988). Moreover, since this legislation is applicable only to units above a certain size, in order to escape its applicability, it has been argued that units at the margin limit the size of their operations and hence do not reap the benefits of economies of scale (*cf.* Anant, Sundaram and Tendulkar, 1999).

(iv) Industrial Relations Legislation

In addition to above three types of legislation, which are supposed to directly, affect the economic condition of workers, there is a fourth category of legislation which does influence the economic status of labour vitally, though in an indirect manner. This important category pertains to various legislative and other measures governing trade union activity and machinery for improving the state of industrial relations. By safeguarding the rights of trade unions and providing a framework for maintaining industrial peace these legislative measures are beneficial not only to labour but employers as well. There are, however, lacunae in effectiveness of the existing industrial relations machinery, which need to be tackled through appropriate policy rationalization (See Subbiah Kannapan, 1993; Navin Chandra, 1998).

It needs to be borne in mind that provisions of most of these legislative measures apply only to labour employed in enterprises in the organized segment of the economy. Labour in unorganised segment by and large remains outside their coverage. Even where some of the measures are applicable to the unorganised segment, as for example, Minimum Wage Legislation for the agricultural workers, their implementation is far from satisfactory and less effective than in the case of organized segment, although in latter also implementation is not cent-percent.

Moreover, in terms of relative size of the organized segment vis-à-vis that of the unorganised one, which is not covered by most of labour enactments, the organized segment as a whole accounts for at the most 10 per cent or so of the total labour employed in the economy, although in some sectors it is substantially higher, particularly in the case of the non-agricultural activities. Thus, although labour legislation does cover a wide range affecting welfare of labour, in its total impact it is rather limited under the prevailing circumstances.

When we consider the case of contract labour, the need to device a framework for dealing with their specific problems was recognised during the British regime itself. The earliest concern was expressed in respect of contract labour employed in plantations during 1860's, in response to which a Commission was set up in 1861. On the basis of this, the Transport of National Labour Act of 1863 was enacted. This was followed by other Commission and Acts, culminating in the Royal Commission on Labour in 1929-31 and the Labour Investigation Committee in 1946 (For details, See M.S. Ramanujam, 2004).

After independence, the Industrial Disputes Act 1948; Mines Act, 1952; and Plantation of Labour Act, 1951, all examined the issue of contract labour and expressed the view that contract labour should be treated at par with regular labour so that contractors may pay fair wages and provide other welfare services. This was followed by a number of steps suggested by the second Five Year Plan to provide continuous employment to contract labour.

JUDICIARY AND CONTRACT LABOUR

The subsequent important steps in this area arose in response to legal pronouncements. The first major decision was that taken by the Supreme Court in Standard Vacuum Refining Company *versus* their Workmen (See Ruddar Datt, 2004; Vasant Gupte, 2004). The Supreme Court recommended that contract labour should be employed where work was of perennial nature, work was necessary for main activity of the factory and required whole time workforce of a considerable magnitude. The National Commission on Labour (Ministry of Labour, 1969) also expressed the view in 1969 that a strict regulatory framework should be adopted for contract labour and that contract labour should be abolished wherever circumstances permitted. It was in response to these major pronouncements that the Contract Labour (Regulation and Abolition) Act of 1970 was passed by the Central Legislature. The Act aimed at abolition of contract labour where work was perennial and conformed to other conditions, which were by and large the same as those enunciated in the Standard Vacuum case judgement by the Supreme Court. In case of other establishments, a strict regulatory framework was provided for. The Act was applicable to establishments and contractors employing more than twenty workers. Further, in case of contractors employing over 100 workers, provision of all basic facilities like drinking water, etc., was made mandatory. However, establishments performing casual and intermittent work were exempted from the Act.

Subsequent to the 1970 Contract Labour (R&A) legislation, there were two other landmark judgments in which again, it was judiciary that took a lead in protecting the interests of contract labour. These were the judgments of the Supreme Court in the case of Gujarat Electricity Board *versus* Hind Mazdoor Sabha (1995) and the cases of Air India (Statutory Corporation) *vs.* United Labour Union & Others. In both these cases, the Supreme Court upheld the view of the 1970 Contract Labour (R & A) Act that contract labour needed to be abolished. It laid down further that on abolishment, the labour so affected had to be automatically absorbed in the ranks of regular labour. Although these judgments clearly laid down the legal position, there have been long delays in implementation making the Act virtually dysfunctional. On the other hand, managements of a number of public sector undertakings expressed the view that judgments of the Supreme Court forced them to take contract labour on their permanent rolls even when they could not afford to do so. They have claimed that labour laws and procedures have reduced the incentive for organized labour to work efficiently and have made it unprofitable for organized industry to generate new jobs through outsourcing. At the same time, it has made it difficult to compete successfully in the external markets, specifically in competition against the Chinese industry.

ECONOMIC REFORMS AND CONTRACT LABOUR

It is evident from the foregoing discussion that after the advent of independence, the government undertook a number of steps for improving welfare of the working class. Most of these have taken the form of legislative Acts aimed at providing decent working conditions like ensuring regulated working hours, Provident Fund, etc., while other have tried to ported interests of the working class in terms of conditions of the employment, like provision of minimum wages or safeguards against arbitrary retrenchment. Two points need to be noted about these. First, most of these measures are primarily applicable to those working in organized sector establishments leaving the much larger unorganized sector workforce without the cover of much of the protective measures outlined earlier.

This has, however, gone to enhance disparity within the two segments of the workforce. In some cases the gulf is quite wide, for example, that between casual agricultural labour on the one hand, and employees of the large private sector and public sector units on the other. Second, while trend of most of post-independence measures was to provide as much protection and improvement in working conditions of the organized sector as feasible, since the advent of economic reforms and globalization in early nineteen nineties, there has been a basic change of outlook amounting to almost complete reversal of direction in some areas. This has been necessitated by shift to the principle of market competitiveness in a globalised environment. The earlier protective measures, it has been argued, by protagonists of economic liberalization, enhanced the costs of employees thus making many of the producers non-competitive in an open market environment unless employers were able to reduce their costs devoted to labour welfare measures.

Economic Reforms, as is widely known, stand on two legs (See, Ashok Mathur, 1999). The first of these, namely, the Stabilization programme primarily aims at achieving aggregate demand compression so as to reduce fiscal deficit in the domestic economy. The second component, christened Structural Adjustment, covers a wide range of policies all of which are based on the proposition that free market economy is more efficient in generating growth and attaining external balance than models of economic management which rely on state intervention either in the form of planning mechanism or various types of control, which had taken the form of industrial licensing, MRTP Act, regulations governing capital issues, FERA, and regulation of imports through customs duties.

In the sphere of labour, Structural Adjustment Programme requires:

(i) Creation of a perfectly free and flexible labour market in which wages are determined by free play of the forces of demand and supply of labour. Thus it implies that in a country like India, which is characterized by surplus labour, real wage should move downwards in order to promote employment expansion.

(ii) In order to facilitate the above process, minimum wage restrictions imposed by law should be withdrawn or at least relaxed.

(iii) Reallocation of labour from declining industries to those which belong to the 'sunrise' category with fast expanding demand and from the chronically sick units, both within the public and private segments, to the more dynamic enterprises with higher productivity levels. This would be possible only if restrictions on reduction and expansion in the size of labour force employed in an enterprise, or on closure of a unit, as for example contained in job security provisions, are relaxed.

(iv) Consequent upon the above changes, lower wage costs would tend to promote exports and strengthen the impulses of export-led growth. This would bring about movement of labour from domestic to the expanding export-based activity. It would thus help to absorb labour surplus in expanding export activities.

According to the Structural Adjustment point of view, if the changes outlined above do materialize, these would ultimately exercise a positive influence on the growth rate and the demand for labour. This would promote a faster pace of employment growth as well as an improvement in the condition of labour, even though it may create adverse conditions in the shortrun.

However, there are certain implicit assumptions in view of which a higher demand for labour may not materialize. This has actually been the case if one looks at trend of growth rate of labour employed in India (See Ashok Mathur 1999 and G.S. Bhalla, 2008). Whereas there was some increase in growth rate during 1994-2000, the reverse has been the case subsequently. Moreover, all throughout the period since 1993-94, the rate of unemployment has been on the rise. It is, therefore, imperative to look at implicit assumptions underlying the Economic Reforms point of view, which is outlined below :

(a) First, downward labour market flexibility may be exercising a positive effect on demand for labour at the level of individual entrepreneurs but at the marco-level, keeping in view the Keynesian framework of analysis, downward movement of wages is likely to exercise a retrogressive influence on the aggregate demand for labour. Thus removal of minimum wage legislation may not always be conducive to reducing the level of unemployment.

Moreover, whereas within the organized sector, minimum wage legislation may be providing a floor to wages to be paid, in case of the unorganized sector, which absorb the bulk of labour force, these is hardly any wage inflexibility (*cf.* L.K. Deshpande, 2004). In much of the rural areas and even in the informal urban economy there is no legal bar on wages an employer may pay. Wages paid are essentially an outcome of the demand and supply forces and individual negotiations between the employers and workers employed by them.

(b) Secondly, the contention that relaxation of job security regulations in India, which have been outlined above, can go to make labour market more flexible and enhance labour efficiency as well as promote employment expansion, has some validity but within limits (*cf.* Papola, 1994). As far as the relationship between job security legislation and employment potential goes, job security of the type assured by the 1976 and 1984 legislations has to a certain extent been responsible for employers within the organized sector attempting to thwart the legislation by the device of sub-contracting, or setting up captive ancillary units within the unorganised segment, or simply by adopting labour replacing capital-intensive technology. But how far these tendencies shall get reversed if job security legislation is withdrawn is a debatable issue.

The relationship between job security legislation and labour efficiency has two facets and conceptually they need to be treated differently. In so far as an individual employee's standard of performance falls persistently below par, it should be within the management's right to dispense with the person's services after due warning / disciplinary action. The industrial relations mechanism should be made speedy enough to dispense the necessary action expeditiously, but judiciously. However, the view that an individual's efficiency would be higher if he/she works under the threat of job loss cannot be taken to be unequivocally justified (*cf.* Sharma and Shasikumar, 1996). Overall standards of performance depend upon a number of factors rather than being simply dependent upon the fear of job loss. Attempt should be to enhance effectiveness of mechanisms through which deliberate negligence of duty or continued sub-standard performance can be adequately punished.

In respect of the provision of overall security of tenure to all the employees within an enterprise, there are two conflicting considerations involved here. From the point of view of managerial decision-making, in situation of genuine non-viability of an enterprise on account of declining demand for the goods produced or similar reasons beyond an employer's control, it should be within managements' right to close down a unit. However, from the point of view of labour's welfare, there is justification for the job security provision, particularly in the case of a poor developing country like India where alternative employment avenues are much harder to come by than in the case of a good many of the developed western economies. In case there is adequate aggregate demand which in turn reflects itself in buoyant labour demand thus enhancing the possibility of quick absorption of retrenched labour in alternative channels, the need for job security regulations being imposed by law becomes correspondingly lower. However, stringent job security provisions is not the most appropriate way of providing means of job security since it does reduce the role which personnel management should play in running an organization efficiently. What is needed is to:

(a) Develop alternative means of job security in the form of unemployment insurance; and

(b) Incorporate policy measures which ensure maintenance of adequate levels of aggregate demand (*cf.* Amit Bhaduri, 1996; Bhaduri and Nayyar, 1996).

Thirdly, in order to gain a competitive edge, as pointed out above, employers in the organized segment have been consistently resorting to use of capital-intensive technology. This has resulted in slow growth of workforce and has contributed to a rise in the rate of unemployment. Contract labour has felt the adverse impact of economic reforms on employment from two ends. First, competitive pressure on employers in the formal sector in the wake of economic reforms and globalization has implied that in order to reduce their commitments under various Acts to protect the interests of labour, they have resorted to contract labour for as many tasks as possible. There has consequently been a continuous rise in the incidence of contract labour since the advent of economic reforms. Despite Contract Labour (R&A) Act of 1970 and subsequent pronouncements of the Supreme Court upholding the interest of contract labour, to which attention has already been drawn, the ground reality is that in the era of Economic Reforms, it is not possible to prevent a rise in the incidence of contract labour although the 2004-05 NSS Survey showed some decline in the proportion of contract labour. As already pointed out, one has to look for ways in which the conflict between social considerations and the dictates of Structural Adjustment can be reduced. Under the circumstances, what is required is to look for alternative ways, other then absorption of contract labour as regular workers, for meeting the challenge of economic reforms. Some of these directions are indicated below :

(i) The guiding principle for reducing clash between imperatives of maintaining decent work conditions and raising competitiveness in the economy should basically focus on measures to improve productivity through improvement in technology but with a low capital intensity, enhancing labour efficiency through improvements in work culture and through adoption of improved managerial practices. These elements should be incorporated in the policy framework rather than on incorporating measures for reducing welfare payments to labour and toning down the conditions for "decent work".

(ii) For the purpose of improving working conditions and welfare of the contract labour, it is imperative to provide alternative means of social security for contract labour somewhat on the lines on which it is taken care of in use of the organized sector workforce. The reference here is not to the Job Security legislation of the type referred to earlier but various forms of entitlements in case of accidents, sickness, maternity, old age, death, etc. However, this issue is better considered in the context of unorganised workforce as a whole, of which contract labour is only one component. This is the way in which NCEUS (National Commission for Enterprises in the Unorganised Sector) has viewed the issue. NCEUS examined the problem of almost complete lack of any social protection to a large segment of Unorganised Workforce in considerable detail. This formed the basis of its Report on Social Security for Unorganised Workers (NCEUS, 2006, 2007) and the Unorganised Workers' Social Security Bill.

According to the NCEUS Report, there is a Skeleton social security framework for the unorganised workers operating at the level of Central and State governments but it covers only 21 million workers, which is only 6 per cent of unorganised informal workers. Another 2 per cent so of the unorganised workforce is provided some social security cover by NGOs. But all the existing social security cover is rather of a fragmented nature. It has been classified by NCEUS into three levels. First of these refers to universal programmes such as mission for literacy, schooling, health care services, drinking water and sanitation, technical training, etc. The second category provides some socio-economic security to working as well as non-working population. These are schemes such as Integrated Child

Development Scheme (ICDS), Development of Women and Children in Rural Areas (DWCRA), Public Distribution System (PDS), National Social Assistance Programme (NSAP), Mid-Day Meal Scheme for School Children, recently introduced National Rural Employment Guarantee Act (NREGA, 2005), etc. The third category is very important but it is either almost completely non-existent in case of unorganised workers or is very feeble in its presence. This refers to deficient and adverse circumstances which can arise for any individual. The former pertain to deficiency in access to credit, loans for upgrading skills, children's education, etc. The latter refer to certain major contingencies like ill health, accidents, death, old age, etc., and belong to the category of protective social security.

Social security is present on rather a limited scale, thus enhancing vulnerability to adversity in case of unorganised workforce. There are five welfare Funds, but they address needs of only selected segments of unorganised workers, e.g. Beedi making, cine workers, workers in certain mining operations, etc. These, together with National Social Assistance Programme (NSAP), National Old Age Pension Scheme (NOAPS), National Family Benefit Schemes (NFBS) and some State Level Schemes, cover only 8 per cent of unorganised workers.

It is the remaining 92 per cent of unorganised workforce which is without any protective social security cover which was the concern of unorganised workers Social Security Bill, 2006. Prior to this, three other National Committees had also mooted the need for establishing a national social security scheme for the unorganised workers, viz. :

(i) The National Commission on Rural Labour (NCRL, 1991) under the Chairmanship of Dr. C.H. Hanumantha Rao;

(ii) The Second National Commission on Labour (NCL, 2002) also suggested the Constitution of a high powered National Social Security Authority and Social Security Fund at the national and State levels.

In the light of these recommendations, The Government formulated the Unorganised Sector Workers' Bill, 2004 and National Advisory Council drafted the Unorganised Sector Workers' Social Security Bill in 2005.

Based on these earlier contributions, the Unorganised Workers' Social Security Bill, 2006, proposed a National Social Security Scheme for taking care of hospitalization, maternity & life insurance and old age security. This was based on the principle of tripartite contributions from the government, the employer and employee at the rate of Rupee one per day by each of these three constituents, thus making available Rs. 1095 per year for providing benefits. Where an identifiable employer is not available or does not exist, as in case of hawkers, rickshaw pullers, etc., the government was supposed to pay Rupee one per day in lieu of an employer. Moreover, BPL workers were to be completely exempted from making any contribution and Government was supposed to pay on their behalf. The scheme was meant to provide old age pension at the Rs. 200 per to all persons above 60 years of age and Provident Fund for all other workers. Entitlement to the benefits was meant to be on the basis of a Social Security Identity Cards issued to each worker.

The above scheme was quite an elaborate one. But the Bill has not found approval of the Government for the time being. Therefore, the contract workers who would have been covered by this Bill are left without any social security cover. Under the circumstances, it would be worthwhile to explore the possibility of drafting a separate bill for contract workers on the lines of the Bill of 2006. It is likely to be easier to handle a social security scheme for a smaller number of workers than the much larger set of all the unorganised workers. The lead in this matter would have to be taken by an appropriate wing of the Ministry of Labour.

(iii) The second direction for improving the lot of contract workers is by helping to create conditions in which the vulnerability of contract workers can get reduced. One of the important ways in which this can be achieved is by raising the educational level, and even more than that, the skill level of contract workers. This can be facilitated by incorporating provisions providing educational loans for enhancing educational level or skill training. Facilities for combining work with part time education / skill enhancement shall be an additional help.

(iv) In the third place, the absorption of contract workers as regular workers is difficult in the era of economic reforms. However, certain minimum conditions for decent work can be incorporated by putting greater emphasis on regulation of working conditions of contract labour rather than on their absorption. For example, provisions can be made for providing crèches, some regulatory framework for normal working hours per day, etc.

REFERENCES

Ahluwalia, Isher (1998), "Industrial Policy and Industrial Performance in India", in Robert, E.B. Lucas and Gustav, F. Papenk (Eds.), (1988), *The Indian Economy*, Oxford University Press Delhi.

Anant, T.C.A., K. Sundaram and S. Tendulkar (1999), "Employment and Labour in South Asia", *SAAT, International Labour Organisation*, New Delhi.

Bhaduri, Amit (1996), "Employment, Labour Market Flexibility and Economic Liberalisation in India", *The Indian Journal of Labour Economics*, Vol. 39, No. 1.

Bhaduri, Amit and Deepak Nayyar (1996), *The Intelligent Person's Guide to Liberalisation*, Penguin Books, New Delhi.

Bhalla, G.S. (2008), "Globalisation and Employment Trends in India", *Indian Journal of Labour Economics*, Vol. No. 51, No.1.

Chandra, Navin (1998), "Employment Relations: Realities and Options", in *Labour and Employment: Emerging Issues*, Published by V.V. Giri National Labour Institute, NOIDA.

Das, Subhash K. (1998), "Fixation and Enforcement of Minimum Wages", *The Indian Journal of Labour Economics*, Vol. 41, No. 2.

Deshpande, L.K. (2004), *Labour Market Flexibility and its Impact on Contract Labour*, in M.S. Ramanujam and J. S. Sodhi (2004).

Gupte, Vasant (2004), *Contract Labour in India : The Legal Position*, in M.S. Ramanujam and J.S. Sodhi.

Kannappan, Subbiah (1993), "Industrial Relations and Employment Policy in India: The Problem of Liberalisation and Strategies for Economic Growth and Equity", *The Indian Journal of Labour Economics*, Vol. 36, No. 2.

Lucas, R.E.B. and Fallon, Peter R. (1991), "The Impact of Changes in Job Security Regulations in India and Zimbabwe", *The World Bank Economic Review*, Vol. 5, No. 3.

Mathur, Ashok (2002), "Economic Liberalisation and the Quality of Employment in India: National and Regional Scenarios", in Raj Kumar Sen, editor, (2002), *India Labour in the Post-Liberalisation Period*, K.P. Bagchi & Company, Kolkata.

Mathur, Ashok (1999), "Economic Reforms, Employment and Non-Employment: Theory, Evidence and Policy", Keynote Paper for Technical Session VI of 82nd Annual Conference of the Indian Economic Association held at Amritsar, published in *Indian Economic Journal*, 1999, Conference Volume.

Ministry of Labour (1969), *Report of the First National Commission on Labour*, Government of India, New Delhi.

Ministry of Labour (2002), *Report of the Second National Commission on Labour*, Government of India, New Delhi.

Ministry of Rural Development (2005), *The National Rural Employment Guarantee Act (NREGA)*, Department of Rural Development, Government of India, New Delhi.

National Commission for Enterprises in the Unorganised Sector (2007), "Report on Conditions of Work and Promotion of Livelihoods in the Unorganised Sector", *NCEUS Report*, Government of India, New Delhi.

National Commission for Enterprises in the Unorganised Sector (2007), "Comprehensive Legislation for Minimum Conditions of Work and Social Security for Unorganised Workers", *NCEUS Report*, New Delhi.

National Commission for Enterprises in the Unorganised Sector (2006), "Social Security for Unorganised Worker", *NCEUS Report*, Government of India, New Delhi.

Ramanujam, M.S. (2004), *Contract Labour in India : As Overview*, in M.S. Ramanujam and J.S. Sodhi (2004).

Ramanujam, M.S. and J.S. Sodhi (Eds.) (2004), *Management of Contract Labour in India*, Shri Ram Centre for Industrial Relations & Human Resources, New Delhi.

Ruddar, Datt (2004), *Contract Labour in India: Role of Judiciary and the State* in M.S. Ramanujam and J.S. Sodhi (2004).

Sasikumar, S.K. (1998), "Social Security for Labour", in *Labour and Employment: Emerging Issues*, published by V.V. Giri National Labour Institute, NOIDA.

Sharma, Alakh N. and S.K. Sasikumar (1996), *Structural Adjustment and Labour* V.V. Giri National Labour Institute, NOIDA (mimeographed).

7

CONTRACTUAL LABOUR MARKET IN THE ERA OF GLOBALISATION

C. S. Verma

This chapter studies the emergence of contractual labour market in India in the aftermath of liberalisation, in organized as well as unorganized sector. While dealing with the organized sector, an attempt is also made to examine the effects of amendments to labour dispute laws, and amendments to job security legislation. The effects of legal amendments related to the Industrial Disputes Act, are also identified. It is observed that laws that increase job security or increase the cost of labour disputes substantially reduce organized sector employment and output but do not increase the labour share. Labour-intensive industries, such as textiles, are the hardest hit by laws that increase job security while capital-intensive industries are most affected by higher labour dispute resolution costs. It becomes obvious that the employment structure of organized manufacturing industries in India has undergone substantial changes with the steep rise in the use of contract workers in place of permanent workers. This process has led to increased wage inequality, discrimination as well as the concern of job insecurity in the labour market. It is also found that the widespread and increasing use of contract labour may have brought some output and employment gains but did not make up for the adverse effects of job security and dispute resolution laws. Regarding unorganized sector, it is observed that liberalisation in many rural parts of India and other developing countries are leading to an increase in contract farming arrangements. Under these arrangements, landowners have contracts with stakeholders such as agribusiness marketing and processing firms. Workers employed by contract producers more often than not experience poor terms and conditions, especially women workers and children.

Organized Sector

The organized sector is usually characterized as enterprises covered by the Factories Act, which applies to units with electrical power employing ten workers or more, or units without electrical power employing twenty workers or more. Although unorganized sector workers would tend to be informal, it does not follow that all workers in the organized sector are formal. A large number of workers not only in the organized private sector but also in the public sector—casual, temporary and contract workers (i.e. those hired through the mediation of a labour contractor)—are also informal, in the sense that they are equally unprotected by labour legislation

One belief about the impact of globalisation gaining ground in India, is that globalisation, through the agency of transnational corporations, the World Bank, IMF and WTO, is driving the dilution of labour standards and assault on workers' rights and that it inevitably leads to an attack on workers' rights. Globalisation has also led to major job cuts and wage cuts in the manufacturing sector. The liberalisation of 1991 was accompanied by a vigorous employer campaign for an 'Exit Policy', i.e. the right to hire and fire workers freely. This was resisted just as fiercely by trade unions, and temporarily withdrawn. However, dismissals and closures continued unabated throughout the decade. Several studies reveal that with globalization, the employment structure in the Indian economy, especially in the organized sector has been undergoing changes (Deshpande *et al.*, 2004). In order to adapt to the fast changing world and compete effectively in a globalized market, firms need flexibility relating to labour, capital, or bureaucracy. In this regard, stringent labour regulations not only put domestic producers at a disadvantage but also deter foreign direct investment and eventually impact adversely on investments, outputs and employment (Hensman, 2001).

Over the last two decades, a number of countries have attempted to liberalize their respective labour markets and have also amended their labour laws so as to make them more investment and employment friendly—a process that has weakened job security and collective bargaining (Agarwal, 2001). In particular, in India also, we observe increasing shares of casual labour over time. It is also observed that in order to effectively compete in a liberalized market economy, firms require flexibility, especially in managing labour. (Bhandari, Heshmati, 2006) Presently, the labour sector is quite restrictive with the labour laws. By empirically looking at labour regulations and their impact on the manufacturing sector in Andhra Pradesh, Besley and Burgess (2002) found that stringent pro-labour regulations lead to negative impact on registered manufacturing firms' output, whereas the effect is the opposite on the output of unregistered firms. In this connection, Kumar (2002) wrote that 'It needs to be realized that any dynamic economy needs flexibility in employment matters. There are many jobs that do not require permanent workers. The kind of permanency that few of the organized sector workers have in India is not prevailing in any other market economy'. Over-protection often leads to industrial disputes and labour strikes, which in turn affect production.

The organized manufacturing sector, suffered a catastrophic erosion of job security from the 1980s onwards. Textile mills, for example, went through a spectacular decline in employment. It is estimated that the Bombay textile strike of 1982-83 was followed by the loss of roughly 75,000 jobs due to closures and downsizing, excluding job where older workers were replaced by new recruits (Wersch, 1992). By the end of the 1990s, this number is estimated to have climbed to 100,000 jobs. In Ahmedabad, another textile centre, the decline started in 1982, with the closure of 50 private mills and 20 government-owned mills and the loss of almost 100,000 jobs over the next fifteen years, the majority in the 1980s (Patel, 2001:6). Other textile centres like Kanpur witnessed a similar decline. The vast majority of these job losses were not due to natural wastage or voluntary early retirement: they were involuntary and sometimes bitterly resisted. The lower wage earned by contract worker is largely due to cost cutting, rather than differences in labour productivity. In other industries like pharmaceuticals and personal care products, although there was rapid automation, downsizing and an increasing sense of insecurity amongst workers throughout the 1980s (created, for example, by events like the Hindustan Lever Sewri factory lockout of 1988-89, which resulted in the loss of several hundreds of jobs, including those of all the women workers), actual closures took place mainly in the 1990s. Most of these were achieved by means of so called Voluntary Retirement Schemes, which, however, contained a large element of intimidation and coercion combined with disinformation designed to create what workers called 'a fear psychosis' (Interviews with plant-level unionists, 1993-99).

Employers thus demonstrated that they could get rid of their workforces even without any change in the law. Nonetheless, Indian employers in particular found it cumbersome to be obliged to negotiate a retirement compensation scheme with the union, or to obtain permission for closure or downsizing from the State government. They, therefore, mounted a systematic campaign to revise (a) the Contract Labour Act, especially Section 10, in order to remove all restrictions on the use of contract labour, and (b) the Industrial Disputes Act, 1947. In October 2000, the State government of Maharashtra, pressurized by Indian industrialists' threats to take their investments to other States, proposed wide-ranging revisions to labour legislation that would render them virtually useless for protecting workers' rights (Samant, 2000; D'Costa 2000). The employer campaign culminated in the announcement by then Finance Minister Yeshwant Sinha, in his Budget Speech of 2001, that the government would liberalize the use of contract labour and permit employers to dismiss workers and close down units employing up to 1000 workers—an announcement greeted with great euphoria by the business lobby (Datta, 2001; Mitra, 2001). The arguments in support of these measures were that by increasing flexibility, they would enable enterprises to restructure, or allow failing enterprises to close down and shift their investments to more profitable lines, thereby also expanding employment.

Responding to the demand for an 'exit policy', trade unions fought back vigorously, and succeeded in defeating any plans for change. However, when employers began using strategies like VRS instead, unions were less successful in fighting them. Some unions could stem the tide of job losses by means of an imaginative campaign demonstrating the miserable fate of most workers who had earlier taken VRS, but on the whole, job losses and closures continued unabated. (Hensman, 2001). A key element of this employer strategy was the transfer of production to informal sector.

Unorganized Sector

While it is true that there are a small proportion of genuinely self-employed persons in the informal sector, the vast majority work for others, and this is the section which will be considered here. Most of them are agricultural or non-agricultural rural labourers, but a large proportion is also to be found in the urban economy. Contract farming in agriculture has occupied a special place in the unorganized sector employment. In some recent studies conducted on the contract farming in agriculture it is pointed out that agriculture is becoming increasingly 'feminized' as men move out of the sector more quickly than women, and as women become the preferred labour type for many employers. While these new labour arrangements have led to marginal increases in real income for some women workers, they have also changed relationships between workers and employers, workers and work, and led to differentiation within labour. Women's wages are generally lower than men's, working conditions poorer and their bargaining power more limited. Of greater concern is the issue of child labour; one of the major problems in contract farming throughout the developing world. India is one of the main users of child labour in the Asian region, with almost 80 per cent of working children employed in the agricultural sector. A study conducted by Bharat Gyan Vigyan Samiti, (an NGO working in 20 States) in the terai region of Uttrakhand on the vegetable farming, reveals that as much as 90 per cent of the production is undertaken under contract farming arrangement. The contractors bring contract labourers from as far as Bihar. The workers are given paltry sum as advance to begin the work on the assurance that the rest will be paid by the end of the season. No facility was available for health or any other emergency at the farms. Yet their employers or contractors have no requirement to take care of them; if any health problems arise, the workers are simply replaced with a new group. With no social security obligations, there is hardly any cost involved for the employers. Children miss out on their schooling to work in the fields, yet child labour under contracting is not subject to any legal or public disapproval.

It is suggested that there is a need to take a gender perspective to address the whole question of a changing agrarian production structure under contract farming, especially issues associated with transfer of skills, choice of technology, organisation of labour, working conditions and terms of work. Banning child labour is not the answer; instead conditions for these children need to be made more tolerable, and their education and skills need to be built so as to release them and their families from the vicious cycle of poverty and exploitation. He also calls for industry-regulated codes of conduct, along with legal provisions, to increase the voice and influence of contract labourers.

Employment Trend

While keeping in mind that employment statistics may not be totally reliable, especially with respect to the informal sector [Nagaraj, 1999 (a), CSO, 1999, Nagaraj, 1999(b)], a general picture emerges.

1. In the most recent period, it is estimated that while organized sector jobs increased at an average annual rate of 0.5 per cent during 1993-99, non-agricultural unorganized sector jobs grew at an average rate of 2.8 per cent per annum (*Economic Times*, 2001).

2. Looking now at the proportion of informal labour, one estimate puts it at 90.5 per cent. In 1972-73, 90.1 per cent in 1987-88, and 91.1 per cent in 1993-94 [Mahendra Dev, 2000(b): 48]. The total labour force was 314.13 million in the 1991 census while the Economic Survey 1997-98 estimated the labour force as being 397.2 million in 1997.

According to the Statistical Outline of India 1998-99, employment in the organized sector, rose from 26.73 million in 1991 to 28.25 million in 1997, so the proportion of permanent employees in the organized sector declined from 8.5 to 7.1 per cent in the period 1991-97. Finally, it was estimated that organized sector employment fell from 8 per cent of total employment in 1994 to 7 per cent in

1999-2000 (*Economic Times*, 2000). While these figures may not be directly comparable, since some pertain only to the private sector, some to private and public, some only to manufacturing, some to employment as a whole, and so on and so forth, there is agreement on the overwhelming and growing preponderance of informal labour.

Conclusion

It becomes obvious that the employment structure of organized manufacturing industries in India has undergone substantial changes with the steep rise in the use of contract workers in place of permanent workers. This process has led to increased wage inequality, discrimination as well as the concern of job insecurity in the labour market. It is also found that the widespread and increasing use of contract labour may have brought some output and employment gains but did not make up for the adverse effects of job security and dispute resolution laws. As a matter of fact, the employment has declined in this period. Regarding unorganized sector, it is observed that liberalization in many rural parts of India and other developing countries is leading to an increase in contract farming arrangements which are exploitative in nature with no consideration for the minimum social security measures for the contract labour.

Future of Contract Labour Market

The contract employment in India is facing social stigma and bottlenecks at present. However, the trend is definitely moving in favour of increased utilization of contract labour. While the overall perception of the general populace has remained unchanged, the trends are definitely supporting the cause of contract employment. But with such a wide exposure to the concept and experience of contract employment, it has to be a wait-and-watch game of will Indian workforce embraces contract labour whole-heartedly. As of now, the trend is moving in favor of contract employment.

REFERENCES

Amin, S. (1964), *Accumulation on a World Scale: A Critique of the Theory of Underdevelopment*, Monthly Review Press, New York.

Amin, S. (1998), "Towards a Progressive and Democratic New World Order", *Economic and Political Weekly*, Vol. XXXIII, No. 23, 6 June.

Antony, M.J. (2001(b), "Bid to Dilute Contract Labour Law Fails", *Business Standard,* 21 February.

Banaji, J. and Hensman, R. (1990), *Beyond Multinationalism: Management Policy and Bargaining Relationships in International Companies,* Sage Publications, New Delhi.

Banerjee, N. (1981), "Is Small Beautiful?" in Bagchi, A.K., and Banerjee, N. (Eds), *Change and Choice in Indian Industry,* K.P. Bagchi, Calcutta, 177-295.

Banerjee, N. (1984), "Women's Work and Discrimination", chapter presented at a Conference in Bogota, Colombia (mimeo).

Basu, K. S. Bhattacharya and A. Mishra (1992), "Notes on Bribery and the Control of Corruption", *Journal of Public Economics,* 48, 349-359.

Besley, Timothy and R. Burgess (2002), "Can Labour Regulation Hinder Economic Performance?", Evidence from India, CEPR Discussion Paper 3260, Institute for Human Development, New Delhi.

Chandrashekhar, C.P. (1997), "The Economic Consequences of the Abolition of Child Labour: An Indian Case Study", *The Journal of Peasant Studies,* Vol. 24, Number 3, April, pp. 137-179.

Chauhar, Paro (1998), "Living on the Edge", *Labour File,* Vol. 4 Number 8, August, 17-20.

Central Statistical Organisation (1999), "CSO's Comments - How Good are India's Industrial Statistics?" *Economic and Political Weekly,* Vol. XXXIV, No. 23, 5 June, pp. 1461-63.

Datta, Kanika (2001), "Employers of India may Lose their Chains", *Business Standard,* 2 March.

Deshpande, Rajeshwari (1999), "Organising the Unorganized – Case of Hamal Panchayat", *Economic and Political Weekly,* Vol. XXXIV No. 39, 25 September, L-19-26. *Economic and Political Weekly,* 1997, "Bihar: More Bloodshed", Vol. XXXII No. 13, 29 March, p. 622.

Goldar, Bishwanath (2000), "Employment Growth in Organized Manufacturing in India", *Economic and Political Weekly,* Vol. XXXV No. 14, 1 April 1991-95.

Hensman, C.R. (1971), *Rich Against Poor: The Reality of Aid,* Allen Lane, The Penguin Press, London.

Hensman, R. (2000), "World Trade and Workers' Rights: To Link or Not to Link?", *Economic and Political Weekly,* Vol. XXXV No. 15, 8 April, pp. 1247-54.

Hensman, R. (2001), "World Trade and Workers' Rights: In Search of an Internationalist Position", in Waterman, Peter, and Wills, Jane (Eds), Place, Space and the New Labour Internationalisms, Blackwell Publishers, Oxford.

Hobson, J.A. (1938), *Imperialism—A Study*", Allen & Unwin, London.

Holmstrom, M. (1984), *Industry and Inequality—The Social Anthropology of Indian Labour,* Cambridge University Press, Cambridge.

Iyer, Sabarinath M. and Arun (2001) "Garment Cos. Want Dumping Duty on Lanka, Bangladesh", *The Economic Times,* 17 February.

Konkani, Magnet (1994), "Theories of the Soviet System—A Retrospective Critique", *Economic and Political Weekly*, Vol. XXIX, No. 31, 30 July, pp. 2036-39.

Kumar, Nagesh (1995), "Industrialisation, Liberalisation and Two Way Flows of Foreign Direct Investments: Case of India", *Economic and Political Weekly*, Vol. XXX, No. 16, December, pp. 3228-37.

Kumar, Arun (2002), "Labour Law Reforms in India: Some Issues for Consideration".

Kumar, V.P. (2001), "2-Wheeler Firms Seek Duty Hike to Counter Chinese Imports", *Business Standard*, 18 April.

Labour File (1998), "Deaths All the Way", Vol. 4, Number 8, August, pp. 26-27.

Mahendra Dev, S. (2000(b)), "Economic Liberalisation and Employment in South Asia", *Economic and Political Weekly*, Vol. XXXV, Nos.1&2, 8 January, pp. 40-51.

Marjit, S. M. Rajeev and D. Mukherjee (2000), "Incomplete Information as a Deterrent to Crime", *European Journal of Political Economy*, pp. 763-773.

Menon, Sindhu (1999), "Spectre of Death Haunts Construction Industry", *Labour File*, Vol. 5, Numbers 1-4, Jan-April, pp. 20-24.

Mitra, Soumya Kanti (2001), "Capitalize on Labour Flexibility", *The Economic Times*, 3 March.

Mookherjee, D. and I. P. L. Pang (1994), "Corruptible Law Enforcers: How Should they be Compensated?", *The Economic Journal*, Vol. No. 105, pp. 145-159.

Rajeev, Meenakshi (2003), "A Search for an Optimal Policy in a Corrupt System: A Note", *The Journal of Developing Areas*, Vol. 37, pp. 159-170.

Roy, Tirthankar (1998), "Development or Distortion of Powerlooms in India, 1950-1997" *Economic and Political Weekly*, Vol. XXXIII, No. 16, 18 April, pp. 897-911.

Sakai, J. (2000), "Aryan Politics and Fighting the WTO", in *Anti-Fascist Forum* (Ed), My Enemy's Enemy—Essays on Globalization, Fascism and the Struggle Against Capitalism, Anti-Fascist Forum, Toronto, 7-23.

Shah, Suresh [2001(b)], *Textile Imports Seen Crossing Rs. 4,000 Crores*, 30 March.

Sharma, D.P. (1999), "Fishing and Aquaculture Policies Debates Continue", *Labour File*, Vol. 5, Numbers 1-4, Jan-April, pp. 68-71.

Teerink, Rensje (1995), "Migration and its Impact on Khandeshi Women in the Sugar Cane Harvest" in Loes Schenk-Sandbergen (Ed.), *Women and Seasonal Labour Migration*, Sage (IDPAD), New Delhi, pp. 210-300.

Thomas, Cherian (1999), "Sica Amend Bill to Plug BIFR Loopholes", *Business Standard*, 15 October.

Zhu, Xiaohua (1997), "Anti-Dumping Measures—Time to Roll them Back," *Economic and Political Weekly*, Vol. XXXII, No. 18, 3 May, pp. 936-37.

8

EARNING PATTERN OF CONTRACTUAL EMPLOYMENT IN INDIAN LABOUR MARKET

L. S. Singh

Emergence

The impact of global integration of markets on the quantity and quality of jobs has been a contentious issue. This is not surprising as the labour market is one of the main channels through which globalization affect a country's economy and workers. Globalization (a world without barriers to trade and investment) is widely perceived to result in negative labour market outcomes, that is, job losses and reduction in earnings. Three major areas of concern have been the loss of good jobs in industries losing competitiveness, biased technological change against unskilled workers and the informalization of the workforce 'race to the bottom'. All these reasons taken together suggest that globalization could put labour markets under pressure. This outcome could lead to greater social conflicts as a consequence of unemployment and increasing wage inequalities. In the context of India, accelerating output growth in recent years has not been accompanied by a faster rate of job growth, in particular, the slow growth of regular jobs and the intensification of duality in labour markets has become a serious problem.

India has experienced robust economic growth due to liberalization and globalization. Globalization has induced greater competition among national players, and between national players and international players. Such a competition has necessitated the need to be more productive, with an aim to generate profit, if a firm has to sustain its business. Thus, firms are seeking various ways of reducing cost, increasing efficiency and still remain profitable. The new game of profitability and competitiveness has forced companies to identify ways of using labour as efficiently a possible, with the motto of the 'right worker in the right job at the right time'. Flexibility has become an unavoidable strategy for the firms to ensure the efficient use of labour, because of the low availability of human resources that can be flexibly employed with the capability of multi-tasking, temporary staffing has emerged as an attractive option. However, while temporary staffing is a cost-effective answer to the challenge of flexibility, the loyalty of the temporary workers towards the firm is very limited.

It has been argued in this context that the Indian labour market is highly regulated causing rigidities in the adjustment in the use of labour in enterprises, which result in high direct transaction costs, reduce efficiency in production and make it difficult for them to successfully operate in a competitive environment, These rigidities also tend to discourage investment, both domestic and foreign, expansion in output and increase in employment. It is, therefore, considered necessary that 'reforms' be brought about in the labour market through changes in the legislative framework for labour regulation, not only to encourage investment and growth of output, but also for expansion of employment in industry.

Changes in government policies and programmes bring about changes in the labour market. Further, and in particular adjustment programme introduced in 1991 is intended to make the economy more efficient and competitive through a widening of the role of the market and a reduction in that of the state. As a result of these changes permanent workers are being replaced by contract labour and casual workers melting in an employment shift towards informal activities (ILO-ARTEP, 1992; Ascher, 1987; Das, 1998a). All formal sector organisations today engage contract labour and the current trend indicates that more and more jobs are now being off-loaded to contractors and small suppliers. This is justified on the grounds that it reduces wage cost, ensures flexibility in labour deployment, and minimizes management problems. While the workers directly employed by the organizations get high wages and have secure jobs are secured, the contractor workers and casual workers are poorly paid and their working conditions are less regulated. These workers are also to be included in the definition of informal sector and more precisely the term 'informal sector labour market' is to be replaced by "informal labour market" (Papola, 1992).

By the early twenty-first century the workforce structure in particular and the world of work in general reflected the profound impact of the global reorganizations of production. The industrialized world, as could be seen from the OECD countries, experienced considerable changes in the pattern of employment (ILO, 2001). Labour markets in the OECD were tending to be increasingly segmented. Firms organise employment into 'core' and peripheral components. Core employment includes stable employment. Peripherals, marked by high turnover, are on the increase. Groups which are increasing in members in relation to the core, include part-time and job-sharing employees, those on short-term contracts, probationers and public- subsidy trainees. Extensive use, is also made of external groups, such as outsourcing, sub-contracting and self-employment, resulting in increasing vulnerability of these workers Part-time work has tended to increase as a proportion of total employment. Relative importance of temporary employment is increasing. There has been growing inequality between the unskilled and skilled in their earnings and gradual disappearance of labour-intensive manufacturing from the North (Munck, 2002).

Indian labour markets have been dualistic, and the process of liberalization and globalization was expected to widen this dualism. In fact, it was found that dualism did accelerate during the post-liberalization era—the share of permanent manual workers declined from about 69 per cent in 1991 to 62 per cent in 1998, increasing sharply in industries such as non-metallic minerals, beverages and tobacco. Not only did the share of non- permanent workers increase but the share of casual workers in the non-poor permanent category increased even faster. The big firms resorted to greater use of non-permanent workers. With all other factors remaining the same, firms employing 50-99 workers and those employing 500 or more workers increased their share of non- permanent workers significantly between 1993 and 1998. Casual employment did not show any relation with the size of employment. Gender-wise, women workers were mostly employed in large firms. Firms employing 1,000 workers or more accounted for more than 75 per cent of all women workers. Firms, which employed a higher share of non-permanent workers, also employed a higher share of women workers (Sharma, 2006). What is needed is protection for workers from the vagaries of flexibilisation and this could he done only by the state extending social protection to casual workers.

Following these views, over the last two decades, a number of countries have attempted to liberalise their respective labour markets and amend their Labour Laws so as to make them more investment and employment-friendly—a process that has weakened job security and collective bargaining (Agrawal, 2001).

This in turn has given rise to different types of non-permanent employment structures in the form of casual Labour, consultants, subcontractors, contract labour, tele workers and others, among which contract labour is one of me most prominent kind in the Indian industrial sector today. There may be different kinds of contractual employment in vogue in a firm. As it can be expected that in India the use of such non-permanent employment will only increase over time (from the annual Survey of Industries data on contract labour one can see that the use of contract labour is on the rise (Rajeev and Roy Chowdhuri, 2005).

Conceptualization and Dimension of Contract

The contract workers as a result do not enjoy organizational legal, institutional (collective bargaining) rights and these have left a 'rights vacuum'. The 'contract labour' is applied to labour which is employed to perform some work through a contractor and hence no direct employment relationship exists between the ultimate employer for whom she does work and herself (MKI, 2001).

The contract workers and the contractor have contractual relationship. The contract workers provide their labour services to the principal employer. There exists a common zone, the 'tripartite zone' which becomes the basis for legal and non-legal course of actions for trade unions. Contract labour in India is regulated under the Contract Labour (Regulation and Abolition) Act 1970.The aim of the Act is to provide for the regulation of contract labour in certain economic activities and for abolition in other circumstances.

Under this Act, contract labour has been prohibited in certain industries. The Act does not apply when a contractor employs less than 20 workers and this has led to manipulations by employers and contractors (SNCL, 2002). The aim of the Act was to provide for the regulation of contract labour in certain economic activities and for abolition in other circumstances. Under this Act, contract labour has been prohibited in certain category of jobs. For example, with a notification in 2001, contract labour was prohibited in handling of foodgrains including loading and unloading, storing and stacking in godowns and depots of the Food Corporation of India (FCI). The Acts also bars use of contract labour in 'core' and perennial activities and regulates employment of contract labour in other activities. The act applies to (a) every establishment in which 20 or more contract workers are/were employed, and (b) to every contractors who employs or who has employed 20 or more contract workers, on any day in preceding 12 months. In the debate on labour market reforms, the employment of contract labour has been one of the most contested issues. It is argued that the nature of the 'core' and 'perennial' activities has changed in the wake of globalised production systems and production based on orders. So even in its 'core' activity, an enterprise does not have same amount of work throughout the year and requires varying magnitude of labour from season to season. Greater flexibility in the use of contract labour is, therefore, necessary. It seems illogical not to allow an enterprise to employ workers on a non-regular, contract basis if the work that it carries out is not of a regular nature and varies in volume from time to time. At the same time, absence of restriction on the practice of contract labour may result in greater use of this form of employment by employers primarily to deny job security and other benefits to workers. Regulation on the use of contract labour notwithstanding, the extent of contract labour has significant increased in Indian industry since early 1990s. According to an estimate, the share of contract labour in the organized factories sector in the country increased from about 12 per cent in 1985 to about 23 per cent in 2002 (Pages and Roy, 2006). In this period the increase in the share of contract labour varied across States, declining in very few such as Assam and Karnataka, while increasing in most others. Among the States, Andhra Pradesh had the highest increase in the share of contract labour in the organised sector, an increase from 33.8 per cent in 1985 to 62 per cent in 2002 (Papola, 2007).

Originally, the intention of the Contract Labour (Regulation and Abolition) Act 1970 (CLA) was that contract labour would be employed in those operations that are not of perennial nature. The current legal position about the employment of contract labour is that it can be employed in any operations including core operations unless it is "specifically prohibited" under the CLA by the appropriate government in a particular operation. Many State governments have prohibited contract labour in very few operations. Often, contract labourers are employed under a "sham contract" which if brought to the notice of a court can lead to regularization of contract workers for violation of the CLA. But most such contracts are continuing as per collusions between the employers and State agencies, and often due to the indifference of the trade unions. Only two State governments—the Government of Andhra Pradesh and the Government of Gujarat—have succeeded in effecting amendments to the effect that a contract worker cannot be employed in core operations. Such amendments help in preventing excessive exploitation of contract labourers.

Though contract workers enjoy provident fund (PF) benefits on chapter , it is often a burden to them rather than an aid. It is a burden in the sense that every month some fixed amount is deducted from their meagre salary for provident fund contribution. However, these workers often change the contractor they work for and a new provident fund account then gets opened. Unfortunately once a worker leaves a contractor, he/she never gets any cooperation from the contractor in retrieving the money paid. Many contract agencies also close down and then retrieving the PF dues becomes very difficult for the employee. It is also the duty of the principal employer to verify the PF details, which is however, not often done. Furthermore, in order to recover the PF amount, a contract worker has to have a bank account into which the sum due should be deposited by a cheque.

Contract workers often cannot maintain accounts because of minimum deposit requirements by banks. This makes recovering their PF dues even more difficult. In addition, it has been observed that there are a number of unregistered contract agencies that deduct PF contributions from the workers but never deposit the same in the provident fund office. Thus the provision of contractual employment seems at least to help a segment of the population that is temporarily in distress due to causes beyond their control. In the absence of a contract agency as an intermediary, the only option would have been to employ oneself as a casual labourer, whose condition a separate survey (Rajeev, 2005) shows even more pathetic than that of the contract labourer.

Social Security Perspectives

A vast majority of the workers working as contract labour works under very poor conditions of work, for excessively long hours and for very low wages as compared to workers doing similar work with a permanent status. Many of the fringe benefits like provident fund, sickness, insurance, gratuity, and privilege leave with pay and so on, are usually not available to contract workers. On the whole, conditions of service of contract workers are substantially poorer as compared to those of regular employees of an employer. Because or non-regular system of employment, uncertainty of tenure, frequent changes in contracts and contractors, lack of proper employment records and such other factors, contract workers find it extremely difficult to get organised into strong trade unions. So providing some minimum social security measures and legal protection to this vulnerable section assumes paramount importance. Though there is no direct ILO standard on contract labour yet much of the ILOs contribution focuses on promoting the parameters of acceptable and fair work place relationships. At the core of all ILO's efforts lies the consensus that has been achieved around what is popularly known as 'Declaration on Fundamental Principles and Rights at Work' comprising the minimum acceptable global principles and rights such as freedom of association and the right to organize and collective bargaining, freedom from forced labour, freedom from child labour and equal opportunities—equal remuneration for men and women for work of equal value and an end to discrimination in various areas of work such as access to training, wages and access to good quality jobs. The ILO deems the declaration to be a powerful tool to achieve socially equitable and economically sound development. It is further argued that there are several other standards, which provide models for regulation of most aspects of work. Thus, in spite of the absence of any specific ILO standard on contract labour, the overall framework of ILO standards and ILO declaration on 'Fundamental Principles and Rights at Work' offers an international model for regulation of conditions of workers not covered by any specific legislation, on employment relationship.

The division between permanent and contract workers reflect the basic difference in organisational power of them. Permanent workers are organised and have better conditions of work and are a pampered lot. The contract workers are not so. There are layers in the working class and are not homogeneous. The absence of organisation and collective bargaining rights and the disparities in the legal framework (say in the definition of workmen or wages) in case of contract workers diminish their status. The organisation of contract workers whereas bridges this gap. The employers should ideally adopt a 'community of interests' approach and realise that contract labourers are as much as responsible as other stakeholders in the companies. The contract labourers might perform tasks that are not core in the technical sense but their jobs are as much essential to the completion of tasks as the core jobs. The jobs on an ethical scale are weighted equally though on a technical scale disparities could be imparted. The firm is the result of multiple activities and all stakeholders play an important role. The economic logic of rewards based on their marginal contributions often may not mean a living wage for workers, which is not only a constitutional assurance but also a moral wage. The moral wage not only maximizes labour and thereby social welfare but also leads to social peace. The inequalities within the firm should not be radical enough to cause discontent. Firm is a microcosm of the society. If each firm strives to establish some measure of equity within it, then the society will approximate towards social equity. Values like equality and fairness are components of their corporate social, responsibility and constitute good corporate governance. Wages differentials are required to act as a price signals for efficient allocation of labour. This is 'technical efficiency' of the market, but markets are embedded in an ethical context. And 'social efficiency' involves reducing the inequalities to the extent that social welfare is maximized and social, discontent is toned down. There are companies in Mumbai Like Reliance, Godrej, Larson & Tubro, which employ more contract labour than permanent workers and are doing well (Samant, 2004). But there are also companies like Crompton & Greaves, Johnson & Johnson, German Remedies, Hercules Hoist, etc., which have not employed contract or casual labourers and they are performing equally well. The latter have better corporate governance than the former. The trade unions have made progressive steps by embracing the vulnerable groups like contract workers into their fold and cleaned their 'historical blemish'. But more needs to be done. They have been knocking at the doors of the judiciary for legal relief and the government for 'systemic solutions'. These are conventional methods. While the trade unions need not give up theses they should adopt 'social' and 'market' routes also. The trade unions need to strengthen and widen their social coalitions and forge a social movement to press for equity both at the workplace and in the larger society. The institutional and social power is a weapon to be wielded by vulnerable workers. The case studies (Shyam Sundar, 2007) reveals to contract workers struggle in Airports Authority and Reliance Energy demonstrate the role played by institutional powers. Trade unions also need to embrace the 'community of interest' approach. It is often the case that trade unions and regular workers seek to solely protect their interests in collective bargaining. The organisational assumption is/was that contract and casual labourers do not belong to their community. Trade unions and regular workers working especially in a hostile environment succumb to this. This strikes at the roots of ethical and organisational basis of the labour movement. The insider-outsider rhetoric gains strength and unions are verified, though justifiably. The 'community of interests approach' is an answer to such criticisms.

It has been the general feeling of a large number of firms that contract labour is indeed paid very low wages. Many enterprises revealed during our field survey that they are ready to enhance the wage level of contract workers provided minimum wage norms are revised accordingly. However, rather than fixing auniform minimum wage rate for all firms, wage rates for contract labour should be linked to the wages paid by the firm to direct worker.

This would not only reduce wage disparity between regular and contract workers, but also lessen the feeling of discrimination amongst contract workers. Furthermore, given the current status of provident fund benefits, building an effective social security net which can enhance the bargaining power of labour is essential (Meenakshi, 2006). In a planned economy with a large public sector, government plays an important role as producer. However, in a market economy, government's responsibility as a regulator becomes foremost. In the case of contract labour, it has been observed that a collusive agreement between the contractor and principal employer or the labour inspector leads to various corrupt practices. Being on the long side of the market, labour has often been victimised. Careful steps need to be taken to curb corruption to ensure that labouring class gets its due. To ensure this, first and foremost it is necessary to educate labour about their rights and responsibilities, contract labour should be able to voice their complaints to an independent authority, which in turn should take it up with the labour inspector. The governments both at the Centre and in the States have been more liberal in respect of other aspects of labour regulation also in recent years. In fact, they do not seem to be very keen on carrying a 'pro-labour' image that governments in the past seemed to be proud of. Though no significant changes in labour laws have taken place, changes in implementation practices to make labour regulation more 'enterprise-friendly' have taken place (Nagaraj, 2004). Routine inspections by labour officials have been curtailed in many States (Reddy, 2007; Shyam Sundar, 2007; Sharma and Kalpala, 2007).

Relaxations of various kinds have been allowed, say in the use of contract labour and in hours of work and so on in export oriented units and IT establishments (e.g. Government of Gujarat, 2006). At the State level, governments competing with each other to lure investments have resorted to the mechanism of making changes in the regulatory framework through amendments to the central labour laws and the use of executive orders.

According to a study on Andhra Pradesh, 'there have been State amendments to central Acts and certain executive orders modifying the implementation of legal regulatory measures with far-reaching implications for the protection of rights of labour relating to basic working conditions' (Reddy, 2007). It says, the main essence of the CLA has been diluted and a whole range of activities that would not be permitted to contract out is now permitted. This has led to a sudden surge in the use of contract labour in Andhra Pradesh.

Some provisions of CLA should give way to a wider perspective on labour reforms that will go towards reducing rigidity in labour use in general and provide minimum modicum of human conditions of work and social protection. It must also be recognised that in order to be acceptable to all parties, the reforms have to be balanced, and not one-sided. While it is legitimate to ask for greater freedom to industry in the modes of use and adjustment of labour, it is also equally important that all workers irrespective of the size and sector of their employment are ensured reasonable conditions of work including wages and social protection. Similarly, there is ample justification to have another look at the CLA with a view to allowing use of contract labour when the activity is not of even quantity throughout the year. Here again, the provision of conditions of work and social security must be strictly adhered to, which does not seem the case at present. The most important, area of reforms in labour regulation relates to the provision of minimum conditions of work and social security to the workers not covered by the existing labour regulations. It may not necessarily mean replication of what presently exists for the regulated sectors either in terms of the levels of protection or implementation mechanism. The SNCL recommended enactment of a law for unorganized sector workers. The government followed it up by drafting a bill. Some non-governmental organizations and individuals have also made proposals in this regard. Taking all these into consideration, the NCEUS has already made comprehensive proposals for social security cover and conditions of work for the workers in the unorganized sector. The Commission has submitted draft legislations on both these aspects to the government. These proposals need to be carefully considered and seen as part of labour reforms in the direction of reducing dualism in the regulatory framework of the Indian labour market.

The NTUI put forward three basic aspects of 'regulation' that could constitute "post-SAIL agenda" for contract workers, viz. (a) 8-hour day, (b) a fair statutory minimum wage, and (c) the principle of equal wage for equal work. The new agenda of the trade unions in Maharashtra consists of issues such as minimum wage, 'equal wage for equal work' and 'continuation of contract workers irrespective of change in contract workers', The unions in the government sector (like the municipal corporation) demand wages for contract workers equal to Class IV employees and retention of contract workers even when the contractors change. They no longer demand abolition of contract labour system. In a few cases like the Navi Mumbai Municipal Corporation case, the unions have succeeded in achieving the latter demand. This seems to be a new approach of the Contract Labour Advisory board also (Proceedings at the Meeting of the board in Maharashtra on June 6, 2007).

REFERENCES

Breman, Jan (2004), *Making and Remaking of an Industrial Working Class*, Oxford University Press, New Delhi.

Das, S. K. (1998 a), "Privatisation and its Impact in Labour", *Management in Government*, Govt. of India, Deptt. of Administrative Reforms and Public Grievances, April-June, New Delhi.

I.L.O. (2001), *World Employment Report*, ILO Geneva.

ILO-ARTEP (1992), *Social Dimensions of Structural Adjustment in India*, ILO, Geneva.

Kumar, Arun (2002), "Labour Law Reforms in India: Some Issues for Consideration", *Manpower Journal*, Vol. XXXVIII, 4.

Maniben Kara Institute (2001), *Contract Labour in India—The Legal Position*, Mumbai.

Munck, Ronald (2002), *Globalization and Labour*, Madhyam Books, Delhi.

Nagaraj, R. (1994), "Fall in the Organised Manufacturing Employment: A Brief Note", *Economic and Political Weekly*, July 24.

NCEUS (2007), "Social Security for Unorganised Workers", *Report by National Commission for Enterprises in the Unorganised Sector*, Government of India, New Delhi.

Pages, Carman and Roy, Tirthankar (2006), "Regulation, Enforcement and Adjudication in India Labour Markets: Historical Perspective, Recent Changes and Way Forward", chapter presented at Conference on India: Meeting the Employment Challenge, 27-29 July 2006, New Delhi, IHD and World Bank.

Papola, T.S. (1992), "Informal Sector: Concept and Policy", M. K. Rao, *Growth of Urban Informal Sector and Economic Development*, Kanishka Publishers and Distributors, Delhi.

Papola, T. S. (2004), "Globalization, Employment and Social Protection: Emerging Perspectives for Indian Workers", *Indian Journal of Labour Economics*, Vol. 47, No. 3, July- Sept., New Delhi.

Papola, T. S. (2007), "Debate on Labour Market Reforms in India: A Case of Misplaced Focus", *Indian Journal of Labour Economics*, Vol. 50, No. 2.

Rajeev, Meenakshi (2005), "Contract Labour Status: Problems and Options" (unpublished).

Rajeev, Meenakshi (2006), "Contract Labour in Karnataka Emerging Issues and Options", *Economic and Political Weekly*, May 27.

Rajeev, Meenakshi and Supriya Roy Chowdhuri (2005), "Contractual Employment in Selected Manufacturing Enterprises in Karnataka", Project Report No. SRTT/4, Institute for Social and Economic Change, Bangalore.

Reddy, D. Narasimha (2007), *Labour Regulations, Industrial Growth and Employment: A Study of Recent Trends in Andhra Pradesh*, Institute for Studies in Industrial Development, New Delhi.

Scherk, A. (1987), *The Politics of Privatisation Contracting Out Public Service*, MacMillan, London.

Sharma, Alakh N. (2006), "Flexibility, Employment and Labour Market Reforms in India", *Economic and Political Weekly*, Vol. XLI, No. 21, May 27.

Sharma, Alakh N. and Kalpana, V. (2007), *Labour Regulations and Industrial Development in Uttar Pradesh: Some Recent Trends*, Institute for Studies in Industrial Development, New Delhi.

Shyam Sunder, K.R. (2007), *Impact of Labour Regulation on Industrial Development and Employment: A Study of Maharashtra*, Institute for Studies in Industrial Development, New Delhi.

Shyam Sunder, K. R. (2007), "Contract Works: The Need for Community of Interest Perspective", *Indian Journal of Labour Economics*, Vol. 50, No. 4.

Shyam Sundar, K. R. (2007), "Trade Unions and Civil Society: Issues and Strategies", *Indian Journal of Industrial Relations*, Vol. 42, No. 4.

Team Lease (2005), *India's Labour Market: Case for Temporary Staffing Reform to Reduce Unemployment*, A White Paper and Team Lease Services.

Varghese Rajan, K. E. (2004), "Contract Labour: Judicial Trends", in Ramanujam, M. S. and Sodhi, J. S. (eds.), *Management of Contract Labour in India*, Shri Ram Centre for Industrial Relations and Human Resources, New Delhi.

9

EMERGING PATTERN OF CONTRACTUAL EMPLOYMENT IN INDIAN LABOUR MARKET

Rashmi Tripathi

Introduction

Staffing is broadly defined as the process of attracting, selecting, and retaining competent individuals to achieve organizational goals. Every organization uses some form of a staffing procedure, and staffing is the primary way an organization influences its diversity and human capital. The nature of work in the twenty-first century presents many challenges for staffing. For example, knowledge-based work places greater demands on employee competencies; there are widespread demographic, labour, societal, and cultural changes creating growing global shortfalls of qualified and competent applicants; and the workforce is increasingly diverse.

Staffing should be one of the most important strategic mechanisms for achieving competitive advantage; organizational decision makers do not understand staffing or use it optimally. Given that the war for talent is very real and relevant to organizations around the globe, it is critical that organizations and organizational scholars recognize the value of staffing (Barney & Wright, 1998). There is growing recognition that recruiting—by itself and irrespective of selection—is critical not only for sustained competitive advantage but basic organizational survival (Taylor and Collins, 2000).

Factors Affecting the Recruitment Process

One clear finding in recent recruitment research is the importance of the employer's image or reputation (Saks, 2005). Employer image has been examined by different researchers using different operationalizations (e.g., image, reputation, brand, symbolic attributes), but all converge around the finding that this image has important effects on recruitment outcomes (Collins and Stevens, 2002).

The reputation of an organization, operationalized as the organization's ranking in various popular business publications had an effect on objective applicant pool characteristics. Firms with more positive reputations increased the number of applicants and influenced applicant behaviour. On the downside, both low- and high-ability applicants were likely to apply to organizations with a favourable reputation, thus increasing recruiting costs. On the upside, having more applicants should allow the organization to make finer distinctions and be more selective of top talent (Cable and Turban, 2003). Applicants use the firm's reputation as a signal about the job attributes and as a source of pride from being a member. There are many similarities facing marketing and recruiting departments. For example, brand equity research suggests that organizations can create marketing advantage by fostering recognition and favourable impressions of the organizations' brand.

More important, brand image allows people to differentiate the product from competitors' products. When the image is positive, it creates positive attitudinal reactions to the organization and the product's attributes (Collins and Stevens, 2002). In the early stages of recruitment, organizations can use publicity, sponsorship of universities and schools, word-of-mouth, and advertising to create a positive brand image. These practices are particularly important in the early stages because the applicants have little information about the firm. They found these practices (excluding sponsorship) influenced employer brand image, which in turn influenced applicant decisions. Using multiple practices produced a stronger effect (Collins and Hans, 2004). They found these practices and information positively influenced applicant quality and quantity, demonstrating recruiting practices and organizational information can have organizational-level consequences. Advertising was the most important determinant of multiple measures of quality and quantity (Collins and Stevens, 2002) has borrowed from the marketing literature to consider the concept of brand equity.

Overall, employer brand image offers another possibility of sustained competitive advantage because it is rare, difficult to imitate, valuable, and cannot be substituted (Turban & Cable, 2003). Fostering favourable employer brand image can be accomplished through advertising and similar practices (Collins & Stevens, 2002) and can influence both applicant and organizational-level recruiting outcomes (Collins & Hans, 2004; Turban & Cable, 2003). Employer brand image offers a way for organizations to differentiate themselves among applicants, even when they cannot compete in terms of location or wages.

The Challenges and Constraints for Recruitment

1. Poor image of the company
2. Unattractive job package
3. Conservative internal policies
4. Limited financial support
5. Restricted policies of government

Recruitment is the process of locating and encouraging potential applicants to apply for existing job opening. Recruitment is influenced by variety of environmental factors like economic, social, technological, political, legal, etc. Recruiter these days wants special skills such as ability to work in a team, problem solving, creativity and communication skills and strong leadership potential. The main problem of recruitment is retaining. Employer brand identity is increasingly important to compete for talented people who have numerous options. Rebuilding a damaged employer brand often takes years.

Understanding Talent Acquisition

Talent acquisition involves all the sub-processes around finding, attracting and engaging highly talented individuals into your organization. Now-a-days traditional recruitment is re-emerging as a broader 'talent acquisition' concept—An approach that is becoming more and more critical in the 'War for Talent'.

Encouraging your own 'star' players to identify other outside top performers is an extremely powerful tool that is being used more and more. Corporations are offering a wide range of rewards in order to get these names and then act on them.

Once the talent has been identified, the next stage is to start building on-going relationships and look for that all elusive 'trigger point' in someone's career that would get them to change jobs. This can be a number of things but it is often a negative experience or an outstanding opportunity. Gathering intelligence from their 'friends' and from previous market research will help in uncovering exactly what excites top players.

Educating line managers that talent acquisition must also be an every day duty is also a success criterion. Most managers, rightly so, look at hiring only when there is a 'box' vacant on purely transactional basis.

Money is of course essential in the talent acquisition quest, but it is not the only element. Many corporations are using traditional job classification and job grading systems in order to remain competitive in the 'cash compensation' side. Being able to mould an opportunity and make it exciting will also attract top performers, the notion of a *la carte* job descriptions is becoming more and more adopted as a way of finding the "hot button", and excite people enough to make the move. That will prove to be more and more essential in giving corporations a leading edge and competitive advantage over others. If you have it you will be one of the survivors, if not then a 'market correction' may be soon be coming your way.

Difference between Recruitment and Talent Acquisition

Recruitment is nothing more than filling open positions. It is an entirely tactical event. Strategic talent acquisition takes a long-term view of not only filling positions today, but also using the candidates that come out of a recruiting campaign as a means to fill similar positions in the future.

These future positions may be identifiable today by looking at the succession management plan, or by analyzing the history of attrition for certain positions. This makes it easy to predict that specific openings will occur at a pre-determined period in time. In the most enlightened cases of Strategic Talent Acquisition, clients will recruit today for positions that do not even exist today but are expected to become available in the future.

Strategic talent acquisition allows us access to a pool of competitive talent that would otherwise have been missed or even worse, ignored. Clearly, the business case for acquiring talent strategically is far more compelling than simply paying to fill positions today. What we are doing is adding a small incremental effort, in exchange for a huge potential reward.

Importance of Talent Acquisition

- Understanding workforce demographics (current and future)
- Identifying economic issues impacting organizational sustainability
- Identifying organizational and cultural issues impacting talent acquisition
- Knowledge of industry trends and emerging issues linking organizational strategy to HR Strategy
- Understanding the organizational strategy
- Translating the organizational strategy into a HR strategy
- Reviewing key components of the HR strategy
- Identifying talent acquisition and retention issues

Designing and Implementing a Talent Acquisition Strategy

- What is an employer of choice?
- Demystifying the generational implications on recruitment
- Reviewing the base elements of a talent acquisition strategy
- Utilizing talent acquisition tools and templates
- Identifying considerations when implementing a talent acquisition strategy

- Learning from best practices
- Analyzing performance metrics (business impacts, financial considerations, etc.)
- What is meant by strategic talent acquisition
- How HR strategy, policies, and practices support and facilitate corporate strategy
- Key design elements required in an HR talent acquisition strategy
- Practical application of a talent acquisition strategy
- Knowledge of emerging trends and best practices in attraction and retention of talent

The Role of Information Technology on Recruitment

The internet never before in the history of mankind has there been such an enabling technology. Candidates can now advertise their desire to change jobs within minutes of making the decision and receive enquires about their talents within hours.

Potentially, it is feasible that a high quality employee of yours, having received the final 'straw which broke the camels back' (bad appraisal, inappropriate negative response from boss, extra workload stress etc.) can post their CV/resume up on a particular jobs board at midday today, receive three interested requests for contact with third party recruiters or headhunters within hours, be interviewed for an outstanding role (at one of your competitors) tomorrow, receive an offer in writing the following day and resign that afternoon (within 2 days). Scary, isn't it? But if the Internet has enabled this process for candidates, it has also brought significant advantages for organizations.

Organizations have been using the Internet as a recruiting mechanism almost as soon as it became popular. This use ranges from massive job search engines such as *Monster.com*, to providing job and career information on the organization's Website, to using the internet as a means to screen and process applicants. The internet has become an important job search tool for applicants, and it appears that the job search behaviour of a sizable minority is influenced by

Websites (Karr, 2000).

Recruitment efforts are likely to be most effective when an organization emphasizes fit information, provides details about the job and organization; selects and trains recruiters, treats applicants with fairness and respect, uses job-related procedures and explains the purpose of the selection process, articulates the right employer brand image, and ultimately creates a unified, consistent, and coherent recruiting campaign (perhaps marketing and recruiting departments should work together?). Furthermore, organizations that use Websites for recruitment should ensure they are aesthetically pleasing, easy to use, and provide the appropriate content for their purpose.

Nearly every major staffing firm has adapted some form of internet-based testing, and many organizations have already migrated from chapter to Web-based selection. The rush to use this delivery platform is appealing: efficiency and cost savings, ability to administer the test globally in real time, and standardized scoring and administration. The issues involving Web-based selection are quite different from Web-based recruitment, in large part because there is more legal scrutiny with selection practices.

Thus, through the processes of human capital emergence and human capital advantage, hiring more competent employees through the use of valid selection systems should contribute to better organizational performance.

Because of the advent of the Information Technology people are switching the job very frequently and now employee is like transnational employee, for this reason there is need for the study of the culture of that country. They have to look after their language, dress, eating habits, times consciousness, values and norms, beliefs and attitudes, work habits and practices to make their self adaptable.

Direct Access to the Candidate Market

Now organizations can go direct to the candidate market, thereby cutting the time it takes to find the right people, whilst dramatically reducing their recruitment costs. However, simply posting up jobs on various jobs boards is not the answer.

Best Practice Process

Talent acquisition needs to be addressed at the most senior levels within all organizations—big or small, public or private. This means that talent acquisition needs to fit 'hand in glove' with your overall organizational strategy. It needs to have the appropriate level of resources behind it; it needs to be monitored and reported on at all board meetings and it needs to involve many people within the organization who attribute to it the importance that the organization requires. But don't despair, given the correct focus we can help ensure that your organization becomes 'an employer of choice' in this brave new world.

Conclusion

Staffing sits in a curious position at the dawn of the twenty-first century: Economic, societal, and cultural changes make organizational success and survival dependent on staffing, but many organizational decision makers and even organizational scholars fail to recognize staffing's value. Managers often plea for tools to attract and hire better people. Often times, we can give managers these tools if they would only believe in them. Staffing should reign supremely strategic in the war for talent and sustained competitive advantage, but it is incumbent on staffing researchers and practitioners to show the organizational value of their science and practice (a concern of HR more generally). Multi-level staffing research and models were offered as one mechanism for conveying business unit value. Every single organization in the world uses some form of staffing procedure, but there is no guarantee they use them optimally or even appropriately. This is unfortunate but is likely to continue unless research-practice gaps are closed to show the business unit strategic value of staffing (Anderson, 2001; Anderson & Ostroff, 1997; Herriot, 1989; Tissen, 1989), the relationship between a person and an organization begins before the person's first day on the job. Instead, we must view the relationship as beginning at the first point of contact between the person and organization. With the emergence of the World Wide Web and associated technologies, this first point of contact is, increasingly, at the organization's website or other web-based employment advertisement (Cober *et al.*, 2000). Just as these technologies have revolutionized many aspects of business operations, they offer tremendous potential for recruitment, selection and socialization processes as well. However, with the potential benefits come potential consequences. In particular, the ability to provide hi-tech, customizable recruitment messages to a virtually infinite number of people at relatively little cost makes understanding job seeker reaction to such messages all the more important.

The realities of today's demographics have elevated the issue of talent attraction and retention to become a critical leadership concern, receiving significant attention. Given the projected labour market and demographic trends, an organization's approach to talent acquisition can become a key differentiator and source of competitive advantage. The changing market has revealed that prevailing "one size fits all" HR practices are no longer effective. Organizations must develop specific people strategies for their most critical segments that directly align with and support the business strategy. While individual approaches are customized to the needs of each organization, all approaches are based on key critical success factors. This course focuses on the issues and challenges organizations face in attracting and retaining key talent. While introducing participants to emerging recruitment trends in the industry, this course will also provide participants with a selection of tools and best practices from which to draw as they design their own strategy to win the war for talent.

REFERENCES

Alba, J.W. and Marmorstein, H. (1987), "The Effects of Frequency Knowledge on Consumer Decision Making", *Journal of Consumer Research*, 14, pp. 14–25.

Anderson, N.H. (1981), *Foundations of Information Integration Theory*, New York: Academic Press.

Anderson, N. (2001), "Towards a Theory of Socialization Impact: Selection as Pre-entry Socialization", *International Journal of Selection and Assessment*, 9, 84–91.

Bauer, T. N. Truxillo, D. M. Sanchez, R. J., Craig, J. Ferrara, P. & Campion, M. A. (2001), "Applicant Reactions to Selection: Development of the Selection Procedural Justice Scale", *Personnel Psychology*, 54: 387-419.

Binning, J.F. and Barrett, G.V. (1989), "Validity of Personnel Decisions: A Conceptual Analysis of the Inferential and Evidential Bases", *Journal of Applied Psychology*, 74, 478–494.

Bless, H., Bohner, G., Schwarz, N. and Strack. F. (1990), "Mood and Persuasion: A

Cognitive Response Analysis", *Personality and Social Psychology Bulletin*, 16, 331–345.

Bliese, P. D. (2000), "Within Group Agreement, Non-independence, and Reliability: Implications for Data Aggregation and Analysis" in K. J. Klein & S. W. J. Kozlowski, (Eds.), *Multilevel Theory, Research, and Methods in Organizations: Foundations, Extensions, and New Directions*: 349-381. San Francisco: Jossey-Bass.Boudreau, J.W. and Rynes, S.L. (1985), "Role of Recruitment in Staffing Utility Analysis", *Journal of Applied Psychology*, 70, 354–366.

Boxall, P. F. (1996), "The Strategic HRM Debate and the Resource-based View of the Firm", *Human Resource Management Journal*, 6: 59-75.

Breaugh, J.A. and Starke, M. (2000), "Research on Employee Recruitment: So Many Studies, So Many Remaining Questions", *Journal of Management*, 26, 405–434.

Bretz, R.D. and Judge, T.A. (1998), "Realistic Job Previews: A Test of the Adverse Self-Selection Hypothesis", *Journal of Applied Psychology*, 83, 330–333.

Brief, A.P., Butcher, A.H. and Roberson, L. (1995), "Cookies, Disposition, and Job Attitudes: The Effects of Positive Mood Inducing Events and Negative Affectivity on Job Satisfaction in a Field Experiment", *Organizational Behaviour & Human Decision Processes*, 62, 55–62.

Bureau of National Affairs. (1998), *Recruiting and Selection Procedures: Personnel Policies Forum*, Survey No. 146, May, Washington, DC.

Cable, D. M. and De Rue D. S. (2002), "The Convergent and Discriminant Validity of Subjective fit Perceptions", *Journal of Applied Psychology*, 87: 875-884.

Cable, D. M. and Edwards, J. R. (2004), "Complementary and Supplementary Fit: A Theoretical and Empirical Examination", *Journal of Applied Psychology*, 89: 822-834.

Cappelli, P. (2001), *Making the Most of On-line Recruiting*, Harvard Business Review, 79, 139-146.

Carlson, K.D., Connerley, M.L. and Mecham, R.L. (2002), "Recruitment Evaluation: The Case for Assessing the Quality of Applicants Attracted", *Personnel Psychology*, 55, 461–490.

Clevenger, J., Pereira, G. M., Wiechmann, D., Schmitt, N., & Harvey, V. S. (2001), "Incremental Validity of Situational Judgment Tests", *Journal of Applied Psychology*, 86: 410-417.

Cober, R.T., Brown, D.J., Blumental, A.J., Doverspike, D. and Levy, P.E. (2000), "The Quest for the Qualified Job Surfer: It's Time the Public Sector Catches the Wave", *Public Personnel Management*, 29, 479–495.

Cober, R. T.; Brown, D. J.; Keeping, L.M. and Levy, P. E. (2004), "Recruitment on the Net: How Do Organizational Web Site Characteristics Influence Applicant Attraction?," *Journal of Management*, 30: 623-646.

Cober, R. T.; Brown, D. J. and Levy, P. E. (2004), "Form, Content, and Function: An Evaluative Methodology for Corporate Employment Web Sites", *Human Resource Management*, 43: 201-218.

Cober, R.T.; Brown, D.J.; Levy, P.E.; Cober, A.B. and Keeping, L.M. (2003), "Organizational Web Sites: Web Site Content and Style as Determinants of Organizational Attraction", *International Journal of Selection and Assessment*, 11: 158-169.

Collins, C. J. and Han, J. (2004), 'Exploring Applicant Pool Quantity and Quality: The Effects of Early Recruitment Practices, Corporate Advertising, and Firm Reputation' *Personnel Psychology*, 57: 685-717.

Jeff Grout, Sarah Perrin, *Recruiting Excellence: An Insider's Guide to Sourcing Top Talent.*

Johanna Rothman, *The Secrets & Science of Hiring Technical People.*

Lance A. Berger and Dorothy R. Berger, "*The Talent Management Handbook: Creating Organizational Excellence by Identifying, Developing, and Promoting Your Best People*", (Hardcover).

Martin Yate Techies and Nerds, "Hiring the Best: A Manager's Guide to Effective Interviewing", *Hiring the Best Knowledge Workers.*

Nicholas Corcodilos, *Nicholas Cordilos Ask the Headhunter: Reinventing the Interview to Win the Job.*

10

INDIAN CONTRACTUAL LABOUR MARKET, MIGRATION AND GLOBAL COMPETITION

VINOD KUMAR SRIVASTAVA

This chapter aims to give an overview of Indian contractual labour market, migration and global competition. The chapter is divided into four sections. Section first covers a brief introduction about the theme. Second section deals with nature, causes and effects of migration of contractual labour in India. Section three deals with the different provisions of Contract Labour (Regulation and Abolition) Act, 1970. The chapter concludes with Section four which gives a brief account of conceptual facts about migration of contractual labours in global competition.

Labour, however, is manifestly different from other factors of production and has got certain characteristics which give rise to various labour problems in all the economies across the globe. Labour is a living being and that makes all the difference. The first characteristic of labour is that it is inseparable from the person of the labourer. The labourer has to go himself to deliver the goods. The environments in which labour has to work are, therefore, of utmost consequence. Secondly, the worker sells his work, his labour only, but himself retains his own property. The investment in labour, that is, his training and efficiency, therefore, are of great importance. Thirdly, labour is a perishable commodity. One day lost is lost forever. Labour cannot be stored up like other commodities. It has no reserve price. Hence, workers cannot afford to wait, and so they are in a weak bargaining position as compared to employers. Fourthly, the supply of labour cannot be curtailed immediately even if wages fall, and it also takes time for children to grow up or for people to get trained in order to increase the labour supply. Hence, there can be no rapid adjustment of the supply of labour to its demand. Fifthly, capital, which helps labour in production, is more productive than labour itself. A man stands in no comparison with the productive capacity of a modern machine. Therefore, under the competitive economy, the owners of capital claim and take away a larger share of the national dividend than what goes to the labourers. Sixthly, labour is not so mobile as capital. Therefore, there are differences in environments, fashions, habits, and languages, etc. which make people prefer to remain at home rather than move from place to place. Seventhly, it has also to be kept in mind that labour is not only a factor of production but is also the ultimate end of production. The economic problems of labour as a consumer, such as the standard of life, cost of living and poverty, constitute important subjects of labour economics. Lastly, labour being a human factor, not only economic but moral, social and other considerations, having a bearing on human beings, have also to be taken into account in the discussion of problems connected with labour. Labour problems, thus, have many aspects—economic, political, psychological, sociological, legal, historical and administrative. Labour economics, therefore, cannot be studied without an inter-disciplinary approach.

Contract labour is a significant and growing form of employment. It is prevalent in almost all industries, in agriculture and allied operations and in service sector. It generally refers to workers engaged through an intermediary and is based on a triangular relationship between the user enterprises, the contractor including the sub contractor and the workers. These workers are millions in number and generally belong to the unorganized sector. The concern for providing legislative protection to this category of workers, whose conditions were found to be abysmal by various commissions and committees, coupled with the judgment of the Supreme Court of India in the standard Vacuum Refinery Company case, resulted in the final enactment of the Contract Labour (Regulation and Abolition) Act, 1970.

Nature, Causes and Effects of Migration of Contractual Labour in India

One of the characteristic features of the industrial labour in India is that it has been mostly of a migratory character in the sense that the workers employed in most industries do not claim as their hometown the place at which they work. In other words, the Indian factory labourers do not constitute wage-earning class exactly corresponding to the factory labourers in the western countries. In the west, where industrialization has taken deep roots, there are big industrial centres, which attract a permanent class of industrial workers, completely divorced from land. In those countries the workers have no ties with the villages or adjoining areas—most of them have been brought up in the towns—and they depend upon their wages as the only means of livelihood. But in India most of the unskilled factory workers come from the adjoining villages and continue to keep contact with their village homes. The workers are, thus, immigrants and may not be called as migratory in the sense in which the word is commonly understood. The tendency to migrate from one centre to another is noticeable only amongst casual labourer, while other workers generally try to continue at one place and in one industry, especially in places where high wages prevail, or in those industries, which require a high degree of skill. By the migratory character of Indian labour, therefore, is meant the absence of any permanent industrial population claiming industrial towns as their homes—the majority of the workers coming from the rural areas—and the problem is that this migration has not been permanent but only temporary in nature though in recent years a change in this migratory character has been noticed and there is a trend towards stabilization of industrial labour in urban areas.

However, it has to be noted that the industrial worker, though comes from the village, is not essentially an agriculturist, who has only temporarily forsaken his agricultural work in order to add to his income by a brief spell of industrial work in the city. Only in seasonal industries, dealing largely with agricultural products, and in the mines, there is a substantial class directly interested in agriculture. In regular factory industries the employer has passed the stage of being compelled to employ only those workers who are prepared to work for a few months and go back to the village at the time of harvesting or sowing the crops. An investigation undertaken by the Labour Investigation Committee (1946) clearly showed that the bulk of factory workers though immigrant in character, had little stake in agriculture and their occasional visits to their village homes were more for rest and recuperation than for attending to cultivation. Their interest in agriculture may be only this much that some may be members of a joint family having an agricultural holding or may have close relations actively engaged in agriculture. The truth behind the assertion of the agricultural character of the factory population is that the great majority of those employed are at heart villagers. They are born in the villages, their childhood is spent in them, they have got village traditions, many leave their families behind in their villages and even when the wife accompanies the husband to the city she is generally sent back to the village at the time of confinement. The labourer visits his village as frequently as his financial circumstances permit, especially at the time of social ceremonies, urgent family matters, illness, repair of his house or meting of relations, etc. Some of the workers may be even prepared to give up industrial work if remunerative work can be secured in their village and in any case some earnestly hope to retire there permanently. Except this contact with the village, which in many cases may also be in the form of sending remittances to the family relations or to the village money lender, the workers, in majority of the cases, continue to work in the industries for a considerable period once they join them, and cannot be called merely "birds of passage". Besides, it is also not true that all workers have a longing for the village. In the words of the Royal Commission on Labour, "with some, the contact is close and constant, with others it is slender or spasmodic, and with a few it is more an inspiration than a reality."

The causes for this migration are complex. The main cause has been the increasing pressure of population on land on account of decline of cottage industries and village handicrafts and absolute increase immolation. There have been more people depending on agriculture than land can support resulting in uneconomic holdings poverty, unemployment and indebtedness in the villages. Besides, a fairly large class of landless agricultural labourers has long been in existence, obtaining a somewhat precarious living even in good years and subjected to series of hardships in bad years and the less of land owing to the accumulation of debt, the eviction of tenants due to the desire of landlords to increase their own cultivation quarrels between the tenant heirs after the death of permanent tenant, have been some of the factors leading to an increase in the number of families in this class, these landless rural labourers are the first to feel the pinch of agricultural distress, and improved means of transport enable them to leave the villages in search of work and higher wages in the urban areas in many places the petty landholders are under the necessity of migrating every year to the towns in order to earn a livelihood. The joint family system also facilitates such migration as some members of the family can leave the village without having to break up their homes or give up their lands and can leave their women and children to the care of other members of the family besides sometimes the agriculturists have taken employment in the towns to evade the village money lenders or to earn enough for buying cattle or more land. Many village craftsmen, after the decline of cottage industries, also migrated to industrial areas in quest of work further, depressed classes in the villages find that they receive far better social treatment in industrial curtness than in village and are spared much humiliation, as industrial employment tends to break down social and caste distinctions. It is significant that in Kanpur percentage of the woman workers belong to the backward or untouchable castes the Koris, Shaikhs, Pasis and Bhangies, and about 30 per cent of men belong to the depressed castes. Majority of them being koris. Some villagers also migrate to the industrial centres on account of family quarrels and worries or to avoid punishment and social boycott due to some or moral offence, love affair, etc.

Evil effects of the migration, as a result of migration, as already pointed out many actions of factory workers find themselves in an entirely unfamiliar environment of customs and traditions and sanctions is weakened the ties which give village life its corporate and organic character are loosened; new ties are not easily formed and life tends to become more individualistic this fact has got a serious effect on the psychology of the workers and lowers their efficiency the health of the worker is subjected to a severe strain due to many reasons, e.g., difference of ultimate and condition of work, a defective dietary excessive congestion lack of sanitation and the temptations of enforced separation from the family. The worker lives and works under conditions and circumstances which are new to his experience and completely at variance with many things that he had to face previously in the village the work is spasmodic with loans intervals of leisure, while in the cities the workers find themselves caught within the great walls of the factory and are stupefied by the clang and whirl of the machinery. The efficiency of the worker also suffers because with the constant changing of the labour force the workers are not able to get full training. Recent official statistics show that Rural-Rural migration continued dominant, accounting for roughly 62 per cent of all movements in 1999-2000. People from backward states like Bihar, Uttar Pradesh, Orissa and Rajasthan out-migrateto the developed "Green Revolution States of Maharashtra, Punjab and Gujarat for the transplant and harvesting season.

An estimated 20 million people migrate temporarily each year in India. High levels of temporary migration are reported in a number of village studies. For example, a study of Bolangir District in Orissa estimated that nearly 60,000 people migrated during the drought of 2001 from that District alone (Wanschneider and Mishra, 2003). Bolangir is one of the three in famous KBK (Koraput-Bolangir-Kalahandi) districts in Orissa with persistently high levels of poverty. Studies in the drought prone areas of West Bengal by Rogaly *et al.*, (2002) observe that over 5,00,000 lakh tribals, Muslims and lower caste people migrate seasonally to the rice growing areas of the State.

An important but under researched dimensions of migration in India is the relationship between migration and the caste system. In some studies it is noted that certain castes and tribes have a higher propensity to migrate. Deshingkar and Starts (2003) for example found that the scheduled tribes had higher migration rates in Andhra Pradesh and Madhya Pradesh. Similar observations have been made by Dayal and Karan (2003) regarding Jharkhand: whereas 15 per cent of scheduled castes and scheduled tribes migrated, only 8 per cent of upper castes and 3 per cent of other backward castes migrated. In 2001, India had a population of over one billion. Of these 67.2 per cent lived in rural areas and 32.8 per cent in towns and cities. During 1951-2001, people in urban areas as a percentage of the total population increased gradually from 17.3 per cent to 32.8 per cent. Of the total work force, 73.3 per cent remained in rural areas, a marginal decline from 79.3 per cent in 1981, and 77.7 per cent in 1991. In India migration by individuals and/or households is

Table 10.1: Percentage of the Distribution of Migrants by Place of Last Residence, Age, Sex and Reason for Migration, 2001

Reason	Sex (M/F)	Rural	Urban	Total
Work employment	Male	16.9	38.0	27.45
	Female	1.2	3.2	2.2
Business	Male	1.5	3.5	2.5
	Female	0.2	0.3	0.25
Education	Male	2.1	3.0	2.55
	Female	0.2	1.1	0.65
Marriage	Male	4.0	0.8	2.4
	Female	77.9	44.2	61.05
Moved after birth	Male	13.5	6.8	10.15
	Female	2.4	4.4	3.4
Moved with household	Male	17.9	20.7	19.3
	Female	6.2	26.8	16.5
Others	Male	44.1	27.3	35.7
	Female	11.9	20.0	15.95

Source: Computed on the basis of Census of India: 2001 Table D-5.

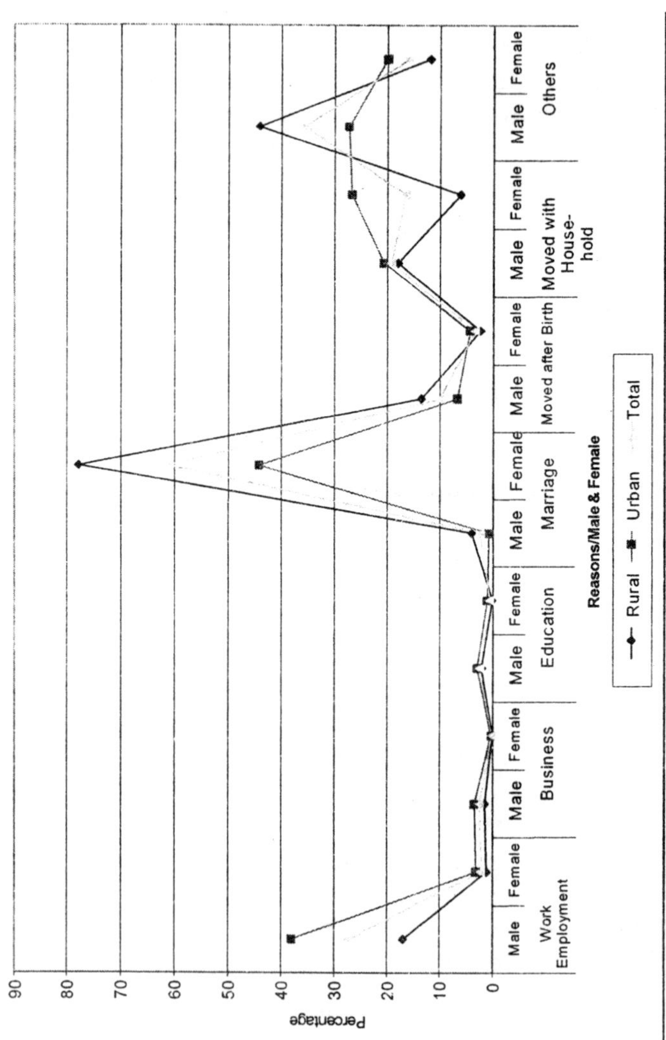

Fig. 10.1: Percentage of Distribution of Migrants by Place of Last Residence 2001

undertaken for both economic and social reasons. These include migration by virtue of marriage, as has been the case of large majority of the female migraines or due to economic reasons such as for seeking better employments opportunities. Migration can be with in the country, i.e. internal migration which can be with in the district, intra-/inter-district or intra-/inter-state (rural to rural, rural to urban, urban to rural and urban to urban) or it can be international migration. Here we primarily deal with the working conditions of internal migrant wage workers and focus on semi-permanent or seasonal migrants in the informal sector, who are at the lowest end of the spectrum of migrant workers.

Table 10.2 reveals the fact that employment continues to be the main reason for men while marriage is the main reason for women migration in the case of man, employment as a reason for migration was seen to rise in the nineties. This could be a reflection of the impact of structural changes on availability of employment opportunities, largely generated in urban centre and that too for the more skilled among the workers. According to the 2001 census, the

Table 10.2 : Percentage Distribution of Total Migration by Duration of Stay, 2001

Duration of residence	Sex (M/F)	Rural	Urban	Total
Less than one year	Male	6.2	3.0	4.6
	Female	2	2.5	2.25
1-4 years	Male	17.2	18.3	17.75
	Female	12.9	17.0	14.95
5-9 years	Male	11.3	14.5	12.9
	Female	13.1	14.9	14.0
1-9 years	Male	28.5	32.7	30.6
	Female	26.0	31.9	28.95
10 years & above	Male	32.7	45.0	38.85
	Female	64.0	50.1	57.05

Source: Computed on the basis of Census of India: 2001 Table D-3.

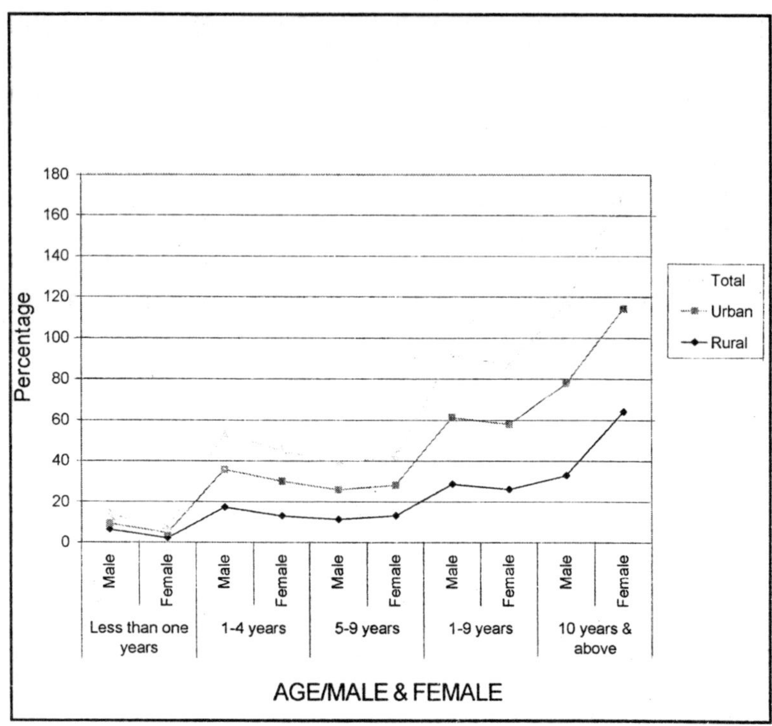

Fig. 10.2 : Percentage Distribution of Total Migration by Duration of Stay, 2001

total migrate population in the country was 314.5 million. Among those migrating for work and employment purpose is long term/ permanent migration (above 10 years) has the highest share in India. Percentage of the distribution of migration by duration of stay 2001 is given in Table 10.2.

Table 10.3 : Percentage Distribution of Migrants who stated Work/ Employment as the Reason for Migration by Duration of Stay, 2001

Duration of residence	Sex (M/F)	Rural	Urban	Total
Less than one year	Male	13.8	3.1	8.45
	Female	21.0	5.6	13.3
1-4 years	Male	28.4	21.0	24.7
	Female	27.0	26.4	26.7
5-9 years	Male	17.2	18.3	17.75
	Female	14.1	18.0	16.05
1-9 years	Male	45.6	39.3	42.45
	Female	41.1	44.4	42.75
10 years & above	Male	40.6	57.6	49.1
	Female	37.8	49.9	43.85

Source: Computed on the basis of Census of India: 2001 Table D-3.

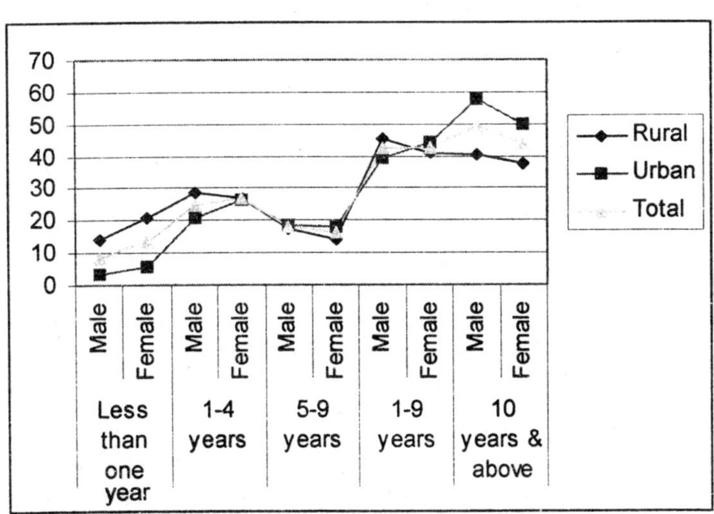

Fig. 10.3 : Percentage Distribution of Migrants who stated Work/ Employment as the Reason for Migration by Duration of Stay, 2001

As per the 1999-2000 NSSO, 10.9 million workers migrated for to 6 months of which 8.5 million ware in rural areas. Among the rural migrants 3 million were females. Short duration out migrants constituted 2.1 per cent of the rural employed persons and 1.3 per cent of the urban employed of which 3.1 per cent (rural) and 1.5 per cent (urban) were casual labourers.

Contract Labourers (Regulation and Abolition) Act, 1970

The system of employing contract labour is prevalent in most industries for different jobs including skilled and semiskilled. It is also prevalent in agricultural and allied operations, and to some extent, in the services sector. A contract labour is a person who is hired, supervised, contracted and remunerated by a contractor, who in turn, is compensated by the user enterprises. The concern to improve the working and living condition of contract labour, and the Supreme Court of India's observations in the case of Standard by Vacuum Refinery Company *Vs* Their Workman resulted in the Act meant of the Contract Labour (Regulation and Abolition) Act 1970. The Act seeks to regulate the employment of contract labour in certain establishment and to provide for its abolition in certain circumstances and for matters connected therewith. The Act and the Contract Labour (Regulation and Abolition) Central Rules, 1971 came into force on 10th February 1971. The Act provides for the constitution of Central and State advisory contract labour boards to advise the respective governments on matters arising out of the administration of the Act. The Act contains specific provisions to ensure payment of wages and certain amenities to be provided by the contractor to the contract labour. The Central and the State governments are empowered to prohibit employment of contract labour in any activity in an establishment and so to grant exemption to establishment/contractors in the case of an emergency from the applicability of the provisions of the Act. The Central government has issued a number of notifications prohibiting employment of contract labour in different categories of works in deferments fields. In the central sphere, the central Industrial relation machinery (CRIM) has been interested with the responsibility of enforcing the provisions of the Act and Rules made thereunder. In a landmark judgment relating to contract labour, a five judge Constitutional Bench of Supreme Court in the case of Steel Authority of India Ltd. *Vs* National Union of Waterfront expressly or by necessary implication, provide for automatic absorption of contract labour. Consequently, the Principal Employer cannot be required to order absorption of the contract labour working in the concerned establishment

General Terms and Conditions for Contract Labour in India

- Rates/quotations duly filled in, will be received up to the date and time mentioned in the letter.
- Commissioner of Authority for Advance Rulings reserves the right to postpone and/or extend the date of receipt/ opening of Rates/Quotations or to withdraw the same, without assigning any reason therefor.
- The contractors are required to submit the complete rates/ quotations only after satisfying each and every condition laid down in the annexure enclosed.
- All the rates must be written both in figures and in words. Correction, if any is to be made by crossing out initializing, dating and rewriting. In case of discrepancy between the words and figures the rates indicated in figures shall prevail. All overwriting/cutting, insertion shall be authenticated and attested.
- Rates/quotations should be submitted and signed by the firm with its current business address.
- The rates shall be valid for a period of at least three calendar months from the date of opening.
- The contractors should satisfy themselves before submission of the rates/quotations to the Commissioner, Authority for Advance Rulings that they meet the qualifying criteria and capability as laid down in the annexure.
- The contractor must comply with the rates/quotations, specification and all terms and conditions of contract. No deviation in the terms and conditions of the contract shall be entertained unless specifically mentioned by the contractor

in the rates/quotations and accepted by the Commissioner Authority for advance Rulings.

- The contract will be awarded initially for 90 subject to further extension from time to time. However, extension will be considered keeping in view the various factors such as the prevailing market price, satisfactory performance of the firm etc.

Contractual Labour and Global Competition in India

The Contract Labour (Regulation and Abolition) Act, 1970 was brought on the Statute Book to regulate the employment of Contract Labour in certain establishments and to provide for its abolition in certain circumstances and for matters connected therewith. The Act and the rules came into force on 10th February, 1971. The Act applies to every establishment/contractor in which 20 or more workmen are employed or were employment on any day on the preceding 12 months as contract labour and to every contractor who employs or who employed on any day of the preceding 12 months 20 or more workmen. It does not apply to establishments where the work performed is of intermittent or seasonal nature. An establishment wherein work is of intermittent and seasonal nature will be covered by the Act if the work performed is more than 120 days and 60 days in a year respectively. The Act also applies to establishments of the Government and local authorities as well. With a view to facilitate the outsourcing of certain activities of an establishment and at the same time to protect the interests of contract labour in terms of wages, social security, welfare, health and safety, consequent to Court judgments and feedback received from social partners, a proposal was prepared by the Ministry of Labour for enacting a new law on Contract Labour. The Hon'ble Prime Minister constituted a Group of Ministers (GOM) to examine these proposals before the same is brought before the Cabinet. The Ministry of Law & Justice (Legislative Department) has been requested to draft the amendment proposals, which would be placed before the Group of Ministers for its finalization. The migration of races across countries and continents has been a regular feature of human history. However, the quantum of international migration has now reached an extent where it has become a major factor in global change. Never before have such large numbers of people left their country of origin, either permanently or for short duration, as economic migrants, or as refugees and asylum seekers. The World Development Report 1999/2000 estimates that more than 130 million people now live outside the countries of their birth. At the outset, it is important to highlight the basic characteristics of the labour flows from India to the industrialized countries in the period since Independence:

- Such outflows are made up almost entirely of permanent migration in so far as the proportion of emigrants, who return to India, after a finite period, is almost negligible.
- A large proportion of these migrants are persons with professional expertise, technical qualifications or other skills.
- For an overwhelming proportion of these migrants, the destinations are United States, Canada and the United Kingdom.

The Ministry has drawn an ambitious plan for the welfare and development of Labour during the Tenth Plan. Special emphasis would be laid for elimination of child labour, welfare or unorganized sector workers, skill up gradation and strengthening of labour statistics and research. Earlier a zero-based budgeting exercise was carried out during 2001-2002. As an outcome of this exercise, the numbers of on-going plan schemes were reduced from 142 to 101 during 2001-2002. The number after rationalization is around 94 in 2003-2004 and 73 during 2004-05 including those schemes, which were earlier, proposed for transfer from Plan to Non-plan. The total outlay of the Ministry during the Tenth Plan has been placed at Rs. 1500 crore, which is 90 per cent higher, compared to Rs. 792 crore in the Ninth Plan. Rs. 181 crore has been earmarked for the Ministry of Labour during 2004-05 as against Rs. 170 crore during 2003-04.

Liberalization and globalization have changed the economic scenario and demand in the labour market. The high quality skilled workforce has gained performance, as there is greater emphasis on increase in productivity, which has a direct bearing on the skill available with the labour force. Investment in skill development and training by all the stakeholders and modernization of training system are important so as to equip the labour force with employable skill. The government has accorded high priority to the creation of a skilled labour force as well as skill upgradation in the country to avail the advantages of globalization. Accordingly, 9 obsolete trades were deleted, 42 new trades introduced and curriculum of 42 trades revised in the Craftsman's Training. By way of low cost solution to improve the functioning of DGE &T during 2003-04, the intake capacity of trainees increased from the targeted level of 13,530 to 16,949, which represents an increase of 25.24 per cent Further, a target of training 21,984, 23,678 and 27,060 trainees has been fixed for the years 2003-04, 2004-05 and 2005-06 respectively which would result in doubling the capacity in four years without creating any infrastructure or new posts. The expansion has been possible by starting additional short-term courses, running classes on Saturdays, engaging some guest facilities etc. Over the past two decades, labour market around the world has become increasingly integrated. Political change and economic reform have transformed, India and the former eastern block countries, effectively involving there large labour forces in open market economies. At the same time, the development of technology, combined with the progressive removal of restriction on cross-border trade and capital flows, has made it possible for production processes to be unbundled and located further from target markets for growing universe of goods and services. The location of production has become much more responsive to relative labour cost across countries. There have also been increasing flows of migrants across border, through both legal and information routes. This ongoing globalization of the labour market has drawn increasing attention from policymaker and the media, particular in the advance economies. The most asked question is whether the addition of this unprecedented large pool of labour from emerging market and developing countries is adversely affecting compensation and employment in the advance economies.

It may not be inappropriate to infer from the aforesaid analysis that in the era of liberalised trade regime new vistas of opportunities and better remunerations have attracted people across the region and social strata to go for them and leave less remunerative and least productive spheres of economic activities. Inadequate infrastructure coupled with poor quality of life has also been one the reasons which compelled people to think in this direction. Consequently, all these circumstances have made the feeling of insecurity more prominent in the minds of the people, especially the casual workers to migrate on continuous basis.

REFERENCES

Amjad, Rashid (Ed.) (1989), *To the Gulf and Back: Studies on the Economic Impact of Asian Labour Migration*, New Delhi: ILO-ARTEP.

Andhra Pradesh Rural Livelihood Project (2003), *Role of Migration in People's Lives: A Qualitative Study of Four Villages in Mahaboobnagar and Anantapur Districts*, Andhra Pradesh Rural Livelihood Project, Government of Andhra Pradesh.

Athukorala, Premachandra (1993), "Statistics on Asian Labour Migration: Review of Sources, Methods and Problems", in *International Labour Migration Statistics and Information Networking in Asia*, New Delhi: ILO-ARTEP.

Bhagat, B.R. (2005), "Conceptual Issues in Measurement of Internal Migration in India", chapter presented at the XXV IUSSP International Conference held in Tours, France.

Bhat, Ela R. (1994), "The Unprotected Labour", *The Indian Journal of Labour Economics*, 37(3).

Census of India (2001), *Migration Tables-India*, Office of Registrar General, India.

Clawen, A. (2002), "Female Labour Migration to Bangkok: Transforming Rural Urban Interactions and Social Networks through Globalization", *Asia Pacific Population Journal*, 17 (3):53-78.

Connell, J, B., Dasgupta, R. Laishley and M. Lipton. (1976), *Migration from Rural Areas: The Evidence from Village Studies*, Delhi: Oxford University Press.

Dev, S.M. and R.E.Evenson (2003), "Rural Development in India: Agriculture, Non-Farm and Migration", (mimeo), *http://scid, stanford.edu/events/India2003/Rural Development.*

Eevit, Zafer and Zachariah, K.C. (1978), "International Labour Migration", *Finance and Development*, Vol. 15, No. 4.

Emigration Act, 1983 (No. 31 of 1983), Government of India.

Government of India, *Economic Survey (2006-2007),* Ministry of Finance, Ministry of Finance, New Delhi.

Government of India, Ministry of Labour (2000), *Annual Report - 1999-2000*, New Delhi: Government of India.

Government of Kerala (1977), *Survey on Employment and Unemployment*, Department of Economic and Statistics, Trivandrum: Bureau of Economics and Statistics.

Government of Kerala, Department of Economics and Statistics (1987), *Report of the Survey on the Utilisation of Gulf Remittances in Kerala*, Trivandrum: Government of Kerala.

IFAD (International Fund for Agriculture Development) 2001, *Rural Poverty Report 2001: Challenge of Ending Rural Poverty*, Oxford University Press, Oxford.

ILO-ARTEP (1993), *International Labour Migration Statistics and Information Networking in Asia*, New Delhi: ILO-ARTEP.

Isaac Thomas T.M. (1992), *Economic Consequences of the Gulf Crisis: A Study of India with Special Reference to Kerala*, New Delhi: ILO-ARTEP.

Karan, A. (2003), "Changing Pattern of Rural Bihar", in G. Iyer (Ed), *Migration Labour and Human Right in India*, Kanishka Publisher, New Delhi, pp.102-139.

Kundu, A (2003), "Urbanisation and Urban Governance: Search for Perspective Beyond Neo-liberalism," *Economic and Political Weekly*, XXXVIII (29): 3079-98, 19 July.

MOLE (2007), *Annual Report 2006-2007*, Ministry of Labour and Employment, Government of India.

Madhavan, M.C. (1985), "Indian Emigrants: Numbers, Characteristics and Economic Impact", *Population and Development Review*, Vol. 11(3).

Mathew, E.T. and P.R. Gopinathan, Nair (1978), "Socio-Economic Characteristics of Emigrants and Emigrants Households: A Case Study of Two Villages in Kerala" in *Economic and Political Weekly*, Vol. XIII, No. 28, July 25.

Mowli, Chandra. V. (1992), *Bridging the Gulf: India's Manpower Migrations to West Asia*, New Delhi, Sterling.

Murthy, R.R.V. (1991), "Seasonal Labour Migration in Semi-arid Areas: A Case Study of Palamuru Labour'', M.A. Dissertation, Department of Economics, University of Hyderabad, Hyderabad.

Nair, P.R. Gopinathan (1981), *Primary Education, Population Growth and Socio-Economic Change*, Allied Publishers Pvt Ltd., New Delhi

Nair, Gopinathan P.R. (1988), *Enhancement of Household Capacity in the Post-Migration Phase: A Case Study of India*, The United Nations University, Tokyo.

Nair, Gopinathan P.R. (1989), "Incidence, Impact and Implications of Migration to the Middle East from Kerala (India)", in Rashid Amjad (ed.) *To the Gulf and Back: Studies on the Economic Impact of Asian Labour Migration*, pp. 343-364, New Delhi: ILO-ARTEP.

Nair, Gopinathan, P.R. (1993), *International Labour Migration Statistics in India*, New Delhi: ILO-ARTEP.

Nayyar, Deepak (1989), "International Labour Migration from India: A Macro-Economic Analysis" in Rashid Amjad (ed.) *To the Gulf and Back: Studies on the Economic Impact of Asian Labour Migration*, pp. 95-142, New Delhi: ILO-ARTEP.

Nayyar, Deepak (1994), *Migration, Remittances and Capital Flows: The Indian Experience*, New Delhi: Oxford, University Press.

Nayyar, Deepak (1999), *Globalisation and Migration: Retrospect and Prospect*, V.V. Giri National Labour Institute, Noida.

Oberai, A. and H. K. Singh (1980), "Migration, Remittances and Rural Development: Findings of A Case Study in the Indian Punjab", *International Labour Review*, 119(2): 229-41.

Prothero, Mansell, R. (1990), "Labour Recruiting Organisations in the Developing World: Introduction", *International Migration Review*, Vol. XXIV, No. 2.

Rogaly, B; J. Biswas, D.Coppard, A. Rafique, K.Rana, and A. Sengupta (2001), "Seasonal migration, Social Change and Migrants' Rights: Lessons from West Bengal", *Economic and Political Weekly*, 8 December, pp. 4547-59.

Rao, Omakant, R. (1981), "Exploitative Practices by Recruiters in Overseas Employment: A Case Study of India", ARPLA Working Paper Series No. 1, Asian Regional Project for Strengthening Labour/Manpower Administration (ILO-UNDP), Bangkok.

Sasikumar S.K. (1995b), "International Labour Migration Statistics in India", *Asian and Pacific Migration Journal*, Vol. 4, No. 4.

Sasikumar, S.K. (1998a), *Emerging Trends in International Labour Mobility: The Indian Case*, Research Report, V.V. Giri National Labour Institute, Noida.

PART - III

Social Security in the Contract Labour Market

11

SOCIAL SECURITY OF CONTRACTUAL WORKERS

RAJESH KUMAR

INTRODUCTION

The mass employment of workers has been a regular feature in India. We may divide the Indian workforce in two sectors. The first part comprises organized sectors. The second parts consist of unorganized sectors. Both the sectors employ contractual workers in large numbers. The employment of contractual workers has been a cause of various problems in India. The system of employment of contractual workers leads to many abuses by the employers/contractors because the migrants' natures of workers are involved in the contractual employment in India. They are informally low paid and exploited workers; employed, employable unemployed and self-employed and include contract labour, casuals, temporaries, home workers, time rated or piece rated, part time workers, account workers, agriculture workers, share-croppers, marginal farmers, and also women, child labour and old aged workers. They are very poor and live at subsistence level. They do not get protection of labour laws due to ignorance and very loose enforcement.

The unorganized workers are denied social security, welfare measures, and health covers. The plight of contractual workers led the Government of India to pass an act namely, "The Contract Labour (Regulation and Abolition) Act 1970". The act aims at abolition of contract labour in a progressive and phased manner in certain circumstances, wherever possible and practicable, and that in cases where this system could not be abolished altogether, the condition of contractual workers should be regulated for improvement in their service condition including providing social security. The abolition of contractual labour system is still a long dream despite passing of the above Act in 1970. In fact, employments of contractual workers are increasing day by day due to globalization of industrial workforce.

Social security is utmost importance for the well-being of workers and their families. The world community recognizes the right to social security including social insurance for every regular workers or contractual workers. Social security is an indispensable part of any Government policy and an important tool for prevention and alleviation of poverty in India.

For unorganized sector of workforce, a bill named as unorganized workers social security bill 2007 introduced recently in the parliament, which is likely to be passed within a short period. Presently contractual workers associated with the organized sector come within the preview of ESI Act 1948.

Social security can be understood as the protection, which society provides to its members through a series of measures against the social and economic distress resulting from sickness, maternity, employment injury, unemployment, death, old age, etc. Social security can be divided into following branches, viz, Medical care, Sickness benefits, Employment injury benefits, Maternity benefits, Old age benefits, and Unemployment benefits and Death benefits.

Social Security Under Employees' State Insurance Act 1948

The Government of India has enacted many schemes for the welfare of the workers. The following are important ones in the field of welfare of workers like Factories Act, Employees Provident Fund and Miscellaneous Provisions Act, Minimum Wages Act, Maternity Benefit Act, Bonus Act, Workmen's Compensation Act, etc. But the social security of contractual workers mainly comes within the preview of ESI Scheme formulated under Employees' State Insurance Act 1948, an integrated social security scheme tailored to provide social protection to workers in the organized sector and their dependants in contingencies, such as, sickness, maternity or death and disablement due to an employment injury or occupational disease. The ESI Scheme is administered in some pockets of implemented industrial areas in States with the co-operation/participation of State Governments with the ESI Corporation, an autonomous body under Ministry of Labour, Government of India. It comprises members representing Central and State Governments, Employers, Employees, Parliament members and the medical profession. Union Minister of Labour functions as Chairman of the ESI Corporation, whereas the Director General, as chief executive, discharges the duty of running the day-to-day administration.

The definition of employee in ESI ACT 1948 covers regular employees, as well as Contractual/Casual workers as defined in Section 2 (9) of the Act. The definition of employee is so exhaustive that it includes all type of workers, contractual or casual, or regulars. The relevant portion is reproduced below for better understanding and applicability as:

Section 2(9)—"employee" means any person employed for wages in or in connection with the work of a factory or establishment to which this Act applies and—

(i) who is directly employed by the principal employer on any work of, or incidental or preliminary to or connected with the work of, the factory or establishment, whether such work is done by the employee in the factory or establishment or elsewhere; or

(ii) who is employed by or through an immediate employer, on the premises of the factory or establishment or under the supervision of the principal employer or his agent on work which is ordinarily part of the work of the factory or establishment or which is preliminary to the work carried on in or incidental to the purpose of the factory or establishment; or

(iii) whose services are temporarily lent or let on hire to the principal employer by the person with whom the person whose services are so lent or let on hire has entered into a contract of service; and includes any person employed for

> wages on any work connected with the administration of the factory or establishment or any part, department or branch thereof or with the purchase of raw materials for, or the distribution or sale of the products of the factory or establishment, etc.

The perusal of above definition shows that if a worker under contract does work of a factory, shops, or establishment, on part time or regular basis, piece rate basis or hourly basis, he is coverable under the Employees' State Insurance Act 1948 and entitled to social security provided by the Employees' State Insurance Act 1948 subject to conditions prescribed under in the regulations.

The Contractual category of workers includes, house keeping workers, Security Personnel, Canteen employees, Running Staff like contract bus drivers/conductors of the buses, Annual Maintenance staffs like air-conditioning maintenance staffs, building maintenance staffs. The contractual workers, who works on short period contracts for service as electrician, carpenters, plumbers etc for repair work in the shop or workshop or establishments are also entitled for benefits of Employees' State Insurance Act 1948 subject to conditions prescribed.

Coverage of workers engaged by the outside agencies/Job Contractors in connection with the work of the principal employer outside the premises are also coverable as Job work is done outside the factory/establishment premises through contractors, and the supervision is being exercised by the Principal Employer. The employees engaged in jobs outsourced by the Principal Employer to outside factories/establishments which are not having independent Code Numbers, but such outsourced job is being undertaken under the supervision of the Principal Employer or his agent are also covered under Section 2 (9) (ii) of the Act. In this case, also the compliance in respect of employees engaged in such work has to be made by the Principal Employer.

It is possible for an employee to work under different employers and still he can be an employee of the unit even if he works under different employers. It is also held that when the employer has the right to reject the product, if it does not conform to the specifications of the employer and directs worker to re-do it, the element of control and supervision is involved and the worker is coverable and is entitled for the benefits under ESI Act 1948. ESI (Genera) Regulations 1950 provides the mechanism of benefits in respects of part time contract workers where a workers works under different employers during a specified wage period.

Benefits

Two types of benefits are provided under ESI Act—Medical Benefits and Cash Benefits.

ESI scheme aims at providing medical care and cash benefits to workers in contingencies of sickness, maternity, disablement and death due to employment injury, as envisaged under ESI Act 1948.

The ESI Corporation provides social security to workers/ employees by insuring them in a unique method of Contribution Period of six months i.e. April to September and October to March of a year. In addition, Corresponding Benefit Period is of six months each from January to June and July to December of a year. In a sense, the financial year has been divided in two-contribution period and calendar year has been divided in two benefits period.

The rate of contribution is 4.75 per cent from employer and 1.75 per cent from employees from the wages paid to the employees. The coverage limit of employees is presently Rs. 10,000 per month. The worker whose daily wage is less then Rs. 70 need not pays any employee's contribution but Employer's contribution of 4.75 per cent is required to be paid.

For example (as per approximate figures, depending upon the number of days in a month and wages earned by worker). If a worker gets Rs. 70 per day as wage (for 31 days payment with Sunday as holiday) in a month totalling Rs. 2170. Then he need not pay any contribution, but the employer has to pay Rs 103 as contribution. The worker is entitled for all benefits subject to fulfilment of number of seventy-eight worked days in the factory/shop/establishment. His daily standard rate of benefit will be Rs. 44 and in case of sickness he will get 120 per cent of Rs. 44 i.e. Rs. 52.80 per day of benefit for sickness and 150 per cent i.e. Rs. 66 per day in case of employment injury.

In case of maternity of a female worker the benefit rate will be Rs. 88 for eighty days, if she has worked for 70 days in two consecutive contribution periods.

Similarly if a worker, contractual or regular or casual gets Rs. 5,000 in a month as wage, then he has to contribute Rs.87.50 for monthly contribution and employer has to add Rs.237.50. as employer contribution. The total monthly contribution comes to Rs. 325. His daily standard rate of benefit will be Rs. 98 and in case of sickness he will get 120 per cent of Rs. 98 i.e. Rs. 119.60 per day of benefit for sickness if he worked seventy-eight during the corresponding contribution period. In addition, 150 per cent of standard benefit rate i.e. Rs. 147 per day in case of employment injury is admissible if he gets the injury during the course of employment. In case of maternity of a female worker the benefit rate will be Rs.196 for eighty days, if she has worked for 70 days in two consecutive contribution periods.

Cash Benefits

The following cash benefits are payable to the workers covered under the provisions of ESI Act 1948 with certain conditions of payment of contributions and days of workings relating to the employment.

(a) Sickness Benefits are periodical payments to any insured person in case of his/her sickness certified by a duly appointed medical practitioner or by any other person possessing such qualifications and experience as the Corporation may, by regulations, specify in this behalf. The daily rate of sickness benefit in respect of a person during any benefit period shall be twenty per cent more than the standard benefit rate specified in Rule 54 of ESI (Central) Rules 1950 corresponding to the average daily wages of that person during the corresponding contribution period". Presently, this comes to 60 per cent of the wages, which he receives in the factory. Provision of Extended sickness benefit for long-term diseases has also been incorporated for the workers who suffer from cornice diseases.

(b) Maternity benefit is a periodical payment to an insured woman in case of confinement, miscarriage, or sickness arising out of Pregnancy, confinement, premature birth of child or miscarriage, such woman being certified to be eligible for such payments by an authority specified in this behalf by the regulations. Presently, the rate of benefit comes to more than actual wages i.e. twice the standard benefit rates specified in Rule 54 of ESI (Central) Rules 1950, which she receives in the factory/establishment. The maternity benefit is payable for eighty-four days which can further be extended to thirty more days on the ground of sickness arising out of pregnancy, confinement, premature birth of the child, etc. In case of miscarriage, or medical termination of pregnancy, she is entitled for six weeks, maternity benefits following the date of miscarriage, or medical termination of pregnancy.

(c) Disablement benefits are periodical payments to an insured person suffering from disablement as a result of an employment injury sustained as an employee under this Act and certified to be eligible for such payments by an authority specified in this behalf by the Regulations. The rate of benefit is around 75 per cent of the wages, which he/she receive in the factory/establishment. The disablement benefit is admissible to a worker as under—

  (i) For temporary disablement, at full rate i.e.150 percentage of standard benefit rates.

  (ii) For permanent total disablement, at full rate i.e.150 percentage of standard benefit rates.

  (iii) For permanent partial disablement, at the percentage of disability (loss of earning capacity) as specified in the second schedule.

(d) Death Benefits, (which is also called dependants' benefit) is a Periodical payments to such dependants of an insured person who dies as a result of an employment injury sustained as an employee under this Act, as are entitled to compensation under this Act. The rate of benefit is around 75 per cent of the wages, which he/she received in the factory/establishment at the time of death due to employment injury. The benefit is distributed between the dependants in the ratio like widow 3/5, children 2/5. If the wife or children are more than one then the benefit is divided equally among the dependants. If the wife or children are not available, then the benefit is considered in favour of parents (or second class of dependants) in the ratio of 3/10 each of the rate.

(e) Expenditure on the funeral of the deceased insured workers is a payment paid to the eldest surviving member of the family of an insured person who has died, towards the expenditure on the funeral of the deceased insured person, or, where the insured person did not have a family or was not living with his family at the time of his death, to the person who actually incurs the expenditure. Presently, funeral expenses on death of a worker is paid subject to a maximum of Rs. 3000.

(f) *Unemployment Allowance :* Unemployment Allowance named as Rajiv Gandhi Shramik Kalyan Yojana, is payable to those workers facing involuntary unemployment due to closure of factory/establishment; retrenchment or permanent invalidity arising out of non-employment injury. The daily rate of Unemployment Allowance is at par with the standard Sickness Benefit rate, which is just above 50 per cent of the daily wages. This allowance is payable for a maximum period of six months either in one spell or in different spells of not less than one month's duration.

(g) *Occupational Disease :* If an employee employed in any employment specified in Part-A of the Third Schedule of ESI Act 1948 contracts any disease specified therein as an occupational disease peculiar to that employment, or if an employee employed in the employment specified in Part-B of that Schedule for a continuous period of not less than six months contracts any disease specified therein as an occupational disease peculiar to that employment or if an employee employed in any employment specified in Part-C of that Schedule for such continuous period as the Corporation may specify in respect of each such employment, contracts any disease specified therein as an occupational disease peculiar to that employment, the contracting of the disease shall, unless the contrary is proved, be deemed to be an "Employment Injury" arising out of and in the course of employment. The worker in this situation gets all benefits, which are admissible under employment injury. Presently, the rate is around 75 per cent of the wages, which he/she receives in the factory/establishment.

Medical Benefit

Full medical facilities for self and dependants are admissible from day one of entering insurable employment. The primary, out-patient, in-patient and specialist services are provided through a network of Panel clinics, ESI dispensaries and ESI Hospitals. The super speciality services are provided through a large number of advanced empanelled medical institutions on referral basis. In every State where the scheme has been implemented, one Hospital is being developed as a Model Hospital for the treatment of workers.

The Eligibility to Medical Benefit is as Under

From day one of entering insurable employment for self and dependants such as spouse, parents and children, own or adopted. Firstly, medical benefit is admissible for three months which is regularized for further period if he continues in the employment for whole contribution period and he has paid contribution for seventy-eight days of employment in the corresponding contribution period.

For self and spouse on superannuation from employment and subject to having completed five years in insurable employment on superannuation or in case of having suffered permanent physical disablement during the course of insurable employment, he is entitled for full medical care on payment of Rs. 120 for one year.

In full medical care, the following medical benefits are being provided to all type of workers including contractual workers, under ESI Scheme that includes medical treatment and attendance on insured workers :

Out-door services,

Indoor services,

Specialist consultation,

Supply of drugs and dressing,

Ambulance services,

Laboratory services,

X-Ray services, and

Dental services.

The reimbursement of medical expenses is also part of the scheme when workers are referred to other specialized hospitals for Super-speciality treatment. In many places revolving fund has been established for better and quick medical facility to the workers. However, due to divergent functioning of the State government, a lot of improvement is required to fulfil the expectation of workers.

Some Other Benefits Offered by the Scheme are :

(a) Old age Medical care for self and spouse at a nominal contribution of Rs. 120 per annum with certain conditions of previous employment;

(b) Vocational Rehabilitation in case of disabled insured persons under 45 years of age with 40 per cent or more disablement;

(c) Free supply of physical aids and appliances such as crutches, wheelchairs, dentures, spectacles and other such physical aids;

(d) Preventive health care services such as immunization, family welfare services, HIV/AIDS detection, treatment; etc.

(e) Confinement Allowance @ Rs. 1000 is paid to an insured woman or in respect of the wife of an insured person in case she does not avail medical facilities of the scheme for child delivery.

Demerits in Implementations

- The main drawback is that it is implemented to organized sector in only few industrial areas of the country in the factory, shop, or establishment having ten or more workers are employed with power using and twenty workers in the non -power using factory/establishments.

- The employer is reluctant to maintain records in respect of contractual or casual employees due to prevailing labour laws and its implications.
- The appropriate Government has failed to notify implementation of the scheme in all parts of the country for all type of workers in uniform manner.
- Full medical facility is not uniformly and adequately available in all parts of the country.
- The minimum number of employees fixed at ten is also barrier in the expansion of social security scheme.

Conclusion

In view of the above benefits, it is clear that Employees' State Insurance Act 1948 provides comprehensive social security to not regular workers alone but all types workers which include contractual as well as casual workers. The overall picture of social security is not satisfactory due to non-implementation of social security legislation in a mass way for whole country. We may hope that legislation in the shape of Unorganized Workers Social Security Bill 2007 will bring real social security to entire workforce in India.

12

THE CONTRACT LABOUR (REGULATION AND ABOLITION) ACT, 1970

A Critical Evaluation

PREETI MISHRA AND PRADEEP KUMAR PANDEY

In every establishment, whether governmental or non-governmental, contractual labour to some extent is unavoidable due to pressure of workload and today's high industrial wage costs. The system of contractual labour is prevalent in most industries including skilled, semi-skilled and non-skilled occupations. In this system, there is high probability of misuse of contract labours, because employers/contractors take the advantage of their illiteracy, poverty, helplessness and ignorance. The contractors offer standard form of contracts to the labours with unreasonable terms and conditions. Though judiciary has interpreted standard form of contract in favour of the weaker party on the ground that terms and conditions of standard form of contract should be reasonable and in compliance with natural justice but still a lot needs to be done in this regard to save the poor labours from the clutches of the employers.

With the phenomenal growth in the industrial sector, a lot of changes have taken place in the employment sphere. At one time the establishment being the employer, all persons working there were the employees of such employer. This is no more the case today.

Many of the employers including Central and State governments now get their work done through contractors who employ workers as contract labour. These contract labourers have no direct relationship with the principal employer for whom they work. Many of these contractors exploit the labourers engaged by them in various ways including by payment of low wages.[1]

Contract labours are engaged temporarily on contract basis for a fixed period by the contractor with or without the knowledge of principal employer. 'A workman shall be deemed to be a 'contract labour' when he is hired in connection with the work of an establishment by or through a contractor'.[2] In other words, they are indirect employees who are hired, supervised and remunerated by a contractor who, in turn, is compensated by the establishment. They get daily wages or accumulated daily wages in the end of the month. Casual nature of employment, inferior labour status, lack of job security and poor economic conditions are the major characteristics of a contract labour. Actually, the conditions of contract labour depend on the mercy of contractor. At many times they are exploited and under paid. Their working conditions and working hours are irregular, inhuman and longer in comparison to employees who are directly appointed on regular basis besides they have no employment security. 'The incidence of engagement of contract labour is widespread. They have been found working in industries like textiles, engineering, distillery and brewery, heavy chemicals and fertilizers, cement, beedi industries, brick kilns and khandsari etc. but incidence of their employment is more marked in the construction of power projects, irrigation projects, bridges, canals, construction of roads, generation of electricity, its distribution and maintenance of power stations."[3]

Contractual labour is justified by employers on the ground that :

(a) Requirement is casual and seasonal;

(b) It will improve the productivity and service competitiveness through offering the tremendous opportunities for employment; and

(c) It allows the employers flexibility to choose what is best for them.

But ground reality is different from their justifications. In this system, employer is in most beneficial position as they get production at lower cost and are not under any obligation regarding worker's provident fund, bonus, housing facilities and leave with wages etc. On the other hand, contractual labour is opposed on many grounds as :

1. They work for benefits of principal employer but they are not considered employer's employee.
2. Generally, the contract labours belong to weaker and lower sections of the society so they are unable to take the benefits that accrue to regular employees.
3. Efficiency will decrease, as establishment will be deprived of experienced workers.
4. Regular employments will reduce.

Working conditions of contract labours are unsatisfactory. Their conditions in India have been studied and analysed by many commissions, committees and Ministry of Labour also. All these found their condition to be appalling and exploitative in nature. Due to peculiar nature of their employment the contract labours are unable to get the fruits of the various egalitarian social legislations like Maternity Benefits Act 1961, Employees State Insurance Act 1948, Minimum Wages Act 1948 and Equal Remuneration Act 1976, etc.

In the Second Five Year Plan, the Planning Commission of India made certain recommendations, such as, understandings of studies to ascertain the extent of the problem of contract labour, progressive abolition of the system and improvement of service conditions of contract labour where the abolition was not possible. The matter was discussed at various meetings of Tripartite Committees at which the State Governments were also represented and the general consensus of opinion was that the system should be abolished whenever possible and practicable and that in cases where this system could not be abolished altogether, the working conditions of contract labour should be regulated so as to ensure payment of wages and provision of essential amenities.

Taking into account the poor conditions of contract labours, the Parliament of India enacted 'The Contract Labour (Regulation and Abolition) Act, 1970[4] (here in after referred as Act). Before the enactment of this Act, there was no any specific legislation to deal with the problems of contract labours. This Act is an attempt to achieve some of the objectives contained in Directive Principles of State Policies of the Constitution of India.

The Act is divided into Seven chapters containing 35 sections. Exercising the rule making power[5], the Central Government made rules[6] to carry out the purposes of the Act. Broadly speaking, the Act has aims to :

(a) regulate contract labour where abolition was not possible; and

(b) abolish contract labour in certain establishments.

Actually the objective of the Act is to prevent exploitation of contract labours and also to introduce better conditions of work. Etymologically, it is clear from the above mentioned that Parliament does not want to abolish contract labour *in toto*. In fact, if the contract labour is banned strictly then almost all industries, especially public sector industries will be closed down. Further, this Act legalises the employment of contract labour by any contractor provided that establishment obtains the requisite registration as employer and provided also that the intermediary contractor must be a license holder. In absence of such a license or registration, the legal status of labour would be a direct labour. 'However, workmen hired through a contractor without a valid licence and being paid by the management through that contractor, are workmen employed by the establishment and not contract labour.'[7]

In H.C. Bathra *v.* Union of India[8] the court observed that where a person undertook to collect and manufacture quarry products for and on behalf of railways by engaging workmen to carry out his contract works under the railway establishment, the workmen employed by him for such work are to be deemed as contract labour. The supply of such quarry products would produce a given result for the establishment. Thus, he fulfills all requirement of a contract labour under section 2(1)(c) of the Act and, therefore, is obliged to take licence under section 12(1).

Further, in Steel Authority of India Ltd. *v.* National Union Water Front Workers[9] the Supreme Court said that if the contract is found to be not genuine but a mere camouflage, the so-called contract labour will have to be treated as employees of the principal employer who shall be directed to regularize the services of the contract labour in the establishment concerned, subject to the conditions as may be specified by it.

The contractor is under legal obligation to pay wages to labour and a duty is cast on him to ensure disbursement of wages in the presence of the authorized representative of the principal employer. If contractor fails to pay wages partly or full, the principal employer is liable to pay the same. This Act applies to every principal employer of an establishment and the contractor wherein twenty or more workmen are employed or were employed on any day of the preceding twelve months as contract labours. This Act does not apply to the establishments where work performed is of intermittent or seasonal nature but exceptionally applies if intermittent or seasonal nature of work is done for more than 120 days and 60 days in a year respectively. The Act also applies to establishments of the Governmental and local authorities as well.

In Gammon India Ltd. *v.* Union of India[10] the constitutional validity of the Act and Rules made there under were challenged. Apex Court of India held that both the Act and Rules are constitutional and there is no unreasonableness in the measure.

The Central Government and State governments are required to set-up Central and State Advisory Contract Labour Boards to advise the respective governments on matters arising out of the administration of the Act as are referred to them.[11] Further, the Boards are authorized to constitute committees as they think fit.[12] Every establishment must be registered as principal employer with appropriate authorities. Every contractor is under a legal obligation to obtain a license to execute any work through contract labour. Chapter IV deals with licensing of contractor. 'Every granted/renewed license shall remain in force for 12 months from the date it is granted or renewed.[13] Effect of non-registration of principal employer is provided in Section 9.

Under Section 10 the 'appropriate government' is authorized, after consultation with the Central Board or State Board, as the case may be, to prohibit employment of contract labour in any establishment in any process, operation or other work, by notification in the official gazette. Sufficient guidelines are laid down under Section 10(2) to decide upon the abolition of contract labour in any process, operation or other work in any establishment as appropriate government shall have regard to the conditions of work and benefits provided for contract labour in that establishment and other relevant factors such as :

(a) Whether the work is incidental or necessary for the work of establishment.

(b) Whether the work is of perennial nature.

(c) Whether the work is being done ordinarily through regular workman in that establishment or a similar establishment.

(d) Whether the work is sufficient to employ a considerable number of whole time workmen.

In I.C.M. Engineering Workers Unions *v.* Union of India[14] Delhi High Court ruled that the machinery provided under Section 10 of the Act is complete and effective machinery, which may be termed as efficacious alternate remedy and writ petition under Art. 226 would not be maintainable to seek a direction from the court to abolish contract labour, in a particular process, operation or work etc. in an establishment.

The Madras High Court in a case[15] aptly observed that section 10(1) of the Act is a *non obstante* clause beginning with the words "notwithstanding anything contained in the Act". This section, therefore, overrides other provisions of the Act and once the order prohibiting employment of contract labourers is duly issued under a notification, it operates as a total bar for that class of contract labourers irrespective of the number of workers employed.

Further, the appropriate government is empowered to grant exemption to any establishment or class of establishments or any class of contractors from applicability of all or any provisions of the Act or the rules made thereunder on such conditions and restrictions and for such period or periods, as may be specified in the notification.[16]

Welfare and health provisions are provided under chapter V of the Act and Central Rules. The contractor is under legal obligation to provide such amenities but if any amenity is required to be provided for the benefit of contract labour is not provided by the contractor within prescribed time, such amenity shall be provided by the principal employer. All expenses incurred by the principal employer in providing the amenity may be recovered by the principal employer from the contractor by deduction from any amount payable to the contractor under any contract or as a debt payable by the contractor.[17] The provisions for following facilities have been made under the Act-

1. Canteens — If employing 100 or more labours in one place and if the work is likely to last for 6 months or more.[18]
2. Rest Rooms—Where contract labour is required to halt at night and the work is likely to last for 3 months or more.[19] Further, separate rooms shall be provided for women employees,[20] and effective and suitable provision shall be made in every room for securing and maintaining adequate ventilation is the circulation of fresh air.[21]
3. First-Aid facilities—First-aid box equipped with prescribed contents at every work place be readily accessible during all working hours.[22]
4. Sufficient number of latrines and urinals : Separate for men and women.[23] Every latrine shall be under cover and so partitioned off as to secure privacy and shall have a proper door and fastenings.[24]
5. *Sufficient supply of wholesome drinking water at convenient places*[25]
6. *Washing Facilities* : Separate and adequate for the use of male and female workers.[26] Such amenities shall be kept in clean and hygienic condition.[27]

Besides responsibilities of the contractor have also been fixed under the Act to:

1. Pay minimum wages fixed by the government or pay wages as may be fixed by the Labour Commissioner and in their absence pay fair wages to contract labours.
2. Comply with all the legal requirements of the Act.
3. Issue employment card to his contract labours.
4. Maintain various register and records, display – notices, abstracts of Act, Rules, etc.

Furthermore, for contravention of the provisions of the Act or any rules made thereunder for which no penalty is elsewhere provided, the punishment is imprisonment for a maximum term up to 3 months and a fine up to a maximum of Rs. 1000 or both.

Amendments Suggested by National Commission for Women

National Commission for Women suggested amendments[28] in the following Sections of Act in reviewing the laws and legislative measures affecting the women as:

Section 1: Short title, extent, commencement and application : Sub Section (4) of Section (1) shall be deleted. Also sub-section (5) of Section (1) shall be deleted. Explanation shall be deleted. *Section 2: Definition* – An explanation shall be added in Clause (c) of sub-section (1) of Section 2 as below:

Explanation – The word contractor includes both a licensed and a non-licensed contractor. This section will read as: (c) 'contractor', in relation to an establishment, means a person who undertakes to produce a given result for the establishment, other than a mere supply of goods or articles of manufacture to such establishment, through contract labour or who supplies contract labour for any work of the establishment and includes a sub-contractor. *Explanation* – The word contractor includes both a licensed and a non-licensed contractor. Section 2 : (i) This ceiling of Rs. 500 shall be removed. A suitable amount be replaced, determined by the appropriate government consistent with the living index and the sale of inflation.

Section 2: Definition – For the sake of clarity that the word contractor includes both lincensed and non-licensed contractor.

(B) – The ceiling of Rs. 500 is too low considering the present rate of inflation. It should be reasonably enhanced.

Section 3: Another proviso – After the proviso of this section another proviso shall be added which will read as – 'Provided further that at least half of the members of the Central Advisory Board nominated shall be women' to give equal participation to women in decision making process.

Section 4: Another Proviso – After the proviso of this section another proviso shall be added which will read as – 'Provided further that at least half of the members of the State Advisory Board nominated shall be women' to give equal participation to women in decision making process.

Section 15: Appeal – Following section shall be substituted – (I) any person aggrieved by an order made under section 7, section 8, section 12 or section 14 may within thirty days from the date on which the order is communicated to him, prefer an appeal to the court of Additional District Judge or a specially appointed Judicial Officer by the appropriate government. Provided that the court or specially appointed judicial officer may entertain the appeal after the expiry of the said period of thirty days, if he is satisfied that the appellant was prevented by sufficient cause from filing the appeal in time. (II) On receipt of an appeal under sub-section (1), the Court specially appointed Judicial Officer shall, after giving the appellant an opportunity of being heard dispose of the appeal as expeditiously as possible.

Section 17: Rest-Rooms – In sub-section (1) of Section 17 after the words 'rest room' the words 'separately for male and female' shall be inserted. (1) In every place wherein contract labour is required to halt at night in connection with the work of an establishment – (c) to which this Act applies, and (d) in which work requiring employment of contract labour is likely to continue for such period as may be prescribed. There shall be provided and maintained by the contractor for the use of the contract labour such number of rest rooms separately for male and female or such other suitable alternative accommodation with in such time as may be prescribed. (2) The rest rooms or the alternative accommodation to be provided under sub-section (1) shall be sufficiently lighted and ventilated and shall be maintained in a clean and comfortable condition.

Section 18: Other Facilities – For clause (a) a Section 18 following clause shall be substituted – (b) a sufficient number of latrines and urinal, separately for male and female of the prescribed types so situated as to be convenient and accessible to the contract labour in the establishment; and for clause (c) of section 18 following clause shall be substituted – (c) washing facilities separately for male and female. A new clause (d) shall be inserted, viz., (d) crèche for women with infants and young children.

Section 20: Liability of principal employer in certain cases – For section 20 the following shall be substituted – (i) If any amenity required to be provided under section 16, section 17, section 18 or section 19 for the benefit of the contract labour employed in an establishment shall be provided by the principal employer within such time as may be prescribed. (ii) All expenses incurred by the principal employer in providing the amenity may be recovered by the principal employer from the contractor either by deduction from any amount payable to the contractor under any contract or as a debt payable by the contractor.

Section 21: Responsibility for Payment of Nages – (i) It shall be the duty of the principal employer to make payment of wages to the contract labour employed by the contractor and such wages shall be paid before the expiry of such period as may be prescribed. (ii) The Principal Employer shall recover the amount so paid under section (1) from the contractor either by deduction from the amount payable to the contractor under any contract or a debt payable by the contractor.

Section 26: Cognizance of Offences – Following section shall be substituted – 'No Court shall take cognizance on any offence under this Act except on a complaint made by, or with the previous sanction in writing of the inspector or any person aggrieved or by a voluntary organisation and no court inferior to that of a Presidency Magistrate or a magistrate of the first class shall try any offence punishable under this Act.

Section 27: Limitation of prosecutions – the following shall be substituted – This section will read as 'No Court shall take cognizance of an offence punishable under this Act unless the complaint thereof is made within reasonable time from the date on which the alleged commission of the offence came to knowledge of an inspector. *Explanation* – It will be the discretion of the court to decide that what would be the reasonable time depending on the merit of the cases but it should not be less than 3 months in any case.

Section 28: Inspecting Staff - An explanation shall be added after sub-section (I) of Section 28 as below:

Explanation – Whenever a premises/establishment being inspected is expected to have women contract labour, the inspecting staff should include a woman inspector.

Section 31: Power to exempt in special cases – Shall be deleted.

Justification in Favour of Proposed Amendments by NCW

Sub-section (4) of Section (1): To widen the scope of application of this Act. Application of this Act should not be limited to the establishment in which only twenty or more workmen are employed. It should also not exclude the establishments in which work of intermittent or casual nature is performed. These provisions deprive the workmen from the benefit of this Act if there are less than twenty workmen in any establishment and work of intermittent or casual nature is performed. Consequential amendment in respect of Sub-section (5) of section 1. *Section 15: Appeal* – To ensure that the matter be looked into judicially. *Section 17: Rest rooms* – Separate shelters/rest-rooms for male and female workers would ensure privacy and better relaxation amongst the workers of both sexes. Moreover, when the Act provides male and female workers separate facilities for urinals, toilets, washing places, storing and drying wet clothes (suggested), then separate shelters/rest-rooms would be appreciated. *Section 18: Other Facilities* – The liability to maintain a crèche should not be linked with the number of women workers employed in a factory. Instead, it should be linked with the number of workers, whether male or female. Section 21: To ensure the timely payment of wages to the workmen as it is generally observed that they are not paid proper wages on time. *Section 26: Cognizance of offences* – To give a right to file the complain to an aggrieved person and to an organisation working for social cause. *Section 31*: Power to exempt in special cases – As it grants unfettered discretion to the appropriate government to exempt the application of the Act to certain establishment.

A Bill[29] was introduced in Rajya Sabha to amend Sec. 2(a) and 10 of the Act. Accordingly a proviso was to be added as—

> "Provided that where the appropriate government decides that the process, operation of other work in an establishment is of perennial nature, the contract labour employed for such work shall be given regular employment for such perennial work in the concerned establishment".

But due to lack of commitment on the part of our legislatures, it could not take the form of law. Further, the group of Ministers (GOM) expressed their desire to bring the contract labours under the medical insurance scheme[30] but nothing substantial could be done till today.

Recommendations of the Second Labour Commission

The Commission recognized implicitly the concept of *second-generation reforms while* applauding the example set by the Maharashtra State Government, in bringing about a distinction between the core and non-core functions.[31] The Commission stipulated that prohibition for engaging contract labour would be *limited for only core production/ service activities*. The recommendations thus leave *only the core activities* free from the ambit of contract labour as opposed to *perennial activities* under the present scheme of Section 10 of CLRA. The Commission further pays lip service to the onus of proof being on the employer to show payment of equal wages to the labourer and to ensure social security measures and *ironically* mourns the practice of "*double fraud' perpetrated at the cost of poor contract workers,*" The *double fraud* that the Commission found in many industries was the fact that the management after making deductions from the wages of the contract labourers in the name of Provident Fund and other social security measures refused to redeem their liability in this regard after the termination of service of that labourer.

The report thus widens the scope of application of contract labour tremendously with reservation expressed only with regard to the core sector and thus renders the CLRA absolutely ineffective and meaningless. In its present form, it is submitted, the Report violates the primary objective of the Act which, expressed in the words of the Apex Court of the land, is *to prevent exploitation of contract labourers.*[32]

A mon avis if the recommendations of the Second Labour Commission with regard to the subject are accepted, it will unfortunately result in an indirect validation of *"a modern method of human trafficking"*, a phenomenon decried as *heinous* by the Supreme Court.[33] Insecurity of tenure seems to be the Commission's guiding logic in a self-assured route to economic efficiency. The report fails to take into account, India's consistent pro-labour stand and does not show an iota of concern for the plight of a contract labourer. The discrimination that already exists under the various statutory provisions, between a regular workman and a contract labourer are further magnified to the detriment of the latter by the Commission's stand. There are unimpeachable studies to prove that the perception that efficiency can be brought about by instilling a sense of insecurity among the labourers (which is what the Commission also seems to be guided by, in its whole-hearted endorsement of the system of contract labour) is nothing, but a carefully circulated and assiduously precipitated myth.[34]

Suggestions

Following measures are being suggested to make the present Act more workable :

1. Women Welfare officers should be recruited compulsorily in every establishment where women are working on contract basis.
2. Industrial Disputes Act 1947 must be applicable in contract labours' matters.
3. Principle equal pay for equal work contained in Article 39(d) of Constitution of India should be specifically incorporated in the Act.

4. The application of this Act must be on every establishment and contractor whether the nature of work is seasonal or perennial and whether there are 20 or less workers in the establishment.
5. If any accident occurs during the course of employment, contract labours must be treated as workmen within the meaning of Workmen's Compensation Act 1923.
6. The penalty imposed for contravening the provisions of the Act must be enhanced to make the compliance of the provisions of the act more effective and forceful.

NOTES

1. Thomas Paul, "Contract Labour: Liability of Principal Employer," Vol. 39 : 2, *JILI* 465-469 at 464.
2. Section 2 (b) of The Contract Labour (Regulation and Abolition) Act 1970.
3. J.S.P. Pandey, "Employment of Contract Labour in Factories", Vol. XIV, No. 1: 12, *Labour Bulletin*.
4. Act No. 37 of 1970, came into force on 10.02.1971.
5. Sec. 35 of the The Contract Labour (Regulation and Abolition) Act 1970.
6. The Contract Labour (Regulation and Abolition) Central Rules, 1971.
7. Wormen *vs.* Best & Crompton Engg. Ltd.1985 (1) *Lab LJ 492.*
8. 1976 *Lab I C* 1199.
9. (2001) 7SCC1.
10. (1974) 1 *Lab L.J.* 480.
11. Sec. 3, 4.
12. Sec. 5.
13. Rule 27 of The Contract Labour (Regulation and Abolition) Central Rules, 1971.
14. (2001) 1 *Lab L.J.* 1127 (Delhi).
15. Agarwal H.C. *vs.* State (2002) 2 *Lab L.J.* 650 (Madras)
16. Section 31 of the Act.
17. Section 20.
18. Section 16.
19. Section 17.
20. Rule 41(3).
21. Rule 41(4).

22. Section 19. See also Rules 58-62.
23. Rule 51.
24. Rule 52.
25. Sec. 18(a).
26. Rule 57 (2).
27. Rule 57 (3).
28. www.new.nic.in/page 33.htm#2 accessed on 29-01-2008.
29. The Contract Labour (Regulation and Abolition) Amendment Bill No. XI of 2002.
30. www.hinduonnet.com/2003/08/06/stories/2003080604261 200.htm accessed on 29-01-2008.
31. The concept of 'core' and 'non-core' may be best explained with the help of an example: if we were to take the example of a paint factory, a labourer engaged in an intrinsic activity, in relation the production of that factory, say pigment mixing, will be considered to be a 'core' activity and hence outside the purview of contract labour; another labourer engaged as a security guard or as a housekeeping staff, will be considered 'non-core' and hence within the domain of contract labour.
32. R.K. Panda *vs.* Steel Authority of India Ltd., (1994) 69 FLR 256 (SC).
33. Gujarat Electricity Board *vs.* Hind Mazdoor, AIR 1995, SC 1893.
34. Amartya Sen, *Inaugural K.C. Basu Memorial Lecture Series*, organized by the National University of Juridical Sciences, Kolkata, on 'Law and Economics'.

REFERENCES

The Contract Labour (Regulation and Abolition) Act 1970, Section 2 (b).

The Contract Labour (Regulation and Abolition) Central Rules, 1971.

Pandey, J. S. P. "Employment of Contract Labour in Factories", Vol. XIV, No.1: 12, *Labour Bulletin*.

Act No. 37 of 1970, came into force on 10.02.1971.

Section 35 of the Contract Labour (Regulation and Abolition) Act 1970.

Women *vs.* Best and Crompton Engg. Ltd. 1985 (1) LLJ. 49.

1976 *Lab I C* 1199.

(2001) 7 SCC 1.

1974) 1 Lab L.J. 480.

Section 3, 4.

Section 5.

Rule 27 of the Contract Labour (Regulation and Abolition) Central Rules, 1971.

(2001) 1 *Lab L.J.* 1127 (Delhi).

Agarwal, H.C. *vs.* State (2002) 2 *Lab L.J.* 650 (Madras).
Section 31 of Act.
Section 20.
Section 16.
Section 17.
Rule 41(3).
Rule 41(4).
Section 19. See also Rules 58-62.
Rule 51.
Rule 52.
Section 18(a).
Rule 57 (2).
Rule 57 (3).
www.ncw.nic.in/page 33.htm#2.
The Contract Labour (Regulation and Abolition) Amendment Bill No. XI of 2002
www.hinduonnet.com/2003/08/06/stories/2003080604261 200.htm.

13

THE UNORGANISED SECTOR WORKERS' SOCIAL SECURITY BILL, 2007

Implementation Challenges

I.C. AWASTHI AND A.P. WILLIAM WORDSWORTH

I. Aims

The aims of this Policy Brief are to:

(a) Examine the concept of social security for unorganised workers in the Bill introduced in Parliament;

(b) Evaluate its adequacy and implementation feasibility alongwith practicalities from the wider perspective of stakeholders, primarily the intended beneficiaries (unorganised workers) and the lawmakers, policy makers and others responsible for its implementation; and

(c) Propose modifications in the bill that would enhance the aims underlying this proposed enactment.

II. Status of the Bill

The Unorganised Sector Workers' Social Security Bill (Bill No. LXVII of 2007) was introduced in the Rajya Sabha on September 10, 2007. Subsequently, the Bill was referred to the Standing Committee on Labour for examination and the Standing Committee, after wider consultation with stakeholders, submitted a report to the Lok Sabha and Rajya Sabha on December 3, 2007. The Bill is expected to be debated in Parliament in 2008.

III. Concept of Social Security and its Evolution

The notion of social security as enunciated by the International Labour Organisation (ILO) Convention 102 of 1952, caters to a broad spectrum of nine social security contingencies compensated by benefits, namely, sickness benefit, medical benefit, maternity benefit, employment injury benefit, old age benefit, invalidity benefit, survivors' benefit, unemployment benefit and family benefit. This Convention has not been ratified by India. However, India has ratified other conventions of the ILO: Workmen's Compensation, Occupational Diseases (Convention 18 and Revised Convention 42 of 1934); Equality of Treatment (Accident Compensation) (Convention 19 of 1925); and Equality of Treatment (Social Security) (Conventions 1 and 8 of 1962).

The Constitution of India, through Directive Principles of State Policy, enshrines the obligations of the State for providing social security under various Articles (Articles 38, 39, 41 and 47). However, the Directive Principles of State Policy are not justiciable rights enforceable in a court of law, and have remained cherished ideals.

IV. Social Security for Unorganised Workers

The concept of social security practiced in developed countries evolved from the perspective of growth-meditated social policies and organised workers. High growth was regarded as a panacea for providing social security to the workers. Such a notion of social security is built around two fundamental assumptions. First, as development takes root, unorganised labour would gradually be absorbed in the organised sector with the expansion of industry; and secondly, higher growth rates and industrialisation would ensure greater social security and decent living for workers. However, the validity of such hypotheses in developing countries is questionable, primarily because of slow employment expansion in the industrial sector and very high population growth. An overwhelmingly large part of the workforce in developing countries remains unorganised and is characterised by poverty, illiteracy and absence of social security among the working poors.

Social security measures in India are by and large limited to organised sector workers who constitute less than one-tenth of the total workforce. These social security measures include maternity benefits, workmen's compensation, sickness insurance, payment of gratuity, provident fund, pensions, etc. The unorganised workers forming about 92 per cent of the total workforce and contributing 60 per cent to the GDP have no access to social security measures, except a few welfare schemes for certain categories of workers. Some of the laws applicable to unorganised sector workers, for example, Workmen's Compensation Act, Minimum Wages Act, The Bonded Labour System (Abolition) Act, The Inter-State Migrant Workmen (Regulation of Employment and Conditions of Service (RECS) Act, and The Building and other Construction Workers (RECS) Act are limited in coverage.

Thus, promotional measures such as the provision of work (casual wage employment and self-employment) and welfare measures in the form of food, education and health through targeted interventions to specific population groups, are the main plank of protection for unorganised workers.

The organised sector is unable or unwilling to absorb the growing labour force except as 'working non-employees'. This has increased irregular casual work, depressed wage rates relative to the statutory minimum wages and reduced opportunities for skilling of workers.

The question of providing social security for the unorganised sector workers was carefully examined by the Second National Labour Commission (NLC), and on the basis of recommendations of the NLC, a Draft Bill on "The Unorganised Sector Workers' Bill" was prepared by the Labour Ministry in 2004. Subsequently, the National Commission for Enterprises in the Unorganised Sector (NCEUS) studied the entire issue of social security in consultation with stakeholders and prepared two bills, one on social security, and another on conditions of work and livelihood promotion for unorganised sector workers.

V. Issues for Consideration

Some of the fundamental issues and questions with regard to social security measures for the unorganised workers are:

1. Is 'unorganised sector' a distinctly identifiable category in terms of activities or workers ?
2. Is there any correspondence between the terms 'unorganised sector workers' and 'unorganised workers'? In other words, does it include all non-unionised workers in organised and unorganised sectors? Is it the 'sector' that is unorganised or 'workers' that are unorganised ?
3. Does a separate bill for the 'unorganised' present any advantages over a universal social security system for all workers ?
4. Does the proposed Social Security Bill seek to adequately cover a critical minimum threshold of protection corresponding to decent work or living wage ?
5. Are protective and promotional measures jointly pursuable ?
6. Have the interests of principal stakeholders (workers) been taken into consideration while framing the Bill ?
7. How are different stakeholders involved in the implementation of the scheme and its monitoring and redressal mechanism ?
8. Are benefits proposed in the scheme sustainable ?
9. How would the schemes flowing from this law ameliorate conditions of unorganised workers ?
10. Does the benefit under social security envisage any in-built mechanism to offset price rise ?
11. Is there adequate representation of primary stakeholders (workers) in the proposed Tripartite National and State Social Security Advisory Board, formulating welfare schemes ? Would real power vest with primary stakeholders or the bureaucratic agencies ?

12. What will be the method of funding and disbursal ? Does it ensure the smooth flow of resources without any interruptions ?
13. How does the Bill in its present form take into account the enormous diversity across different regions and activities ?
14. How would the law ensure the 'inclusiveness' for the vast numbers of non-unionised workers ? Does it subserve the broader objective of growth with social justice ?
15. Does the Bill have provisions to look to alternative models for development in public welfare service delivery based on public-private partnership ?

VI. Policy Options

(i) Inclusive Growth for All or Category-specific Segmentation?

Inclusive growth is the plank of India's Eleventh Five Year Plan. The criteria of survey would be measuring coverage, scope and impact on the targeted workers concerned, in terms of the tangible outcome or benefits they derive, not in terms of the legislations passed or the number of boards or committees constituted.

Public expenditure on social security in India at 1.8 per cent of the GDP compares unfavourably with 4.7 per cent in Sri Lanka and 3.6 per cent in China (World Labour Report, 2000). There is a need to move from critical nominal security for few segments of the population to more coverage on the basis that social protection is not just an element of subsistence but also an indication of social inclusion and safeguarding of human dignity.

Preventive, Promotional and Protective Social Security are three forms by which inclusive growth will serve the broader objective of economic growth with social justice.

(ii) Umbrella Legislation or Specific Laws for Specific Worker Categories ?

Bills like (i) Agricultural Workers' Conditions of Work and Social Security Bill, 2007, (ii) Unorganised Non-Agricultural Workers' Conditions of Work and Social Security Bill, 2007 and others have already been placed in the Parliament. Does the Unorganised Sector

Workers' Social Security Bill, 2007 provide something more than these bills; or anything new ? Most of the poors among the unorganised workers are relegated, not because they are unorganised but because they are impoverished, devoid of opportunities, discriminated against, scattered and disguised. This has to be understood within political economy of the poors and disadvantaged.

(iii) Benchmarks or Novelty ?

Social security measures should include basic needs (food, health and housing), education and employment as important components of comprehensive human development. Experience suggests that direct public actions have proved to be more effective than rapid income growth (successful cases, e.g., Chile, Costa Rica, Cuba, China, Jamaica, Kerala and Tamil Nadu States in India, and Sri Lanka). Also, where social security has been an integral part of governance (Kerala and Tamil Nadu are the cases of State-sponsored participation), it becomes an effective strategy in carrying out preventive, protective and promotional security measures.

(iv) Are Unorganised Workers Vulnerable or Discriminated against ?

The aims underpinning employment creation are usually more than providing a dole or relief programme by developing skills and capacities among workers to ensure their participative role in an inclusive growth process. The most vulnerable workers in the unorganised sector are women and children who suffer from multifaceted discriminations and are engaged in the most precarious and hazardous occupations on miserably low wages. The vulnerability is compounded in working from home where piece-rate work is generally carried out. Social protection designed for formal workplaces and jobs can thus be discriminatory.

(v) Market Wages or Minimum Wages ?

Evidences from ongoing studies by the IAMR (Evaluation of NREGS, 2007) reveal that even though the government has prescribed fixed wages at Rs. 80 per day under the National Employment Guarantee Act (NREGA), there are numerous instances where wages paid to workers are, on average, Rs. 25 and the maximum paid is about Rs. 40 only.

In fixing minimum wages, the piece-rate systems also have to be safeguarded with respect to cost of living adjustments. The 'working poors', who contribute to the development of the system, have little left for their own skills enhancing and professional development. The existing wages would not bring many workers above the poverty line even if the duration of employment were increased. The chronic problem of market-determined wages being depressed to levels below the Statutory Minimum Wages remains unsolved.

(vi) Is Indian Labour Market to be regulated only within National Borders on GDP basis or including GATS Modes on GNP basis ?

The Bill is silent about factor incomes of Indian workers engaged abroad which are counted in India's GNP. The labourers (mostly illiterate) are often misused in jobs for which permits were not been given and even skilled workers may remain outside social security coverage, if work given to them is misallocated. There is a need to make social security portable and compatible with systems outside India too. This would provide some modicum of security to unorganised workers.

(vii) Mistrusted by Touts and Middlemen Countervailing Trade Union Power or Political Rights ?

Social security schemes for unorganised workers could be based on the solidarity principle through mandatory registration to enable shift away from crisis-led safety nets towards a system of wage-earner funds administered by trade unions or public-private partnerships.

(viii) Self-help Groups (SHGs) or NGOs ?

Participation of self-help groups (SHGs) and voluntary non-governmental organisations or cooperative agencies could be an alternative for delivery of micro credit with institution of revolving funds at disaggregated level (panchayat or ward). Such micro-credit revolution may be used also to promote enterprise development, and entrepreneurship training after accruing entrepreneurship trainability. The experiences of Grameen Bank and also from our experiences in India, such as Bandhan, Micro Credit Foundation of India, Saadhana Microfin Society, Grameen Koota, Sharada's Women's

Association for Weaker Sections, SKS Microfinance Private Ltd., and Asmitha Microfin Ltd, in the Forbes' 50 List in December, 2007 and others may be worth studying.

(ix) Freedom of Association or Collective Bargaining ?

This Bill intends to encourage unorganised workers to coalesce their interests around social security structures and benefits, aimed at creating a voice and space for them. However, the Bill contains no rights for collective bargaining or modes for assertion of basic rights related to their status as workers.

(x) Occupational Safety or Unsafety Compensation ?

There is no single law that would ensure the implementation of occupational safety measures which are essential above any type of social security envisaged for the future: for instance, people working with stone materials exposed to stone mason's disease (silicosis), tannery workers involved in the process of cleaning raw skin, scavengers cleaning human soils are prone to dangerous diseases at early ages. Special provisions related to occupational prohibitives, safety protections and compensation need to be included.

(xi) Entitlement vs. Charity

Basic minimum social protections for the unorganised workers need to be enforced as entitlements or as statutory rights and not merely as impromptu generosity or charity. When the Second Labour Commission Report reviewed existing laws on social security and labour, it did not review the delivery mechanism of social security schemes and the subsequent outcome of the existing social security benefits accruing to such incumbents.

(xii) Profit Sharing or Residual Claimants ?

Among organised workers, pay for performance is statutorily given as bonus, besides other forms of profit sharing through incentive schemes. In order to facilitate some conceptual parity, unorganised workers also need to be recognised as more than residual claimants.

VII. A Critical Review of the Unorganised Sector Workers' Social Security Bill, 2007 (Bill No. LXVII of 2007) introduced in the Rajya Sabha on September 10, 2007

The bill consists of the following parts:

1. Defining or identifying the unorganised sector (Clause 2);
2. Empowering the Central and State Governments to formulate welfare scheme and funding patterns of Central Government (Clauses 3 and 4);
3. Creating a National Advisory Board and suggesting the composition of its members (Clause 5);
4. Creating respective State Advisory Board and its composition (Clause 6);
5. Funding of the State Governments' schemes and record-keeping (Clauses 4 and 7);
6. Mandating the registration of unorganised sector workers (Clause 9);
7. Enlisting the powers of the Central Government to give directions and to make rules (Clauses 10 and 12);
8. Reiterating the powers of State Governments to make rules (Clause 13)

According to Clause 2(k) of the Bill, "the unorganised sector means an enterprise owned by individuals or self-employed workers and engaged in the production or sale of goods or providing service of any kind whatsoever, and where the enterprise employs workers, the number of such workers is less than ten." A large segment of workers are left uncovered in this definition. Were the definition for unorganised sector workers to be a conceptual one, the scale of an enterprise is irrelevant? It is well known that size can be manipulated by increasing units.

Further, as per the definition, when association of persons is less than ten, the employer can also be counted as a worker. Thus, it provides a loophole for persons making huge profits to evade the burden of paying taxes. The Bill defines unorganised sector workers as of three types, viz.:

(i) Home-based workers [Clause 2(b)];

(ii) Self-employed workers [Clause 2(j)]; and

(iii) Wage workers [Clause 2(m)].

There are workers, who continue to receive salaries/wages but are not on the regular pay roll and unless the nature of the work is deemed as regular, no pension benefits become due to them. Legal obligations for both parties (employer and employee) for temporary staff need to be considered. There are also various forms of public and private works (for example, teachers and tutors with limited rights and no union, and those engaged in funeral work, religious work, etc.) The scope of the bill needs to be comprehensively and exclusively defined on the basis of location, culture, region, craft, discipline, service and seasonal specifics.

Clause 3 (3) of the Bill limits Clause 3 (1) to include or exclude any welfare scheme for unorganised sector workers. This is exclusionary in character. It is incongruous because Clause 3 (3) neither spells out the scope nor rationale to evaluate the efficacy and desirability of including any existing schemes under Clause 3 (4). It is a matter of formulating, including, extending or expanding the coverage of such schemes to the beneficiaries concerned.

Clause 4 (1) of the Bill confers on Central and State Governments the power to formulate welfare schemes for different sections of unorganised workers. The governments in the States and the Central Government have hitherto faced no problems in exercising authority in their defined domains and so this enabling provision merely reiterates what already exists.

The Constitution has clearly laid down the powers, privileges and jurisdiction of the respective governments and labour is on the concurrent list in the Seventh Schedule. Clause 4 of the Bill does not contain anything definite or specific. Since funding such welfare schemes is inevitable, there was no need for a clause without detailing functions that would be meaningful for beneficiaries.

NCEUS and the National Advisory Council have recommended an enforceable 'floor scheme' for each unorganised sector worker beneficiary as a legal entitlement of statutory protection within a specified time frame. In the National Rural Employment Guarantee Act, 2005, 100 days of work with standard minimum wage including penalties for denial of work are already prescribed. The schemes that may be formulated on the basis of this new enactment are contingent on political and enforcement aspects.

The Bill, in its present form, contains no welfare schemes and raises fears that vested interests and scattered political agendas would not enmesh effectively.

(i) Creation of Advisory Boards

Clauses 5 and 6 of the Bill provide for Social Security Advisory Boards, at Centre and States with powers of recommendation, advice, review and monitoring. However, Clause 10 of the Bill suggests that the real powers are still retained mostly with the Central Government and only some with respective State Governments, which may give directions to these Boards in matters concerning the implementation of the legislation. The Boards, Commissions and Committees are typically driven by political will. In a Board pyramid, if the chain of command is structured with more weight at the top, the breadth of administration and its complexity could be plagued by bureaucratic delays.

The Boards are powerless and unduly large in size. The Central Board consists of at least 31 members and the State Boards of 28 members. Since they do not have substantive powers, there is no apparent benefit of such a structure that could accrue to unorganised workers. Rather, it would create a functional conflict among the existing welfare boards in some of the States, where social security schemes for unorganised workers are in place such as Kerala, Tamil Nadu and Maharashtra.

It seems from Clause 5 (4) of this Bill, that the creation of the Boards is the main aim since the Bill details the composition of members, conditions of service, procedure to be followed, discharge of their duties, terms of office, and to give final shape to this clause adequate representations of persons from the SC/ST categories are being prescribed. Such details would have been better thought of by first defining 'workers' and then formulating specific schemes to cater to the diversity of vulnerable forms of wage work that does not qualify as employment.

Clause 5 (5) prescribes a three-year term for the board with recommendatory, advisory, monitoring and review powers. While prescribing the review of expenditure of funds under various schemes, there is no accountability prescribed nor responsibilities of even the board members are specified. In three-year terms, each board would vanish. Similar functions are prescribed for the State Boards. There is no responsibility of permanent bureaucracy in Boards.

There can be a regulatory authority type of machinery put in place by an Act of Parliament to devolve some permanent executive responsibility, which is directly responsible to Parliament and would be autonomously free in exercising its power for the welfare of unorganised workers. Unless the powers and responsibilities are fortified with defined objectives, the aims shared by many and ultimately by none, may get diffused.

(ii) Record-keeping

Although Clause 6 (8) of the Bill provides for a record-keeping function by the district administration, it is silent on devolution of funds to district authorities, viz., District Panchayats and urban local bodies, if the welfare schemes are to be directed through these agencies. In other words, the specific roles of these agencies are not clearly mentioned and there seems to be no mechanism to give teeth to local bodies or specialised agencies to implement, enforce and review the flow of funds.

(iii) Registration

Clause 9 of the Bill facilitates registration of an unorganised sector worker who is above 14 with a 'smart card' as identity card. As the Bill itself does not contain any substantial benefits to which unorganised workers get entitled, there is no incentive for registration of a member. The legislation itself is so weak that it is unwise to spend a lot of money for making and distributing 'smart cards' that would not be useable. Welfare Schemes can benefit unorganised sector workers even without smart cards. If entitlements to schemes for beneficiaries is the aim, registration of membership through wage-earners' funds could be made 'compulsory' for all unorganised sector workers as a redistributive social security system, rather than being as a crisis-overcoming palliative of doubtful value.

The miscellaneous Clause 11 under Chapter VI emphasises that no proceedings of the National or State boards shall be invalid on the ground merely of the existence of any vacancy or defect in the constitution of the National or State Boards. This clause undermines the role and importance of the members, particularly, representatives of unorganised workers; even though such a clause may produce avoidable delay in decisions of the Board or Boards.

VIII. The December 2007 Bill

The Unorganised Workers' Social Security Bill, 2007 prepared by the Standing Committee (herein referred as the December Bill) sought to improve upon the Unorganised Sector Workers' Social Security Bill, 2007 (referred herein September Bill) in terms of contents and coverage and institutional mechanism. The new Bill has made following changes:

Clause 1 (1) : In the title the word 'sector' has been removed. Removal of the term 'sector' is a welcome change from its original form and the term 'unorganised workers' now needs to be defined as a distinct analytical category. This may be done either in terms of size of employment and/or by registration/regulation or system of national accounts (1993) framework treating it as sub-set of household sector. It is still not clear how the term 'unorganised workers' would be defined to inclusively specify its scope.

Clause 1 (3): Different dates for different States have been included; in addition, including 'within six months from the date of the assent'.

Clause 2 (n) : Definition of 'wage worker' has been incorporated.

About 92 per cent workers are estimated to be unorganised including many working in the formal sector without getting any regular and social security benefits (e.g., casual, irregular and part-time workers, etc). The conditions of work and work standards are somewhat protected by assured floor level wages in registered establishments whereas in the unregistered informal employment the work conditions are extremely precarious and wages are determined entirely by market forces.

In the new Clause 2 (a), the definition of 'employer' includes 'natural or juridical' person. However, this is only one aspect of 'employer'. In small establishments with less than 10 persons, it becomes difficult to differentiate between employer and employee and the distinction between the employee and employer may get blurred.

Clause 2 (c) states the *modus operandi* to be followed in issuing identity cards. This is well thought out. However, this still does not ensure that all unorganised workers receive identity cards for accruing benefits.

A multipurpose National Identification Number (NIN) can be thought of instead of issuing ID cards with limited purpose. Issuance of identity cards to each unorganised sector worker on a permanent basis is problematic because their nature of work changes often and workers themselves resort to multiple works. The sort of precautions inherent in ESI system and ESI cards needs to be incorporated. It was reported by some civil society organisations that SCs/STs were not allowed to register for wage employment under NREGS in some States. When such kind of discrimination surfaces and the workers are weak, illiterate and unaware of their entitlements, identification of beneficiaries should be made not on the basis of voluntary membership but on solidarity principles of 'compulsory membership' to all those deemed to be unorganised workers.

In Clause 3(1A) besides prescribing the value of benefits as national common minimum social security benefits, a five-year time limit has been prescribed. Since the selective time frame for identifying beneficiaries, issuing of identity cards, etc., has not been prescribed, the 'within five year' clause does not make any sense. There is a need to work out separate time frames for each clause including notification and implementation.

Clause 3 (1B) needs to specify the time frame for different phases and clarify the role of different agencies to accelerate the process of implementation.

Clause 3(1C) and Clause 3(4): While explaining the scope of enlarging the schemes at national and State level, marriage of daughters has been included as a new feature. It is also for the consideration to include widow, widower and minor children of such widows for such benefits.

Clause 3 (2) could be clubbed together with Clause 2 (h) of definitions in order to simplify the definition itself and make it easier to understand and interpret.

Clause 3(3) seeks to include or exclude welfare schemes. While likelihood of inclusion of schemes has been already stated in Clause 3(1C) and Clause 3(4), this amending clause is a threat to the schemes already in place, and would not ensure stability and sustenance of the schemes.

Clause 4 (2) covers the followings :

(i) Scope of the scheme;

(ii) Coverage and phasing of the scheme;

(iii) Resources of the scheme;

(iv) Manner of implementation of the scheme; and

(v) Any other relevant matter.

The entire crux of the Bill has been placed here without details. If all five points were spelt out in detail, the Bill could sufficiently explain and take care of the purpose.

(i) New Chapter: National Social Security and Welfare Fund (NSSWF)

Creation of National Social Security and Welfare Fund is a constructive idea. However, it may delay the initiative to use the funds as more levels/hierarchies are involved to get in and come out. The Central Government could put in place the proportion of that amount in terms of percentage of GDP that is committed for the National Social Security and Welfare Fund, since this is going to be the major contribution anyway.

It has been proposed in Clause 5 (2a) that the National Social Security Board shall be headed by the Union Minister of Labour and Employment. The Board could be headed by an autonomous entity vested with all powers to execute the schemes not to be seen as an alm of political discretion.

Chapter III deals with the proposed National Social Security Board for Unorganised Workers. Significant changes from the

December Bill are that, the Union Minister for Labour and Employment is to be the Chairperson of this Board, besides it proposes to include five representatives from Central Government Ministries/Departments and two Members of Parliament representing Lok Sabha and one from Rajya Sabha. Total number of members of the board was increased to thirty-four from thirty-one as was in the September Bill (Observations/comments on the September Bill under the sub-head 'Creation of Advisory Boards', Clauses 5 and 6 are applicable to this chapter as well).

Chapter IV deals with proposed State Social Security Board for Unorganised Workers. Besides retaining the proposed State Boards in the September Bill, the December Bill proposes the Minister for Labour and Employment to be the Chairperson of this Board, and also proposes to include seven representatives from Government Departments, Welfare Boards and Public Agencies, and two Members representing Legislative Assembly and one from Legislative Council. Total number of members of the Board was increased to twenty-nine from twenty-six as was in the September Bill. (Observations/comments on the September Bill under the sub-head 'Creation of Advisory Boards', Clauses 5 and 6 of the Bill are applicable to this chapter as well).

Social security administration needs to be kept separately under a regulatory mode while implementing the welfare schemes through public-private partnership (PPP). The stress is on the regulatory type of authority as 'National Social Security Regulatory Authority'. Although regulatory authority type is generally adopted to regulate the commercial activities and to oversee the use of public goods, it may be appropriate to follow such type of organisation to have a single command with uni-directional move, which is also directly accountable to Parliament and not to any individual leader. Such type of organisation can be more efficient and a better agency as delivery mechanism.

Chapter V: Clause 5 [(2c) (vi)] envisages two representatives of Lok Sabha and one representative of Rajya Sabha. The role of Parliamentarians should be limited with the formulation of law.

Clause 9 (1) prescribes two necessary obligations on the part of those who are willing to register: (a) he/she shall have completed 14 years of age; and (b) a self-declaration by him/her confirming that he/she is an unorganised worker.

It is observed in the light of Clause 9 (1a) that though a child above 14 years of age becomes eligible to work, yet considering the need for the development of mind and body, and to attain a complete maturity, they should be engaged in 'earning-while-learning' type of vocations and their registration also be made compulsory under skill development/apprenticeship category, in order to ensure that they are not being exploited and learn a vocation with portable skills useful in adult life.

Clause 9 (1b) recommends a self-declaration system for registration of unorganised workers. However, self-declaration may lead to mushrooming of imposters if it is not suitably devised on certain well-defined criteria, with regard to verifiability.

Clause 9(1c) prescribes income limit and the land ceiling in case of agriculturists for considering a person to be entitled to register as unorganised workers. Again, the concern is that people may fall beyond the borderline and people much above cut-off line might fraudulently obtain registration and get certain benefits. Land-ceiling records could also be wrongly used to get benefits. It is also not clear how size of land could be an adequate criterion for registration under the scheme. Income criterion (below poverty line, for example) appears to be one of the important criteria for inclusion as unorganised worker.

Though Clause 15 (3)(1b) spells that the National/State Board may decide the criteria of eligibility for benefits under specified scheme, a broader specification of eligibility norms to be qualified as worker has to be framed to obviate the impulse for a uniform direction to authorities under one legislation.

(ii) Workers' Facilitation Centres (WFC)

This new section has been incorporated to extend the coverage of the Bill and reach the unorganised workers in remote areas. Workers'

Welfare Board, PRIs, trade unions, associations, cooperatives, SHGs and non-profit organisations has been proposed as WFC at the local levels. These tasks may be entrusted to insurance companies assigned for providing the social security schemes.

Chapter VI, Clause 15 (1) Miscellaneous: This section assures that 'this law will not affect the application of any other State or Central Acts, which applies to the unorganised worker or to the employer under this Act'.

The Second National Labour Commission reviewed the Laws and observed that existing laws do not cater to the welfare of the unorganised sector workers. Rather, they are used against them. It was even proposed to nullify the dead laws, which are not effectively used for the welfare of the unorganised workers. Clause 15 (i) tacitly ignores the weak aspects of the existing laws pertaining to the unorganised workers. Further, Clause 15 (2) assures "notwithstanding anything contained in this Act, wherever any unorganised worker eligible for superior or better benefits under any existing Law in force, the worker shall continue to be entitled for such benefits". However, in practice, the benefits accrued from welfare laws do not reflect in the quality life of the unorganised, marginalised and poor workers.

(iii) Dispute Resolution Bodies (DRB) and their Constitution

Of late, this chapter has been included after the Miscellaneous Chapter and claims that "this chapter to be included before the miscellaneous chapter". It goes like ... "the State government shall constitute at least one Dispute Resolution Council (DRC) in each district for resolution of disputes relating to the non-observance of provisions of this Act, arising amongst the unorganised workers, employers, Workers' Facilitation Centres and State Boards".

Clause (3) of this specific chapter assumes DRC to have the same powers as vested in a civil court under Criminal Procedure Code (CPC),1908. However, it is not clear how this would ensure the due benefits to concerned workers.

Further, a clause recommends punitive actions for the contravening officials as one-year imprisonment or Rs. 5,000 or with both, in addition, Rs.100 for each day of such contraventions. Although this provision appears as well-intentioned, it does not contain the necessary potent clauses in it. In practice, erring officials are rarely held accountable or punished under the Criminal Procedure Code. It is also unclear how far this DRC will act in a balanced way to keep the interests of the workers.

IX. Endnote

Like the 73rd and 74th Constitutional Amendment Acts that brought in sea changes in the working of the Panchayati Raj and Nagarpalikas, by means of a single amendment, the government could bring workers under one unified umbrella after stratifying segments and try to extend the scheme segment by segment instead of trying to do too much and ending up doing little. The Government could formulate and implement this social security law in a way that would empower unorganised workers and enhance their capacities on sustainable basis, by provisioning wage earners' funds and skill development funds for unorganised workers.

NOTE

*Published as IAMR Policy Brief Series PB-1/2008. Authors are grateful to Professor Ajeet Narain Mathur, Formerly Director IAMR, for his guidance and encouragement in preparation of this brief. The authors acknowledge the suggestions received from faculty members in the brainstorming session organised at the Institute on December 28, 2007. The authors especially thank Anil Mathur, Bhoop Singh, Indu Shekhar, Jerry Joseph, Mridula Sharma, Nankhoo Ram, S.L. Arora, Surendra Meher, T. Thankachan, U.S. Bhandari and V.K. Saxena for their comments, and Dipika Sen for editing the draft policy brief.

REFERENCES

National Rural Employment Guarantee Programme (NREGP), IAMR, 2007.

Report of the National Commission on Labour, Vol. I, (Part I & II), 2002.

Report on Social Security for Unorganised Workers, National Commission for Enterprises in the Unorganised Sector, May, 2006.

Twenty-fifth Report, Standing Committee on Labour (2007-08), Lok Sabha Secretariat, November 2007.

The Unorganised Sector Workers' Social Security Bill, 2007 (Bill No. LXVII of 2007).

World Labour Report, 2000.

14

MAGNITUDE AND CONSTITUTIONAL PROTECTION OF INFORMAL CONTRACT CHILD LABOUR IN INDIA

SHAKTI KUMAR

A child is the father of the nation. The future of the nation depends on sound health of these children. The health of the children depends upon number of factors. First, the quality of education interlinked with global requirements. Second, moral, physical, and mental development of children. Third, economic conditions of parents in particular and of nation in general. Fourth, government and political wills regarding child labour. All these factors entail that there should not be any scope of exploitation of child labour to have better future of the nation.

A work for children (age ranged between 5 to 14 years) that harms or exploits them physically, mentally, morally or educationally, called Child Labour. It is demanded in the world because of following reasons. First, it is less remunerative in nature. The study of ILO shows that 70 per cent of child workers are unpaid family workers. Second, overtime work of these labourers is easily undertaken by employers without repayment. It is called wageless overtime. Third, The employer gets bonded labour. Fourth, possibility of profit to employers becomes high. Fifth, they are demanded for smuggling, sex, trafficking and armed conflict. To match this demand, child labour is supplied. A number of factors are responsible for supplying child labour. First, poverty of both the parents and the nation is the foremost cause to supply child labour. Second, family expectations and traditions to support economically, in early stage of children, also cause child labour. Third, lack of good schools and childcare enhances possibility of occurring child labour. Fourth, lack of health care causes child labour. Fifth, public opinion, that downplays the risk of early work for children, encourages child labour. Sixth, uncaring attitudes of employers improve magnitude of child labour. Seventh, lack of political and bureaucratic will to implement the policy causes child labour. These demands for and supply of child labour increased magnitude of child labour in the world, in general and in developing countries, in particular. One out of six children in the world, today, is involved in child labour, doing work that is damaging to his or her mental, physical or emotional development. The study of ILO shows that there are some 250 million children between the age group of 5 to 14 years who are in economic activity in developing countries alone. Asia, being the most densely populated region of the world, has the largest number of child labourers. Out of total child labourers in the world, 61 per cent are found in Asia, 32 per cent in Africa and 7 per cent in Latin America. Moreover, the sex ratio of the child labour scenario goes in favour of girls in which 56 per cent of total child labour engaged in developing countries is boys and remaining 44 per cent are girls. However, particularly, in Asia, this sex ratio is 54 per cent for boys and 46 per cent for girls in different sectors. A number of sectors are available which have engaged these children. First, agriculture, hunting, forestry and fishing, collectively, alone occupy 70.40 per cent of total child labour. While manufacturing sector occupies only 8.30 per cent of total child labour in developing economies.

India is one of the developing countries situated in South Asia. It is the member of SAARC. South Asia alone occupies 7.36 per cent of total children as child labour. Among South Asian countries, India alone occupies 51.64 per cent of total child labour available in South Asia. Its population is 10270.15 lakh. It shares 15 per cent of world population. It occupies 2.5 per cent of world areas but 2.5 per cent of world GDP. The occupational pattern of Indian economy shows that agricultural sector provides livelihood to two-third of its population. All above-mentioned factors encourage for studying magnitude and constitutional protection of child labour in India.

Magnitude of Child Labour

The present study will deal with magnitude focusing three steps for better clarification. First step accounts magnitude of child labour as total number of children in India. Second step analyses magnitude of child labour as total population of India. Third step finds magnitude of child labour as total work force in India.

The magnitude of region wise child labour as total children in India has been shown in Table 14.1. There are 2100 lakh children in India (ILO). The number of child labour in India was 112 lakh in 1991. It shows that almost 5.33 per cent of total available children is employed as child labour in India. This figure was 51.64 per cent of total child labour employed in South Asia. This figure of child labour increased over the period and reached to 126.60 lakh in 2001, which is 5.18 per cent of total children. It clearly infers that the number of child labour, in absolute term, is rising while in relative terms it is lowering. In 1991, Madhya Pradesh and Uttar Pradesh States shared more than 12 per cent of total number of child labour in India, as shown in Table 14.1. While, the respective share of Madhya Pradesh decreased to 9.89 per cent and that of Uttar Pradesh increased to 15.16 per cent in 2001. There were three States having percentage share less than one per cent in total child labour in 1991 and this figure decreased to two in 2001.

The magnitude of child labour may be compared with total population. The population of India increased from 8,463 lakh in 1991 to 10,270.15 lakh in 2001. During this period the child labours employment increased from 112 lakh in 1991 to 126.60 in 2001. It shows that the employment of child labour increased in absolute terms along with rise in the population but decreased in relative terms from 1.32 per cent of total population in 1991 to 1.23 per cent in 2001 as shown in Table 14.1. However, the existence of the child labour employment has its own regional variations. It was the Southern region of India, in 1991, in which there was maximum number of child labour. It occupied 23.82 per cent of total child labour in India.

Table 14.1: Magnitude of Child Labour in India (lakh) for 5 -14 Years of Age Group in India

Region	States	Year 1991			Year 2001		
		Child labour (C.L.)	Population	C.L. as % of population	C.L	Population	C.L. as % of population
Northern	Haryana	1.09 (0.97)	164.63 (1.93)	0.66	2.23 (1.76)	210..82 (2.05)	1.06
	Himachal	0.56 (0.50)	51.50 (0.60)	1.08	0.98 (0.77)	60.77 (0.59)	1.61
	Punjab	1.42 (1.26)	202.81 (2.38)	0.70	1.68 (1.32)	242.89 (2.36)	0.69
	Rajasthan	7.74 (6.89)	440 (5.20)	1.76	12.13 (9.58)	564.73 (5.50)	2.14
Southern	Andhra Pradesh	16.61(14.79)	665 (7.85)	2.49	13.56 (10.71)	757.27 (7.37)	1.79
	Karnataka	9.76 (8.69)	449.77 (5.30)	2.16	8.53 (6.73)	527.33 (5.13)	1.62
	Kerala	0.34 (0.30)	290.98 (3.42)	0.11	0.33 (0.26)	318.38 (3.10)	0.10
	Tamilnadu	5.78 (5.15)	558.58 (6.59)	1.03	4.33 (3.42)	621.10 (6.04)	0.70
Eastern	Bihar	9.42 (8.39)	863.74 (10.19)	1.09	10.73 (8.47)	828.78 (8.06)	1.29
	Orissa	4.52 (4.02)	316.60 (3.73)	1.42	4.23 (3.34)	367.06 (3.57)	1.15
	W. Bengal	7.11 (6.33)	68.77 (8.03)	1.05	8.11 (6.40)	802.21 (7.81)	1.01
Western	Gujarat	5.23 (4.66)	414 (4.89)	1.26	5.01 (3.95)	505.96 (4.92)	0.99
	Maharashtra	10.68 (9.51)	789.37 (9.32)	1.35	8.56 (6.76)	967.52 (9.42)	0.88
Central	Madhya Pradesh	13.52 (12.04)	661.81 (7.81)	2.04	12.38 (9.89)	603.85 (5.87)	2.05
	Uttar Pradesh	14.10 (12.55)	1391.12 (16.43)	1.01	19.20 (15.16)	1660.05 (16.16)	1.16
Others		4.40 (3.91)	527.12 (6.22)	0.83	14.61 (11.66)	1130.74 (11.00)	1.29
India		**112.28 (100)**	**8463 (100)**	**1.32**	**126.60 (100)**	**10270.15 (100)**	**1.23**

Source : Census of India Note: Percentage shares in brackets.

While, it was the Central region of India, in 2001, in which maximum number of child labour was employed. It shared 24.94 per cent of total child labour in India. The region, which occupied maximum percentage share in child labour in 1991, comprises Andhra Pradesh, Karnataka, Kerala and Tamilnadu States which are highly literate and comparatively developed one. These States adopted constitutional protections to child labour and hence the magnitude of child labour decreased to 26.75 lakh in 2001. It shows negative (1.66 per cent) growth rate. While, the region which shares maximum cake of child labour in 2001, comprises most populous States, namely, Madhya Pradesh (M.P.) and Uttar Pradesh (U.P.) The magnitude of child labour increased at the rate of 1.41 per cent per annum in this region because Less constitutional protections were implemented in this region.

Table 14.1 itself shows that the number of States, having percentage share of more than 2 per cent in its population decreased from three in 1991 to two in 2001. At the same point, it was the Andhra Pradesh State, where, there were 2.49 per cent child labourers of its total population in 1991, which was the highest.

An important issue can be viewed in Table 14.1. It is not necessary that child labour will be high where, there, population is high. For example, Madhya Pradesh shares 5.87 per cent in India's population but 9.89 per cent in India's child labour. At the same point, Maharashtra state shares 9.42 per cent of India's population and only 6.76 per cent in India's child labour. Therefore, one can say that population is not the only factor which influences the existence of child labour. Another point may be seen that child labour exists comparatively less where economic development is high. For example, Punjab is the developed State, which accounts only 1.32 per cent of total child labour in 2001. The existence of the child labour gets affected by the level of education. For example, Kerala is the most literate State in India and hence it accounts only 0.26 per cent child labour in India. From above, one can infer that the existence of child labour depends on many factors such as literacy rate, economic development, population, poverty and so on. It will be seen in details later on in this chapter itself.

Table 14.2 : Per annum Growth Rate of Child Labour (Age Group of 5 -14 years) in India in the Year 2001 as compared to the year 1991

Region	States	Child labour (C.L.)	Popul-ation	C.L. as % of population
Northern	Haryana	10.45	2.80	0.40
	Himachal	7.50	1.75	0.53
	Punjab	1.83	1.97	(-) 0.01
	Rajasthan	5.67	2.83	0.38
Southern	Andhra Pradesh	(-) 1.83	1.38	(-) 0.70
	Karnataka	(-) 1.26	1.72	(-) 0.54
	Kerala	(-) 0.29	0.94	0.01
	Tamilnadu	(-) 2.50	1.12	(-) 0.33
Eastern	Bihar	1.39	(-) 0.40	0.29
	Orissa	(-) 0.64	1.59	(-) 0.27
	W. Bengal	1.40	1.78	(-) 0.04
Western	Gujarat	(-) 0.42	2.22	(-) 0.27
	Maharashtra	(-) 1.98	2.25	(-) 0.47
Central	Madhya Pradesh	(-) 0.84	(-0) 0.87	0.01
	Uttar Pradesh	3.61	1.93	0.15
India		**1.27**	**2.13**	**(-) 0.09**

Source : Census of India.

The overall growth rate of child labour is 1.27 per cent per annum while that of population is 2.13 per cent but child labour as percentage of population is decreasing. It shows that child labour is decreasing as compared to population. There are number of States where growth rate of child labour is negative. The population growth rate is very high in the Punjab and Rajasthan while it is negative in Bihar and Madhya Pradesh. It is true that growth rate of child labour is high in those States where population growth rate is high. In general, it can be inferred from Table 14.2 that growth rate of child labour is associated with growth rate of population. In the developed States, the growth rate of child labour is low, which shows that employment of child labour is negatively associated with economic development.

Table 14.3: Child Labour (Age Group of 5 -14 years) as Percentage of Total Work Force in India in the year 2001

Region	States	Child labour as % of workforce
Northern	Haryana	4.85
	Himachal	8.12
	Punjab	3.22
	Rajasthan	8.11
Southern	Andhra Pradesh	7.83
	Karnataka	6.89
	Kerala	0.43
	Tamilnadu	3.78
Eastern	Bihar	4.91
	Orissa	4.32
	W. Bengal	4.52
Western	Gujarat	4.23
	Maharashtra	4.51
Central	Madhya Pradesh	6.87
	Uttar Pradesh	4.01
India		5.00

Source : Census of India.

Now it would be better to know the magnitude of child labour in terms of workforce existed in India and it has been shown in Table 14.3. It is 5 per cent of total workforce in India. It is very high. It is Northern region, which contributes highest percentage share in work force as child labour. It accounts almost one-fourth of total workforce in India.

It is the Western region, which accounts least child labour in total work force. It accounts 8.74 per cent of total child labour existed in India. It is the Himachal Pradesh, which accounts the highest percentage share in child labour in workforce. It accounts 8.12 per cent. It is the Kerala state which employees least child labour as workforce in India.

From above, one may entail that child labour exists in India alongwith the regional and spatial variations. However, it is true that its existence is getting affected by economic development, population, poverty and literacy and so many factors. Now, it would be better to know the economic activity of child labour in India.

Economic Activity of Child Labour

There are some children who are economically engaged for full time to get bread and butter to survive. However, on the other hand, some children are engaged as part time as marginal workers. In both the cases, both the male and female children are engaged economically in different activities.

Over the period, efforts are being undertaken both by domestic and international agencies to combat the child labour problems. This was the reason of declining the proportion of full time workers in 2001 compared with 1991. It declined from 82.35 per cent of total child labour in 1991 to 44.89 per cent in 2001 in India. This promotion of full time child workers was higher than part time workers in all regions and States of India in 1991. But this trend shifted in favour of marginal workers in 2001. The proportion of full time and marginal workers became 45.57 and 54.43 respectively in 2001. It has been shown in Table 14.4 to show the trend variation of full time and part time workers.

Table 14.4 : Marginal Workers as total Child Labour (Age Group of 5 -14 years) in India

Region	States	Year 1991			Year 2001		
		Main workers	Marginal workers	Total workers	Main workers	Marginal workers	Total workers
Northern	Haryana	81.65	18.35	100	47.87	52.13	100
	Himachal	53.57	46.43	100	36.55	63.45	100
	Punjab	92.95	7.05	100	71.87	28.13	100
	Rajasthan	63.30	36.70	100	38.78	61.22	100
Southern	Andhra Pradesh	92.53	7.47	100	60.47	39.53	100
	Karnataka	83.81	16.19	100	51.32	48.68	100
	Kerala	82.35	17.65	100	44.89	55.11	100
	Tamilnadu	90.48	9.52	100	67.84	32.16	100
Eastern	Bihar	84.39	15.61	100	50.37	49.63	100
	Orissa	71.90	28.10	100	40.67	59.33	100
	W. Bengal	83.40	16.60	100	59.71	40.29	100
Western	Gujarat	71.31	28.69	100	51.27	48.73	100
	Maharashtra	75.37	24.63	100	38.83	61.17	100
Central	Madhya Pradesh	73.74	26.26	100	36.83	63.17	100
	Uttar Pradesh	81.20	18.80	100	48.63	51.33	100
	India	**80.47**	**19.53**	**100**	**45.57**	**54.43**	100

Source : Census of India.

Both the male and female child labourers are engaged in different activities as shown in Table 14.5. This Table shows that female participation rate is 57.47 per cent while remaining belongs to 42.53 per cent for male. Female child labour attends mostly in domestic activities. 90.75 per cent of total workers who attended domestic duty only belong to female. It is worst situation in India that female children are asked to attend domestic duty while male children are asked to do something else or to enjoy. This is the reason why school participation ratio of male children is comparatively very high for male children. At the same time, it has been shown that female children who attended Domestic Duty plus free collection of Goods, Tailoring and Weaving is very high rate of 87.73 per cent. It shows worst situation of female children in India. Almost 63 per cent of total children employed belong to female who are at work to earn for livelihood at the age of studying.

In this section itself, it would be better to know the sectoral allocation of child labour employed in different activities. It has been

Table 14.5: Female Participation in Child Labour in India in the Year 2001

Economic activities	Male	Female	Total
Children engaged in economic activities	52.83	46.17	100
Attended domestic duty only	9.25	90.75	100
Children at work	36.29	63.71	100
Attended domestic duty plus free collection of goods, tailoring and weaving	12.27	87.73	100
Attending school	56.04	43.96	100
Children neither at work nor at school	47.50	52.50	100
Total	42.53	57.47	100

Source : www.indiatogether.org/photo/2006/childlabour.

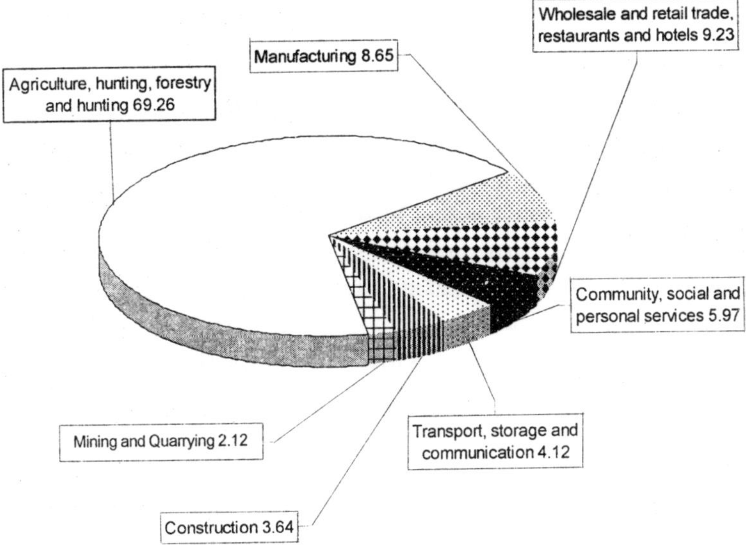

Chart 14.1: Economically Active Child Labour in Different Sectors in 1991 in India

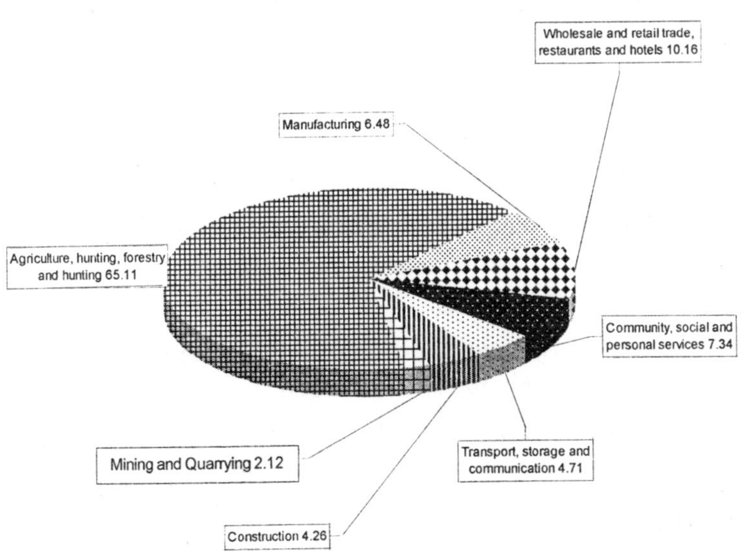

Chart 14.2: Economically Active Child Labour in Different Sectors in 2001 in India

shown in Chart 14.1 and 14.2. They are engaged in agriculture; manufacturing; wholesale, retailer, restaurants and hotels; community, social and personal services; transport, storage and communication; construction and mining and quarying. Most of the child labourers are employed in the agricultural sector for livelihood. However, their percentage share decreased from 69 per cent in 1991 to 65 per cent in 2001 due to various reasons. First, after 1991, the Indian economy was liberalized with structural changes. Second, labour migration took place due to urbanization and industrialization. Wage rate in the non-agricultural sector became comparatively more than agricultural sector. Construction sector resulted with boom during this period.

From Table 14.5, one may conclude that children are economically active in different activities with high participation of female exploitation. At the same time, the marginal workers are proportionally rising in their number in India across the regions and States. Over and above, most of the child labourers are employed in the agricultural sector. However, child labour concentration is shifting from agricultural to non-agricultural sectors with predominance of former.

There are various disadvantages of existence of child labour. First, pillar of the nation becomes weak since beginning due to loss of skilled human capital. Second, children are exploited educationally, mentally, physically, culturally and economically. Third, gap between poor and rich increases. Fourth, bonded child labour emerges. Fifth, it violates children right to educate and their human rights. All these factors encourage policy makers to have constitutional protection to child labour.

Constitutional Protection

A number of constitutional protections have been undertaken to combat child labour in India. These are enumerated as below:

(1) ***Indian Factory Act (IFA, 1881)*:** It fixed the minimum age of employment at seven and maximum number of working hours at nine per day with four months holidays in a year. IFA 1891 and 1954 disallowed the employment of children during night time.

(2) ***Whitely Commission (1929):*** Rege Committee (1944) and Gurupadswamy Committee (1979) recommended to regulating child

labour. Based on these committees, child labour Prohibition and Regulation Act was passed by Government of India in 1986.

(3) ***Indian Constitution (1950):*** Articles 24, 45, 36-e, 39-f and Directive Principles are certain constitutional protections, which are adopted in India to prevent child labour. Both the articles 45 and Directive Principles prohibit the child labour in factories, mines and other hazardous occupations. Article 45 makes provision of free and compulsory education for up to 14 years age group of children. Article 39-e lays down that no child be forced by economic necessity to enter unsuited occupations. Article 39-f makes a provision to provide healthy opportunities to children to maintain their dignities.

(4) ***Bonded Labour Abolition Act (1976):*** It purports to abolish all debt agreements and obligations arising out of India's longstanding bonded labour. It orders the economic rehabilitation of freed bonded labourers by the State.

(5) ***Child Labour Prohibition and Regulation Act (1986):*** It bans employment of children working in hazardous occupations. It defines child as a person who has not completed 14 years of age. It lays down penalties for violation of this provision. This Act accepts that child labour cannot be abolished so long as poverty exists.

(6) ***The National Child Labour Policy (1987):*** All the released children from employment in hazardous industries are provided educational services, non-formal, under the centrally sponsored National Child Labour Project (NCLP). It is operational in 100 districts in 13 States, in the areas of high concentration of child labour throughout the country.

(7) ***Ratification of UNCRC-1989 (1992):*** India ratified United Nations Convention on the Right of the Child (UNCRC) in 1992 according to which India is bound to have international standard of children right. It provides following principles for examining the implementation of the convention: (a) the principle of non-discrimination (Article 2), (b) best interest of the child (Article 3), (c) the right to life, survival and development (Article 6) and (d) respect for the views of the child (Article 12).

(8) ***Unnikrishnan vs. State of Andhra Pradesh (1993):*** The Supreme Court of India lays down a provision according to which right to education for children to be considered a fundamental right. It brought state initiatives to educate child labour.

(9) ***M.C.Mehta vs. State of Tamilnadu (1996):*** When gross violation of Article 24 takes place due to employment of child labour, Article 32 is imposed to stop child labour. The Supreme Court of India gave direction for immediate identification of children in hazardous occupations and their subsequent rehabilitations, including providing appropriate education to the released children.

(10) ***Ratification of UN Convention:*** India has ratified only three conventions namely ILO Convention No. 29, 105 and UNCRC.

Despite these efforts made through constitutional enforcement, there exists child labour exploitation in India due to following flaws.

(1) Almost all laws, in practice, are enforced only in organized sector where only 8 per cent of total child labourers are employed. It ignores unorganized sector where 92 per cent of total child labourers are employed.

(2) So long as the child is not forced to work in an exploitative environment, the State does not take legal action.

(3) The Act provides a list of hazardous occupations. It does not define what constitutes hazardous work.

(4) It does not clarify what the child labour should happen once the employer is prosecuted. However, after the initiative of the Supreme Court of India, a provision of rehabilitation of child labour has been started but separate budgetary provision has not been made yet.

(5) Under the law, the employer is supposed to notify the Labour Department of any children working in the established. This is akin to asking the murderer to report the crime.

(6) The implementation of Act depends on ill-equipped State's bureaucratic machinery.

(7) The education of the child is important more for society rather than parents.

Therefore, law empowers State to take punitive actions against parents who do not send their children to school. In practice, law should empower parents to do so.

After dealing with constitutional remedies, it would be better to provide certain suggestions to stop child labour in India. First, family income should be raised because there is positive relationship between child labour and poverty (Mehra-Kerpelman, 1996). Second, Law should be enforced to eradicate bonded labour through poverty eradication because even if bonded child labourers are released, the same conditions of poverty that caused the initial debt can cause people to slip back into bondage (ILO, 1993). It has been rightly observed that a bonded child is released only after lump sum payment made by parents, which is extremely difficult for the poor (Human Right Watch, 1996). Third, qualitative but equal educational opportunities should be provided as fundamental duties by States. Fourth, Family size is controlled by controlling fertility so that families are not burdened by children.

This study may be summarized by saying that any labour that harms or exploits a child either way of physically, mentally, morally or educationally is known as child labour. This child labour problem is prevalent worldwide with highest concentration in Asia in general and in India in particular. It percolates existence of poverty, lack of good schools, lack of health care, uncaring attitudes of employers and parents, limited choices for women and bad public opinion regarding child labour. Therefore, child labour must be eradicated for better future of the nation.

Note: There is oral or written bilateral agreement between employer and employee in Contract system (Indian Contract Act, 1872). Oral agreement may not be legally enforced as it takes place in child labour. Therefore, the present study deals with informal contract child labour having age group of 5 to 14 years.

REFERENCES

Human Rights Watch (1996), *The Small Hands of Slavery-Bonded Child Labour in India*, New York.

International Labour Organisation (1992), *World Labour Report*, Geneva.

International Labour Organisation (1993), *World Labour Report*, Geneva.

International Labour Organisation (1995), *World Labour Report*, Geneva.

International Labour Organisation, A Dynamic Profile of Child Labour in India 1951-1991, *Child Labour Action and Support Project*, ILO, New Delhi.

Mehra-Kerpelman, K. (1996), "Children at Work: How Many and Where?", *World of Work*.

Nangia, P. (1987), *Child Labour: Cause – Effect Syndrome*, New Delhi, Janak Publishers.

15

CHILD LABOUR AND DEVELOPMENT PARADIGM IN INDIA

P. K. Sinha and Rashi Krishna Sinha

Introduction

Today many people and organizations are concerned about child labour. Various research projects study child labour, and numerous books and studies have been published on the subject. The concerns partly stem from the kinds of work children do, some of which cause irreversible physical or psychological damage or even threaten their lives, and partly from the overwhelming number of children who work. Considerable differences exist between the many kinds of work children do. Some are difficult and demanding, others are more hazardous and even morally reprehensible. Children carry out a very wide range of tasks and activities when they work. One disapproves child labour because of number of reasons of which few are enlisted below :

1. Allowing children to work means stealing their childhood from them;
2. Child labourers are subject to economic exploitation because they are paid at the lowest rates, and sometimes not at all;
3. Children often work under the worst conditions, which can cause physical deformations and long-term health care problems;

4. Some child work can perpetuate poverty because child labourers, deprived of education or healthy physical development, are likely to become adults with low earnings prospects;
5. Children often replace adult labour; employers prefer them because they are cheap and docile;
6. The widespread use of child labour may result in lower wages for all workers; and
7. Countries that allow child labour are able to lower their labour costs; thus they attract investors and also benefit from "unfair trade" due to their low production costs. (Adapted from Arat, 2002).

   Situation in India do not differ to great from this else than point (7).

While both boys and girls work as child labourers, the girl child is often subject to even more dismal treatment than her brothers. Girls consistently earn less money than boys (as women earn significantly less than men in India), and are subject to gender-specific forms of abuse from their employers, including rape. In addition to lower pay and greater abuse, girls suffer from the higher demands placed on them within the Indian household. Girls have to work in the house—they tend to the other children, they clean, they go to market, they cook—even if they are also working long and gruelling hours outside the home. Furthermore, girls are over represented in some of the most brutal industries to employ child labour. There are twice as many girls as boys labouring in India's quarries and factories, and the majority of children working in the construction industry are girls. Two players create the debt bondage arrangement: the creditor-employer, who offers money to an impoverished parent in an attempt to secure the extremely cheap and captive labour of his or her child, and the parent who accepts this money, agreeing to offer the child's labour as surety for the debt. The child is a commodity of exchange. She or he is powerless to affect the agreement or its terms and—whether willing or unwilling to serve the bond master—powerless to refuse.

The arrangements between parents and contracting agents are usually informal and unwritten. The number of years required to pay off such a loan is indeterminate. Many of the children, who had already been working for several years, and even among those relatively new to their jobs, none said that they expected to be released prior to maturity. Some intended to walk away from their bondage when they married, leaving a younger sibling to take over the labour-payment or a parent to somehow extinguish the debt-perhaps by a new loan from a different creditor-employer.

In many industries marked by the use of debt bondage, the child's labour does not function to pay off the original loan at all. Instead, the child's labour serves as both interest on the loan—for the children are paid only a fraction of what their labour would bring them on the open market—and as a surety for the loan's repayment. The original amount loaned to the parent must be repaid in full in a single installment; only then will the child be released from servitude.

There are more children under the age of fourteen in India than the entire population of the United States of America, according to the Embassy of India, Washington D.C. It is also a fact that every fifth child in the world lives in India. Every third malnourished child is an Indian, every second Indian child is under weight, three out of four children in India are anemic and every second new born has reduced learning capacity due to iodine deficiency. According to the SRO 2000, there are 1104 lakh child labour in India. Children born with low weight are 46 per cent and 79 per cent of the children under the age of three are anemic (NFHS-III). Even the immunization coverage is very low—in case of polio 78.2 per cent, DPT 55.3 per cent, and BCG 78 per cent (NFHS-III).

All these statistics enables one to comprehend how pathetic and grave is the State of child in India in the twenty first century. It also highlights the fact for immediate need for effective policy execution to provide safe future to the future citizens of our country. As is well known that the vision and perception of these blooming buds lays the potential of our nation in the future and the deep imprints of the tender age lays the foundation for a bright future. Child's mind is an open horizon, which needs to be inculcated and ingrained with creative ideas, independent thinking and scientific temper. These innocent angels believe in faith and trust in what is being taught to them is for their benefit, if shown the right path can do wonders. The need of the hour is to address the issues affecting the life and growth of the millions of voiceless children, who can dream of dreams and have the potential to make them come true. It becomes but natural and quite natural and pertinent too to analytically examine different dimensions of the problems of the child labour in India.

Constitutional, Legislative and Policy Related Measures

The Constitution of India recognizes the vulnerable position of children and their rights to protection from any form of exploitation. It calls for protective discrimination as Article 15 of the Constitution of India makes special attention to children through necessary and special laws and policies that safeguards their rights. Article 14, 15, 15(3), 19(1), 21, 21(A), 23, 24, 39 (e), and 39(f) reiterate India's commitment to the protection, safety, security and well being of all its people, including children. Article 24 clearly states that, "No child below the age of fourteen years shall be employed to work in any factory or mine or employed in any hazardous employment." At the same time Article 39(e) of the Indian Constitution direct the State policy such, "that the health and strength of workers...and the tender age of children are not abused and that citizens are not forced by economic necessity to enter a vocation unsuited to their age or strength, that children are given opportunities and facilities to develop in a healthy manner, and in conditions of freedom and dignity, and that childhood and youth are protected against exploitation, and against moral and material abandonment." These two articles show that India has always had a goal of taking care of its children and ensuring their safety of the workers. It is also significant to note here that notwithstanding the clear instructions in the Constitution of India and the different legislative measures there is a long way to go and effective enforcement of the policies, programmes and provisions of the Constitution and the legislative measures are a but natural prerequisite to overcome the perplexing problem of child labour. Human Rights Watch (1996) specifically mentions that, "A glaring sign of their neglect of their duties by the officials charged with enforcing child labour laws is the failure to collect, maintain and disseminate accurate statistics regarding enforcement efforts."

Child labour in India is a grave and extensive problem. It is a commonly observed phenomenon that children below the age group of 14 years can be seen at work in glass-blowing, fireworks, most commonly in carpet-making factories, bidi-making, in agricultural practices, home-servants and at the tea stalls etc. According to the Government of India report, there are about 20 million child labourers, while the non-governmental organisations estimates the figure to be around 50 million. It is most prevalent in the northern parts of the country and is socially accepted practice keeping in view the pathetic economic status of the families. It becomes necessary that the meaning of child labour be made clear. Before getting into the various constitutional and legislative measures it would be better to recall what the term child labour connotes. Children, as is usually observed and practiced across the globe, imitate and learn from their grand parents, parents, family members and the immediate surrounding environment. This is a traditional practice followed so as to inculcate, in the new generation, positive traditional practices, good habits and mannerism. Any form of help and work in the family by the child, age 5-14years, without depriving him of his cognitive, psychological and physiological development, is not a child labour. When a family engages a child in an economic activity at the cost of his future, the child is deprived of his basic need of education, freedom etc, which retards his overall development such an act is usually termed as child labour. In other words, the term child labour refers to that work, which deprives children of their childhood, their potential and their dignity and that which is harmful to physical and mental development. From this term one may also infer that it is an act that allows children to work by stealing their childhood from them. The children being innocent follow the direction verbatim even though they are subject to economic exploitation because they work more rigorously but are paid the least and many a time are not paid even. The condition under which a child works usually happens to have an adverse impact upon their overall development. If they continue to work under such circumstances for a long period of time it may also lead to some serious physical ailment. It is also found that child labour displaces the adult labour, it is so because the employer finds them easy to handle and exploit them accordingly. Within the term 'child labour' is inherent that it is a work that –

(a) mentally, physically, socially or morally dangerous and harmful to children; and

(b) it interferes with their schooling: -

(i) by depriving them of the opportunity to attend school;

(ii) by obliging them to leave school pre-maturely; or

(iii) by requiring them to attempt to combine school attendance with excessively long and heavy work.

In its most extreme forms child labour involves children being enslaved, separated from their families, exposed to serious hazards and illness and or left to fend for themselves on the streets of large cities—often at a very early stage. Whether or not particular forms of "work" can be called "child labour" depends on the child's age, the type and hours of work performed, the conditions under which it is performed and the objectives pursued by the individual countries. The answer varies from country to country, as well as among sectors within countries (Inter-Parliamentary Union/International Labour Office, 2002).

People and experts hold divergent views on what children should and should not be permitted to do, and at what age they should be allowed to do certain kinds of work at all ages in their national legislations. Different countries have minimum different ages in their national legislations.

The ILO Convention Number : 138, adopted in 1973, sets 15 as the minimum age for work in the developed countries, but a child can become an apprentice at a younger age, 14 years, or undergo a vocational training. More than 130 countries have ratified this convention. Keeping in view to protecting a child from various forms of exploitations national policies and legislative measures were enforced and adopted. The Fundamental Rights and the Directive Principles of the State Policy of the Constitution of India furnishes the framework for child's rights. The first Act in India relating to child labour has roots in the pre-independent India. It was in the year

1933 that the Enactment of Children (Pledging of Labour) Act, February 1933, came into being. The Employment of Children Act followed this in 1938. Subsequently, a number of legislations were passed that progressively extended legal protection to children. Few of the significant legislative measures for the protection of the child are enlisted below:

- Factories Act, 1954;
- Probation of Offender's Act, 1958;
- Bombay Prevention of Begging Act, 1959;
- Orphanages and Other Charitable Homes (Supervision and Control) Act, 1960;
- Bonded Labour System (Abolition) Act, 1976;
- Immoral Traffic Prevention Act, 1986 [initially it was Suppression of Immoral Traffic in Women and Girls Act 1956 (SITA)];
- Prevention of Illicit Traffic in Narcotic Drugs and Psychotropic Substances Act, 1987;
- Juvenile Justice (Care and Protection of Children) Act, 2000;
- Commission for Protection of Rights of the Child Act, 2005.

Few of the important sections for the protection of a child under Indian Penal Code (IPC) concerning our theme are enlisted below:

- Section 363 considers kidnapping for camel racing, etc., as a crime;
- Section 363-A considers kidnapping for begging a crime;
- Section 367 considers kidnapping for slavery etc. a crime;
- Section 366-A considers procurement of minor girls by inducement or by force to seduce or have illicit intercourse a serious crime;
- Section 372 considers selling of girls for prostitution a crime; and
- Section 373 considers buying of girls for prostitution a serious offence.

The Act of 1986 needs to be elaborated briefly. The Act aims to prohibit the entry of children into hazardous occupations and to regulate services of children in non-hazardous occupations. The Act, in particular,

- Bans the employment of children, i.e., those who have not completed the age of 14 year, in specified occupations and processes (listed in the schedule to the Act);
- Lays down procedure to make addition to the schedule of banned occupations or processes;
- Regulate the working conditions of children in occupations where they are not prohibited from working;
- Lays down penalties for the employment of children in violation of the provisions of this Act, and other Acts which forbid the employment of children; and
- Brings uniformity in the definition of the "child" in related laws.

The protective legal provisions for the working children in other laws are listed at Annexure II. At the same time it would be proper to have a glance over different policies and programmes initiated by the government at different period oriented for the well-being of the children. Few of the major policies formulated while keeping these views in mind are enlisted below:

- National Policy for Children, 1974;
- National Policy on Education, 1986;
- National Policy on Child Labour 1987;
- National Nutrition Policy 1993;
- Report of the Committee on Prostitution, Child Prostitutes and Children of Prostitutes and Plan of Action to Combat Trafficking and Commercial Sexual Exploitation of Women and Children, 1998;
- National Health Policy, 2002;
- National Charter for Children, 2004;
- National Plan of Action for Children, 2005.

The Nation Charter for Children, 2004 has certain section which can be precisely made mention of here :

1. Survival, life and liberty.
2. Protection from economic exploitation and all forms of abuse.
3. Protection of the girl child.
4. Care, protection, welfare of children of marginalized and disadvantaged communities.
5. Ensuring child friendly procedures.

The highlight of the National Plan of Action for Children (NPAC), 2005 regards the child as an asset and discusses a child as a person with human rights.

The impact of all these efforts at all the levels is quite evident from the figures which are emerging out from the Census data of 1971, 1981, 1991 and 2001. Appendix Table 15.1 (*see* Appendices) brings to the surface certain important facts. Over the period covered under the four Censuses the percentage of children working in the age group of 5-14 years has gone down considerable from 26.84 per cent to 12.24 per cent for 1971 Census and 2001 Census respectively.

Involvement of Child Workers in Different Industries

ILO Statistics on Child Labour and Responses in South Asia reveals that in India about 33.3 percentage of the total population was under the age of 15 years (Human Development Report 2004). Elaborating on the issue of Child labour in South Asia, officially available statistics estimates that in India about 11.2 million children, in the age group of 5-14 years, are working children. Of the total number of working children the percentage of children in the category of domestic servants is 23.25 per cent. Out of the total sample, 19.90 per cent children were in this evidence group. 50.30 per cent of these children were boys and the remaining girls. 34.68 per cent children in this evidence group were in the age group of 5 to 12 years, while 22.85 per cent children were in the age group of 13 to 14 and 42.47 per cent children were in the age group of 15 to 18 years. In the age group of 5 to 12 years, 51.92 per cent children were girls, while 52.30 per cent children in the age group of 13 to 14 and 46.48 per cent children in the age group of 15 to 18 years were girls. Among all the children in this evidenced group, 23.16 per cent were child domestic workers, 11.21 per cent were working in tea kiosks and restaurants, 7.83 per cent were engaged in bidi rolling and the remaining were working in 'other' occupations such as lock making, carpet weaving, construction, shops, artisans, etc.

In the year 1981 the Census of India (1981) divided the child labour into nine industrial divisions. They were (i) Cultivation, (ii) Agricultural Labour, (iii) Livestock, Forestry, Fishing, Plantation, (iv) Mining and Quarrying, (v) Manufacturing, Processing, Servicing and Repairs, (vi) Construction, (vii) Trade and Commerce, (viii) Transport, Storage and Communication, and (ix) Other Services.

Within different age groups, as specified in the Appendix Table 15.2 (refer Appendix), majority of them were girls. The recent ban on use of children in domestic work is yet to be functional on ground, as in reality one may easily observe the state which the concerning legislation meets in our day-to-day life. To execute it at the ground level needs to make the people convinced that what they are practicing on different pretext is inappropriate and is violating the basic spirit not only of the legislation but also of humanity. At the same time the children working at tea kiosks is about 11.21 per cent of the total number of working children.

Within the specified age groups the number/percentage of boys are substantially ahead of their girl counterparts. It is worth noting here that an important aspect of the involvement of children is in the bidi making and here the percentage of girl child is far ahead of their male counterparts. As the environment in which these children work affects their mental horizon thereby not only damaging their future but also make inevitable the sociologically impact of the problem consequently leading to the problem of governance. The available statistics on the subject reveals that the children involved in the other such menial occupations are as high as 57.81 per cent of the total number of working children. Even though the percentage of boys in the different specified age groups is higher than the girls yet the percentage of girls involved in different respective categories is quite considerable. Of the total number of children in this the percentage of boys is as high as 61.28 per cent and that of girls is 38.72 per cent.

It is also important to mention here that there are substantial numbers of children on the streets. According to the study on child abuse (2007), of the total number of the respondents 18.6 per cent were street children of which 55.33 per cent were boys and 44.67 per cent were girls. The study also surfaced the fact that 65.9 per cent of the children living on the streets were living on the streets with there families. Of this 51.84 per cent slept on footpaths, 17.48 per cent slept in the night shelters and 30.67 per cent slept in other places like bridges, flyovers, railway platforms, parks, etc.

60.94 per cent children in this evidence group were in the age group of 5 to 12 years, while 19.90 per cent children were in the age group of 13 to 14 and 19.16 per cent children were in the age group of 15 to 18 years. In the age group of 5 to 12 years, 53.97 per cent children were boys, while 55.31 per cent children in the age group of 13 to 14 and 59.68 per cent children in the age group of 15 to 18 years were boys. The gender and age break-up of children on the street indicated two significant findings; first, that girls of all age groups are also living on the streets rendering them vulnerable to abuse and exploitation; second, the number of boys living on the streets is larger than that of girls.

India has the dubious distinction of being the nation with the largest number of child labourers in the world. The child labourers endure miserable and difficult lives. They earn little and struggle to make enough to feed themselves and their families. They do not go to school; more than half of them are unable to learn the barest skills of literacy. Poverty is one of the main reasons behind this phenomenon. The unrelenting poverty forces the parents to push their young children in all forms of hazardous occupations. Child labour is a source of income for poor families. They provide help in household enterprises or of household chores in order to free adult household members for economic activity elsewhere. In some cases, the study found that a child's income accounted for between 34 and 37 per cent of the total household income. In India the emergence of child labour is also because of unsustainable systems of landholding in agricultural areas and caste system in the rural areas. Bonded labour, as we know, refers to the phenomenon of children working in conditions of servitude in order to pay their debts. The debt that binds them to their employer is incurred not by the children themselves but by their parent. The creditors-cum-employers offer these loans to destitute parents in an effort to secure the labour of these children. The arrangements between the parents and contracting agents are usually informal and unwritten. The number of years required to pay off such a loan is indeterminate. The lower castes such as *dalits* and tribal make them vulnerable groups for exploitation.

The environmental degradation and lack of employment avenues in the rural areas also cause people to migrate to big cities. On arrival in overcrowded cities the disintegration of family units takes place through alcoholism, unemployment or disillusionment of better life etc. This in turn leads to emergence of street children and child workers who are forced by their circumstances to work from the early age. The girls are forced to work as sex-workers or beggars. A large number of girls end up working as domestic workers on low wages and unhealthy living conditions.

Some times children are abandoned by their parents or sold to factory owners. The last two decades have seen tremendous growth of export based industries and mass production factories utilizing low technologies. They try to maintain competitive positions through low wages and low labour standards. The child labourers exactly suit their requirements. They use all means to lure the parents into giving their children on pretext of providing education and good life. In India majority of children work in industries, such as cracker making, diamond polishing, glass, brass-ware, carpet weaving, bangle making, lock making and mica cutting to name a few. 15 per cent of the 100,000 children work in the carpet industry of Uttar Pradesh. 70-80 per cent of the 8,000 to 50,000 children work in the glass industry in Ferozabad. In the unorganized sector child labour is paid by piece-by-piece rates that result in even longer hours for very low pay

The National Sample Survey (NSS) 2000 data shows that 9.8 million children (5-14 years) are in economic activities and another

6.6 million in domestic and non-remunerative work. These 16.5 million child labourers, facing physical hardship and educational deprivation during childhood, when adults, would have essential skills to labour, but would lack both physical strength and basic learning to steer their livelihood. Nearly 46 million out-of-school children are not in the workplace either. They are in a state of enforced "idleness", performing some 'marginal, irregular activities'. By not being in school, they lack basic education, and by being idle, lack essential practical skills. Once they become adults, they will join the population of 'ignorant and unemployable'. These 63 million children decisively face an unwelcoming future. In respect of them, the question "are our children really free" has only one answer.

In Mumbai, 446 children were rescued from 226 *zari* workshops. Then, in Delhi, 25 children were rescued from an ill-lit small room converted into *zari* factory. The reality is that interests of the industry and the employers prevail over that of children. The All India Carpet Manufacturers Association claims that child workers, with their soft and nimble fingers, are important for the hand knotted carpet industry.

"Child labour is increasingly becoming an important issue of concern for the world community, with over 250 million children working around the world. India is one of the worlds' leading countries in terms of employing children with an estimated number between 60 and 115 million working children. Most of these children work in the agricultural sector, leaving about 15 per cent of these children in the service and small-scale industries *Child labour in India—An Introspection*, Dibyojyoti Sarkar.

Appendix Table 15.3 (refer Appendix) brings to the surface the fact that the proportion of child labour in certain industries is quite substantial. For instance, in case of the carpet industry in Mirzapur, Uttar Pradesh, 75 per cent of the total workers are children. It may not be difficult to imagine how it would affect the costs and prices of carpet weaving industry if they are rehabilitated and employers are to employ adults in place of them.

The data in Appendix Table 15.4 (refer Appendix) bring out the fact that it is not necessary that a State having high incidence of child labour will also have high percentage of out-of-school children. It is clear from the respective table that the states of Andhra Pradesh, Orissa, Rajasthan, Meghalaya, Karnataka, Chhattisgarh, Uttar Pradesh, West Bengal, and Maharashtra have child labour incidences above the national average, which the States having higher out-of-school children, above the national average, were Bihar, Jharkhand, Uttar Pradesh, Rajasthan, Arunachal Pradesh, Madhya Pradesh, Orissa and Chhattisgarh. It may be noted that Orissa and Arunachal Pradesh are outside the ambit of BIMARU States.

About 67 per cent of the total child workers across Industry were employed in agriculture, as is evident from the data furnished in the Appendix Table 15.5 (refer Appendix). It is followed by manufacturing which employs about 17 per cent of the total number of students employed in the different industry groups. It is important to note that in the respective categories the percentage of girls employed is higher than their male counterparts. In agriculture the percentage of girls employed is 71.1 per cent, which is 8.3 per cent higher than the males employed in agriculture. The figure for the manufacturing as far as the girl child is concerned it stands at 20.5 percent, which is 6.1 per cent higher than the males employed in the respective sector.

Appendix Table 15.6 (refer Appendix) reveals that there were 7 million child workers in the rural areas. The number of child workers for the year 2004-05 in the urban areas, as is evident from the respective table was 1.5 million. That is, the total number of child workers in the urban areas as percentage of them in the rural areas was just 21.4 per cent. It may be safe to infer that the problem is more oriented towards the rural areas where poverty, illiteracy and unemployment are higher. The percentage of child worker in the rural areas was slightly higher than their counterparts in the urban areas, i.e. 0.8 per cent higher in the rural areas than in the urban areas. About two-third of the children were engaged in the family enterprises as helpers, while more than one-third were engaged as paid wage workers. In case of the urban areas the percentage of wage-employed children to the total workers was 49 per cent.

The number of child workers, as is evident from the Appendix Table 15.7 (see Appendices), has declined from 13.3 million in the year 1993-94 to 8.6 million in 2004-05. This is in consonance with the percentage decline in the child labour for the respective period, which was 6.2 per cent in 1993-94 and declined to 3.4 per cent in 2004-05. That is, a decline of 2.8 percentage points during the aforesaid period. This decline can be an outcome of efforts of the government, NGOs, national and international organization working for the complete eradication of child labour.

From the figures Appendix Tables 15.3 and 15.4 (see Appendices), which are based on Appendix Table 15.7, it is quite clear that the magnitude was higher in case of boys than girls. Even in the category of students there is a visible increase in terms of numbers and percentage. This can be viewed as something moving in the desirable direction. In the category of out-of-school category there are positive reflections, as the number of children and the percentage of children in this category has shown a declining trend. It may not be inappropriate to infer that the efforts of the State and the non-governmental organizations have shown their results. The need of the hour is to create awareness among those who are in destitute that for the pretty momentary gains they compromise the future of their children on one or the other pretext. At the same time it is also required to be taken into cognizance that there are families in the destitute who even though recognize that they should send their children to the school and shall not burden their childhood to share their own family responsibilities but because of the compelling economic circumstances they do what they know is incorrect. What they need is a strong support mechanism that will enable them to do what they otherwise will not be able to do.

Conclusion

It is an acknowledged fact that the child policy in India is two-fold. One, a ban on such labour in hazardous industries and second, its regulation in others. It has been found in the studies conducted by the independent researchers and the government agencies—CSO & NSSO that the child continues to work in such hazardous industries and the problem of child labour is yet to be eliminated. A substantial number of children are engaged in agriculture and allied activities at the cost of their overall development and manufacturing, the second highest industry group employing and exploiting the child labour, are unlikely to relent before the law prohibiting child labour and exposing these tender beings to hazardous work because of the wage differentials. These industries are highly fragmented and complex in nature. Enforcement of the law is essential, but it is not enough. The bonded child labourer must have some place else to go. The child's parents must have other options available. The community must support the end of debt bondage for children. In sum, the attack must be holistic-it must work to change the *system* of debt bondage. Elements already in use by community activists and some government officials include: education, including vocational training and popular education, and rural development. The availability of free, compulsory, and quality education is widely regarded as the single most important factor in the fight against bonded and non-bonded child labour. The illiteracy and bonded labour are deeply related with one another, with studies/researches reporting that literacy rates among bonded child labourers are as low as 5 per cent. Precisely, the fight against child labour must be carried out on two fronts : enforcement and prevention.

REFERENCES

Badiwal, Mitesh C. "Child Labour in India: Causes", Governmental Policies and the Role of Education, Child Labour Inquiry.

"Child Labour and India: Embassy of India", Washington D.C.

Devi, R (1985), "Prevalence of Child Labour in India: A Secondary Data Analysis", in *Child Labour and Health: Problems and Prospects*, edited by U. Naidu and K Kapadia: Bombay, Tata Institute of Social Sciences.

"Economic Activities and School Attendance by Children of India: Fifth Quinquennial Survey", NSSO, NSS 50th Round 1993-94, May 1997.

"Employment and Unemployment in India, 1993-94", Fifth Quinquennial Survey, NSSO, Fiftieth Round (July 1993-June1994), and March 1997.

"Employment and Unemployment Situation in India 2004-05", Part-I, NSS Round 61st (July 2004-June 2005), September 2006.

"Employment and Unemployment Situation in India 2005-06",NSS 62nd Round (July 2005-June 2006), January 2008.

Grootaert, C. and R. Kanbur (1995), "Child Labour: An Economic Perspective", *International Labour Review*, 134:187-201.

Human Rights Watch (1996), "The Small Hands of Slavery-Bonded Child Labour in India", New York: Human Rights Watch.

International Labour Organization (1992), World Labour Report, Geneva: International Labour Organization.

International Labour Organization (1993), World Labour Report, Geneva: International Labour Organization.

International Labour Organization (1995), World Labour Report, Geneva: International Labour Organization.

International Labour Organization (2004), *Child Labour: A Text Book for University Students*, International Labour Office.

Jain, S.N. (1985), "Legislation and Government Policy in Child Labour" in *Child Labour and Health: Problems and Prospects*, edited by U. Naidu & K. Kapadia; Bombay, Tata Institute of Social Sciences.

"Key Results on Employment and Unemployment", Fifth Quinquennial Survey, NSSO, Fiftieth Round (July 1993-June 1994), and October 1996.

Mehra-Kerpelman, K. (1996), "Children at Work: How Many and Where?", *World of Work,* 15:8-9.

Nangia, P. (1987), *Child Labour: Cause-Effect Syndrome*, New Delhi: Janak Publishers.

Narayan, A. (1988), "Child Labour Policies and Programmes: The Indian Experience in Combating Child Labour?" in *Young Hands at Work- Child Labour in India*, edited by M. Gupta and K Vol. l, Delhi: Atma Ram & Sons.

Study on Child Abuse: India 2007, Ministry of Women and Child Development, Government of India.

APPENDICES

Appendix Table 15.1 : Statewise Distribution of Working Children according to 1971, 1981, 1991 and 2001 Census in the Age Group of 5-14 Years

Sl. No.	State/UT	1971	1981	1991	2001*	¥	£	$
1	2	3	4	5	6	7	8	9
1	Andhra Pradesh	1627492	1951312	1661940	1363339	19.9	–14.83	–17.97
2	Assam	239349	**	327598	351416	—	—	7.27
3	Bihar	1059359	1101764	942245	1117500	4.003	–14.48	18.6
4	Gujarat	518061	616913	523585	485530	19.08	–15.13	-7.268
5	Haryana	137826	194189	109691	253491	40.89	–43.51	131.1
6	Himachal Pradesh	71384	99624	56438	107774	39.56	-43.35	90.96
7	Jammu & Kashmir	70489	258437	**	175630	266.6	—	—
8	Karnataka	808719	1131530	976247	822615	39.92	–13.72	–15.74
9	Kerala	111801	92854	34800	26156	-16.9	–62.52	–24.84
10	Madhya Pradesh	1112319	1698597	1352563	1065259	52.71	–20.37	–21.24
11	Maharashtra	988357	1557756	1068427	764075	57.61	–31.41	-28.49
12	Chhattisgarh	NA	NA	NA	364572	—	—	—
13	Manipur	16380	20217	16493	28836	23.42	–18.42	74.84
14	Meghalaya	30440	44916	34633	53940	47.56	–22.89	55.75
15	Jharkhand	NA	NA	NA	407200	—	—	—
16	Uttarakhand	NA	NA	NA	70183	—	—	—
17	Nagaland	13726	16235	16467	45874	18.28	1.429	178.6
18	Orissa	492477	702293	452394	377594	42.6	–35.58	–16.53
19	Punjab	232774	216939	142868	177268	–6.8	–34.14	24.08
20	Rajasthan	587389	819605	774199	1262570	39.53	–5.54	63.08

contd...

Appendix Table 15.1 : (*contd...*)

Sl. No.	State/UT	1971	1981	1991	2001*	¥	£	$
21	Sikkim	15661	8561	5598	16457	-45.3	-34.61	194
22	Tamil Nadu	713305	975055	578889	418801	36.7	-40.63	-27.65
23	Tripura	17490	24204	16478	21756	38.39	-31.92	32.03
24	Uttar Pradesh	1326726	1434675	1410086	1927997	8.136	-1.714	36.73
25	West Bengal	511443	605263	711691	857087	18.34	17.584	20.43
26	A & N island	572	1309	1265	1960	128.8	-3.361	54.94
27	Arunachal Pradesh	17925	17950	12395	18482	0.139	-30.95	49.11
28	Chandigarh	1086	1986	1870	3779	82.87	-5.841	102.1
29	D & N Haveli	3102	3615	4416	4274	16.54	22.158	-3.216
30	Delhi	17120	25717	27351	41899	50.22	6.3538	53.19
31	Daman & Diu	7391	9378	941	729	26.88	-89.97	-22.53
32	Goa	NA	NA	4656	4138	—	—	-11.13
33	Lakshadweep	97	56	34	27	-42.3	-39.29	-20.59
34	Mizoram #	NA	6314	16411	26265		159.91	60.05
35	Pondicherry	3725	3606	2680	1904	-3.19	-25.68	-28.96
	Total	10753985	13640870	11285349	12666377	26.84	-17.27	12.24

Note: * The figure includes marginal workers also.

** Census could not be conducted.

Census figures 1971 in respect of Mizoram included under Assam

Computed on the basis of figures of Census 1971, 1981, 1991 and 2001of working children in the age group of 5-14 years

¥ - 4 as % of 3, £ - 5 as % of 4, $ - 6 as % of 5

Appendix Table 15.2 : Percentage of Boys and Girls Working in Different Occupations

Age-group	Boys				Girls			
	A*	B#	C$	D	A±	BØ	Cγ	Dµ
5-12 years	16.33	85.71	14.13	63.36	83.67	14.29	85.87	36.64
13-14 years	23.44	85.96	14.58	56.13	76.56	14.04	85.42	43.87
15-18 years	19.05	85.96	23.08	62.55	80.95	21.13	76.92	37.45
Total	18.84	84	16.77	61.28	81.16	16	83.33	38.72

Courtesy: Study on Child Labour: India 2007, Ministry of Women & Child Development, GOI.

A* & A± % of Boys and Girls respectively working as Child Domestic Workers.

B#& BØ % of Boys/Girls respectively working at kiosks and restaurants.

C$& Cγ % of Boys/Girls, respectively working in Bidi rolling.

D&Dµ of Boys/Girls working, respectively in other occupations.

Appendix Table 15.3: Industrywise Involvement of Child Labour

Industry	Location	Total worker	Child worker	% of child workers to total workers
Carpet weaving	Mirzapur, Bhadohi, UP	2,00,000	1,50,000	75
Carpet weaving	Jammu & Kashmir	4,00,000	1,00,000	25
Match	Sivakasi, Tamil Nadu	Not known	45,000	—
Bidi	India	32,75,000	3,27,500	10
Silk & silk products	Varanasi, UP	11,900	4,409	37
Circus industry	—	—	12% of the entire labour strength	—

Courtesy: "Born to Work: Child Labour in India", Neera Burra.

Appendix Table 15.4 : States with High Incidence of Child Labour and Out-of-School Children (Labour Pool) [5-14 years] 2004-2005

State	Male	Female	Total
Child labour			
Andhra Pradesh	6.1	7.1	6.6
Orissa	5.3	4.6	5.0
Rajasthan	3.8	5.9	4.8
Meghalaya	5.8	3.3	4.6
Karnataka	4.3	4.8	4.6
Chhattisgarh	3.6	5.5	4.5
Uttar Pradesh	4.7	3.4	4.1
West Bengal	4.3	3.2	3.7
Maharashtra	3.2	3.7	3.5
All India	3.5	3.3	3.4

contd...

Appendix Table 15.4 : *(contd...)*

State	Male	Female	Total
Out-of-school			
Bihar	29.9	40.1	34.4
Jharkhand	20.0	27.4	23.4
Uttar Pradesh	20.3	25.7	22.8
Rajasthan	15.6	29.2	22.2
Arunachal Pradesh	19.7	24.1	21.7
Madhya Pradesh	17.3	26.4	21.5
Orissa	17.3	23.7	20.4
Chhattisgarh	14.0	23.0	18.6
All India	15.4	20.8	17.9

Source: Computed on the basis NSS 61st Round 2004-2005, Employment Unemployment Survey.

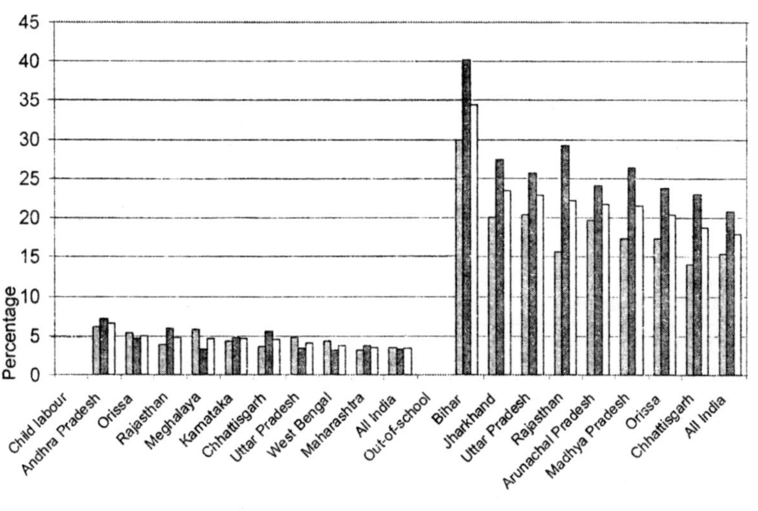

Appendix Figure 15.1: States with High Incidence of Child Labour and Out-of-School Children (Labour Pool) [5-14 years] 2004-2005, (Based on Appendix Table 15.4)

Appendix Table 15.5 : Percentage of Child Workers [5-14 years] across Industry Groups by Gender 2004-2005

Industry group	Boys	Girls	Total
Agriculture	62.8	71.1	66.6
Mining	0.1	0.4	0.2
Manufacturing	14.4	20.5	17.2
Electricity	0.0	0.0	0.0
Construction	3.0	0.8	2.0
Trade	10.6	1.6	6.4
Hotels	4.4	0.4	2.5
Transport	1.2	0.0	0.6
Real estate	1.2	0.0	0.6
Education	0.0	0.0	0.0
Health	0.0	0.1	0.0
Community	1.8	1.6	1.7
Household	0.5	3.4	1.8
Total	100.0	100.0	100.0

Source: Computed on the basis NSS 61st Round 2004-2005, Employment Unemployment Survey.

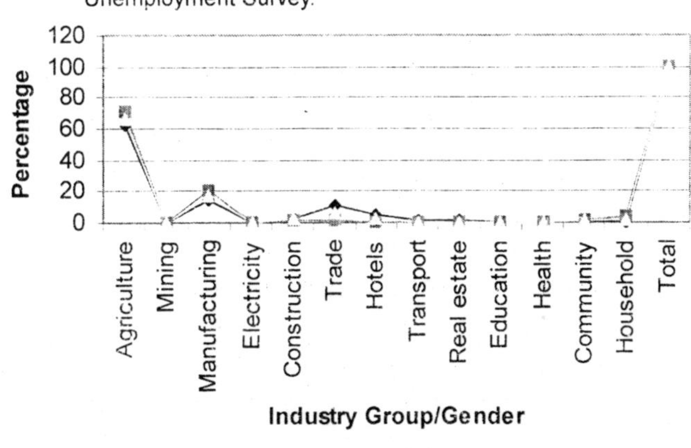

Appendix Figure 15.2 : Percentage of Child Workers [5-14 years] across Industry Groups by Gender 2004-2005. (Based on Appendix Table 15.5)

Appendix Table 15.6 : Child Labour [5-14 years] by Sector 2004-2005

	Rural	Urban	Total
Child labour (million)	7.0	1.5	8.6
Child labour (as percent of all children)	3.7	2.5	3.4
% of self-employed to total workers	66.5	51.0	63.9
% of wage-employed to total workers	33.5	49.0	36.1

Source: Computed on the basis of NSS 61st Round 2004-2005, Employment Unemployment Survey.

Appendix Table 15.7 : Number and Percentage of Children [5-14 years] across Usual Status by Gender.

Usual status	2004-2005			1993-1994		
	Boys	Girls	Total	Boys	Girls	Total
Numbers (million)						
Labour	4.7	3.9	8.6	7.3	6	13.3
Non-worker	16.1	20.5	36.6	22.2	32	54.1
Out-of-school	20.8	24.4	45.2	29.4	38	67.4
Students	113.9	93.2	207.1	84.4	61.3	145.8
All (5-14)	134.7	117.6	252.3	113.9	99.3	213.2

contd...

Appendix Table 7 : *(contd...)*

Usual status	2004-2005			1993-1994		
	Boys	Girls	Total	Boys	Girls	Total
Percentage						
Labour	3.5	3.3	3.4	6.4	6.1	6.2
Non-worker	12	17.4	14.5	19.5	32.2	25.4
Out-of-school	15.4	20.8	17.9	25.9	38.3	31.6
Students	84.6	79.2	82.1	74.1	61.7	68.4
All(5-14)	100	100	100	100	100	100

Notes :

1. Labour includes the unemployed
2. Labour pool includes child labourers and non-workers.
3. Non-workers are children who are neither in school nor at work.

Source : Computed .on the basis of NSS 61st and 50th Rounds, 2004-2005 and 1993-1994, Employment -Unemployment Survey

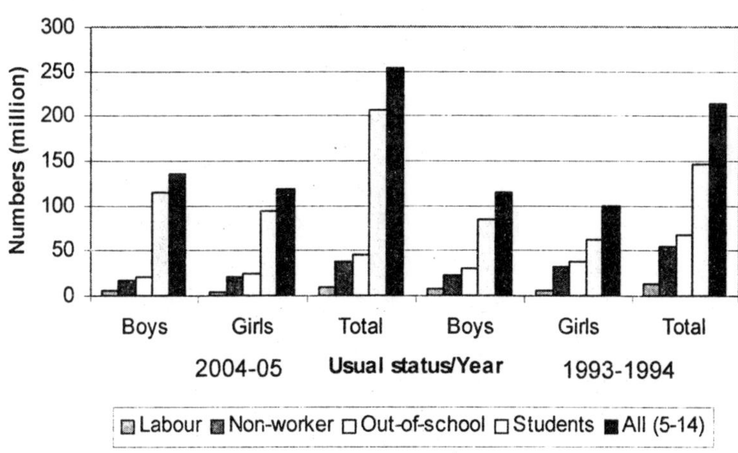

Appendix Figure 15.3 : Number of Children [5-14 years] across Usual Status by Gender (Based on Appendix Table 15.7)

PART - IV

Diversities in Contract Labour : Regional Perspective

16

CONTRACTUAL LABOUR AND DEPRIVATION OF TRIBAL RIGHTS

An Assessment of Community Forest Management in Visakhapatnam District of Andhra Pradesh

V.M. Ravi Kumar

INTRODUCTION

Human rights based approach to development process has acquired prominence in the development discourse, particularly in the third world countries. This has been projected as a missing link to equitable and sustainable development policies related to natural resource management. The human rights based approach along with the sustainable livelihood framework has been recognized as an important framework to analyze the contractual labour problem in India. Forest sector offers an interesting insight on the interplay between human rights advocacy, participatory development process and contractual labour relations. Participatory forest management (PFM) introduced in the names of Joint Forest Management (JFM) in the early 1990s and the Community Forest Management in 2002 in Andhra Pradesh (AP) promised an important role to forest dependent communities to improve their livelihoods by making them equal partners in the forest management. Andhra Pradesh represents one of the progressive forest departments in India, credited to have gone 'beyond' JFM to 'Community Forest

Management' (CFM) with the support of the World Bank funding. This process has initiated a wide range of micro and macro level changes in forest management in terms of governance and livelihoods of the people. However, after one and half decade of implementation, PFM found to have negatively affected the customary rights and livelihoods of people in general and tribals in particular. This chapter examines the process of usurpation of tribal rights in the context of Participatory Forest Management (PFM) in Andhra Pradesh with special focus on the condition of contractual labour in the context of implementation and outcomes of this programme Andhra Pradesh.

To analyze the impact of CFM on tribal rights and livelihoods in Andhra Pradesh, the present study organized into four sections: introduction followed by analytical framework and methodology were mentioned in the first section; section two analyses how the tribal people were excluded in the decision making process related to forest governance; section three shows how the tribal livelihoods were effected after implementation of PFM and final section documents some broad summary and conclusions.

Analytical Framework

After the 1990s, in the context of globalization and free trade policies, people's livelihood systems in the rural areas have undergone significant change. This change could be tracked in two changing livelihood trajectories. One, due to inherent and structural advantages, certain communities experienced upward trajectory of livelihood change. Second, certain communities, mainly majority of SC/ST and to some extent BCs lack of voice and bargaining powers experienced downward trajectory of livelihoods systems (Farrington *et al.*, 2006). It is the downward trajectory that majority of tribal and the rural marginalized poor experienced in the context of globalization in India. In this context, human rights approach to development gained prominence in development discourse. It is argued that "the right to development is an inalienable human right by virtue of which every human person and all people are entitled to participate in, contribute to and enjoy economic, social, cultural and political development, in which all human rights and fundamental freedom can be fully realized".

Apart from important ecological and economic values, forests support livelihoods of the poorest of the poor who are prone to vulnerability and high risk with regard to livelihood options (Profemberger and MecGean, 1998). The World Bank estimated that 240 million people live in forest areas, constituting 18.5 per cent of the 1.3 billion people living on environmental fragile regions (cited in Sunderlin *et al.*, 2005). The Bank also estimated that about 80 per cent of people living in absolute poverty depended on forests as an important source of livelihoods (Castern, 2004). In India, the Bank has estimated that 275 million people depended on forests for various livelihood sources (World Bank, 2006). Tribal people, known in India as *adivasis*, constitute about 8 per cent of India's population (FSI, 1998), or more than 73 million people mainly depended on forests for survival. In Andhra Pradesh, about 10 million, predominantly tribals depended on forests as an important source of livelihood. There has been consistent debate on the question of whether conservation and development processes go together? Studies on livelihood systems attempted to answer this question. They proposed that the efficient institutional arrangements not only improve forest-based livelihoods but also protect environment and wild life (Convey *et al.*, 2002, Farrington *et al.*, 2006). Thus, decentralized institutional structure, which would ensure the equitable distribution of forest resources and sustainable forest management, had acquired prominence in development and policy discourse.

The advocacy of decentralized forest management put forwarded in the context of five macro level process: one, structural adjustment reform introduced in the name of liberalization, where scaling down of the State functions in several sectors was advocated (Burden, 1996; Hobley, 1996; Harris, 2000; Manor, 1999; Sharma, 2006); second, application of livelihood centre approach to forest management (Casten, 2005; Sunderline, 2005; Solesburey, 2003; Baumann, 2000; Norten and Foster, 2001; Hobley and Shelids, 2000) and third process is that the wakening of single party domination and emergence of regional parties, which were compelled to address the voices of marginalized sections (Desai, 2000; Chatterjee, 1999; Kaviraj, 1999; Farrington *et al.*, 2006). And fourth one is that advocacy of human rights based approach to development by various international organisations (World Bank, 1999; Piron and Francis, 2004; Convey, 2002). And fifth process is, emergence of strong social activities trend advocated for restoration of tribal customary rights undermined by the British colonial forest policies (Guha and Gadgil, 1990; Prasad, 2006).

Ever since declaration of international human rights, there has been consistent debate on how to improve the quality of human life by guiding development process. Conventionally, human rights studies mainly focused on civil and political rights for the poor and marginalized. In the context of participatory development paradigm, the human right-based approach to development has acquired prominence. Some studies proposed that development process should be oriented towards achieving human rights. It has been argued that the Human rights based approach to the development process enables the policy makers to create proper space into policy framework for addressing the concerns of marginalized people. In fact, it is lack of decision-making power that is root cause for perpetuation of poverty (Conway, 2002). Development professionals argued that human rights approach not only concentrate on civil and political rights but also with economic, social and cultural rights. It is this study that enables us to locate the sections, which were denied of basic human rights (ODI, 1999).

There has been increasing concern within the international community on the miserable and vulnerable conditions of the rural poors and tribals who depended on forests as an important livelihood source. In the context of participatory development, which aimed to empower poor and vulnerable population, human rights approach to development increasingly becoming popular (Frankovits, 2005; Prion and O'Neil, 2005). Thus, linkages between human rights and development have been projected as a potential factor to address the equity issue in development process. Justice A.S. Anand argued that the main aim of human rights is empowerment of people through human development. For him, human rights approach to development includes an enhancement of capabilities widening of choices and an expansion of freedom (Anand, 2006).

In India, Adivasi communities' integration into mainstream economy, polity and social process has been done forcefully and quit often victimized their livelihoods (Farrington, *et al.*, 2006). A series of government actions weakened the existing management systems substantially over the course of the last century (Serien *et al.*, 2002). This process to a large extent undermined the traditional livelihood systems, which were mainly subsistence oriented. The forceful intrusion of the state into tribal areas was historically resisted by tribal in different parts of the Indian sub-continent in colonial and postcolonial India (Guha, 1989; Shiva, 1986; Rangan, 2005). In Andhra Pradesh, the state intervention in the tribal areas for exploitation of forests was vehemently resisted by the tribals in several occasions (Murali, 1989; Arnold 1990; Himondorf, 1992).

Participatory forest management promises a significant role to tribal communities in forest management to improve their livelihoods (Amitabh Behar, 2002). It provided certain rights to local communities in terms of sharing benefits from the forests, which were given to their management (Profemberger, 1998; Tukka, 2005). But, at implementation level, it negatively affected the livelihoods of the tribes. Some studies argued that the objective of equitable distribution of benefits has fallen short in participatory development resulting in poor performance in poverty eradication effort (Blair, 1996; Adhikari, 2005; Chotracy, 2004; Agrawal and Gupta, 2005). A study, on performance of decentralized governance in natural resource management in Andhra Pradesh and Karnataka, (Baumman *et al.*, 2003) proposed that decentralized forest resource management has not significantly increased access of the rural poors and tribals to forest resources. Some of the works demonstrated that envisaged economic benefits have not been achieved in PFM in India (Agrawal and Gupta, 2005, Kumar, 2002, Reddy *et al.*, 2004, Samata, 2005). In fact, PFM negatively affected the traditional livelihoods of tribals (Sarin *et al.*, 2002). The main reason for this underperformance has been that the ineffectiveness of institutional structure created by forest management. Recently, some studies have demonstrated constraints for efficient institutional functioning in India (Johnson, 2001). Madhu Sarin argued that the attitudinal change in forest department, essential for successful PFM has not been achieved in India (Sarin *et al.*, 2003; Sarin, 2005).

As PFM perceived to be failed to deliver the expected benefits, UNDP advocated that attention to human rights to policy process add the missing link to development and strengthen the equitable development process. This approach based on recognition of real success in tackling poverty and vulnerability requires making the poor and vulnerable a stake, a voice, and real protection in the societies where they live. It is argued that the human rights approach to development enable every person to participate in development not simply as subject rather as a right which would have profound consequence for the design and implementation of developmental activities (UNDP, 2005). Regarding the importance of human rights based approach to development, the ILO conference proposed that 'the people concern shall have the rights to decide their own priorities for the process of development as it effects their lives, beliefs, institutions and spiritual well-being and land they occupy or otherwise use, and to exercise control to the extent possible, over their own economic, social and cultural development' (DFID, 2002).

PFM implementation in India in general and Andhra Pradesh in particular, excluded tribals from meaningful participation and deprived their legitimate rights and livelihoods. They were excluded from decision-making process related to forest management. At the same time, by reclaiming the customary *podu* lands under the CFM, it hampered the livelihood of the tribals (Samata, 2005 and World Rainforest Movement, 2002). The present study shows how the PFM implementation process which has excluded people from governance and deprived livelihoods in Andhra Pradesh.

Methodology of Study

For empirical study, Visakhapatnam district located in costal Andhra Pradesh was selected. It represents high tribal population and density of forests. Three villages VSS were selected by using a stratified random sampling on the basis of the VSS ranking by FD in terms of performance. Qualitative methods such as focused group discussions with different stakeholders, semi-structured discussions, personal interviews, case studies, transect walks and village public meetings were mainly used in the present study.

Table 16.1: Details of the Sample Villages

District	VSS Villages
Visakhapatnam	Sobhakota Gudlamveedi Nandivalasa

Source: Field Survey.

Community Forest Management and Policy Pronouncements

CFM in AP was introduced in 2002 by incorporating several flexible rules to facilitate peoples' participation in forest management.[2] Under CFM, 5000 villages, spread over 14 districts and covering 13, 79,862 hectares of forest area were extended funding. It is funded by the World Bank with the total outlay of Rs. 652 crore for the period of five years. The CFM targeted to benefit 55,000 families living in below poverty line (GoAP, 2002). The main object of the CFM scheme is "to reduce rural poverty through improved forest management with community participation" (GoAP, 2002).

Institutionalization of CFM Process

Envisaged object of CFM is to create an institutional platform for participation of tribals in forest management to improve their livelihoods. But at ground level, FD authoritarian attitude on the one hand and lack of people's awareness on the other narrowed the participatory scope of CFM programme in Andhra Pradesh.

Tribal communities, due to inhospitable environment and geographical isolation stayed away from mainstream socio-economic process (Verma, 1986). However, tribal communities evolved diversified mechanisms in order to co-exist with harsh nature. Through various taboos and regulations sanctioned by traditions and belief systems they conserved the local resources (Gadgil and Guha, 1992). For instance, felling of Mahua trees, which provide multiple benefits was prohibited in tribal areas of Adilabad district. Fruit bearing tress like tamarind were protected by tribals by attributing divinity status to them. These patterns were brought under homogenized and normative management system initiated under JFM resulting in deprivation of traditional knowledge and livelihoods.

Formation Management Committee

General Body is an association consisting of all villagers a members and this body elect a Management Committee (MC) is a representative agency to execute VSS works. As per CFM guidelines 15 elected members constitute a MC. Thus, MC is a democratically elected body and accountable to people in VSS management. But MCs were generally dominated by the FD officials. It was observed that elections for MC posts were rarely conducted, and mostly FD officials nominate the members for MC. Generally, FD officials nominate the members belong to socio-economic dominate sections and show loyalty to the department.

Institutional Structure of VSS Village Preparation of Micro Plan

The concept of Micro Plain (MP) in CFM is aimed at incorporating the local priorities and management practices in VSS management. In CFM policy, emphasis was given to involvement of communities while conducting the Participatory Rural Appraisal (PRA). But as (Profemberger, 1998) argues, since FD field staff needs to create thousands of VSS, they do not have time and training to prepare indepth plans with community members.

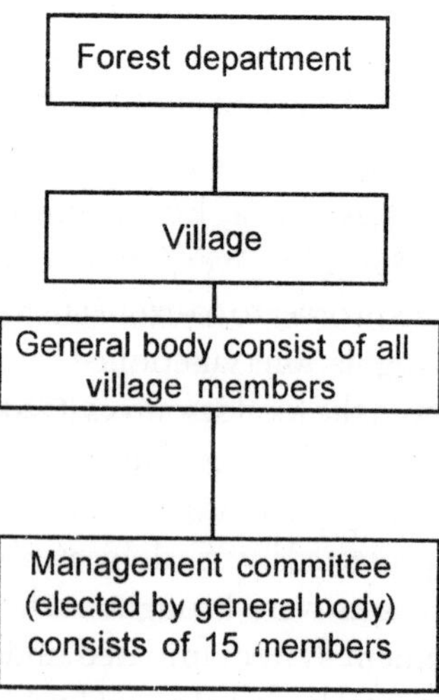

In the tribal areas of Visakhapatnam MPs were prepared by FD officials without interaction with local communities and their priorities. In case of species selection, design of various works, and other decisions, FD officials played a dominant role. For instance, in Gudlem Vedi and Sobhakota villages, the plants selected were not of villagers' choice but by the FD. In many occasions, villagers did not resist FD officials and their fear that funding may not come to their village. Due to this, local tribal forest utilization practices and their priorities were not incorporated into MP.

Decision-Making Process in VSS Management

MC is a representative body to carry out the management of VSS works. They are expected to take decisions in VSS management with the consent of all GB members. But at implementation level in villages, FD officials hold enormous power in implementation of the programme. This led to prioritisation of FD choices in decision-making process in VSS management. As per CFM guidelines, GB meeting should be conducted once in a six months and MC meeting should be organized in every month. In the sample villages, frequency of meetings and attendance of members have come down. In Visakhapatnam it is observed that MC/GB meetings are conducted at the time of fund arrival. As and when fund arrives, FD officials conduct GB/MC meetings and take all-important decision on management of VSS. Due to illiteracy and lack of awareness tribals simply obeys the guidance of FD officials.

The nature of the role played by different actors in decision-making process related to VSS management indicates that important decisions of VSS management like the forest area to be given to VSS for management, identification of works, species selection, supervision of works, management and conservation models to be adopted by VSS and other important decisions are generally taken by mainly FD officials (Table 16.2). Tribals were not given due role in decision-making process related to VSS management. In fact, tribal women, old people who depended on firewood selling, and small grazers were not given any role in decision-making process. It is observed that majority of women in tribal areas still could dare to come before officials.

Table 16.2: Nature of the Decision taken for VSS Management

Functional aspects	VSS, GB/MC	FD	Other NGO
1. Organization of meetings, GB/MC	√	√	√
2. Selection of forest areas for VSS		√	
3. Micro plan preparation	√	√	√
4. Identification of works		√	
5. Species selection		√	
6. Carrying out of works		√	
7. Supervision of works		√	
8. Estimating the costs		√	
9. Funds allocation		√	
10. Distribution of harvesting income		√	
11. Distribution of forest products	√		
12. Entry point activities	√	√	√
13. Minute writings		√	√
14. NTFP value additions		√	
15. Distribution of livelihood enhancement activities		√	
16. Marketing of forest products		√	
17. Selection of training programme		√	

Source: Data from Field Survey.

Apparently little autonomy has been given to MCs to act independently. The decision-making process in MC dominated FD (Table 16.3). Important decisions like species selection, identification of works, allocation of funds for works was taken by FD officials in MC meetings. Especially in tribals areas decisions related to VSS management taken by FD officials with less consideration to people's views. In marketing of VSS harvesting products, FD plays a monopolistic role.

Transparency

Transparency in financial transactions is an important prerequisite in any developmental programme to achieve success. In case of CFM, people were dissatisfied with the transparency issues, particularly with allocation of funds to their estimates of VSS works.

All passbooks, muster role registrars, estimate copies and other documents in our sample village were not given to VSS MCs. They were kept with the range officers. Community Extension Worker for Sobhakota VSS in Visakhapatnam informed that in the entire Paderu range no VSS has their documents with them. In spite of several complaints to DFO no action was initiated to address this problem.

Women Empowerment

Women participation in participatory development schemes has been perceived as an important factor for successful implementation of scheme. CFM policy proposed 50 per cent membership in GB/MC. Besides either of VSS chairperson or vice-chairperson posts are reserved for women.

Though the CFM rules ensure the equal membership for women in GB/MC, women participation in VSS activities found to be passive. In the tribal areas of Visakhapatnam district, women participation found to be very low in VSS management activities. FD officials found it easy to manipulate women than men. In three-sample district of Visakhapatnam district, women were given vice-president posts. It was observed that on many occasions, women are not called for MC meetings. In fact, decisions being taken by MC were not even informed to women.

Table 16.3 : Women Representation in MC

District /VSS	No. of MC members	CP	V. C P
Visakhapatnam			
Sobhakota	8	Male	Woman
Gudlamveedi	8	Male	Woman
Nandivalasa	8	Male	Woman

MC= Management Committee, CP= Chairperson, VCP= Vice-Chairperson.

The Panchayat Extension Act to Scheduled Areas Act (PESA), 1996 and VSS

Under the 73rd Constitutional Amendment Act, Panchayats has emerged as one of the potential stakeholders in forestry management and sharing of benefits derived from it. The Panchayat is now empowered to legislate on matters (the powers and functions devolved to the Panchayats as specified in the Eleventh Schedule of the Indian Constitution. 15 of the States are yet to devolve the powers to the Panchayats, Andhra Pradesh is also one such State which has not devolved all the powers to the Panchayat) relating to forestry that include land improvement, soil conservation, watershed development, SF, farm forestry, minor forest produce, fuel and fodder etc. Extension of this Act to Schedule V areas has wider implications on forest resources in tribal areas (as specified in the V Schedule). The Gram Sabha or the Panchayat is endowed with right to ownership of NTFP. These rights to Gram Sabha on decision making related to NTFP management could give better voice to communities. But the PESA in AP has not yet been operationalised.

The local governance process initiated after community forest management appears to be sound on paper, but in practice, tribal people were not given practical role in decision-making process. It is also observed that FD often encourages village conflicts within villages.

Some villagers in Sobhakota felt that community forest management, instead of giving prosperity to villagers, it crating rift between different groups. Thus, the envisaged goal of people's involvement in decision-making process in forest management still remained as distant reality in the case of tribal of Visakhapatnam.

IMPACT OF PFM ON LIVELIHOODS

Livelihood Impact of Community Forest Management

In Andhra Pradesh, as per latest estimates, about 10 per cent of population, predominantly belong to scheduled caste and tribes and the rural poors have been critically deepened on forest products as an important source of livelihood. The CFM programme, aimed meeting the livelihood needs with multidimensional strategies. Table 16.4 shows the livelihood dependency of people on forests in our study sites.

Table 16.4: Different Livelihood Activities in Study Cities (in terms of proportions)

District/ VSS	Own culti-vation	Podu	Farm activities, labour	Non-farm activi-ties	Fores-ts/ NTFP/ podu	VSS works	Migration	Total
Visakhap-atnam								
S. Kota	10	35	25	–	25	10	–	100
G. Veedi	15	40	15	–	20	10	–	100
N. Valasa	20	25	20	5	20	5	5	100

Source: Field study.

The Table 16.4 shows that forests provide an important source of livelihoods, particularly in agricultural lean season. In tribal villages, forest dependency is significantly high, together with VSS works. In Visakhapatnam, it constitutes above 50 per cent. Having completed most of the treatment practices in JFM, CFM focused on income generating activities with diversified practices. Due to this, wage based works have significantly declined. The Table 16.5 shows the wage works undertaken in CFM.

Table 16.5: Pattern of Wage Employment in different VSS Villages

Name of VSS village	Number of the wage days promised	Actual number of work days	Wage rate for male	Wage rate for female	Number of days taken for payment
S. Kota	60	30	45	35	40
G. Veedi	55	25	40	40	38
N. Valasa	60	32	48	40	35

Wage Employment

After PFM, neighbouring forests of particular villages were given for the management of local communities. The management responsibility was given to them under the guidance of the forest department. The communities were empowered to undertake different forms of works ranging from forest produce collection to building of social assets such as schools, wells and community halls. However, this process was carried out by the labour within the members of general body committee. The nature of the labour employed was basically a contractual labour in nature. It is in the sense that the works of VSS after estimation and sanction of money were undertaken general body, which appoints labour for execution of work. Their wages rates were not fixed; rather, they share the money after completion of works. Thus, the old concept of daily wage labour was replaced by the contractual employment based upon the requirements of works and financial support.

The component of wage employment to tribal people under CFM comes under unorganized contractual labour. In fact, this is the only substantial benefit to the people as part of this scheme. In tribal areas, less wages were paid to people. As tribal people afraid of FD do not question the low wages in VSS works. At the same time, time taken for payment of wage is on an average about 40 days. This resulted in widespread discontentment on VSS works among people. In Visakhapatnam district, *podu* lands were brought under VSS management with the promise of providing wage employment to the tribes. It was observed that the wage employment days per year are not more than 30 with the wage of Rs. 20-25. Tribals informed that this income is inadequate and cannot compensate the income from *podu*.

Income Generating Activities

In CFM, FD undertook income generating activities with diversified strategies such as NTFP value addition initiatives, honey bees keeping, preparation of vermi compost, supply of leaf plates preparation machinery, harvesting of valuable wood and other initiatives. These are meant for generating income from forest products under the supervision of VSS MC Committee. However, our interviews with FD officials in Adilabad and Visakhapatnam inform that these experiments were not successful due to lack of conducive atmosphere. At the same time, while introducing NTFP value edition activities, FD did not impart necessary skills and training to tribals. Due this, they could not utilise these opportunities and convert them into good income generating source.

Tenural Issues

Colonial and post-colonial State policy interventions in the tribal areas in Andhra Pradesh aimed at exploiting forests at the cost of tribal livelihoods. The Madras Forest Act of 1882 had imposed the State control over forests in Coastal Andhra and Rayalaseema. It divided forests into reserved forests and unreserved forests (Brandis, 1883). Under this act, most of the agency forests were declared as state forests and traditional access of tribals was treated an illegal entry. In Telangana, the Hyderabad Forest Act 1945 imposed the State ownership over forests. Under these Acts, the State had declared forests as its property by not recognizing customary peoples' access. During forest settlement, the access of people to forests was defined by forest settlement officers as concession or privileges allowed to be exercised as long as the State permits. Having lost their livelihoods tribals actively participated in the Manyam Rebellion under the leadership of legendary Ramaraju in 1922 (Murali 1989). In Telangana region, the Gonds' leader Komeram Bhiem led massive revolt against the Nizam government (Himondorf, 1985). These were the example of tribal discontent on the intrusion of the State policies, which affected their livelihoods.

The Social Forestry programme was introduced in Andhra Pradesh in the 1980s to promote mono-cultural plantations in encroached forestlands to serve the needs of industry. This had severely affected livelihoods and food security of the tribes in AP. Participatory forest management in the form of JFM, or CFM appears as yet another attempt of FD to consolidate its position and control forest encroachment and people's access to forests. In Andhra Pradesh, JFM was funded by the World Bank. Local communities were granted usufructory rights to enjoy 25 per cent of forests products in return to their protection. It was increased to 100 per cent on all NTFPs. However, this policy did not give any tenurial security to communities. Thus, PFM in Andhra Pradesh did not ensure any tenurial security to local communities. As a result, PFM in Andhra Pradesh remained as wage employment generation scheme to the forest dependent communities. Entire programme is linked with external funding. Villagers and FD take interests and conduct meetings only when fund arrives.

Podu Cultivation/Encroachment

Shifting cultivation or *Podu* in Visakhapatnam has been an important source of livelihoods for the tribals. This has been a contentious issue between the tribals and FD. By 1994, over 3,27,742 ha of forestland was under illicit cultivation. However, though tribals do not have legal *pattas* on these lands, they have been cultivating for long period of time and an important source of livelihood. Tribal people critically depended on *podu* for survival (Reddy *et al.*, 2006).

Especially *podu* cultivation practiced by the tribals mainly in Visakhapatnam has been a problematic issue in CFM. Generally about 20 per cent of income of tribes comes from *podu*, besides providing food security. There has been continuous struggle between FD and tribals on *podu* practice. FD treats *podu* as ecologically detrimental, though its scientific credentials are in vague[3]. Under JFM, about 37,000 ha of *podu* land was brought under treatment practices (Samaj Vikas, 2006). It is estimated that in Visakhapatnam, about 20,000 hectares of *podu* was brought under JFM treatment (Mamata, 2002). Though natural cycle of *podu* had come down and became settled agriculture, tribals with highly diversified cropping pattern (on an average they cultivate 10 varieties of crops in each *podu* patch) protect soil fertility and nutrients.

FD claims that *podu* reclamation under JFM/CFM was done voluntary. But according to local NGOs *podu* land surrender was not voluntarily surrendered by the tribes, it was done with two methods. One, compensation promises by FD, which were not honoured and second forceful surrender. Due to this, many Adivasi families lost their livelihoods (Samata, 2005). Local NGOs informed that FD treats *podu* lands as encroachment and threaten tribals to surrender land to VSS management.

Podu has been practiced in all the three sample villages in Visakhapatnam, and most of the tribal households had *podu* land, although they had only temporary *patta* ('D')[4]. FD considers *podu* cultivators as *de jure* and *de facto* encroachers, and do not recognize their rights which were not recorded in legal documents. After the inception of JFM, the FD has taken away most of the *podu* land from tribals not having 'D' *pattas*. Some times, FD bribed the VSS members to identify the lands of households without 'D' *pattas*. Eventually these lands were brought under JFM treatment. Tribal activist groups have strongly criticized FD methods as they deprived the livelihood of tribes. Even the DFO of Padure felt that *podu* is a social problem and needs to be treated more sympathetically.

Podu/Encroachment and JFM in the Study Villages

In the Sobhakota village, the FD had taken away a few hectares of *podu* land well before the inception of PFM. But strangely, there was no serious resistance except for mild protests. This silence was mainly due to the compensation and rehabilitation promises made by the FD, although they have not been kept. The FD promises of compensation were kept in the case of Nandivalasa, where the

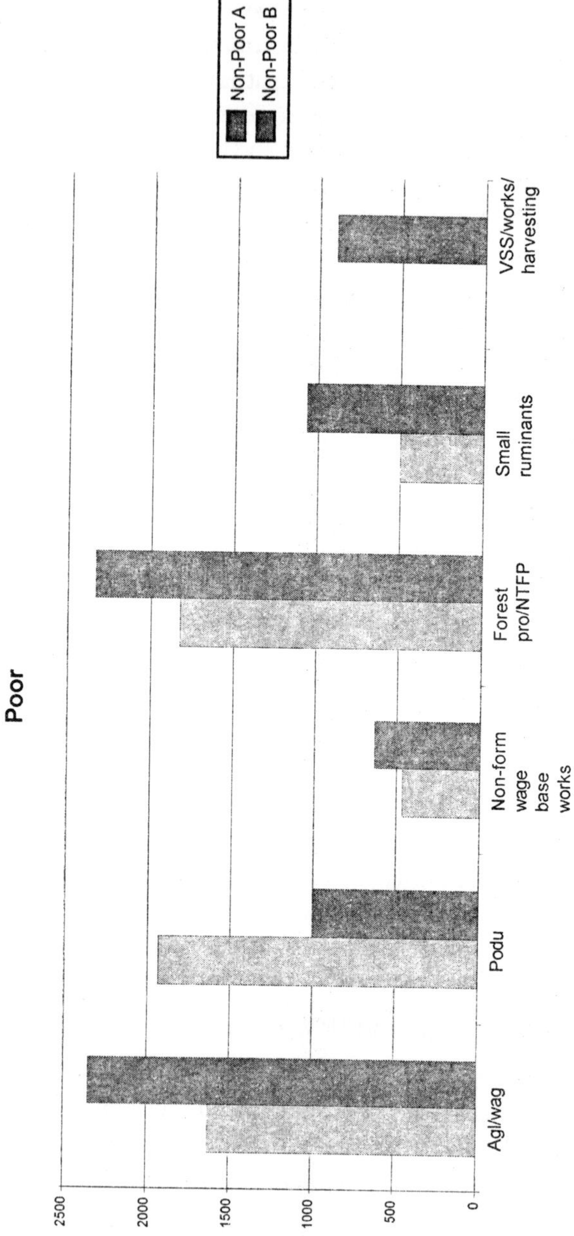

Fig. 16.1 : Change in Income for Poor Households Before/After JFM in Visakhapatnam District

Fig. 16. 2 : Change in Income for Non-Poor Households Before/After JFM in Visakhapatnam District

affected families were helped with "roof tiles" (about Rs. 2,000-4,000 per household). Twenty of the 30 families were also promised the award of *pattas* (tenure rights) to the lower part of the hillock where they were practicing *podu*.

Income Lost Due to CFM

In Visakhapatnam, income from *podu* constitutes 30 per cent for the poor and 28 per cent for the non-poor. Total income has declined due to the reclamation of *podu* lands under the JFM. This is one of the reasons for the relatively low growth in gross households' income in this district. Decline of income from *podu* is 18 per cent for poor and 20 per cent for non-poor. This decline is not only in terms of income but also food security. Though the decline of *Podu* income is compensated to some extent by the VSS wage works, which constitutes 11 per cent for poor and 10 per cent for non-poor, tribals lost their regular income and food security due to JFM (Figs. 16.1 and 16.2).

Cut across all sections in tribal areas, *podu* cultivation not only provides regular income but also constitute an important coping up mechanism of tribes in terms of food security. Moreover, in majority cases tribals have been cultivating *podu* for more than 25 years and it was reported that fresh clearing for *podu* has become uncommon owing to scarcity of fresh patches. However, tribals protect soil fertility with different mechanisms. Importantly, they grew diversified crops sometimes more than 20 varities in one field, which not only protect soil nutrients but also provide food security.

Most of the *podu* lands were brought under JFM and CFM, mainly under coffee plantation. This has deprived the tribals who deepened on *podu* for not only income but also food. It shows the importance of *podu* in the livelihoods of the tribals in Andhra Pradesh. It also shows the relevance of the Scheduled Tribes and other Traditional Forest Dwellers Bill 2006, which intends to recognise the rights of forest dependent communities over the land they have been cultivating. Tribal activities and some of the academicians are demanding that historical injustice done to tribals could be undone by recognition of traditional rights of tribals (Prasad 2006). The Resettlement Action Plan proposed by the FD to compensate tribals who lost *podu* land mainly concentrated on land development which again mainly likely to benefit landed communities within tribal and landless who depended on *podu* continue to be deprived of income and food security.

SUMMARY AND CONCLUDING OBSERVATIONS

Community forest management projected as an efficient instrument to reduce poverty in tribal areas has negatively affected the livelihood of tribals. PFM has destroyed the traditional dependency of the tribals on forests, which was used for subsistence requirements. Especially old people, women and other vulnerable groups within the tribal society were kept out of CFM implementation process. Tribals were not given autonomy in VSS management. FD officials dominated the VSS management and tribals choices and preferences in forest management were neglected. This had undermined the meaningful participation of the tribals in CFM programme implementation process. Reclamation of *podu* lands under JFM/CFM and reduction of wage employment increased the vulnerability of the poor tribes. This resulted in threat to livelihood security of the tribals in Visakhapatnam district. RAP to *podu* victims is yet to take place. Therefore, capacity-building needs to be coupled with creation of rights could make the tribals as equal partners in forest management.

NOTES

1. This is from Article 1 of the Declaration of the Rights to Development, 1986, quoted in S.R. Osmani, Globalization and the Human Rights Approach to Development, University of Ulster, U K, 2005.
2. Number of VSS committees constituted under Participatory Forest Management in Andhra Pradesh has significantly increased, at present 8,343 VSS are in function and covers 23.18 Lakh Hectares of the Forest land under the control of the Forest Department. (Government of Andhra Pradesh, Economic Survey 2005-06, Hyderabad, 2006, p. 46).
3. Some works have argued that podu is a suitable form of cultivation in hill slopes in India, Ramakrishna " Shifting Cultivation in India" NBT, Delhi, 1995. N. Gopala Rao, Impact of Rehabilitation Programmes on Shifting

Cultivation in Andhra Pradesh, in K. Mohan Rao and others (Ed), Displacement and Rehabilitation of tribes in India with special reference Andhra Pradesh; M.D. Subash Chandran, "Shifting Cultivation, Sacred Groves and Conflicts in Colonial Forest Policy in Western Ghats". *Nature and Orient: the Environmental History of South and Southeast Asia*, Ed, Richers Grove and others. Pp. 674-707.

4. 'D' form patta is a temporary patta granted by revenue authority to people with the consent of FD for a temporary period of time. It does not conform legal rights, FD or Revenue department may cancel it at any point of time. These pattas were periodically reviewed by both FD and Revenue department.

REFERENCES

Adhikari Bhim (2005), "Poverty, Property Rights and Collective Action: Understating the Distributive Aspects of Common Property Resource Management", *Environment and Development Economics*, Vol. 10, pp. 7-31.

Agrawal Arun and Gupta, Krishna (2005), "Decentralization and Participation: The Governance of Common Pool Resources in Nepal's Terai", *World Development*, Vol. 33, pp. 1101-1114.

Anand A.S. (2006), *Right to Development*, NHRC Convention held in Geneva.

Blair W. Mary (1996), "Democracy, Equity and Common Property Resources Management in the Indian Sub-continent", *Development and Change*, Vol. 27, pp. 475-499.

Bardhan Pranab (1996), "Decentralized Development", *Indian Economic Review*, Vol. XXXI, No. 2, pp. 139-156.

Baumann, Pari, Rajesh Ramakrishnan, Manish Dubey, Rajiv K. Raman, and John Farrington, (2003), "Institutional Alternatives and Options for Decentralized Natural Resource Management in India", *Overseas Development Institute*, Working Paper 230.

Brandas D. (1883), *Suggestions regarding Forest Administration in Madras Presidency*, Government Press, Madras.

Castern Tukka, (2005), "Ownership and Incentives in Joint Forest Management: A Survey", *Development Policy Review*, Vol. 23, pp. 78-104.

Chaterjee, P. (1999), *State and Politics in India*, Oxford University Press, New Delhi.

Convey Tim, Caroline Moster, Andy Norton and Jhon Farrington (2002), "Rights and Livelihoods Approaches: Exploring Policy Dimensions", Overseas Development Institute.

Desai, M. (2000), *Development and Nationhood: Essays in the Political Economy of South Asia*, Oxford University Press, New Delhi.

Farrington J, Priya Deshinkar, Crig Johnson and Daniel Start (2006), *Policy Windows and Livelihood Futures: Prospects for Poverty Reduction in Rural India*, Oxford University Press, New Delhi.

Frankovits A, (2002), *Rules to Live By: The Human Rights Approach to Development*, Vol. XVII.

Gadgil M. and Guha (1992), *This Fissure Land: An Ecological History of India*, Oxford University Press, New Delhi.

Haller Tobias (2002), "The Understanding of Institutions and their Link to Resource Management from a New Institutionalism Perscriptive", IP, Institutional Change and Livelihood Strategies, Working Paper No. 1.

Harris J. (2000), De-politicizing Development: The World Bank and Social Capital, *Left Word*, New Delhi.

Hobbley, Mary (1996), *Institutional Change Within the Forestry Sector: Centralized Decentralization*, Working Paper 92, Overseas Development Institute.

Kaviraj, S. (Ed), (1998), *Politics in India*, Oxford University Press, New Delhi.

Kumar, Sanjay (2002), "Does Participation in Common Pool Resource Management Help the Poor?: A Social Cost-Benefit Analysis of Joint Forest Management in Jharkhand, India", *World Development*, pp. 763-782.

Manor, James (1999), *The Political Economy of Democratic Decentralization*, Washington, DC, The World Bank.

Prasad, A. (2006), "Conservation and Tribal Development in the Forest Rights Bill", *Social Scientist*, Vol. 34, No. 7-8, July-August 2006.

Prion and O'Neil (2005), *Integration of Human Rights into Development: A Synthesis of Down Approach and Experiences*, Overseas Development Institute, Briefing Paper.

Piron, L. H, Watkins F. (2004), *DFID Human Rights Review: A Review of How DFID Has Integrated Human Rights into its Work.*

Poffenberger, M, McGreen (Eds.), (1996), *Village, Voice, Forest Choices: Joint Forest Management in India*, Oxford University Press, New Delhi.

Samatha (2005), *Andhra Pradesh Community Forest Management Project: A Preliminary Independent Evaluation of a World Bank Forestry Project*, Hyderabad.

Sharma, C.H. (2006), "Decentralization Dilemma: Measuring the Degree and Evaluating the Outcomes", *The Indian Journal of Political Science*, Vol. LXVII, No. 1, Jan-Mar, 2006, 49-64.

Solesbury, Willam (2003), *Sustainable Livelihoods: A Case Study of the Evolution of DFID Policy*, Working Paper 217, Overseas Development Institute.

Solesbury Willam (2003), *Sustainable Livelihoods: A Case Study of the Evolution of DFID Policy*, Working Paper 217, Overseas Development Institute.

Sundar Nandini, Roger Jaffery and Neil Thin (Ed.) (2001), *Branching Out: Joint Forest Management in India*, Oxford University Press, New Delhi.

Sunderline, W. Angelsen A. Brian, *et al.* (2005), "Livelihoods, Forests and Conservation in Developing Countries: An Overview", *World Development*, Special Issues, Vol. 33, No. 9, pp. 1383-14302.

World Bank (2006), *Unlocking Opportunities for Forest Development People in India*, Vol. 1, Oxford University Press, New Delhi.

APPENDIX

HH Income Sources before/after JFM in Visakhapatnam District

Sl. No.	**Sources**	**Poors**	
		Before	**After**
1	Agl/wages	1625	2350
2	Podu	1933.33	1000
3	Non-form wage base works	466.66	633.33
4	Forest produce/ NTFP	1816.66	2333.33
5	Small ruminants	500	1066.66
6	VSS works/ harvesting	—	900.00
7	**Total**	**6341.65**	**8283.32**
Sl. No.	**Sources**	**Non-poors**	
		Before	**After**
1	Agl/Wages	2333.33	3400
2	Podu	1833.33	666.66
3	Non-form wage base works	400	683.33
4	Forest produce/ NTFP	1516.66	2000
5	Small ruminents	500	1000
6	VSS works/ harvesting	—	900
7	**Total**	**6583.32**	**8643.99**

17

WAGE-EMPLOYMENT PATTERN OF CONTRACTUAL LABOURERS IN U.P.'S RURAL ECONOMY

Some Facts and Possibilities

BHASKAR MAJUMDAR

The Problem

It has been well acknowledged now that agriculture by itself cannot ensure productive employment on a regular basis to the size of population settled in India's rural economy. Rapid urbanization of the rural economy is also not a feasible choice. It has also been accepted by the alert economists that forced migration—rural huts to urban slums—is not a sensible option. It has also been acknowledged that Lewis-type frame failed to deliver results in India's limited industrialization attained so far by entry of increasing workers released from rural-agricultural economy. The problem, thus, has been identified as ensuring measures to keep the locally settled population in India's rural economy confined within. This population is thought to be unskilled and dependent on manual works. The solution has been identified as public works in India's rural economy (Majumdar, 2008).

The Scope

The basic assumption is that there exists post-Green Revolution co-existence of surplus stocks of foodgrains with the government than what is distributed. This can be utilized as food for (in exchange of) works for the job seekers. The second assumption is that there exists rural unemployment and underemployment in a situation of limited possibility of additional labour absorption in agriculture. In parallel, this assumption is perhaps associated with limits to extension of area under cultivation as well as India's low-growth land-based economy. The Third assumption was the existence of Common Property Resources (CPR) useable for absorption of workers on the queue. Based on these assumptions, the Food for Work (FFW) programme was launched in India in April 1977 to create wage-employment and public productive assets, particularly rural infrastructure. The programme was supposed to ensure also post-Green Revolution utilization of surplus foodgrains stored in the Food Corporation of India (FCI) in a state of poverty and hunger (Ghosh, 1988, p. 656; Sharma, 1980, p. 2-3; Narayana *et al.*, 1991, p. 210).

Food for Work is essentially a rural works programme that evolved to employ the rural workforce, particularly during off-peak agricultural season and drought-prone areas. This, at the same time, was expected to accelerate the growth of the rural economy directly through creation and utilization of rural productive assets. The rural works can also play a positive role for the workers in situations of oligopsonistic labour markets by reducing the power of a single buyer of labour and the employer as a rent-seeker (Narayana *et al*, 1991, p. 207, 209, 216). During the 1980s, the Food for Work Programme came to be redesigned as the National Rural Employment Programme (NREP) and Rural Landless Employment Guarantee Programme (RLEGP).

This chapter explores the possibilities of labour absorption in the rural economy of India through the Food for Work programme. The exploration is based on an empirical study carried out recently in some districts in Uttar Pradesh. The rest of the chapter is structured as follows. In Section III, we present the objectives, methodology, study zone and sample of the study. In Section IV, we explain the functioning of the Food for Work programme through work opportunities and wages. In Section V we present the major problems inherent in execution of Food for Work programme. Finally, in Section VI we offer conclusions and recommendations.

Objectives, Methodology, Study Zone and Sample

We covered four districts from four regions by administrative-geographic division of the State of Uttar Pradesh (UP). These districts were Chitrakoot, Deoria, Pilibhit and Pratapgarh. We selected two blocks from each district, thus selecting a total of eight blocks. From each block we selected two Gram Panchayats (GPs), thus, selecting a total of 16 GPs. We selected public works undertaken by the Panchayati Raj Institutions (PRIs) in a three-tier system, namely, Zilla, Block and Gram. We considered the selected works into two categories. One category included watershed development, soil conservation and minor irrigation. The other category included works related to roads, buildings and other infrastructure. The selected works thus come under 'public rural' category as opposed to 'private rural' and 'public urban' like micro enterprises, khadi and village industries, self-employment, etc. Rural non-farm works are either demand-driven or poverty-determined. In case of the latter, it becomes the State concern. Thus, the 'public rural' works become the State-space for execution. The selected activities in the study were non-farm in nature. But the operationalization of these non-farm activities will obviously have impact on farm behaviour.

We selected two works from these two categories randomly. These selected works as planned were executed by each of the tiers, namely, ZP, BP and GP. We selected five (5) workers from each work randomly. These workers were linked with works executed by ZP, BP and GP. In addition, five (5) beneficiaries were selected from each district and block under beneficiary-oriented scheme (BOS) implemented by ZP and BP. The total number of workers in the sample was six hundred twenty (Table 17.1 and Flow Chart 17.1).

Table 17.1 : Sample Size

Units	Description	Number
Districts	4 districts from U. P.	4
Blocks	2 blocks from each district	2 × 4 = 8
Gram Panchayats	2 Gram Panchayats from each block	2 × 2 × 4 = 16
Works	4 works from each district, block and Gram Panchayat	4 (4 + 8 + 16) = 112
Beneficiaries	(i) 5 beneficiaries from each work	5 × 112 = 560
	(ii) 5 beneficiaries from each district under beneficiary oriented scheme of Zilla Prarishad	5 × 4 = 20
	(iii) 5 beneficiaries from each block under beneficiaries oriented scheme of Block Samiti	5 × 2 × 4 = 40
Total beneficiaries		760

Source: Majumdar, Bhaskar, 2004, Sampoorna Grameen Rozgar Yojana (Food for Work Component), Report submitted to Planning Commission, India.

We collected secondary data on rural employment from the Muster Roll maintained by the Government by selected indicators under Food for Work for a period of three years, 2001-04. The indicators include works executed by types, number of days worked, wage rate and wage bill paid, gender division of labour, regional pattern of employment, types of workers like local or migrated etc.

Flow Chart 17.1 : Sample Procedure and Size

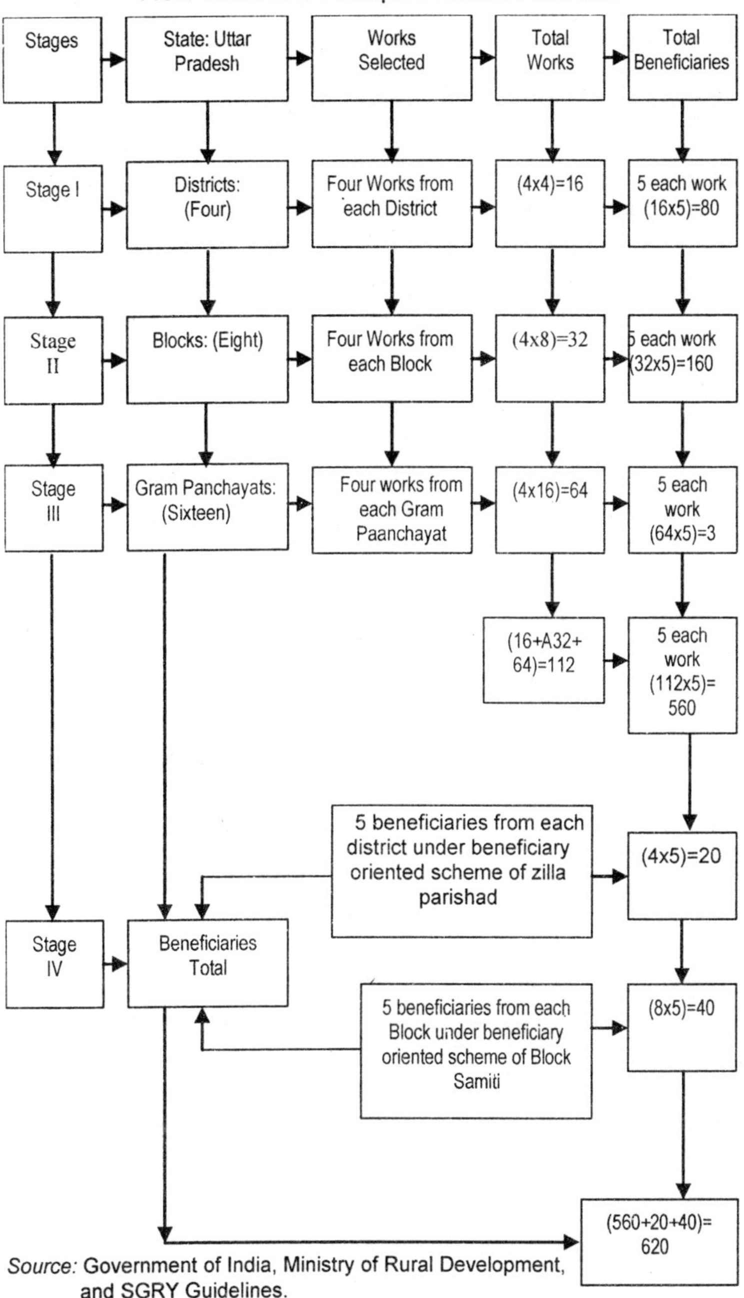

Source: Government of India, Ministry of Rural Development, and SGRY Guidelines.

Work Opportunities and Wages in Food for Work programme

The study was conducted in the broad frame of India's informal or unorganized economy that envelops 92.0 per cent of the country's workforce (NCEUS, 2008, p. 5). In the selected regions and works by types covering all the tiers of PRIs, 94.0 per cent of the wageworkers got work opportunity at least once during 2001-04. Around 40.0 per cent of the total workers got work opportunity twice. The workers were mostly engaged in the construction of rural link roads. Other construction activities e.g. construction of '*Nali*' (narrow drain), Hand Pump and rejuvenation of sources of drinking water also absorbed workers. The works like forestation and construction of school buildings were neglected most.

On average, workers' days per household during the three-year period, 2001-2004, were 27.7. Thus, per year it was 9.2 days. It was highest for drought-prone district Chitrakoot (38.3 per cent). Of the total workers' days generated in this district, women workers' days were 30.67 per cent. Workers' days created by women workers over

Table 17.2 : Workers' Days Generated and Average Workers' Days Worked Per Household (Total and Percentage of Beneficiary Population)

Districts	Male	Female	Total*	Workers' days per household (In reference period)**	Workers' days per year per household
Chitrakoot	4115	1821	5936	38.3	12.8
Pratapgarh	3374	50	3424	22.1	7.3
Deoria	4134	36	4170	26.9	8.9
Pilibhit	3626	24	3650	23.5	7.8
Total	15249	1931	17180	27.7	9.2

Note: *The workers' days calculated on the basis of response from households. We have substituted workers' day for man-day.

** Reference period covered 2001-02, 2002-03 and 2003-04.

Source: Field Survey, 2004.

Table 17.3 : Workers' Days Generated and Average Number of Days Worked Per Worker

Districts	**2001-02**			**2002-03**			**2003-04**		
	Workers' days generated	No. of workers	No. of days Pper worker	Workers' days generated	No. of workers	No. of days per worker	Workers' days gene-rated	No. of workers	No. of days per worker
Chitrakoot	464	40	11.6	868	140	6.2	239	15	15.9
Pratapgarh	216	46	4.6	1769	140	12.6	331	32	10.3
Deoria	290	27	10.7	2420	145	16.7	249	18	13.8
Pilibhit	1208	105	11.5	1689	130	13.0	254	23	11.0
Total	2278	218	10.4	6746	555	12.2	973	88	11.1

Source: Field Survey, 2004.

all the selected districts were one-tenth of the total. Of total workers' days generated by women workers in all the districts, Chitrakoot alone shared 94.3 per cent (Table 17.2).

The number of days that each worker worked was similar for each of the three years, 2001-02, 2002-03 and 2003-04 for all the districts considered together. It was 11.1 days per worker per year (Table 17.3).

We found large gap in creation of workers' days between the actual number of days worked as reported by the workers and the days recorded by the Government officials in Muster Roll for all the three levels of PRIs (Table 4).

We found a huge gap in wage rate prescribed and wage rate actually paid for works executed under Food for Work for all the levels of PRIs and for all the selected districts. A sum of Rs. 2187.55 crores (29.8 per cent of prescribed wages) did not reach the workers employed under Food for Work as reported by workers. In all the selected districts at all the layers of works executed, a high percentage of wages was siphoned off. The highest leakage was reported at GP level, followed by BP and ZP. Most of the wage payments and wages prescribed were also in that order, Gram to Block to Zilla Panchayat (Table 17.5).

Under Food for Work, a worker was entitled to a wage rate of Rs. 58.00 per day during 2001-04, of which 5 kg. of foodgrains was to be paid as kind payment and the rest in cash. In practice, over all districts and all Panchayat levels, each worker received Rs. 32.8 in cash and 1.8 kg. in rice/wheat (Table 17.6).

The average wages paid in cash per worker per day at ZP level were highest in Deoria (Rs. 51.95) and lowest in Chitrakoot (Rs. 35.53) at GP level. The wage rate per day per worker on average for all works at all levels in the selected districts was Rs. 41.71. The wage rate paid per worker at ZP level was also higher than at Block or Gram Panchayat level for any district considered over all types of works executed under Food for Work. At the BP level, Pilibhit paid highest average wage (in cash) while Deoria paid the lowest. In case of GPs, highest wage in cash was paid in Deoria and lowest average

Table 17.4 : Workers' Days Recorded in Muster Roll and Actual Number of Days Worked as Reported by Workers (Gap in Workers' Days)

PRIs	Workers' days generated	Chitrakoot	Pratapgarh	Deoria	Pilibhit	Total*
Gram panchayat	Actual	1988	2099	2048	2018	8153
	Muster roll	2651	2667	2351	2727	10396
	Gap (%)	25.0	21.3	12.9	26.0	**21.6**
Block panchayat	Actual	1074	512	863	691	3140
	Muster roll	1480	787	1219	1163	4649
	Gap (%)	27.4	34.9	29.2	40.6	**32.4**
Zilla panchayat	Actual	523	392	468	407	1790
	Muster roll	909	543	641	656	2749
	Gap (%)	42.5	27.8	27.0	37.9	**34.9**
Total	Actual	3585	3003	3379	3116	13083
	Muster roll	5040	3997	4211	4546	17794
	Gap (%)	28.9	24.9	19.7	31.4	**26.5**

*Note:*Gap (per cent) is calculated as actual (physical) gap as a percentage of actual (Muster Roll) workers' days.
*The workers' days calculated only for respondent workers under Food for Work.
Source: Field Survey, 2004.

Table 17.5 : Wages (Rs.) Received by Workers and Siphoning off under Food for Work (Gap between Prescribed Wages and Wages Actually Received by Workers)

PRI levels	Wages	Chitrakoot	Pratapgarh	Deoria	Pilibhit	Total
Zilla panchayat	Paid	24224	15026	24313	20906	84469
	Prescribed	30334	18386	27144	24558	100422
	Siphoning off	6110 (20.1)	3360 (18.3)	2831 (10.4)	3652 (14.9)	15953 (15.9)
Block panchayat	Paid	25769	25122	34452	35220	120563
	Prescribed	37125	36656	50460	41284	165525
	Siphoning off	11356 (30.6)	11534 (31.5)	16008 (31.7)	6064 (14.7)	44962 (27.2)
Gram panchayat	Paid	62736	74694	96075	77365	310870
	Prescribed	107484	119858	127484	113884	468710
	Siphoning off	44748 (41.6)	45164 (37.7)	31409 (24.6)	36519 (32.1)	157840 (33.7)
Total	Paid	112729	114842	154840	133491	515902
	Prescribed	174443	174900	205088	179726	734657
	Siphoning off	62214 (35.7)	60058 (35.7)	50248 (24.5)	46235 (25.7)	218755 (29.8)

*Note:*Figures in brackets show siphoning off of wages as per cent of prescribed wages.
Source: Field Survey, 2004.

Table 17.6 : Wages Paid per Day per Worker (Wages in both Cash and Foodgrains)

Districts	Wages per day per worker	Zilla panchayats	Block panchayats	Gram panchayats	Average in sample
Chitrakoot	Cash in Rs.	36.35	31.07	25.53	28.91
	Wheat in kg.	2.00	1.90	2.00	2.00
Pratapgarh	Cash in Rs.	37.40	29.75	27.37	29.50
	Wheat in kg.	2.00	2.00	2.00	2.00
Deoria	Cash in Rs.	44.95	32.60	36.71	36.32
	Rice in kg.	1.00	1.00	1.00	1.00
Pilibhit	Cash in Rs.	41.76	40.70	31.92	36.34
	Wheat in kg.	2.00	2.00	1.96	1.97
Total	Cash in Rs.	40.24	33.40	30.40	32.77
	Wheat/rice in kg.	1.80	1.89	1.79	1.82

Source: Field Survey, 2004.

wage per worker was paid in Chitrakoot. Among the selected districts, lowest wage rate per worker per day was paid at GP level (Table 17.7).

Table 17.7 : Wages Paid in Cash per Day per Worker

PRIs	Chitra-koot	Pratap-garh	Deoria	Pili-bhit	Average
Zilla panchayats	46.35	47.40	51.95	51.76	49.24
Block panchayats	41.20	39.75	39.60	50.70	42.85
Gram panchayats	35.53	37.37	43.71	41.72	39.41
Total average	38.91	39.50	43.32	46.19	41.71

Note: The calculation was based on price of rice at Rs. 7.0 per kg. and wheat at Rs. 5.0 per kg. as informed by the concerned district officials.

Source: Field Survey, 2004.

Most of the workers received cash wage for work on a weekly basis, which was the highest at ZP level and the lowest at BP level. The number of workers that received fortnight payment of cash wages was negligible and this mode of payment was absent at ZP level. The phenomenon of daily wages was lowest at GP level and highest at BP level. Wage payments on a monthly basis were higher at BP level and lower at ZP level.

The contribution of Food for Work in total income of the households was highest for workers who were in the income category per annum between Rs. 501.00 and Rs. 1,000.00. This was followed by the workers were in the income category per annum above Rs. 2,000.00. Food for Work, thus, provided support income of the rural poor through wage-employment.

Food For Work: Major Problems

In most of the selected regions, the available job seekers were found to be agricultural workers. The workers actually employed were paid extremely low wage rate that was an outcome of the existence of locally settled less mobile reserve army of workers as well as prevailing low agricultural wage rate.

The employed workers were forced to accept the wage rate much lower than the prescribed one (Rs. 58 per worker per day) prevailing in 2004 because of absence of positive opportunity cost. One method of payment of wages less than the stipulated one was through manipulation in muster roll that showed lesser number of days recorded than what the workers were actually engaged in. Also, contrary to daily receipt of wages at the end of the working hours per day, the workers had to wait for the whole month to get wages.

The problems in execution of Food for Work were found to be the following:

- Generally the local unemployed people in the working age expected to get any wage-work rather than remaining jobless-wage less insecure. Thus, they were in the queue to accept any positive wage rate to be employed.
- There existed wage-differential in paid wage rates between works and areas of execution of works. The wage rate was higher in areas adjoining towns/markets and lower in the remote areas.
- The workers had no knowledge about the minimum wage rate. Thus, they accepted any wage rate. Even if they knew the wage rate, they were in no bargaining position to claim it because of political-economic-institutional-demographic factors.
- Absence of any general body meetings in most of the Gram Panchayats led to the absence of consensus in decision-making. There was no 'grievance agency' in case of non-payment or underpayment of wages.
- The large positive gap of 26.5 per cent between official data and primary data on workers' days generated during the survey period raises questions on the transparency and reliability of the official data.

- There was the allegation of the practice of black marketing in foodgrains by the fair price shop dealers, delayed lifting of foodgrains by the FCI, under-allocation by District Rural Development Authority (DRDA) and delayed distribution of foodgrains.
- Women workers were mostly bypassed at different levels of works. They were paid wage rate lower than the male workers.
- By underpayment of wages, there was an aggregate siphoning off of Rs. 2,18,755.00 (i.e. 30.0 per cent from the total wage fund) meant for the workers. This reveals both incompetence and malfunctioning of the agencies.
- 45.2 per cent of the workers did not receive foodgrains while official data showed that 85.6 per cent of the lifted foodgrains was utilized. Thus, the programme was sabotaged to a large extent so far as distribution of foodgrains for execution of works was concerned.
- Tools and implements were not supplied by the implementing agency.
- There was no first aid facility at the work site.
- A large number of workers were brought from outside. Thus, the local workers felt crowded out. The entry of migrant workers in works executed at the local level also violated the norms of the programme.
- There was large gap in the actual days worked by the workers and workers' days mentioned in the muster roll. The dependency and ignorance of the workers helped the implementing agencies.
- Under the BOS, most of the toilets constructed were redundant as the quality standards were not maintained.
- No prior survey was conducted for the identification of the workers. Ignorance regarding the programme, the unorganized work pattern of the Panchayats, and lack of awareness hindered the implementation of the programme.

- Most of the Panchayats were biased in selection of works and workers.
- The manipulated marketing of distributable foodgrains by the agents delayed the payments of food wages to workers engaged under Food for Work.
- Time lag and hence delay in allocation, off take and distribution of funds and foodgrains at the State, district and block levels under the programme led not only to delay in payment of wages but also to non-completion of works.
- Inadequate number of technical personnel at ZP and BP levels led to involvement of contractors in carrying out works leading to delay in distribution of food-cum-cash wages.
- The implementing agencies like DRDAs, Block Offices, and GP Secretariat hardly understood the intricacies of the programme. The subordination of the bottom poor to the local elite also obstructed the effective implementation of the programme. The local poor did not even know the purpose and the components of the programme.
- There was non-transparency in selection of workers, real wages paid, works executed by the PRI representatives and public officials. Thumb impressions on the Muster Roll did not reveal anything.

Thus, though the Food for Work programme aimed at regular employment of the rural income-asset poor and creation of durable productive assets by utilizing food stock as wage payment, it failed in ensuring employment as planned in addition to leakage by non-payment of wages prescribed.

Conclusions and Recommendations

In spite of the problems in execution, the programme provided support income to the workers. Thus, we argue for the effective continuation of the programme for which we recommend the following:

- The State Government should ensure timely release of funds to the implementing agencies. This will help the PRIs at different levels in time-bound implementation of the works and timely payment of wages in cash and foodgrains for the works executed. This may lead to ensuring adequate work opportunities during the non-agricultural season or non-peak season in agriculture.

- The implementing agencies should ensure that the works are planned by the PRIs and executed by assigned priority. The priority will be based on the demographic-geographic-need related parameters of a particular region. This will ensure intra- and inter-regional balanced development.
- The money expenditure should be made in proportion to the allocated budget for the various components of the programme.
- The programme should exclude the non-poor households, children, and students.
- The State Government has to ensure full utilization of budget. The government at the centre should take into consideration the utilization capacity of the States prior to allocation and sanction of funds. This, in turn, would not only check the misallocation but also ensure utilization of funds.
- A State level High Power Committee should be set up to check the actual expenditure incurred on construction works like culverts, roads, buildings, drains in the physical infrastructure sector.
- Public awareness campaign should be organized by the Block Office with support from GP members. This campaign should be accompanied by public display of all the on-going State-sponsored welfare/development schemes at public locations (schools, Panchayat Bhavan etc) for a long period within each village.
- Villagers should be made aware of the Government-sponsored Schemes, made them involved in formulating the programmes and make them employable. They should be given the scope to develop skill and hence make them employable in skill-specific areas. The catalysts for this may be the PRIs, the NGOs, and the Vocational Training Institutes.

- The accounts and records should remain transparent.
- The work plan and hence asset creation should be bottom up and not top down. The Gram Sabha meetings have to be convened regularly and work plan thoroughly discussed and decision taken by consensus. This will ensure need-based works selection. There is no alternative to public awareness in this regard.
- Each available worker is to be provided a job card ensuring the number of days in the specific year he/she is guaranteed job at a specified wage rate. In absence of employment, equivalent unemployment allowance has to be paid to the worker and recorded on the job card.
- In case of partial payment of wages in kind (foodgrains), the cash equivalent of foodgrains is to be recorded on the job card.
- The works selected by ZP, BP and GP have to be of different types.
- There are State government departments like minor irrigation and soil conservation who implement works like watershed, ponds, and land related activities. Similar works are also executed under Food for Work through ZP and BP. There is, thus, need to maintain a pre-project formulation and post-project implementation-related links between the departments like minor irrigation and Food for Work schemes. This may lead to avoiding same end-use projects for implementation in the same region.
- There has to be multi-level vigilance on the quantity and quality of food wage distributed. For this purpose, in addition to the responsibilities currently being exercised by the district administration jointly with the FCI, the representatives of the PRIs should be involved in joint sampling test of distributable foodgrains. A village-level committee should be constituted to look after the distribution of foodgrains.
- One-third of total works by workers' days should be reserved for women.

- The voice of the women workers should be recorded so far as their work-specific and skill-specific employability is involved. The women representatives in the PRIs may ensure this.
- The time lag between the sanction/approval of a work selected under Food for Work and work executed should be minimized. The time lag between the work executed and wage payment should be minimized. The catalyst for this has to be the representatives in the PRIs.
- The selected works should be completed in time to save waste of capital by saving repetitive execution of the same work at the same locality. Generation of workers' days should not show destructive Keynesianism. The responsibility lies on PRIs.
- The rules and norms for selection and execution of works have to be circulated in local languages among all the Panchayat Representatives (PRs) particularly at the bottommost layer. In case of PRs who are literacy-challenged, the locally settled school teacher or Siksha Mitra or any other functionally literate local person may be assigned the responsibility to help the PRs. The responsibility to assign the task rests on the State/district administration.
- Training of the PRI representatives for each layer should be organized at ZP office at least once every year to make them aware of their assigned responsibilities under Food for Work. The responsibility lies on district administration in consultation with ZP representatives.
- The priority of works should be decided in the open general meetings of the PRIs, given the sanctioned fund and foodgrains at different levels.
- For the efficient functioning of the programme, the functioning agencies through the PRIs (Zila, Block, and Gram Panchayats) should be entrusted with the responsibility of distribution and allocation of foodgrains. Hence, the prevailing control of the fair price shop dealers in the

distribution system should be stopped. This would eliminate delay and leakage.

- At the GP level, the Panchayat should undertake surveys to identify the BPL households and then issue BPL cards. These BPL cards must display information related to the number of members of the family, occupation, caste, and landownership.
- The Panchayats have to identify and enlist the workers. Each enlisted worker has to be provided a worker's identity-cum-work entitlement card.
- There has to be a local legal body where the workers can register their grievances and ask for remedial measures.
- Implementation of works should be need-based and top priority should be given to the villagers' opinion before carrying out any work. Towards this end, open general meetings of the Gram Sabha should be held at least twice a year, preferably during lean/off agricultural season and/or during the local festival period. This may ensure inclusive development through participation of local people.
- PRIs have to identify village-specific, cluster of villages-specific, and block-specific and district-specific need-based public works.
- A land ownership-cum-use record at the GP level should be maintained. This record has to show particularly the land owned/used/distributed by Gram Sabha. This will show the possibilities of effective use of Gram Sabha land for long-term productive use by adoption and implementation of public works. This also may show the path of creation of durable public productive assets.
- The work plan for the GP has to be non-conflicting and non-repetitive with those of BP and ZP for the same region.

The promises latent in the programme can go a long way by not only retaining the local workers in the locality by productive wage-employment but also stopping forced migration and associated unwarranted outcome. This is in addition to providing support income, ensuring food security through payment of wages partly in food, creation of rural assets for multiple and repetitive use without destroying the root. The Food for Work is a step in the right direction for uplift of the rural income-poor people if it is implemented through 'inclusive' development path.

REFERENCES

Ghosh, Arun (1988), "Development Planning: West Bengal Experience", *Economic and Political Weekly*, Vol. XXIII, No. 13, March 26.

Majumder, Bhaskar (2004), *Sampoorna Grameen Rozgar Yojana (Food for Work Component)*, Report Submitted to Planning Commission, Govt. of India.

——(2007), *Rural Non-Farm Employment in India: A Focus on Food for Work*, Kanishka Pub., New Delhi.

——(2008), "Food for Work Programme in India: Modus Operandi and Measures for Inclusive Development", paper Presented in the Conference on Reforming Rural Non-Farm Activities for Benefits of Globalization, Organized at IRMA, Anand, Gujarat on 11-12 Jan. 2008

Narayana, N.S.S. *et al.*, (1991), *Agriculture, Growth and Redistribution of Income*, North Holland, Amsterdam.

Sengupta, Arjun *et al.*, (2008), National Commission for Enterprises in the Unorganized Sector, GOI, *Report on Conditions of Work and Promotion of Livelihoods in the Unorganized Sector*, Academic Foundation, New Delhi.

Sharma, R.D. (1980), *Food for Work Programme (A Case Study of Banda District)*, Agro-Economic Research Center, University of Delhi, Delhi, Research Study No. 80/6.

18

DIMENSIONS OF INTERLOCKING LABOUR MARKET IN BACKWARD INDIAN AGRICULTURE

D. M. DIWAKAR

Introduction

Labour market generally denotes to a condition in which labour power is purchased and sold. In agriculture labour market is yet to become commoditised and, therefore, this transaction is linked and tied with various factors and conditions, which influence and interlock a labour market. This exercise is an attempt to understand labour process, dimensions of contracts through labour relations and labour tying contracts and credit labour linkages in backward Indian agriculture. In addition to dealing with theoretical underpinnings this chapter is an endeavour to examine through empirical evidences from West Bengal, Bihar, and Uttar Pradesh.

Labour Process

Labour market linkages are the reflection of labour process as one of the important determinants to understand the process of transformation of a society. Labour process begins with the interactions between nature and creature, as nature provides objects of labour on which labour is applied to effect and modify them suitably through instruments, (i.e., means of labour) for the requirement of creature. Means of labour and skills (which have been created and acquired by a society in historical process of transformation) and objects of labour together constitute means of production, i.e., productive forces.

In this process, human beings inevitably enter into relations and get involved in production, exchange, distribution and consumption. To be precise, productive forces reflect the development of technology through which human being tries to exercise control and dominate over nature. And production relation explains the nature of ownership and control over means of production by human being. Thus, people's relations with the means of production determine their position and places in production and the mode of distribution of the production of labour. Therefore, identification of the labour process, relations of production and development of productive forces decide place of labour in a society. In other words, modes of production help in understanding the labour process and condition of labour at a given stage of transformation of a society and the nature and course of surplus appropriation and distribution. As Marx said: "When we speak of production, we always have in mind production at a definite stage of social development, production by individuals in a society, i.e. various phases in the historical process of development. All stages of production however, have certain common features, elements and categories without which production is inconceivable. For example, no production is possible without an instrument of production (simplest form may be hand), without past accumulated and materialised labour (may be the skill acquired by repeated practice and concentrated in the hand of savage). Thus, capital is a universal and eternal relation, which turns the instrument of production or accumulated labour into capital. Production is always appropriation of nature by individual within and with the help of a definite social organisation". (Marx, 1970, 189-90)

Labour process in a primitive society is different than other historical stages, i.e., slave, feudal, capitalist and communist modes of production, as every system of production has its own system of exchange and distribution. In primitive society there was hardly any scope of exploitation through contractual arrangements as the means of production remains at the disposal of society through communal ownership arrangements. In slave mode of production there is hardly any contract. There is complete subordination and labour remained reduced to speaking tools at inhuman subsistence level. In feudal society landlords, appropriate surplus from labourers and tenants through contractual arrangements for depressed wages, bondage for supply of labour for cultivation and rents operating through interlocking them into land and usury networks. In capitalist mode of production profit maximisation through extracting surplus value of labour by extending hour of works, employing females and children. However, competition and technological replacement of labour becomes self-defeating for maximisation of surplus appropriation. In communist mode of production there is collective ownership over means of production, exchange and distribution. People work according to their capacity and get according to their need. Thus, "The total product of our community is a social product. One portion serves as fresh means of production and remains social. But another portion is consumed by the members as means of subsistence. A distribution of this portion amongst them is consequently necessary. The mode of this distribution will vary with the productive organisation of the community and the degree of historical development attained by the producers" (Marx, 1954; 83). Therefore, epochs of development are so much associated with the institutional and structural set-up that any analysis of transformation in isolation from modes of production is an exercise in futility (Prasad, 1989; 3). Because "it is not the article made, but how they are made and by what instrument, that enables us to distinguish different economic epochs" (Marx, 1975; 175).

In primitive stage of society there was hardly any scope for indirect control on production and distribution through subordinated labour and, therefore, the society remained almost free from any individual contractual arrangement. With the changing pace of productive forces and control over the ownership of means of production slave mode of production replaced the earlier arrangement. In this system human labour was controlled by the owners of the slaves and slaves were treated as speaking tools whose subsistence and lives were dependent at the mercy of the owners. Thus, until irreversible resistance of stronger slaves made impossible to be exploited by the owners of the slave, there was hardly any contractual arrangement. Consequent upon resistance to secure tenancy rights for subsistence, contractual arrangement to appropriate surplus through rents, unpaid labour, usury bondage, etc., from slave convert peasants and labour was put in place. With this arrangement, feudal mode of production came into existence in many parts of the world. Transformation of productive forces and resistance of peasants in due course of history has changed the modes of surplus appropriation significantly, with the advent of capitalism and commodification of labour. Since, the changes have not been universal, multiple contractual arrangements and interlocking factors market emerged to appropriate surplus. Many regions still continue with feudal contractual arrangements modified in due course of time under semi-feudal social formation whereas many regions have witnessed capitalist contractual arrangement with labour in agriculture.

In this backdrop of theoretical underpinnings, this chapter is an attempt to examine the linkages of labour market and contractual arrangements in backward Indian agriculture, which witnessed modifications in feudal contractual arrangement but still remained operative. However, emergence of capitalist contractual arrangement of labour in agriculture is also encountered. This exercise is intended to present a brief account of a few micro studies to understand interlocking of labour through lease market, usury, inputs and other forms of markets operating in agrarian economy of Bihar and Uttar Pradesh (Diwakar, 2000; 2000a; 2001; 2005).

Dimensions of Labour Contracts

Broadly there are two dimensions of contracts between employers and labourers. One deals with employer's interest and the other with that of employee's, (i.e., labourer's). Employer's basic objective remains to maximise their returns at minimum cost whereas labourers exercise their bargaining powers at their disposal subject to the availability of opportunity cost that they have. In classical framework of analysis labourers are paid at best to their subsistence but in neoclassical framework employers intend to pay at best equivalent to marginal productivity of labour and are tempted to pay even less than that if opportunity cost of labour is lower than their marginal productivities, which restrict labourers from deserting their employers. Employee's interest is determined *inter alia* countervailing bargaining power of labour through which labour enters into contracts of working condition including wages and other facilities. In Marxist framework, employers extract maximum surplus value out of labour by extending hours of work, employing females and children. Interlocking has been possible through exercising control over means of production, i.e., objects and instruments of labour including productive forces. Objects of labour include natural resources, and instruments of labour include technology and labour includes capital as exchange value of the utility created by labour and appropriated by non-labour elements as profit, which is nothing but accumulated labour part of which in turn becomes capital.

In case of feudal society tenancy relation emerged as a contract between labour and landlords to ensure supply of labour as rent of the land for tenancy. Thus, land labour interlocking in the labour market became pervasive. With the growing bargaining strength in due course of historical necessity terms of tenancy got revised time and again from share cropping with variation of shares to fixed kind and cash rents after crops and also advance rents beforehand in some cases. Another form of interlocking emerged through usury network. Often landlords operated as moneylender to appropriate surplus in the forms of exorbitant rate of interests, which often compelled labourers to enter into contract of bondage—formal and informal as well. After abolition of *zamindari* system in post independent India, in many cases tenants got ownership rights on land and were practically liberated from bondage. However, in absence of appropriate support system for backward and forward linkages they were forced to depend on moneylenders not only for credit, seeds, fertiliser and irrigation but also to meet their consumption need of the family for which they have to enter into contract in one form or the other.

Labour Relations

Dimensions of interlocking of labour market can be comprehended through labour relations that exist in various forms in Indian agriculture. Rudra (1992) observed broadly two forms of labour relations – (a) family labour, and, (b) hired labour. Generally poor peasants and poor middle peasants operate their land with their family labours in the subsistence farming. However, occasionally in emergency situation they explore and enter into labour exchange and in the event failing this possibility they even hire labourers, which are essentially casual in nature. In case of middle peasant besides using their family labours they hire in labour, which are casual and attached, may be formal or informal. Another category of farmers is of big peasants and landlords. This category of farmers enters into many forms of contracts and uses not only casual labourers but also attached, farm servants, annual farm servants, permanent farm servants, etc., which indicates various dimensions of employer labour relations in terms of duration of contracts, modes and frequency of payments and nature and degree of attachments.

Duration of contracts may be on the basis of days, month, season, year, etc. Basis of payments may be hourly, daily or other time wage, piece rate, share of product, etc. Hours of work may be fully delimited, not delimited, etc. Hired labour with wide variety of contracts with very different terms and conditions and remunerations and modes of payments cannot be categorised only through casual and annual. Casual labour contracts may have daily basis, contracts for longer period on daily basis (CLP), piece rate contracts (PRC) as in case of West Bengal, Bihar, Orissa and Uttar Pradesh. Frequency of payment may be in terms of daily, weekly, monthly, yearly, several irregular instalments during the year, bonus during festivals, etc. Medium of payments may be in terms of cash, kind, meals, snacks and their different combinations. Nature of works may vary and may specify only for farm works and nature of duties may not be specified.

Interlocking of labour market may vary in terms of the nature of dependence and dominance through the allotment of cultivable land, homestead land, consumption loan as a regular practice, inherited or long standing debt, employment of other members of the family in the same farm, etc. Interlocking may also restrict in terms of the degree of freedom to work for different employers. Labourers may enjoy full freedom, conditional or restricted freedom or may experience total absence of such freedom to work for others.

Labour Tying Contracts in Agriculture

Labour tying contracts in agriculture has many dimensions. Bardhan (1984) observed that in order to save on recruitment cost employer enters into short and long term contracts with labour to ensure supply of labour in the peak season when the wage rate is lower than marginal product of labour. In this process employers have to pay higher wage than the marginal product of labour in the lean season. Inter-seasonal adjustment, however, reduces the fluctuation of wages (pp. 67-68). Employer enters into labour tying contracts in terms of wage uncertainty for peak operations. In the beginning of the years employers contracts with some tied labourers, feeding them at a steady rate across the season (i.e., giving them consumption credit to survive the lean season) in exchange for their delivering committed labour supply in the peak season. If the peak labour demand is higher than that of supplied by tied labourers, the employer then enters the spot or casual market, hiring the additional labour at the uncertain wage rate of that time.

Yield increasing improvements increase the importance of tied labour as a proportion of total labour employed. Labour saving technical progress, like some kind of agricultural mechanisation, reduces the importance of tied labourers as a proportion of total labour employed. The larger the total number of workers, the smaller is the importance of tied labourers as a proportion of total labour employed. Migration plays an important role towards entering into contracts with women labour in agriculture. Migration cost is fetched through ensuring women labour supply, which is cheaper also because of wage differential. In general, the more the demand-pressure in the labour market, relative to supply, the larger is the proportional importance of tied labour. Tied labourers are considered more reliable than casual labourers and keep supervisory on casual labour and creating divide and rule policies. However, divide and rule policy is effective for the employer when tied labour is carefully interlocked with personalised credit transactions, provision of homestead land, or cultivable land.

Efficiency of animal control remains higher with tied labourers. Mobilisation of labour for better contracts or wages has positive role but interlocked tied labours have lesser chances to participate in mobilisation. Labour from other regions enters into contract with employers sometimes with lower wage bill than local when mobilisation of local labour against unfavourable contracts takes place. Study of Rudra-Bardhan (1978) for West Bengal and Bhalla (1976) for Haryana confirmed long term contracts even in developed agricultural regions. Evidences of interlinking between land-lease and labour contract, particularly in agriculturally progressive areas and that too largely for a section of unrecorded tenancy were found in West Bengal. Large number of lessee gives option and bargaining power to land owners and they enjoy monopolistic power to opt between lower and higher ability tenants. Fixed rent from lower ability tenants and share cropping from batter ability tenants (Bhowmik, 1993: 166-67).

In case of North Bihar, tied labourers get many indirect concessions and rewards if they are tied with land owners. However, they have to perform free labour on many occasions (Diwakar, 2000). Emerging labour contract is found in almost all agricultural operations. Harvesting, mango orchard, soil cutting by musahar, etc. (Diwakar, 2000; Chakravarti, 2001:252-54) in order to maximise their earnings at minimum labour days. Land owner in the case of contract is free from hassles of control over labour for efficiency. Migrant labour from Bihar to work through agricultural operations in Punjab are mainly on contract. Harvest operation is normally controlled by contract/attached/permanent labours who devoted labour services in transplantations.

International evidence suggests that permanent labourers remained major part of agricultural operation even after emancipation of serfdom in Danish agriculture until large-scale mechanisation was introduced (Bent Hansen, 1971). Erickson and Rogers (1978) for Sweden and Richards (1979) for Germany suggest commercialisation in agriculture with permanent labour. Muqtada and Alam (1986: 45-46) suggests that only medium/large holdings hire-in permanent/ attached labours in agricultural operation in Bangladesh. Attached labour is positively though weakly associated with land productivity in India and attached labour is more important in the areas where the maximum to minimum wage ratio across seasonal operations is higher (Bardhan, 1984:80).

Credit Labour Linkages

Recovery is easier if lent to attached labourers (Bardhan-Rudra, 1978). Lending to attached labour helps in cementing implicit contracts (Bardhan and Rudra, 1978). In case of eastern UP, tenancy and credit locking labour has been found. In this case contrary to West Bengal, depressed wages are paid to the tied labourers (Mishra and Diwakar, 2005). Barter transaction of future labour services tied with living cost consumption loan in the lean season in backward agrarian agriculture is pervasive in West Bengal, Bihar and Uttar Pradesh as survival strategies of agriculture labour. This acts as informal bondage for labour.

Conclusion

Above analysis suggests that agrarian labour contracts are rooted in the situation of agricultural development, which varies with respect to time and space. It depends on the staying power of labourers to agree and disagree with a contract, which are not beneficial for them. Interlocking of labour with tenancy and credit through various dimensions of contracts makes them vulnerable. Non-economic linkages for tying labourers towards formal and informal bondages are equally important in this regard. With the development of technology although freedom of labour could have increased but the evidence suggests that technology and credit control of land owners put further interlocking of the labour market in agriculture.

REFERENCES

Bardhan, P.K. (1984), *Land Labour and Rural Poverty (Essays in Development Economics)*, Oxford University Press.

Bardhan, P.K. and Rudra, A. (1978), "Interlinkages of Land Labour and Credit Relations: An Analysis of Village Survey Data in East India", *Economic and Political Weekly*, Vol. 13, No. 6-7, February.

Bhowmik, S.K. (1993), *Tenancy Relations and Agrarian Development – A Study of West Bengal*, Sage Publication, New Delhi.

Chakravarti, Anand (2001), *Social Power and Everyday Class Relations: Agrarian Transformation in North Bihar*, Sage Publication, New Delhi.

Diwakar, D.M., (2000a), 'Agrarian Transformation in Uttar Pradesh', *Journal of*

Social and Economic Development, Vol. 3 No. 1, January-June.

Diwakar, D.M. (2000), *Emerging Agrarian Relations in India: A Study of Micro Realities*, Manak Publications, Pvt. Ltd., New Delhi.

Diwakar, D.M. (2001), *Purvi Uttar Pradesh ke Krishi Maen Punji Ka Vikas (Hindi)*, Samkalin Lokyudha, Patna, Vol. 10, No. 45 and 46, November-December 2001.

Diwakar, D.M. (2005), "Growth Linkages of Agriculture of Uttar Pradesh: Constraints, Options, and Strategies", *Convention Journal*, Lucknow Management Association, Vol. 1, No. 1, 2005 pp. 76-95.

Marx, K., (1970), *Critique of Political Economy*, Progress Publishers, Moscow.

Marx, K. (1954), *Capital*, Progress Publishers, Moscow, Vol. I, Reprint 1986.

Marx, K. (1975), *Capital*, Progress Publishers, Moscow, Vol. I.

Mishra, G.P. and Diwakar, D.M. (2005), *Land Reforms and Human Development*, Manak Publications, Pvt. Ltd. New Delhi.

Muqtada and Alam (1986), "Hired Labour and Rural Labour Market in Bangladesh in Hirashima", S. and Muqtada, M. (Eds.), *Hired Labour and Rural Labour Market in Asia*, International Labour Organisation, ARTEP, New Delhi.

Prasad, Pradhan H. (1989), *Lopsided Growth*, Oxford University Press, New Delhi.

Rudra, Ashok (1992), *Political Economy of Indian Agriculture*, K.P. Bagchi & Company, Calcutta, New Delhi.

19

VARIOUS TRENDS AND DIMENSIONS OF CONTRACTUAL LABOUR

With Special Reference to Teaching on Contractual Basis in Uttar Pradesh

ALOK CHANTIA

A is a married lady of 44 years. She has been working as contractual lecturer since 1999. Initially she was getting Rs. 3000 per month but this amount was enhanced in the year 2000 by Rs. 5000.Today she is getting Rs. 160 per lecture and maximum Rs. 8000 per month. She has two daughters one has completed intermediate and other one has completed high school. Higher education is not cheap and she is also worried about their marriages. It is very hard for her to survive in this world with two grown up daughters in the petty amount that she gets as contractual lecturer.

Case two is of an unmarried girl she belongs to a good family. She is working as contractual lecturer in a college since 2006. Today in a marriage alliance one not only looks for a girl but also for her job. Groom generally prefers a girl who is in permanent job so as to ensure smooth survival for both. A number of boys have rejected her only because of her nature of job, which has no future. Today she is in depression.

Another case is of 'B' who is an unmarried male. He has been working since 2000 as contractual lecturer on Rs.100 per lecture. Now this amount has been enhanced to Rs. 160 per lecture or to a maximum of Rs. 8000 per month. He migrated from his native place to this metropolitan city of Lucknow in search of better livelihood and dignified life. Because of nature of appointment he cannot get his salary for more than 6 to 7 months as payment is not made for the calendar year or for the academic year but for the classes actually taken. If anybody absents himself/herself from the duty for whatsoever reason a sum of Rs. 300 per day is deducted from this meager amount of salary. There is no HRA or D.A. facility. Rent of the house along with water and electricity bill has to be paid out of this sum only.

Timings of the college are such that one cannot go for alternative assignments to support the meager amount. Besides selection committee also says that since you are working let others get the job as the rate of unemployment is very high in this country.

Since man is a social animal, he has to fulfil not only personal obligations but social responsibilities also. He has to attend social functions, he needs to travel for both personal and professional reasons. He has to attend seminar and conferences, write papers and participate in other academic activities so as to show what has been his/her academic achievements during an academic year to ensure his assignment for next year also. In such circumstances one also cannot think of marriage, as good marriage proposals are not meant for contractual lecturers.

Since 1998 thousands of contractual lecturers have been working in pathetic socio-economic conditions but nothing has been done so far. Every year landlord enhances rent, inflation is also going higher and higher. Permanent teachers get D.A. every six months but so far as contractual lecturers are concerned they are not getting any relief, amount once fixed continues for year to year.

All the above-mentioned cases are of well-qualified people. All three are UGC NET qualified with additional degree of Ph.D. also. They were appointed under the guidelines of Government Order (GO) of 1998.

Table 19.1 : Thinking about Contractual Teaching

Sl. no.	Sex ratio	What do you think about contractual teaching?						Total	
		Exploitation as bonded labour		Against student's interest		A white collar crime			
		Nos.	%	Nos.	%	Nos.	%	Nos.	%
1.	Male	16	21.43	33	58.93	07	12.5	56	56
2.	Female	12	27.27	26	59.09	06	13.64	44	•44
	Total	28	28	59	59	13	13	100	100.0

In order to analyse the position of contractual teachers and their satisfaction with the current mode of payment on per lecture basis 100 contractual teachers, both male and female, working in different degree colleges of Lucknow and Kanpur were interviewed. The analysis of data revealed the facts as given in Table 19.1.

Table 19.1 shows that 28 per cent respondents feel that in the name of contractual teaching they are being exploited as bonded labours. No provision is there for any kind of leave either casual or medical. Instead Rs. 300 is deducted per day if a contractual teacher absents himself or herself from the duty in case of any emergency. 59 per cent respondents think that this policy of government is working against the interests of the students. Since there is no job security and contractual teacher is always under the fear of being thrown out on one reason or the other, he does not take full interest in the teaching. He is always in search of some other source of earning too, so that he may lead a peaceful and secured life. 13 per cent respondents think that contractual teaching is nothing but white collar crime in disguise. On condition of anonymity some respondents told that in order to keep their jobs secured they have to surrender some part of their income either to the management or to the principal of the college concerned, besides they have to fulfil unlawful, unjustified demands of the authorities too. Respondents were of the view that these persons are nothing but education mafias.

A contractual teacher used to get Rs. 100 per lecture and maximum Rs. 5000 per month. Looking at the procedure followed in the selection of contractual teachers, we notice that he/she gets only 20,000 in an academic year. Every creature has some basic needs and when we talk about human being, culture defines three necessities namely food, sex, protection. After the inception of State certain rights of human beings were protected in the constitutions of different nations. Our Indian Constitution is no exception. It guarantees certain fundamental rights such as right to life, right to livelihood, right to shelter, right to food, right to health and right to education. All these fundamental rights are well protected by law and can be enforced through the court of law. One can well imagine how these fundamental rights can get protected by the contractual teachers in a meager amount of 20,000 a year or Rs. 1667 per month.

Table 19.2 : Satisfaction with Payment

Sl. No.	Sex ratio	Are you satisfied with current mode of payment?								Total	
		Labour like payment		Difficult to run family		Cannot ensure dignified life		Insult to education			
		Nos.	%	Nos.	%	Nos.	%	Nos.	%	Nos.	%
1.	Male	11	19.64	27	48.21	13	23.11	5	8.93	56	56%
2.	Female	9	20.45	19	43.18	10	22.73	6	13.64	44	44%
	Total	20	20	46	46	23	23	11	11	100	100.0

From 2006 the State government of Uttar Pradesh has enhanced the payment of contractual lecturers due to rising cost of living etc. Now they are getting Rs.160 per lecture or a maximum amount of Rs.8000 per month. But in case of leave, or if contractual teacher absents himself/herself from teaching then Rs. 300 per day is deducted from his monthly payment. Now a contractual teacher gets Rs.32000 per annum or Rs. 2667 per month.

Table 19.2 shows the respondent's view regarding the mode of payment for contractual teachers. 20 per cent respondents feel that they are being treated like labours on daily wages. They have no job security; no facilities of any kind of leave etc.46 per cent respondents find it difficult to run their family in meager amount. Most of the contractual teachers are married and having children, they find it very difficult to keep their body and soul together. 23 per cent respondents lamented that dignified life ensured by Indian Constitution and in various Supreme Court cases is not meant for them. Whatever, amount they are getting is not just sufficient for leading an ordinary life, what to say of dignified life. 11 per cent respondents said that such meagre amount paid to contractual teachers is a shame and insult to higher education. A person burns mid night oil, he labours day and night in the pursuit of knowledge, but when he sees that even an unskilled worker can earn better than him, he feels frustrated and insulted.

More than 800 contractual lecturers are working in different degree colleges of Uttar Pradesh since 1998, 1999 and are struggling for their survival. We see that no leave or leisure is granted to a contractual lecturer, which is ensured in Indian Industrial laws and in various international conventions and by International Labour Organisation (ILO). Indian Contract Act, 1872 too demands that terms of contract cannot be unjust, unfair, unreasonable, immoral or against public policy. We can also notice the paradox that in Uttar Pradesh, the present government has decided to give Rs. 100 to a worker on daily basis. Thus there is no difference between skilled labour and unskilled labour, between contractual labour and contractual teacher. According to Supreme Court judgments teachers are not workers/labourers. They are on a noble mission (A. Sunderambal *v.* Govt. of Goa, Daman & Dieu (1989)1 L.L.J. 61 SC). But without any proper facility and allowance this noble mission cannot be carried out. The contractual teachers' position is no better than that of a contractual labour who works on daily payment basis. Both are at par, the only difference is that one is doing physical labour and another is doing mental labour. Since working conditions for both are the same, the human rights of contractual teachers should also be protected as enshrined in various national and international conventions. The United Nations Declaration of Human Rights also makes provisions for the protection of family, as maximum contractual teachers are married and having children, they are finding it very difficult to lead their life with dignity.

A contractual teacher is bonded labour in disguise, as they do not get any kind of leave either casual or medical. If one is unable to attend his/her duties for one reason or the other Rs. 300 per day is deducted from his/her payment. The bonded labour like situation amongst contractual teachers is continuing not only because of problem of unemployment but also because of poor government policies that had banned regular appointments. In this precarious situation a person being meritorious and holding higher degrees is forced to join contractual teaching on unfair terms and conditions.

It is submitted that just because a teacher is not worker and is not subjected to industrial laws, he should not be devoid of right to live with dignity, casual and duty leave (UGC recently provided that even temporary teachers should attend training programmes such as refresher course etc. so as to improve their teaching quality), medical facility, insurance policy, D.A., T.A., etc.

A. Etiology of Selection of Contractual Lecturer in Higher Education

Teaching is an essential part of academics and well-qualified teachers are the requirements of each and every educational institution. Though appointment of teachers in degree colleges is done by Higher Education Commission but to fill the gap sometimes contractual teachers are appointed by the Government itself. The desire of keeping the standard of education at par excellent, expressed by the legislature at the time of enactment of Act, 1973, has been negated by providing for regularization/absorption of ad hoc teachers, temporary teachers and part-time teachers from time to time. Vide U.P. Act No. 05 of 1977 under Section 31 (3)(b), persons appointed on temporary posts up to the date of commencement of the Act of 1973 were directed to be absorbed on substantive basis against the post which were temporary at the time of appointment but had subsequently been converted into a permanent posts or against a newly created posts or against any other post substantively vacant in the same department. This absorption/regularization was followed by the U.P. Act No. 01 of 1992 whereby short term appointees were directed to be substantively appointed by the Executive Council against the substantive posts in the same cadre provided that such short term appointees were in fact appointed on or before 30.06.1991 subject to the conditions stipulated therein. The process of appointment by direct recruitment was further diluted with the enforcement of Act No. 09 of 1985 and Act No. 04 1996 whereby personal promotion on the post of Reader and Professor was provided for. Since the provision Act, 1973 qua selection and appointment of teachers in affiliated Degree Colleges (other than minority and government institutions) failed to achieve the desired results, the State of Uttar Pradesh decided to establish a Service Commission for selection of teachers for appointment to colleges affiliated/recognized by Universities vide Commission's Act. Section 12 of the said Act provided procedure for appointment of teachers that:

(1) Every appointment as a teacher of any college shall be made by the management in accordance with the provisions of this Act and every appointment made in contravention thereof shall be void.

(2) The management shall intimate the existing vacancies and the vacancies, likely to be caused during the course of the ensuing academic year, to the Director at such time and in such manner, as may be prescribed.

(3) The Director shall notify to the Commission at such time and in such manner as may be prescribed a subject-wise consolidated list of vacancies intimated to him from all colleges.

(4) The manner of selection of persons for appointment to the posts of teachers of a college shall be such, as may be determined by regulations: provided that the Commission shall with a view to inviting talented persons give wide publicity in the State to the vacancies notified to it under sub-section (3). Provided further that the candidates shall be required to indicate their order of preference for the various colleges, vacancies wherein have been advertised." Section 12 of the Commission's Act, therefore, provided that appointment on the post of teachers to be made on the recommendation of the Higher Education Services Commission only and any appointment made in contravention thereof shall be void. As the legislature was aware that establishment of the Commission and regular appointment by direct recruitment on the post of teachers on its recommendation is to take some time, it provided for ad hoc appointment under Section 16 of the Act pending regular selection by the Commission. Thereafter, vide U.P. Act No. 02 of 1992 power of the State to issue Removal of Difficulties Order as provided under Section 31-A of the Commission's Act was circumscribed by providing that no such order shall be made after expiry of two years from the date of commencement of the Amending Act of 1992.

At this stage the Court took note of the various advertisements and selections made by the said Commission for the purpose of filling up the vacancies on the post of Lecturer in various Degree Colleges as disclosed by the Director of Higher Education in his affidavit. The details are as follows :

Between 1980 to 1994 only six advertisements for the post of Lecturers were published by the Commission namely :

Advertisement No.	No. of post advertised	No. of candidates selected
a. Adv. no. 02 of 1983	97	73
b. Adv. no. 03 of 1983	207	Cancelled
c. Adv. no. 06 of 1985	264	239
d. Adv. no. 07 of 1985	111	107
e. Adv. no. 09 of 1986	86	64
f. Adv. no. 10 of 1986	317	222
g. Adv. no. 17 of 1991	194	119
h. Adv. no. 19 of 1991	259	Cancelled
Total		**824**

Advertise ment No.	Total No. of vacancies available notification to the commission	Total No. of vacancies advertised	Total No. of selection and placements
20/1994	722	722	557
24/1998	149	149	52
26/1998	870	870	631
27/2000	97	97	34
28/2000	183	183	49
29/2000	1640	1640	1253
30/2002	57	57	31
31/2002	128	128	68
32/2002	842	842	791
The results of different subjects were received during the period of 2 years (2003 to 2005)			
37/2003	838	838	

(contd...)

(contd...)

Advertise-ment No.	Total No. of vacancies available notification to the commission	Total No. of vacancies advertised	Total No. of selection and placements
Selection process completed but result stayed by the Hon'ble Court's order dated 18-7-05 passed in writ petition no. 48149 of 2003			
38/2005	281	281	
Selection process is on but result is stayed under the aforesaid order dated 18-7-2005			
40/2006	245	179	179
41/2007	552	552	Selection yet to start
42/2007	337	337	

Vacancies advertised and last date for filling the application was 15.2.2008 Selection yet to start (From 1994 up to December, 2007 total 6941 vacancies were advertised while selection and placements were made against only 3635 vacancies).

It may be seen from the aforesaid that in the last 27 years of its existence the Higher Education Service Commission could select only 824 + 3656 = 4459 candidates. As on date nearly 9,000 vacancies on the post of Lecturer in the Aided Degree Colleges remained unfilled. If the efficiency of the Higher Education Commission in last 27 years is an indication of the things to come it would mean that the Commission will take nearly 54 years to fill all the existing vacancies as of date. We at this stage can only hope that the State would take some radical steps to save the Higher Education in U.P. from getting bad to worse. Another reason for the inordinate delay in the selection of teachers for affiliated Degree Colleges is that the State Government enforced U.P. Act No. 04 of 1994, namely, the Uttar Pradesh Public Services Reservation for Scheduled Caste and Scheduled Tribe Act, 1994 where-under the post of teacher and other staff of educational institutions receiving grant in aid from the State Government have been included. The Act provides for reservation in favour of Scheduled Caste to the extent of 21 per cent, Scheduled Tribes 2 per cent and Other Backward Classes 27 per cent. Despite the enforcement of the reservation, no corresponding amendments have been introduced in the Commission's Act and there exists a serious dispute with regard to the cadre strength against which the percentage of reservation is to be applied. Parties are at a variance as to whether (a) the reservation is to be applied with reference to number of post in a particular subject taught in the college; (b) to the number of total posts in a particular faculty of the College or (c) against the total posts of Lecturers in the College as a whole. It should also be noted that with every change of the Government in the State, there has been a change of Chairman and the members of the Commission and for the period 26.06.1997 to 23.02.1999 (i.e. 01 year 08 months), and thereafter between 14.09.2001 to 05.08.2002 (11 months), there has been no Chairman of the Commission. This has also contributed to the delayed selections.

B. Regularization of Contractual Lecturers

The State legislature has taken various steps for regularizing ad hoc/ hort term appointment etc. because of the failure of the Commission to recommend suitable candidates against the vacant posts from time to time. The first amendment in that regard was enforced by addition of Section 31 (1) (b) to the Commission's Act vide Act No. 21 of 1988 whereby ad hoc teachers and Principal directly appointed on or before 03.01.1984 were directed to be regularized. Thereafter by addition of Section 31-B(2)(a) (added vide Act No. 26 of 1989) regularization of ad hoc teachers appointed on or before 03.01.1984 against a vacancy referable to paragraph 2 of the U.P. Higher Education Service Commission (Removal of Difficulties) Order, 1982 and 1983 were directed to be regularized. Thereafter vide U.P. Act No. 02 of 1992, Section 31 (C) was added to the Commission's Act whereby a teacher appointed on ad hoc basis after 03.01.1984 but not later than 2.11.1991 was directed to be regularized. Sub Clause 4 of Section 31-C of the Act, 1973 provided that all such teachers who are not offered substantive appointment under earlier sub-section would be removed from service. However, by U.P. Act No. 10 of 1997 Sub-Section 5 was added to Section 31-C and it was provided that all those teachers who were not found suitable for substantive appointment earlier, may now be reconsidered for substantive appointment, and it was declared that it would be deemed that they had never ceased to hold the post.

With the enforcement of Act No. 02 of 1992, Section 16 of the Act, 1973 which provided for ad hoc appointment of teachers pending regular selection by the Commission was deleted. As a result whereof there remained no power to make ad hoc appointment against the substantive vacancies. Similarly the power of the State Government to issue directions for removing the difficulties faced in the enforcement of the Commission's Act stood lost after expiry of two years from the date of enforcement of U.P. Act No. 02 of 1992 (subsequent to 02.03.1991) as is apparent from the language of Section 31-A (proviso) itself. Thus the legislature realised that power to make ad hoc appointment was the root cause for regularization being claimed and granted by the State, it decided to do away with such a power of ad hoc appointment itself with a clear purpose that all appointments against substantive vacancies should be made on the recommendation of the Commission after due selection.

The State of U.P. now decided to exercise its executive powers and came out with the Government Order dated 07.04.1998. This Government Order for the first time provided for a new category of Stop Gap appointment of teachers in affiliated Degree Colleges commonly termed as part time teachers. The appointment of part time teachers was required to be made against substantive vacancies of Lecturers against duly created post in affiliated Degree Colleges. The appointment were to be made with the following stipulations :

(a) The part-time teacher had to be appointed for a fixed period which would expire at the end of the academic session, automatically.

(b) The part time teacher was to be paid @ Rs.100 per lecture subject to the maximum of Rs. 5000 per month (now enhanced to Rs. 8000).

(c) Part time teacher will have no right to renewal of his appointment and he would be offered engagement in the ensuing academic year only if he is successful in the selections to be held a fresh for the said subsequent year.

(d) Part time teacher shall have no right to claim regularisation.

U.P. Act No. 42 of 2006 whereby Section 31-E has been added to the Commission's Act, which reads as follows :

"31-E (1) Subject to the provisions contained in Section 12 and 13, if any vacancy exists, which cannot be filled under the provisions of said sections, a teacher on honorarium shall be absorbed in the manner prescribed under sub-section (2), who is working in grant in aid college, possessing educational qualifications determined by the State Government, receiving honorarium. Thereby working for a minimum period of three academic sessions and has been working till the date of commencement of the Uttar Pradesh Higher Education Services Commission (Third Amendment) Act, 2006.

(2) Where any substantive vacancy in the post of a teacher in a grant in aid college is to be filled by direct recruitment, such post shall, at the instance of the Director, be offered by the management to teacher on honorarium referred to in sub-section (1).

(3) Where any teacher on honorarium who has been offered appointment in accordance with the provisions of sub-section (2) fails to join the post within the time allowed, which shall not be less than Fifteen days, his further claim shall cease automatically. Explanation for the purposes of this section : "teacher on honorarium" means a person working in Grant-in-aid College and is engaged in teaching a course of study and receiving payment from the Funds of State aid on a fixed honorarium appointed on a contractual basis with the prior approval of the Director.

(4) Where the Management fails to offer any post to a teacher on honorarium in accordance with the provisions of sub-section (2) within the time specified by the Director, the Director, may himself issue the letter of appointment to such teacher on honorarium and the teacher on honorarium concerned shall be entitled to get his salary as teacher, from

the date, he joins the post in pursuance of such letter of appointment."

C. Constitutional and Legal Implications of Absorption of Contractual Lecturers

Everyone wants a dignified life with all rights such as right to food, shelter, medicine, education etc. But all these rights cannot be availed in the meager amount of contractual lecturership.

A bunch of nearly 169 petitions, was filed in respect of appointment of part-time teachers, in various Degree Colleges of the State of Uttar Pradesh affiliated to Universities covered by the U.P. State Universities Act, 1973 (hereinafter referred to as the Act, 1973), in terms of the Government Order dated 07.04.1998, on honorarium @ Rs. 100 to be paid on per lecture basis subject to the maximum of Rs. 5000 per month (now enhanced to Rs. 8000, against duly created posts of Lecturers, as well as absorption of such part-time teachers against substantive vacancies of Lecturers in terms of Section 31-E of the U.P. Higher Education Service Commission Act, 1980 (hereinafter called the Commission's Act) added vide 3rd Amendment Act No. 42 of 2006. While a set of prospective applicants question the process of absorption as per Section 31-E of the Commission's Act itself. The aforesaid writ petitions may be categorized into four groups—(a) Writ petitions filed by part-time teachers appointed under Government Order dated 07.04.1998 subject to the maximum of Rs. 5000 per month (now enhanced to Rs. 8000) seeking salary at par with the regularly appointed Lecturers with a further relief for a writ of mandamus commanding the College as well as Directorate of Higher Education not to interfere in the working of such part-time teachers till regularly selected teachers recommended by the Commission joins. (b) Writ petitions filed by the part-time teachers with the prayer that they be absorbed against substantive vacant post of Lecturers in affiliated Degree Colleges in terms of Section 31-E of the Commission's Act. (c) Writ Petition No. 1722 of 2007, Writ Petition No. 31429 of 2007 as well as Writ Petition No. 10858 of 2008 have been filed by part-time teachers who have already obtained an order from this Court in an earlier writ petition for their continuance till regularly selected candidates from the Commission join. They now seek the relief of payment of salary at par with the regularly selected Lecturers. (d) Writ Petition No. 5210 of 2007 (Anurag Tripathi and others *vs.* State of U.P. and others challenges the vires of Section 31-E of the U.P. Higher Education Services Commission Act, 1980 as added by U.P. Act No. 42 of 2006 which provides absorption of part-time teachers against substantive vacancies on the post of Lecturers.

This Court was not required to examine the issue as to whether the Government Order dated 07.04.1998 providing for appointment of such part-time teachers was in accordance with law or not inasmuch as a Division Bench of this Court in the case of Malvika Shekhar *Versus* Director of Higher Education U.P. & Others 2004 (1) AWC[1], 321 has held that such appointments are void being contrary to the provisions of the Commission's Act and, therefore, directed that such appointments be terminated forthwith. Against the said judgment of Court, a Special Leave Petition (Civil) No. 84 of 2004 is pending consideration before the Hon'ble Supreme Court wherein interim orders have been passed in favour of such part time appointees where under they still continue in the employment. Reference may also be had to another Division Bench judgment of this Court in the case of Alok Kumar Singh & Others *Versus* State of U.P. & Others; 2002 (2) UPLBEC, 1373 wherein this Court after noticing the provisions of the Commission's Act and the Government Order dated 07.04.1998 held that petitioners who were appointed in terms of the Government Order dated 07.04.1998 had no right to the post. Their process of selection is quite different, the nature of duties performed are also not similar to that of regularly appointed Lecturers. While the aforesaid issues qua the legality of appointment of part time teachers under Government Order dated 07.04.1998 was pending consideration before the Hon'ble Supreme Court the State legislature has come up with U.P. Act No. 42 of 2006

Section 31-E has provided for absorption of such part time teachers against substantive vacancy of Lecturer available in Degree College. The validity of Section 31-E has been challenged by way of Writ Petition No. 5210 of 2007 (Anurag Tripathi & Others *Vs.* State of U.P. & Others)[2] on the basic plea that such absorption is violative of Article 14 of the Constitution of India and amount to denial of opportunity of consideration to open market candidates like the petitioner of the said petition. The Court heard Shri Ashok Khare, Senior Advocate, Shri P.S. Baghel, Shri Shailendra and Smt. Arti Raje along with other counsels on behalf of the part-time teachers in various writ petitions, Shri G.K. Singh on behalf of the petitioners in Writ Petition No. 5210 of 2007, Additional Advocate General, Shri Zafar Naiyar, on behalf of the State respondents.

The Court may first deal with the right of the part-time teachers to claim salary at par with regular Lecturers appointed in various Degree Colleges on the principle of Equal Pay for Equal Work. The issue is no more *res integra*, a Division Bench of this Court in the case of Alok Kumar Singh (*Supra*) has specifically held that the mode and manner as well as the nature of appointment of such part time teachers including the duties and responsibilities discharged by them are altogether different vis-a-vis a regularly appointed teachers. In paragraph numbers 8 and 9 it has been recorded as follows: "The Government Order dated 07.04.1998 only provides a summary process of selection on local arrangement, and the Advertisement was localized. In view of the transitory nature of such engagement highly qualified persons generally retrain from such job. Such candidates cannot be equated with full time regular teachers appointed by the U.P. Higher Education Service Commission. It is stated in Paragraph 5 (p) of the counter-affidavit filed by the State Government that petitioners participated in the selection process in pursuance of the impugned advertisement and hence they cannot challenge the same. In view of the averments made in the counter-affidavit of the State Government it is evident that the petitioners are working only on contract basis without any regular selection through the Commission, and they cannot be equated with regularly selected teachers. Hence, they have no right to the post. Their appointment was under the Government Order dated 07.04.1998 to deliver lectures for a very short span of time and they cannot claim regularization. Their duties and function are also different from the regularly selected teachers. These appointments were made only due to the shortage of regularly selected candidates so that the teaching work may not suffer. However, the appointees cannot claim any right to continue."

The Court also considered the plea for such parity as claimed by the petitioners with reference to Article 23 of the Constitution of India. According to the petitioners, they are required to discharge identical duties of teaching requisite number of classes (periods), examination duties and other administrative responsibilities like any other regular Lecturers in the Degree College. Despite performance of such identical duties they are being paid only on per lecture basis and that to subject to the maximum prescribed, while pay package for a regular Lecturer is about Rs. 15,000 per month at the age of initial appointment. It is, therefore, contended that the respondents are taking *begar* from the petitioners, which is prohibited under Article 23 of the Constitution of India. The petitioners, therefore, claim an entitlement for similar pay.

This very Bench had considered the duties which are required to be performed by part-time teachers in terms of their appointment in the Writ Petition No. 12931 of 2008, Tarun Kumar *Vs.* State of U.P. & Others decided on 05.03.2008 and rejected the case that such teachers were being exploited and were forced to do *begar* observing as follows : "In the instant case, the aforesaid anti-*begar* law does not apply at all. It is not the case of the petitioner that he had been working as full time teacher or had ever been appointed as full time lecturer nor he has stated that he had been forced to work in contravention of the terms of his appointment letter or the Government Order under which he has been appointed. Court clarified that it is at the option of such teacher appointed on per lecture basis to take as many lectures as he wants and for each lecture he is entitled to get Rs. 100 per lecture subject however the maximum of Rs. 5,000 (now enhanced to Rs. 8,000), meaning thereby that the day an appointee completes 50 lectures in a month now 80 lectures in a month, he has a right to refuse any further responsibility to teach the students and in such a situation the management would have to make alternative arrangements. In view of the above, the petition is devoid of merit and is accordingly dismissed. However, if the petitioner feels aggrieved that he is being exploited by the Committee of Management and is being forced to work in contravention of the said Government Order dated 17th April, 1998 or terms and conditions incorporated in his appointment letter, he is at liberty to approach the Civil Court for damages against the management of the college. However, he cannot be permitted to have any claim against the public exchequer. The court held that petitioners are not required to discharge same duties and responsibilities as are to be performed by a regular Lecturer. Payment for the duties performed by the part-time Lecturer is being made on the scale provided by an expert body namely University Grants Commission, on per lecture basis @ Rs. 100 such payment has not been shown to be insufficient or a pittance as alleged by the petitioners. The plea of *begar* has, therefore, been stated only to be rejected. Reference may also be had to the judgements of the Hon'ble Supreme Court wherein the principle of equal pay for equal work has been explained and it has been now settled that persons who are appointed after following a different procedure, the appointment being of different nature and who do not perform identical duties as are performed by regularly appointed persons are not entitled to the benefits of the said principle. In State of Haryana & Others *Vs.* Jasmer Singh & Others, (1996) 11 SCC 77, the Hon'ble Supreme Court considered the provisions of Articles 39 (d), 14 and 16 of the Constitution and held that the principle of 'equal pay for equal work' is not always easy to apply. There are inherent difficulties in comparing and evaluating the work done by different persons in different organisations, or even in the same organisation. There may be differences in educational or technical qualifications, which may have a bearing on the skills, which the holders bring to their job although the designation of the job may be the same. There may also be other considerations, which have relevance to efficiency in service which may justify differences in pay scales on the basis of criteria such as experience and seniority, or a need to prevent stagnation in the cadre, so that the good performance can be elicited from persons who have reached the top of the pay scale. There may be various other similar considerations, which may have a bearing on efficient performance in a job. The evaluation of such jobs for the purposes of pay scale must be left to expert bodies and, unless there are any *mala fides*, its evaluation should be accepted. The Court further observed as under :

> "The respondents, who are employed on daily wagers cannot be treated as on a par with persons in regular service of the

> State of Haryana holding similar posts. Daily-rated workers are not required to possess the qualifications prescribed for regular workers, nor do they have to fulfill the requirement relating to age at the time of recruitment. They are not selected in the manner in which the regular employees are selected. In other words, the requirements for selection are not as rigorous. There are also other provisions relating to regular service such as the liability of a member of the service to be transferred, and his being subject to the disciplinary jurisdiction of the authorities as prescribed, which daily-rated workmen are not subjected to. They cannot, therefore, be equated with regular workmen for the purposes for their wages. Nor can they claim the minimum of the regular pay scale of the regularly employed."

In Union of India & Others. *Vs.* Nanda Kumar & Others, (1997) 11 SCC 661, the Hon'ble Supreme Court after considering large number of its earlier judgements including Daily Rated Casual Labour Employed under P &T Department through Bhartiya Dak Tar Mazdoor Manch *Vs.* Union of India, (1988) 1 SCC 122; Jacob M. Puthuparambil *Vs.* Kerala Water Authority, (1999) 1 SCC 28, held that the daily wagers or casual labourers employed on temporary basis by the railway administration would not be granted pay parity. A similar view has been reiterated in State of U.P. & Others *Vs.* Ministerial Karamchari Sangh, AIR 1998 SC 303 observing that the issue of pay parity should be assigned to the Expert Body as it cannot be done by the Courts.

In Gujarat Agricultural University *Vs.* Rathod Labhu Bechar & Others, AIR 2001 SC 706, the Hon'ble Supreme Court considered a similar issue of pay parity to the daily-rated workers working since long considering large number of its earlier judgments including Surinder Singh *Vs.* Engineer-in-Chief, C.P.W.D., AIR 1986 sc 584; Ghaziabad Development Authority *Vs.* Kikram Chaudhary, (1995) 5 SCC 210; Basudev Pati *Vs.* State of Orissa, (1997) 3 SCC 632; Jasmer Singh (*supra*); State of Haryana *Vs.* Piara Singh, AIR 1992 SC 2130; Bhagwati Prasad *Vs.* Delhi State Mineral Development Corporation, AIR 1990 SC 371; and held that for their absorption etc. the University may frame the Scheme for regularisation and as regularisation cannot be directed in absence of regular post and such employees can be entitled for minimum wages under the Statute, if any, or the prevailing wages in the locality but the question of claiming the minimum of the pay scale of a regular employee would not arise. In State of Haryana & Anr. *Vs.* Tilak Raj & Others AIR 2003 SC 2658, the Hon'ble Supreme Court held as under :

> "A scale of pay is attached to a definite post and in case of daily wager, he holds no post. The respondent workers cannot be held to hold any post to claim even any comparison with the regular and permanent staff for any or all purposes including a claim for equal pay and allowances. To claim a relief on the basis of equality, it is for the claimants to substantiate a clear-cut basis of equivalence and a resultant hostile discrimination before becoming eligible to claim rights on a par with other group vis-a-vis an alleged discrimination . . . Equal pay for equal work is a concept which requires for its applicability complete and wholesome identity between a group of employees claiming identical pay scales and the other group of employees who have already earned such pay scales. The problem about equal pay cannot always be translated into a mathematical formula."

While deciding the said case, reliance had been placed by the Hon'ble Supreme Court on its earlier judgments including State of U.P. *Vs.* J.P. Chaurasia, AIR 1989 SC 19; Harbans Lal *Vs.* State of Himachal Pradesh, (1989) 4 SCC 549. In Harbans Lal (*supra*), it has been held that a mere nomenclature designating a person is not enough to come to a conclusion that he was doing the same work. A comparison cannot be made with counterparts in other establishments with different locations though owned by the same management. The quality of work which is produced may be different, even the nature of work assigned may be different. It is not just a comparison of physical activity. The application of principle of pay parity requires consideration of various dimensions of given job.

In State of Haryana & Others *Vs.* Charanjit Singh & Others, AIR 2006 SC 161, a similar view has been reiterated for rejecting the claim of 'equal pay for equal work' observing that persons may do the same work, their quality of work may differ. Where persons are selected by a Selection Committee on the basis of merit with due regard to seniority, a higher pay scale granted to such persons who are evaluated by a Competent Authority cannot be challenged. A classification based on different educational qualifications may also justify different pay scale.

In State of Karnataka & Others *Vs.* KGSD Canteen Employees Welfare Association & Others, AIR 2006 SC 845, after considering very large number of its earlier judgments and considering the provisions of Articles 14, 16 and 39 (d) of the Constitution of India, the Hon'ble Supreme Court held that daily wagers cannot claim pay scale as that of government employees. The Court again reiterated the law laid down by it in its earlier judgment in Mahendra L. Jain & Others *Vs.* Indore Development Authority & Others, (2005) 1 SCC 639, wherein it has been held that the daily wagers do not hold the post, therefore, they were not the employees of the State. Salary of a regular scale of pay, it is trite, is payable to an employee only when he holds a status. In U.P. State Sugar Corporation Ltd. & Anr. *Vs.* Sant Raj Singh & Others, AIR 2000 SC 2296, the Hon'ble Supreme Court held that the doctrine of 'equal pay for equal work' as enshrined under Article 39 (d) of the Constitution read with Article 14 thereof, cannot be applied in vacuum. The constitutional scheme postulates equal pay for equal work for those who are equally placed in all respects. Possession of a higher qualification has all along been treated to be a valid basis for classification of two categories of employees. Accordingly the relief prayed for in all the writ petitions qua payment of salary at par with regular Lecturers is hereby rejected. We may now examine the issue of continuance of such part-time teachers till regularly selected candidates join. On behalf of the petitioners it has been contended that under the Government Order dated 07.04.1998, it has been provided that a part time teacher if appointed would not be entitled to continue automatically in the next academic session. In the next academic session the entire process for fresh recruitment has to be re-initiated and if the candidate is again selected as part time teacher in terms of the Government Order dated 17.04.1998, he would then only become entitled to continue in the subsequent session. It is submitted that such an arrangement on the face of it, is arbitrary and inasmuch as it amounts to replacement of a part-time teacher by another part time teacher. It is contended that once a person has been selected for appointment as part time teacher after following the procedure prescribed, there is little or no justification for any fresh selection being held after the end of the earlier academic year for like nature of appointment to be made in the subsequent year. It is submitted that the part-time teachers appointed in a Degree college are not to be treated as a daily wage labourers nor they can be asked to undergo the process of selection again and again for continuance as par-time teacher only. Teachers by the profession are liable to be treated with respect.

In view of the final orders passed by the Hon'ble Supreme Court in the Special Leave Petition (Civil) No. 84 of 2004 it was held that part time teachers appointed strictly in accordance with the Government Order dated 07.04.1998 would be entitled to continue on same terms and conditions as were applicable at the time of their first appointment (subject, however, to the revision of a maximum amount prescribed on per lecture basis) till regularly selected candidates join.

This took the Court to the hotly contested issue qua absorption of part time teachers against substantive vacancies on the post of Lecturers in Degree Colleges as per Section 31-E (added by U.P. Act No. 46 of 2006) to the Commissions Act. In the case of Malvika Shekhar (*supra*), Division Bench of the Court held that appointment of part time teachers under the Government Order dated 17-04-98 were void being violative of Article 12 of the Commission's Act. It is no doubt true that against the said judgment of the Division Bench, Special Leave Petition was filed before the Hon'ble Supreme Court wherein operation of the judgment and order of this Court was stayed. It merely meant that such part time teachers who were to be removed from employment in terms of the Division Bench judgment have been permitted to continue till the issue of the legality of their appointment is finally adjudicated upon by the Hon'ble Supreme Court.

A issue does arise as to whether even after appointment of such part time teachers having been declared null and void by a Division Bench of this Court and the matter of such appointments being *sub-judice* before of the Hon'ble Supreme Court is it proper and appropriate to direct for regularization of such part-time teachers under Section 31-E to the Commission's Act. Reference may be had to the judgment of the Hon'ble Supreme Court in the case of Committee of Management, Arya Nagar Inter College, Arya Nagar, Kanpur & Anr. *Vs.* Sree Kumar Tiwary & Anr; AIR, 1997 SC, 3071, wherein the Hon'ble Supreme Court has considered that a teacher continuing under an interim order of the Court cannot be held to be in continuous service in his own right under an order of appointment. The relevant portion of the judgment is as follows :

> "...But the crucial question is: whether the respondent was continuously serving the institution under Clause (c) of Section 33-B (i)? Admittedly the service of the respondent came to be terminated w.e.f. June 30, 1988. Though he had obtained the stay order and continued to be in service, it was not by virtue of his own right under an order of appointment, he continued in the office with permission of the Management."

No litigant can derive any benefit from mere pendency of case in a Court of Law, as the interim order always merge in the final order to be passed in the case and if the Special Leave Petition is ultimately dismissed, the interim order would stand nullified automatically. Even otherwise interim orders are passed to maintain the status as is prevailing on the date of the order. Normally there should not be any change of status of the litigant during the pendency of the proceedings.

In view of the aforesaid it can be said that the part time teachers who have been appointed under the Government Order cannot be considered for absorption in terms of Section 31-E of the Commission's Act so long as Special Leave Petition against the judgment of this Court in the case of Malvika Shekhar (*Supra*) is not decided by the Hon'ble Apex Court. The Court may also examine as to whether the provision incorporated under Section 31-E providing for absorption of such part time teachers is *ultra vires* to the provisions of the Constitution of India or to the Commission's Act or not. At the very outset this Court may record that absorption under a statutory provision cannot be provided qua an appointment which was null and void at the inception, inasmuch as no life can be infused in a dead body. More so, if an order is bad in its inception, it does not get sanctified at a later stage. (Vide Upen Chandra Gogoi *Vs.* State of Assam & Others, (1998) 3 SCC, 381; Satchidananda Mishra *Vs.* State of Orissa & Ors., (2004) 8 SCC 599; and Regional Manager, SBI *Vs.* Rakesh Kumar Tewari, (2006) 1 SCC 530). In C. Albert Morris *Vs.* K. Chandrasekaran & Others, (2006) 1 SCC 228 the Hon'ble Apex Court held that a right in law exists only and only when it has a lawful origin.

In State of U.P. *Vs.* Neeraj Awasthi & Others (2006) 1 SCC, 667 wherein it has been held that regularisation cannot be a mode of appointment. Illegal appointments cannot be regularised. Neither temporary nor permanent status can be conferred by regularization. An attempt to induct an employee without following the procedure for selection prescribed by law would amount to back-door entry, the practice whereof has been deprecated.

From the history of the legislation qua appointment on the post of Lecturers in the aided recognized Degree Colleges, it would be seen that in the last 37 years the State has come up at least with six orders/statutory provisions wherein ad hoc, temporary appointments and part time appointments have been directed to be either regularized or absorbed against the substantive post of Lecturers.

It may be recorded that post of Lecturers/Principal/Readers/ Professor in Degree Colleges and Universities were treated to be a class in themselves and, therefore, all these posts were provided to be filled by way of direct recruitment only, meaning thereby that any other factor except merit was irrelevant for the purposes of appointment on the posts. Every candidate is required to compete in the process of selection with candidates from open market for appointment at every stage of the hierarchy of the posts in Degree Colleges/Universities. The purpose is obvious. Education is the back bone of any civilized country. If compromises are permitted to be made in the quality of education to be imparted, there is little or no doubt that the back bone of the country would at least bend if not broken. Such a situation would not be in the interest of the public at large. The State, Executive the legislature have to ensure that best qualified faculty members are made available for imparting education in Degree Colleges and Universities and no attempt to marginalise the said concept of best teachers by any executive or legislative Act can be approved of by this Court.

It is no doubt true that the legislature in respect of a subject within its legislative domain may make law, subject to the constitutional scheme as in the circumstances and conditions is required, including a provision for regularisation/absorption of ad hoc or part-time employees. It is also not in doubt that the Court shall not normally interfere with such legislations, which are within the legislative competence except if they violate some of the fundamental rights guaranteed by the Constitution. The power of the Court to interfere with the legislative act has been dealt with in series of judgments by the Hon'ble Supreme Court.

In A.K. Roy *Vs.* Union of India & Ors., AIR 1982 SC 719, the Hon'ble Supreme Court has held that Ordinance cannot be struck down on the ground of non-application of mind or *mala fides* or that the prevailing circumstances did not warrant issue of Ordinance. In can be struck down either on the ground of want competence of the legislature or being violative of the provisions of Part III of the Constitution. The Courts are precluded from inquiring into the proprietary to exercise the legislative power as it has to be assumed that the legislative discretion is properly exercised. The motive of the legislature in passing a Statute cannot be scrutinised by the Courts, nor the Courts can examine whether the legislature had applied its mind to the provisions of the Statute before passing it. The proprietary necessitated by a legislature is for the determination of the legislative authority and not for determination by the Court. In State of Andhra Pradesh *Vs.* McDowell & Company, AIR 1996 SC 1627, the Supreme Court held that an enactment cannot be struck down on the ground that the Court thinks justified. The Parliament and the Legislatures composed, as they are the representatives of the people, are supposed to know and be aware of the needs of the people and what is good and bad for them. The Court cannot sit in judgment over their wisdom.

In Greater Bombay Coop. Bank Ltd. *Vs.* United Yarn Tex (O) Ltd. & Others (2007) 6 SCC 236, the Apex Court had taken a similar view that an Ordinance can be struck down either on the ground of want of competence or being violative of the provisions of Part III of the Constitution. There is always a presumption regarding the constitutional validity of the legislation. Reference has been made before us to the judgment of the Hon'ble Supreme Court in the case of Reserved Pool Teachers who were directed to be substantively appointed under Section 21 (B) of the U.P. Secondary Education Services Selection Board, 1982 even when they had worked for a few days only when the regular teachers throughout the State of U.P. were on strike. Such appointment of Reserved Pool Teachers was approved by the Hon'ble Supreme Court, in the case of Prabodh Verma & Others *Vs.* State of U.P. & Ors., AIR 1985 SC, 167 and it was held as follows:

> "The reserve pool teachers thus formed a separate and distinct from other applicants for the posts of teachers in recognized institutions. The differentia which distinguished the class of reserve pool teachers from the class of other applicants for the posts of teachers in recognized institutions is the service rendered by the reserve pool teachers to the State and its educational system in a time of crisis and this differentia bears a reasonable and rational nexus or relation to the object sought to be achieved by Ordinances Nos. 10 and 22 of 1978 read with the Intermediate Educational Act, namely, to keep the system of High School and Intermediate Education in the State functioning smoothly without interruption so that the students may not suffer a detriment."

The Court may also notice the judgment of the Hon'ble Supreme Court which has been the sheet anchor of the petitioners qua their absorption namely State of Karnataka & Anr. *Vs.* B. Suvarna Malini & Anr. (2001) 1 SCC, 728. The Hon'ble Supreme Court no doubt upheld the competence of the State legislature to provide for absorption of part time teachers however what is worthwhile to notice is the paragraph 9 of the said judgment which reads as follows:

> "From the materials on record, it appears that the State Government has been regulating the mode of appointment of part-time Lecturers and it is not correct that there has been no process of selection before such appointment of part-time Lecturers. Even though the selection had not been made by the Public Service Commission, yet there was a process of selection and it further appears that unqualified people were not being appointed as part-time Lecturers. Part-time Lecturers having formed a class by themselves and for some reason or the others, they having been deprived of the benefits of the earlier directions of this Court on account of inaction on the part of the State Government, the matter was re-examined by a Committee of experts as to how best, the services of these part-time Lecturers can be utilized and at the same time, there will be no dilution in the quality of teaching nor can there be any infraction in the minimum qualification necessary for appointment as a Lecturer. The concept of equality before the law does not involve the idea of absolute equality among human beings, which is a physical impossibility. All that Article 14 guarantees is a similarity or treatment contra-distinguished from identical treatment. Equality before law means that among equals the law should be equal and should be equally administered and that the likes should be treated alike. Equality before the law does not mean that things which are different shall be treated as though, they are the same. It of course means denial of any special privilege by reason of birth, creed or the like. The legislature as well as the executive Government, while dealing with diverse problems arising out of an infinite variety of human relations must of necessity have the power of making special laws, to attain any particular object and to achieve that object, it must have the power of selection or classification of persons and things upon which such laws are to operate. Mere differentiation or inequality of treatment

does not *per se* amount to discrimination. When the Absorption Rules are examined from the aforesaid standpoint and when we consider the circumstances under which the said Rules were made to solve a human problem and that the Rules made were put to objection to the general public and even the Public Service Commission was consulted and finally matter was laid before the State Legislature to have their concurrence, we are of the considered opinion that the High Court committed an error in striking down the Rules on the ground that they were discriminatory. When this Court deprecates the regularization and absorption, when it comes to the conclusion that such regularization and absorption has become a common method of allowing back-door entries and then regularizing such entries, it is not that in every case, the Court would be justified in striking down the process of absorption or regularization, more so when such absorption has been made as a legislative measure and that also as a one-time measure, and at the same time insisting upon the essential qualifications to be duly complied with, by the persons intended to be absorbed on regular basis."

It would be seen that the Hon'ble Supreme Court deprecated the practice of regularisation when it is used as a common method of allowing back-door entries. It saved the regularization in the case of State of Karnataka (*Supra*) after specifically noticing that it was a one time measure. The facts in hand before us depict an entirely different picture as already stated above that in the last 37 years the State has amended the Act with at least six times for regularization/ absorption of temporary teachers/ad hoc teachers while the process of regular open market selection has been given a back seat. The State earlier experimented by providing Selection Committee under the Act, 1973 for regular appointment on the post of Lecturers. It changed the procedure in its entirety by enforcing the Commission's Act. The Commission had hardly been able to do justice to the object for which it had been created. The number of selections made against the total number of vacancies available is insufficient to the extent of negligible. Huge number of vacancies as of date i.e. nearly 9000 are awaiting regular selection by the Commission. For various reasons the Commission has not been able to function e.g. non- requisition of vacancies as per the rules applicable, because of absence of members and the Chairman for long durations. Every change of the Government has resulted in change of the Chairman and its members, which has made the situation worst. In such circumstances the problem which has been generated qua non-availability of selected teachers of the required member for Degree Colleges is hand made of the government itself. The legislature decided to delete the provision for ad hoc appointment as provided under Section 16 of the Commission's Act, so that appointment through regular selection alone could be made. The Commission fails to deliver the goods and the number of vacancies continue to rise and as of date stand at nearly 9000. The State Government come up with the Government Order dated 17.04.1998 providing for part-time teachers to be paid on a per lecture basis through local process of selection based on marks obtained in various academic examinations. Such part-time teachers are now to be regularized under Section 31-E of the Commission's Act.

What had been taken away by deleting Section 16 of the Commission's Act, has indirectly been provided for under the Government Order dated 17.04.1998 and now such appointees are sought to be absorbed under Section 31-E of the Commission's Act. The Court fails to comprehend the exact intention of the State except that there is an attempt to somehow or the other to resort to appointments, which are initially, stop gap/part-time/ad hoc and thereafter to regularise such appointments. The total outcome of such practice is that the quality of education by teachers duly selected by the Commission has been made a casualty and the ultimate sufferers are the students for whom neither the State nor the authorities appear to have any concern.

D. Opinion about Contractual Lecturership

The earning of livelihood became an important aspect of life after coming into existence of culture as many physiological changes occurred during the process of evolution. In cultural set-up it became very difficult for a human being to survive, therefore he became victim of circumstances. After the coming into existence of state, man searched for employment and other resources so as to earn his livelihood and survive in this cruel world.

In present world education provides a new way of earning and subsistence. Now a person can lead a decent way of life with the help of education. Today specialized education is required due to the advancement of technology and knowledge. Catering to the need and requirement of students various educational institutions have been established of higher learning by the University Grants Commission (UGC).

In back years UGC had launched National Eligibility Test (NET) as minimum qualification for the purpose of applying for the post of Lecturer in any University or College. The purpose was to introduce quality education in the system. After clearing this test a young boy/girl of 24 or 25 years old could become eligible for lecturership in his/her specialized subject. Apart from this Ph.D. holders in a particular subject are also entitled to apply for lecturership. In present scenario candidates for lecturership have been exempted from taking this test if they have doctorate degree in their subject. But it remains essential qualification for others. The idea is to provide quality education by bringing qualified and quality candidates for lecturership. Besides UGC and State government provide various grants to the University and Colleges for improving the standard of Higher Education.

But in the name of funds crisis, lack of posts, ban on government jobs and continuous retirement of teachers the higher education standard has reached to its nadir. Today neither government nor institutions are serious and interested in providing quality education, they are only interested in running their institutions any how for earning huge profits as an industry. The idea of appointing teachers on contractual basis to meet the crisis of teachers has done no good to the higher education. It has only adversely affected the quality of higher education and life of contractual teachers also.

The contractual teacher means a teacher who works on payment for per lecturer basis. He is not entitled to any other facilities as enjoyed by their fellow permanent teachers to enjoy the life of dignity as ensured by our Constitution and other international conventions. The recruitment process itself explains the pathetic condition of contractual teachers. In the month of June or July vacancies regarding teaching positions for various subjects on contractual basis are advertised in local newspapers by different institutions. A number of candidates apply for these posts without any proper course. After some screening names of successful candidates on merit basis are sent to the Higher Education Directorate, Allahabad for approval. The candidate has to wait for long as approval from Directorate comes in the month of October or November. After getting information of his appointment a candidate joins on the affidavit that he/she will not demand his/her regularization in future.

All this procedure adversely affects teaching as well as future of students too, as every college is either affiliated or associated with some University where academic calendar begins in July itself. Some Departments in colleges are having only one or two posts of teachers and whole of the department is to be run by contractual teachers only. Presently in the Lucknow University Academic Calender runs from 16 July to end of February as final exams are held from First of March. The whole procedure shows that a contractual lecturer gets only 3 to 4 months of teaching as various holidays are there during this period of teaching. It is well known and there have been various Supreme Court pronouncements that Teaching is a Mission, but we should not overlook the personal life of a teacher who is involved in this mission.

Conclusion

It can be concluded that contractual teaching is nothing but another kind of contractual labour, it is an important dimension of contractual labour which can be governed by the provisions of Indian Contract Act, 1872, by various international conventions ensuring human rights and by The Contract Labour (Regulation and Abolition) Act, 1970 ensuring all the human rights of a contractual teacher. It should also be noted that contractual lecturer is appointed after fulfilling all the requisite qualification for the post and he continues to prove his /her worth throughout the academic year. All the contractual lecturers in U.P. are proving their worth at their places of appointments since 1998. They should be treated at par with lecturers appointed on regular basis by the selection committee of the Commission and not merely as short term gap arrangements. Contractual lecturers are also human beings and they have a right to live with dignity.

NOTES

1. In civil miscellaneous writ petition No.44332 of 2003 (Malvika Shekhar *vs.* Director Higher Education, U.P. and others.) Allahabad High Court has passed an across the board direction to the concerned authorities to dismiss all the teachers appointed on the honorarium basis (even without notice to the effected parties) in following terms :

   "We therefore direct the concerned authorities including Secretary and Director of Higher Education and the U.P. Higher Education Services Commission that they must see to it that manday appointment i.e. (honorarium basis) are not made any more and any appointment already made are terminated forthwith. The posts of lecturer in the Degree/P.G. college should be filled strictly in accordance with the provisions of the Act i.e. by selection through the U.P. Higher Education Services Commission".

   The petition is dismissed with the above observation. In the light of this verdict SLP (Civil) No. 8840/2004 filed in the Hon'ble Supreme Court of India which gave its verdict as follows :

   The said order, which is quoted herein above, is passed even without hearing the affected parties. Therefore, to that extent alone, we set aside the above quoted part of the order and we direct the High Court Allahabad to once again consider the said civil miscellaneous writ petition No. 44332 of 2003 in the light of the later developments, namely, selection of certain candidates by U.P. Higher Education Service Commission.

   Still final verdict of the Allahabad High Court has yet to come.

2. Anurag Tripathi & Others *vs.* State of U.P. & Others, Civil Misc. Writ Petition No. 5210 of 2007 Lucknow.

20

CHIKAN CRAFT AS A SUBSISTENCE OCCUPATION IN LUCKNOW

S. S. A. Jafri

INTRODUCTION

Extremely beautiful, sophisticated, fine, delicate the floral tracery of white on white clothes is actually called *Chikankari* or *Chikan*. Chikankari is a distinctive integral part of Lucknow culture. In India it is guessed that Chikan embroidery may have existed, or may have been known by some other name from time immemorial. Ancient books revealed bronze needle dating 1500 – 2300 BC and figurine wearing embroidered drapery has been mentioned and seen in the ancient Buddhist stupa sculpture. The *Babur Nama* accounts for the clothes worn then, and the mention of very fine muslin with white embroidery, which is in fact the chikan. The famous historian Abul Fazal documented the clothes decorated with fine embroidery.

Akbar patronized and established the industries for fine embroidery work. He invited the expert chikan craft masters from Nishapur, Iran. All the craftsmen like cutting masters, tailors, embroiderers, gold-silversmith manufacturers of fine wires used to sit under one roof. The cross-cultural exchange encouraged an advance embroidery craft, which spread in all parts of the country. Indian embroidery craft was influenced by middle east, European and Chinese embroidery, when cross-border cultural exchanges improved. Dhaka was an important centre of chikan craft. It is said that Jahangir brought this craft to Lucknow and later it was whole-heartedly adopted by the Nawabs of Lucknow, thus it became a part of the culture of Lucknow. Throughout the history of Indian textile, we see the embroidery work on clothes was a common feature. In ancient and medieval periods embroidery may be more popular among the elites but in modern period it is common even among masses. Thus, due to increasing demand within and foreign countries, chikan craft has become an important industry of Lucknow and Avadh. About 2500 entrepreneurs are engaged in manufacturing the chikan for local, national and international markets. By rough estimates about 2.5 lakh chikan workers are engaged in this industry and who are residing in Lucknow and around Avadh region. The consumption of chikan produce is approximately 15 per cent locally in Lucknow market, 10 per cent in other parts of Uttar Pradesh, 50 per cent in rest of India and 25 per cent for export. Chikan craft entrepreneurs are almost equal in numbers among Hindus and Muslims. Chikan craft workers are divided amongst Hindus and Muslims in a proportion of 30 and 70 per cent respectively. Participation of Hindus as chikan craft workers is a recent phenomenon. With a rare exception most of the chikan craft entrepreneurs are male, majority of chikan craft workers are females, who do the needle work—embroidery. The core of chikan craft is the embroidery, which is successfully done by chikan craft women workers. On question, why has Lucknow become famous for chikan craft? Why not other parts of the country? Some give explanation that those wooden stamps for making the designs on cloth is carved only in Lucknow, and nowhere in the country it can be made of this quality. This argument seems to be untrue as nothing is impossible to be created in any part of the country. The truth is that in Lucknow about 40 per cent population belongs to minority community, among them mostly they don't have any alternative, e.g., agricultural land in rural areas or any employment for their livelihood. Since chikan craft industry is an unorganized enterprise, whose entrepreneurs thrive on exploitation of chikankar women workers, whose average per month income is less than Rs. 600, when the average reported income of entrepreneurs is Rs. 21231, which is roughly 35 times higher than the chikankar women workers.

In chikan craft industry, chikan craft women workers are in majority who do the delicate embroidery work (needle and thread work) and their eyesight is maximum affected leading to total blindness. Related to chikan craft, there are few other artisans like cutting master, tailor, printer, washermen and agent, but they enjoy the better income, i.e. more than Rs. 2500 per month. About one-fifth of the households of chikankar embroiderer have more than one chikankar. Average annual item-wise production per sample entrepreneur is Kurta 3,601, Ladies top 2,829, Shalwar-Kameez 2,824, Saree 2215, Shirts 1,742, Aba-Chadar-Dupatta 248, Sherwani 78 and Lahanga 12. About 12 per cent sample entrepreneurs have reported that they export their products to foreign countries (mostly middle-eastern countries). The impact of income is reflected from the living condition of people engaged in chikan craft. Average size of residential house of chikan craft entrepreneurs is about 2,321 sq.ft. When in case of chikankar it is only 469 sq.ft. About half of the sample entrepreneurs have taken loans from various sources at the average rate of 12 per cent interest, which they expect to be given by the government at lower rate of interest.

At first, designs are printed on the cloth with washable colours mainly indigo. This is a specialized job done by a printer mainly men who use the traditional wooden blocks. Once the design is printed, the garments are transferred from printer to the chikankar, who are mainly women, for needlework. The main stitches of chikan are called: Jali, Murri, Phanda, Bakhia, Hool, Keel, Tepachi, Dhoour, Joda-Pattee, Ghaspattee, Hath-Katee, etc. Each stitch form has a wide variety of motifs. Quite a number of workers specialize in one of the stitch forms, but their proportion in the total workers is still quite low. Chikan embroidery is done on a number of products such as Kurta, tea-shirts, ladies' top, shalwar-kameez, saree, Sherwani-kurta, dupatta-chadar-aba, curtain, table-cloth, etc.

ABOUT CHIKANKAR WORKERS

Population Dynamics

Since there is no authentic information is available about the chikan craft industry or people engaged in it, on random basis chikan craft workers and their households (not necessarily related to our sample entrepreneurs) were surveyed through a well planned detailed questionnaire. For our study we surveyed randomly 6 cutting masters, 14 printers, 6 tailors, 63 chikankars, 6 washermen and 9 agents, means 104 total Chikan craft workers were extensively surveyed. Out of our survey 28 were Hindu workers and 76 were Muslim workers, means percentage-wise they are 26.67 per cent and 73.33 per cent respectively. If the entire family members of the 104 respondent chikan workers are added, it came altogether 579 populations in which male and female are 276 and 303 respectively. The overall sex ratio among the family members of chikan craft workers is high, i.e. 1,098 females per 1,000 males. In overall 579 populations of family members of chikan craft workers, 146 are Hindus and 433 are Muslims. The sex ratios among Hindu and Muslim population are 1,116 and 1,092 females per 1,000 males. The reason of high sex ratio among Hindus is due to high proportion of Scheduled Castes in its population. The highest sex ratio is found among the families of chikankars, i.e. 1,407 females per 1,000 males. It is proved that high sex ratio along with extreme poverty compels the females to take up extremely low paid chikankari, i.e. embroidery. A single female in a household may be very poor cannot take up the chikankari work. For survival and flourishment of chikan craft

Industries, high proportion of widow/divorced among female combined with high sex ratio and poverty are the necessary conditions, which unfortunately is met by the majority of Muslim households. Once a prominent clergy of the community, Dr. Kalbe Sadique in his speech on rampant poverty among Muslim community said that "Chikan is the *Nasur* (leprosy) of the community", which is difficult to be cured unless government intervenes. Entrepreneurs are able to extract high profits despite of vagaries of market forces by squeezing the wages of poor female Chikankar (embroiderer) as they have no other alternative for their survival.

By seeing the age group among Hindu chikan craft workers, it appears that dependents of 0-14 and 60+ years are comparatively less than the Muslim workers. Overall females of above 60 years age group are least in both the communities. Unusually very high proportions of widow/divorced females are found in families of

Table 20.1 : Religion-wise Population and Caste among Households of Chikan Craft Workers

Religion-wise chikan craft workers	Sample House-hold of workers	Household population of workers			Percentage to total population		
		Total	Male	Female	SC	OBC	Others
Hindu							
Cutting Master	1	6	3	3	—	—	100.0
Printer	1	3	2	1	100.0	—	—
Tailor	1	3	2	1	—	100.0	—
Chikankar	22	116	52	64	30.17	31.04	38.79
Washerman	3	18	10	8	100.0	—	—
Agent	—	—	—	—	—	—	—
Muslim							
Cutting master	5	30	18	12	—	40.00	60.00
Printer	13	80	51	29	—	10.00	90.00
Tailor	5	34	19	15	—	—	100.0
Chikankar	41	221	88	133	—	51.58	48.42
Washerman	3	18	8	10	—	100.0	—
Agent	9	50	23	27	—	12.00	88.00
Total							
Cutting master	6	36	21	15	—	33.33	66.67
Printer	14	83	53	30	3.61	9.64	86.75
Tailor	6	37	21	16	—	8.11	91.89
Chikankar	63	337	140	197	10.39	44.51	45.10
Washerman	6	36	18	18	50.00	50.00	—
Agent	9	50	23	27	—	12.00	88.00

Source: Based on survey conducted by the author and his team at Giri Institute of Development Studies, Lucknow, for the project "Diagnostic Study of Chikan Craft in Lucknow", July-August, 2006.

Table 20.2 : Religion-wise Age-Structure, Widow/Divorced and Sick Among Households of Chikan Craft Workers

Religion-wise chikan craft workers	Percentage to total male and female									
	0-14		15-59		60+		Widow/ divorced		Reported sick	
	Male	Female	Male	Female	Male	Female	Male	Female	Male	Female
Hindu										
Cutting master	—	—	100.00	100.00	—	—	—	—	—	—
Printer	—	—	50.00	100.00	50.00	—	—	—	—	—
Tailor	50.00	—	50.00	100.00	—	—	—	—	—	—
Chikankar	25.00	18.75	67.30	78.13	7.70	3.12	—	14.06	13.46	11.54
Washermen	—	12.50	100.00	87.50	—	—	—	—	20.00	—
Agent	—	—	—	—	—	—	—	—	—	—
Muslim										
Cutting master	50.00	25.00	38.89	50.00	11.11	25.00	—	—	—	—

(contd...)

Table 20.2 : (*contd.*)

Religion-wise chikan craft workers	**Percentage to total male and female**									
	0-14		**15-59**		**60+**		**Widow/ divorced**		**Reported sick**	
	Male	Female	Male	Female	Male	Female	Male	Female	Male	Female
Printer	13.73	27.59	84.31	72.41	1.96	—	—	3.45	—	3.45
Tailor	47.37	33.33	52.63	66.66	--	—	—	—	—	6.67
Chikankar	27.27	27.07	69.32	72.18	3.41	0.75	—	12.03	9.09	1.51
Washermen	37.50	20.00	50.00	80.00	12.50	—	—	—	10.00	—
Agent	21.74	11.11	69.56	88.89	8.70	—	—	3.70	8.70	—
Total										
Cutting master	42.85	20.00	47.63	60.00	9.52	20.00	—	—	—	—
Printer	13.20	26.67	83.02	73.33	3.78	--	—	3.33	—	3.33
Tailor	47.62	31.25	52.38	68.75	--	--	—	—	—	6.25
Chikankar	26.43	24.36	68.57	74.11	5.00	1.53	—	12.69	10.72	4.06
Washermen	16.67	16.67	77.78	83.33	5.55	--	—	—	16.66	—
Agent	21.74	11.11	69.56	88.89	8.70	--	—	3.70	8.70	—

Source: Based on survey conducted by the author and his team at Giri Institute of Development Studies, Lucknow, for the project "Diagnostic Study of Chikan Craft in Lucknow", July-August, 2006.

Chikankar workers (embroiderers) both among Hindu and Muslim families, i.e. 14.06 and 12.03 per cent respectively. Among families of Muslim printer and agent, there are 3.45 and 3.70 per cent females widow/divorced. Above one-tenth males among chikankar, i.e. 10.72 per cent and washermen 16.66 per cent were found with some sickness (see Table 20.2).

Literacy and Education

Quite a good proportion of household population of chikan craft workers is engaged as students, i.e. 20.29 and 22.44 per cent males and females respectively. The highest proportions of male and female are studying in households of cutting masters, e.g. 38.10 and 40.00 per cent respectively, who are generally Muslims. Similarly in households of other different traders of chikan craft, at least one-fifth among males and females are students. Among families of chikan craft workers, the male and female literacy is roughly about 56.16 and 50.17 per cent respectively. About 44.20 and 38.61 per cent among male and female population of chikan craft households are below High School. Those who are High school and above are quite few (see Table 20.3).

Occupation and Income

It is observed that in most of the cases if male or female is engaged in chikan craft then their counterpart male or female would work for other than chikan craft occupation. In case of washermen community, who traditionally carry out their jobs, where younger male or female help the head of the household in washing, but don't report their separate income or occupation. Chikankar female are in majority among chikan craft workers, whose income is on an average Rs. 575.00 per month. Income of female agent is about Rs. 2171.00 per month, which is highest even in comparison to female's working in other than chikan craft jobs. Though male workers in chikan craft are less than the females, but their earning is between Rs.1680.00 to Rs.3750.00 per month, which is quite high, when the fellow brothers of their family who work in other than chikan craft trade are comparatively less paid (see Table 20.4).

Table 20.3 : Religion-wise Students, Literates and Educated Among Households of Chikan Craft Workers

Religion/ caste-wise chikan craft workers	Percentage to total male and female population											
	Students		Literate		Below H.S.		High school		Intermediate		B.A.& above	
	Male	Female	Male	Female	Male	Female	Male	Female	Male	Female	Male	Female
Hindu												
Cutting master	--	33.33	66.67	66.67	33.33	33.33	33.33	--	--	33.33	--	--
Printer	--	--	50.00	--	50.00	--	--	--	--	--	--	--
Tailor	--	--	--	--	--	--	--	--	--	--	--	--
Chikankar	19.23	26.56	69.23	60.94	36.54	32.81	5.77	17.19	3.85	6.25	15.38	6.25
Washerman	10.00	25.00	50.00	37.50	20.00	12.50	20.00	--	10.00	--	--	25.00
Agent	—	—	—	—	—	—	—	—	—	—	—	—
Muslim												
Cutting master	44.44	50.00	71.22	50.00	50.00	41.66	5.56	--	--	--	--	--

(contd...)

Table 20.3 : *(contd.)*

Religion/ caste-wise chikan craft workers	Percentage to total male and female population											
	Students		Literate		Below H.S.		High school		Intermediate		B.A.& above	
	Male	Female	Male	Female	Male	Female	Male	Female	Male	Female	Male	Female
Printer	15.69	24.14	62.75	44.83	52.94	41.38	7.84	--	1.96	3.45	--	--
Tailor	31.58	20.00	47.37	53.33	47.37	46.67	5.26	6.67	--	--	--	--
Chikankar	15.91	20.30	45.45	45.86	42.85	40.60	--	6.02	1.14	0.75	1.14	--
Washerman	31.50	37.50	50.00	50.00	50.00	30.00	--	10.00	--	--	--	--
Agent	26.07	11.11	56.52	59.26	56.52	48.15	13.04	14.81	--	--	--	--

(contd...)

Table 20.3 : *(contd.)*

Religion/ caste-wise chikan craft workers	Percentage to total male and female population											
	Students		Literate		Below H.S.		High school		Intermediate		B.A.& above	
	Male	Female	Male	Female	Male	Female	Male	Female	Male	Female	Male	Female
Total												
Cutting master	38.10	40.00	71.43	53.33	47.62	40.00	9.52	--	--	6.67	--	--
Printer	15.09	23.33	62.26	43.33	50.94	40.00	7.55	--	1.89	3.33	--	--
Tailor	22.57	18.57	42.86	50.00	42.86	43.75	4.76	--	--	--	--	--
Chikankar	17.14	22.34	54.29	50.76	40.00	38.07	2.14	9.64	2.14	2.54	6.43	2.03
Washerman	16.67	16.67	50.00	38.89	33.33	22.22	11.11	5.56	5.56	--	--	11.11
Agent	26.07	11.11	56.57	59.26	56.52	48.15	13.24	14.81	--	—	—	—

Source: Based on survey conducted by the author and his team at Giri Institute of Development Studies, Lucknow, for the project "Diagnostic Study of Chikan Craft in Lucknow", July-August, 2006.

Table: 20.4 : Religion-wise Occupation and Income among Households of Chikan Craft Workers

Religion-wise chikan craft workers	Percentage occupation of household population				Average income (Rs. p.m.)			
	Chikan		Other		Chikan		Other	
	Male	Female	Male	Female	Male	Female	Male	Female
Hindu								
Cutting master	33.33	--	33.33	--	2500	--	1000	--
Printer	50.00	--	50.00	--	2500	--	1500	--
Tailor	50.00	--	--	--	2600	--	--	--
Chikankar	--	39.06	42.31	3.13	--	632	1995	750
Washerman	40.00	--	--	--	3100	--	--	--
Agent	—	—	—	—	—	—	—	—
Muslim								
Cutting master	27.27	--	--	--	1700	--	--	--
Printer	43.14	--	19.61	--	2546	--	1930	--

(contd...)

Table 20.4: *(contd.)*

Religion-wise chikan craft workers	Percentage occupation of household population				Average income (Rs. p.m.)			
	Chikan		Other		Chikan		Other	
	Male	Female	Male	Female	Male	Female	Male	Female
Tailor	26.32	--	31.58	--	2497	--	750	--
Chikankar	—	37.59	55.68	3.01	—	544	1851	600
Washerman	37.50	--	--	--	2867	--	--	--
Agent	8.70	25.93	34.78	--	3750	2171	1900	--
Total								
Cutting master	28.57	--	4.76	--	3300	--	1000	--
Printer	43.40	--	20.75	--	2543	--	1890	--
Tailor	28.57	--	28.57	--	1680	--	750	--
Chikankar	—	25.38	50.00	3.05	2000	575	1896	650
Washerman	38.89	--	--	--	2817	--	---	--
Agent	8.70	25.93	34.78	—	3750	2171	1900	--

Source: Based on survey conducted by the author and his team at Giri Institute of Development Studies, Lucknow, for the project "Diagnostic Study of Chikan Craft in Lucknow", July-August, 2006.

Housing Condition

A good proportion of chikan craft workers do not own the house like, printers 64.29, washermen 50.00, cutting masters 33.33, tailors 33.33 and chikankar 19.05 per cent live in rented houses. Only all the agents have their own houses. Majority of households of chikan craft workers live in an accommodation of less than 400 sq. ft. and that also majority live in an unhygienic condition. Among Hindu chikan craft workers, except washermen, all the other workers live in two or more room houses, while among Muslim chikan craft workers, except household of agents, rest households of workers live in smaller houses with less than two rooms. Living condition reflects the poor condition of chikan craft workers (see Table 20.5).

While observing the housing condition, we find that more than 15 per cent house belonging to chikan craft workers have dry latrines, which is banned by the government. Overall 50.00 per cent tailors, 33.34 per cent washermen, 22.23 per cent chikankar, 22.22 per cent agents and 14.28 per cent printers do not have their own latrines in their premises and they have to go out to defecate on roadsides or in sulabh-shauchalayas (public latrines). Similarly, hardly one-third of chikan craft workers have bathrooms in their premises and rest three-fourth households take bath in open areas, mainly out of their premises. About 40.00 per cent chikan craft workers do not have water source in their house premises and they fetch water from outside water sources. Electricity and streetlight is provided in and around 65.00 to 70.00 per cent houses of chikan craft workers. At least one-third houses are yet to be electrified. In family assets, except printers, majority of workers have scooter or motor bike and television is available in majority of the houses of workers. While sewing machines, which are so essential for chikan craft workers, roughly about one-third households of chikan craft workers have it (see Table 20.6).

Earning of Chikan Craft Workers

Among total 104 chikan craft workers, there were 2 male and 7 female agents, who were each earning Rs. 3750.00 (highest) and Rs. 2171.42 per month respectively, when 6 male cutting masters each earning Rs. 3300.00 per month; 8 washermen, each earning

Table 20.5 : Religion-wise Housing Status of Chikan Craft Workers

Religion-wise chikan craft workers	Sample HH	Percentage to total household					
		House owned	Size of houses				Average No. of rooms
			<200 sq.ft.	200-400 sq.ft.	400-600 sq.ft.	600+ sq.ft.	
Hindu							
Cutting master	1	100.00	--	--	100.00	--	2.00
Printer	1	100.00	--	--	100.00	--	2.00
Tailor	1	--	--	100.00	--	--	2.00
Chikankar	22	95.45	13.64	22.72	31.82	31.82	2.14
Washerman	3	66.67	--	66.67	33.33	--	1.67
Agent	—	—	—	—	—	—	—
Muslim							
Cutting master	5	60.00	20.00	60.00	--	20.00	1.60
Printer	13	30.77	23.08	38.46	15.38	23.08	1.77
Tailor	5	80.00	20.00	40.00	20.00	20.00	1.62
Chikankar	41	73.17	14.64	58.53	24.39	2.44	1.66
Washerman	3	33.33	--	66.67	33.33	--	1.67
Agent	9	100.00	--	44.45	33.33	22.22	2.22
Total							
Cutting master	6	66.67	16.67	50.00	16.66	16.67	1.67
Printer	14	35.71	21.43	35.71	21.43	21.43	1.79
Tailor	6	66.67	16.67	50.00	16.66	16.67	1.67
Chikankar	63	80.95	14.29	46.03	26.99	12.69	1.83
Washerman	6	50.00	--	66.67	33.33	--	1.67
Agent	9	100.00	--	44.45	33.33	22.22	2.22

Source: Based on survey conducted by the author and his team at Giri Institute of Development Studies, Lucknow, for the project "Diagnostic Study of Chikan Craft in Lucknow", July-August, 2006.

Table 20.6 : Religion-wise Houses of Chikan Craft Workers having Latrine, Source of Water, Electricity and Family Assets

Religion-wise chikan craft workers	Percentage to total household										
	Latrine		Bath-room	Source of water			Electricity		Family assets		
	Dry	Flush		Pipe	Hand Pump	No water	Home	Street light	Scooter/ M. bike	T.V.	Sewing machine
Hindu											
Cutting master	—	100.00	—	—	100.00	—	100.00	—	100.00	100.00	—
Printer	—	100.00	100.00	100.00	—	—	100.00	100.00	—	100.00	—
Tailor	100.00	—	—	—	—	100.00	100.00	100.00	100.00	—	100.00
Chikankar	13.64	77.27	45.45	50.00	4.55	45.45	72.73	72.73	63.64	72.72	45.45
Washerman	33.33	33.33	66.67	66.67	—	33.33	100.00	100.00	100.00	66.67	—
Agent	—	—	—	—	—	—	—	—	—	—	—
Muslim											
Cutting master	20.00	80.00	40.00	40.00	40.00	20.00	100.00	80.00	80.00	80.00	40.00
Printer	15.38	69.23	38.46	69.23	7.69	23.08	46.15	84.02	—	53.85	15.36
Tailor	—	40.00	20.00	20.00	40.00	40.00	60.00	60.00	60.00	60.00	80.00
Chikankar	17.07	53.66	26.83	65.85	2.44	29.37	60.98	58.54	56.10	43.90	19.51
Washerman	—	33.33	—	33.33	—	66.67	66.67	100.00	100.00	100.00	—
Agent	11.11	66.67	33.33	88.88	11.11	—	77.78	66.67	88.98	100.00	22.22
Total											

(contd...)

Table 20.6 : *(contd...)*

Religion-wise chikan craft workers	Percentage to total household										
	Latrine		Bath-room	Source of water			Electricity		Family assets		
	Dry	Flush		Pipe	Hand Pump	No water	Home	Street light	Scooter/ M. bike	T.V.	Sewing machine
Cutting master	16.67	83.33	33.33	33.33	50.00	16.67	100.00	66.67	83.33	83.33	33.33
Printer	14.29	71.43	42.86	71.43	7.14	21.43	50.00	85.71	--	57.14	14.29
Tailor	16.67	33.33	16.67	16.67	33.33	50.00	66.67	50.00	66.67	50.00	66.67
Chikankar	15.87	61.90	33.33	60.32	3.17	34.92	65.08	63.49	58.73	53.97	28.57
Washerman	33.33	33.33	33.33	50.00	--	50.00	83.33	100.00	88.99	100.00	22.22
Agent	11.11	66.67	33.33	88.88	11.11	--	77.78	66.67	100.00	83.33	--

Source : Based on survey conducted by the author and his team at Giri Institute of Development Studies, Lucknow, for the project "Diagnostic Study of Chikan Craft in Lucknow", July-August, 2006.

Rs. 2816.66 per month, 14 male printers, each earning Rs. 2542.85, 6 male tailors reported each earning Rs. 1680.83 and 63 female chikankars reported each earning an average of Rs. 574.60 per month, which is least. Overall 45.19 per cent chikan craft workers reported that they get their work through the agents. Caste-wise maximum work was given by agents to Scheduled Castes, then to OBC and least to general caste workers. It means that the general caste workers get their work mostly from the entrepreneurs directly. Cutting masters and agents were getting their work directly from the chikan craft entrepreneurs and no one was reported getting work from the agents. While 28.57 per cent printers, 33.33 per cent tailors, 63.49 per cent chikankar women and 16.67 per cent washermen reported getting work through the agents (see Table 20.7).

Time and Cost of Manufacturing

For each item of chikan the maximum time taken to finish the respective jobs by cutting master, printer, tailor and washerman is not more than 60 minutes whereas the longer time is taken in embroidery by the chikankar woman. For example, the time duration depends upon the quality of embroidery, which has no limit. For rough idea a single chikankar woman takes minimum and maximum time in embroidering a quality kurta are 61 to 138 hours, a Shalwar-kameez 119 to 218 hours, ladies' top 24 to 49 hours, Sherwani-kurta 451 to 606 hours, saree 178 to 389 hours, bed sheet 240 to 360 hours and dupatta 228 to 430 hours. For expediting the embroidery work many ladies are engaged on one item at a time to finish the job quickly (see Table 20.8).

Cutting master is a specialized mobile man, he visits the entrepreneurs on request and cutting work is done at the door step of the entrepreneur and the cost of work is paid and received according to fixed rates as mentioned in Table 20.8. As customary the cutting master charges the new enhanced rates from newly established entrepreneurs, while the old established entrepreneurs, generally pay the old rates, which are never disclosed. Generally printers are stationary except very few, they hardly move and agents, helpers or entrepreneurs bring the work at the doorstep of printer's work place and according to number of impressions (prints) charges are

Table 20.7 : Religion and Caste-wise Number of Chikan Craft Workers and their Average Income per Month in Rupees

Religion-wise chikan craft workers	Workers/income	Number of workers and their average income per month (in Rupees)							Percentage reporting work given by agents
		Cutting master	Printer	Tailor	Chikankar	Washer-man	Agent		
		Male	Male	Male	Female	Male	Male	Female	
Hindu total	No. of workers	1	1	1	22	3	—	—	35.71
	Income (Rs. p.m.)	2500.00	2500.00	2600.00	631.81	2766.66	—	—	
Hindu General	No. of workers	1	—	—	9	—	—	—	10.00
	Income (Rs. p.m.)	2500.00	—	—	744.44	—	—	—	
Hindu OBC	No. of workers	—	—	1	6	—	—	—	42.85
	Income (Rs. p.m.)	—	—	2600.00	516.66	—	—	—	
Hindu SC	No. of workers	—	1	—	7	3	—	—	54.54
	Income (Rs. p.m.)	—	2500.00	—	585.71	2766.66	—	—	
Muslim total	No. of workers	5	13	5	41	3	2	7	48.69
	Income (Rs. p.m.)	3460.00	2546.15	1497.00	543.90	2866.66	3750.00	2171.42	
Muslim General	No. of workers	3	12	5	21	--	1	7	42.85
	Income (Rs. p.m.)	2933.33	2591.66	1497.00	514.28	--	3500.00	2171.42	
Muslim OBC	No. of workers	2	1	--	20	3	1	--	59.26
	Income (Rs. p.m.)	4250.00	2000.00	--	575.00	2866.66	4000.00	--	
Total	No. of workers	6	14	6	63	6	2	7	48.19
	Income (Rs. p.m.)	3300.00	2542.85	1680.83	574.60	2816.66	3750.00	2171.42	
Percentage reporting work given by agents			28.57	33.33	63.49	16.67			

Note: Male or Female columns having no workers are deleted.

Source: Based on survey conducted by the author and his team at Giri Institute of Development Studies, Lucknow, for the project "Diagnostic Study of Chikan Craft in Lucknow", July-August, 2006.

Table 20.8 : Religion-wise Average Minimum and Maximum Time (in minutes) for Manufacturing Items by Chikan Craft Workers

Religion/caste-wise chikan craft workers		Kurta	Shalwar kameez	Ladies' top	Sherwani kurta	Saree	Bed sheet	Dupatta
Hindu								
Cutting master	Minimum	10	20	10	60	—	—	—
	Maximum	—	—	—	—	—	—	—
Printer	Minimum	5	5	5	10	10	60	60
	Maximum	10	10	10	15	15	120	120
Tailor	Minimum	35	60	3	60	—	—	—
	Maximum	—	—	—	60	—	—	—
Chikankar	Minimum	8280	9780	1980	43920	16500	14400	30720
	Maximum	1302	17160	4760	610080	24500	21600	60000
Washerman	Minimum	23	25	10	30	35	--	10
	Maximum	—	—	—	—	—	—	—
Muslim								
Cutting Master	Minimum	11	16	12	17	—	—	—
	Maximum	5	10	10	15	—	—	—
Printer	Minimum	7	7	7	10	9	60	65
	Maximum	11	11	11	14	14	120	125
Tailor	Minimum	48	63	38	120	—	—	—
	Maximum	45	45	30	—	—	—	—

(contd...)

Table 20.8 : (*contd.*)

Religion/caste-wise chikan craft workers		Kurta	Shalwar kameez	Ladies' top	Sherwani kurta	Saree	Bed sheet	Dupatta
Chikankar	Minimum	1231	5757	1131	14537	7583	—	2400
	Maximum	5776	10890	3047	20197	22715	—	43200
Washerman	Minimum	32	25	20	28	25	60	—
	Maximum	38	45	32.50	53	60	—	—
Total								
Cutting Master	Minimum	11	16	12	28	—	—	—
	Maximum	5	10	10	15	—	—	—
Printer	Minimum	7	7	7	10	9	60	65
	Maximum	11	11	11	15	15	120	124
Tailor	Minimum	46	63	37	100	—	—	—
	Maximum	45	45	·30	60	—	—	—
Chikankar	Minimum	3690	7165	1433	27072	10700	14400	13680
	Maximum	8311	13072	2940	36360	23347	21600	25800
Washerman	Minimum	28	25	15	29	30	60.00	10.00
	Maximum	38	45	33	52	60	—	—

Source: Based on survey conducted by the author and his team at Giri Institute of Development Studies, Lucknow, for the project "Diagnostic Study of Chikan Craft in Lucknow", July-August, 2006.

made. There are very few entrepreneurs who possess their own printing blocks, which are costly and employ occasionally a full time printer on salary. Tailors are also moving and stationary both, according to quantity of workload, he fixes the time with the entrepreneurs and tailoring rates are fixed with some fluctuations. If workload is more, then tailor stitches the clothes at the doorstep of entrepreneurs, but for less number of pieces, stitching is done at tailor's residence and clothes are brought by the helper, agent or entrepreneur. Washermen are stationery, either they collect the clothes themselves from the entrepreneurs or the clothes are brought to his doorstep by the agents and washing charges are demanded according to fixed rates for number of pieces. The entire family of washerman is engaged in washing, drying and ironing the clothes. Generally, females iron the clothes. Generally maximum money is paid by the entrepreneurs on per piece of embroidered cloth, but this money is distributed among number of chikankar women who together finish the work in quite number of days. Chikankar women are trained easily and they are easily available in and around Awadh region, as the distance increases from Lucknow heartland, where entrepreneurs live, middlemen involve more and wages of embroiderer goes on decreasing. Cutting master, tailor, printer and washerman are all men, who are expert and required to be within the city are rarely available, thus, their wages are higher than the chikankar women (see Table 20.9)

Training, Job Satisfaction, Loan Required and Rise of Income

All chikan craft workers of different trades are in fact trained, though they might have not received the formal training, but by virtue of their living in the atmosphere of chikan craft culture, they automatically get trained by trial and error. Table 20.10 shows the proportion of workers who are virtually formally trained. It is interesting to note that on an average a Hindu chikankar woman took 108 days in training in comparison to a Muslim chikankar woman only 28 days, obviously, Hindu chikankars are the recent entrants than the Muslims who are born in chikan culture. Most of the chikan craft workers devote 8 to 12 hours daily, but chikankar ladies devote less than 8 hours, as they also work in embroidery centres, which are away from their residence

Table 20.9 : Religion-wise Average Minimum and Maximum Rate (in Rupee) for Manufacturing Items by Chikan Craft Workers

Religion/caste-wise chikan craft workers		Kurta	Shalwar kameez	Ladies' top	Sherwani kurta	Saree	Bed sheet	Dupatta
Hindu								
Cutting master	Minimum	1.50	3.00	1.00	4.00	—	—	—
	Maximum	—	—	—	—	—	—	—
Printer	Minimum	0.75	0.75	0.75	1.0	1.00	4.00	4.00
	Maximum	1.50	1.50	1.50	1.50	1.50	6.00	5.00
Tailor	Minimum	8.00	8.00	3.00	10.00	—	—	—
	Maximum	—	—	—	15.00	—	—	—
Chikankar	Minimum	168.00	176.00	32.00	787.00	346.00	100.00	250.00
	Maximum	231.00	251.00	47.00	977.00	520.00	1250.00	570.00
Washerman	Minimum	7.66	8.00	2.00	10.00	8.00	--	10.00
	Maximum	—	—	—	—	—	—	—
Muslim								
Cutting master	Minimum	1.70	2.00	1.10	2.00	—	—	—
	Maximum	2.00	2.25	2.00	3.00	—	—	—
Printer	Minimum	1.63	1.63	1.63	1.76	1.76	4.30	4.69
	Maximum	2.26	2.26	2.26	2.46	2.46	5.39	5.31
Tailor	Minimum	7.00	8.00	3.80	9.00	—	—	—
	Maximum	10.00	12.00	8.00	—	—	—	—
Chikankar	Minimum	31.36	152.17	33.97	417.14	286.09	—	1500.00
	Maximum	174.14	338.84	86.89	706.15	777.80	—	2000.00
Washerman	Minimum	6.33	9.33	3.33	9.00	9.66	8.00	—
	Maximum	10.50	14.00	9.00	13.00	15.00	—	—

(*contd...*)

Table 20.9 : (*contd.*)

Religion/caste-wise chikan craft workers		Kurta	Shalwar kameez	Ladies' top	Sherwani kurta	Saree	Bed sheet	Dupatta
Total								
Cutting master	Minimum	1.66	2.16	1.08	2.50	—	—	—
	Maximum	2.00	2.25	2.00	3.00	—	—	—
Printer	Minimum	1.57	1.57	1.57	1.71	1.71	4.29	4.64
	Maximum	2.21	2.21	2.17	2.39	2.39	5.43	5.29
Tailor	Minimum	7.16	8.00	4.40	9.33	—	—	—
	Maximum	10.00	12.00	8.00	15.00	—	—	—
Chikankar	Minimum	79.07	160.33	33.33	857.25	306.96	100.00	437.50
	Maximum	194.04	307.88	72.82	371.04	570.31	125.00	642.50
Washerman	Minimum	7.00	8.66	2.66	7.83	8.83	8.00	10.0
	Maximum	10.50	14.00	9.00	13.00	15.00	—	—

Source: Based on survey conducted by the author and his team at Giri Institute of Development Studies, Lucknow, for the project "Diagnostic Study of Chikan Craft in Lucknow", July-August, 2006.

and they have also to perform household duties. Almost all the chikan craft workers enjoy weekends and also their important festivals are celebrated, thus, on an average 25 days are working days in a month. Availability of work with chikan craft workers depends upon the entrepreneurs who provide the work according to demand and supply of chikan items in the market. All the cutting masters reported that they don't get the work regularly. Similarly 78.57 per cent printers, 66.67 per cent tailors, 36.51 per cent chikankar women, 50.00 per cent washerman and 44.44 per cent agents reported that they don't get work regularly. A good proportion of chikan workers have shown dissatisfaction on timely payment of their wages/salary. For example 83.33 per cent cutting masters, 50.00 per cent printers, 33.33 per cent tailors, 42.86 per cent chikankar women, 16.67 per cent washermen and 11.13 per cent agents are not satisfied on timely payment of their wages/salary (see Table 20.10).

Majority of chikan craft workers in different trades have desired to get loan, if it is provided on low interest rate. The requirement of loan amount is expressed roughly between Rs. 50,000 to Rs.125,000. Only rarely chikan craft workers have taken very small amount of loan from their known persons or relatives. Only 14.29 per cent printers have reported that their income has increased between 10 to 20 per cent during last five years. Only 7.14 per cent printers, 19.05 per cent chikankar and 16.62 per cent washermen have reported that their income has increased less than ten per cent during last five years (see Table 20.11).

CONCLUSION

There is no mechanism where entrepreneurs may be compelled to give proper minimum wages, as the work force is in surplus and they compete among themselves to work on least wages for their survival. Government can help the Chikan workers by providing them soft loan on line of Kisan Credit Card (KCC). Another possible solution may be if government helps the entrepreneurs in getting the export orders in order to enhance the Chikan production and ultimately empowering the Chikan craft workforce to work on proper wages.

Table 20.10 : Religion-wise Chikan Craft Workers Reporting about Training, Working Hours and Work Satisfaction

Religion-wise chikan craft workers	Sample House Hold	Percentage trained	Average no. of training days	Daily working hours	Working days in a month	Percentage reported	
						Getting work regularly	Satisfied with timely payment
Hindu							
Cutting master	1	100.00	30.00	8.00	25.00	--	100.00
Printer	1	100.00	15.00	10.00	25.00	—	—
Tailor	1	100.00	90.00	10.00	26.00	100.00	100.00
Chikankar	22	81.82	107.61	6.95	23.91	86.36	81.82
Washerman	3	33.33	30.00	10.67	18.00	33.33	100.00
Agent	—	—	—	—	—	—	—
Muslim							
Cutting master	5	100.00	36.00	7.80	25.40	—	20.00
Printer	13	61.54	243.38	10.15	23.00	23.08	53.85
Tailor	5	100.00	33.00	9.40	23.40	20.00	60.00
Chikankar	41	65.85	27.52	7.34	26.20	60.98	43.90
Washerman	3	33.33	30.00	10.00	25.33	66.67	66.67
Agent	9	11.11	15.00	7.56	28.00	55.56	88.89

(contd...)

Table 20.10 : *(contd.)*

Religion-wise chikan craft workers	Sample HH	Percentage trained	Average no. of training days	Daily working hours	Working days in a month	Percentage reported	
						Getting work regularly	Satisfied with timely payment
Total							
Cutting master	6	100.00	35.00	7.83	25.33	—	16.67
Printer	14	64.29	218.00	10.14	23.14	21.43	50.00
Tailor	6	100.00	42.50	9.50	23.03	33.33	66.67
Chikankar	63	71.43	59.56	7.21	25.40	69.84	57.14
Washerman	6	33.33	30.00	10.33	21.67	50.00	83.33
Agent	9	11.11	15.00	7.56	28.00	55.56	88.87

Source: Based on survey conducted by the author and his team at Giri Institute of Development Studies, Lucknow, for the project "Diagnostic Study of Chikan Craft in Lucknow", July-August, 2006.

Table 20.11 : Religion-wise Chikan Craft Workers reporting about Loan and Income Increases

Religion-wise chikan craft workers	Per cent wanted low interest loan	Average amount of loan wanted (Rs.)	Average loan taken (Rs.)	Percentage reported Per cent income increased		
				>20	10-20	<10
Hindu						
Cutting master	—	—	—	—	—	—
Printer	—	—	—	—	—	—
Tailor	—	—	—	—	—	—
Chikankar	31.82	52142	2045	--	--	22.73
Washerman	66.67	125000	—	—	—	—
Agent	—	—	—	—	—	—
Muslim						
Cutting master	80.00	87500	—	—	—	—
Printer	69.23	55556	—	—	15.38	7.69
Tailor	60.00	116667	—	—	—	—
Chikankar	60.98	58000	—	—	—	17.07
Washerman	66.67	55000	—	—	—	33.33
Agent	77.78	35786	—	—	—	—

(contd...)

Table 20.11 : *(contd.)*

Religion-wise chikan craft workers	Per cent wanted low interest loan	Average amount of loan wanted (Rs.)	Average loan taken (Rs.)	Percentage reported		
				Per cent income increased		
				>20	10-20	<10
Total						
Cutting master	80.00	87500	—	—	—	—
Printer	64.29	55556	—	—	14.29	7.14
Tailor	50.00	116667	—	—	—	—
Chikankar	50.80	56719	—	—	—	19.05
Washerman	66.67	90000	—	—	—	16.62
Agent	**77.78**	**35786**	**1000**	—	—	—

Source: Based on survey conducted by the author and his team at Giri Institute of Development Studies, Lucknow, for the project "Diagnostic Study of Chikan Craft in Lucknow", July-August, 2006.

REFERENCES

Hasan, Ameer (1983), *Palace of Culture*, Shabdniketan Printers.

Mishra, Amresh (1998), *Lucknow Fire of Grace*, Surabhi Printers Ltd., Noida.

Praveen, Yogesh (1986), *Dastane Lucknow*, Lucknow Mahotsava Patrika Samiti.

Praveen, Yogesh (1984), *Lucknow Nama*, Lucknow Mahotsava Patrika Samiti.

Sharar, Abdul Haleem (1975), *Lucknow the Last Face of an Oriented Culture*, (Translated and edited by Mr. E.S. Harcourt and Fakhir Husain), Anchor Press Ltd., Great Britain.

Taque, Roshan (2001), *Lucknow 1857*, New Royal Book Co., Lucknow.

Taque, Roshan (2005), *Images of Lucknow*, New Royal Book Co., Lucknow.

21

PATTERNS OF EMERGING LABOUR FORCE AND GROWING UNEMPLOYMENT IN NORTH-EAST INDIA

Some Issues

NIRANKAR SRIVASTAV

Introduction

Widespread unemployment and under-employment along with poverty have been two major challenges to development planning in India since independence. Consequently, alleviation of poverty and removal of unemployment have been the major objectives of earlier five-year plans. These two problems still persist though the degree and extent varies across regions in the country. Out of these States, the most of the States in the North-Eastern region (NER) are considered economically backward in many respects.

The NE region of India consists of seven States, namely, Arunachal Pradesh (ARP), Assam (ASS), Manipur (MAN), Meghalaya (MEG), Mizoram (MIZ), Nagaland (NAG) and Tripura (TRI). Individually, most of these States depict lower level of economic development compared to even national averages as suggested by the various indicators for which information is available except for higher literacy rates.

There had been growing concern about increasing unemployment as a vital economic problem in NER. However, the extent and nature of unemployment is not properly known for these States. In fact, very few attempts have been made in the past to explain the various facets of unemployment at regional levels in India. This is more so in the case among States in the NER where we have not come across any systematic study dealing with this issue.

In this chapter we provide an elaborate exposition of different facets of unemployment with in the NER. The main purpose of this chapter is to analyse the incidence of unemployment among the seven northeastern states. This study also highlights other relevant issues like relationship of unemployment with education and poverty.

Rest of the chapter is divided in three parts. Next section deals with data and methodology issues. This is followed by the discussion of empirical findings in section 3. The conclusions are reported in section 4.

Data and Conceptual Issues

In this chapter we use household level survey (unit record) data on employment and unemployment in India. The data were collected by the National Sample Survey Organization (NSSO). The reference period was the agricultural year (i.e. July to June) 1993-94 (50th round). The survey covers all the States, including NER and union territories of India, which are divided into 78 relatively homogeneous agro-climatic regions.

The employment and unemployment data is further supplemented by expenditure data collected from the same households during the survey. The expenditure data provides the distribution of households according to their per capita monthly total expenditure (PCTE). This has been used in this chapter to measure the incidence of poverty, which in turn was used to study its relationship with the incidence of unemployment. For the purpose of identifying the poor households in NER States, we have applied the official poverty line (OPL) used by Dubey and Kharpuri (1999).

To analyse the nature of unemployment, it is necessary to understand a few technical terms. In this connection first comes the concept of labour force, because entire population is not included in the labour force. Traditionally, adult segment of population in the age group of 15 to 59 years (both included), is considered economically active population and constitute labour force. Though there is no restriction that people below and above this age group cannot participate in economic activities. However, those out of this age group will not be considered for calculating incidence of unemployment.

The population in the labour force is divided in two groups, those who are working and those who are not working, but the seeking and/or available for work, observe that all those who are within the working age group but neither working nor seeking or available for work are treated outside the purview of the set of labour force, e.g., students, persons engaged in domestic duties, rentiers, pensioners, living on alms, disabled persons, etc.

The well-accepted norm of employment stipulates that it is sufficient for a person to be engaged in an economic activity for at least one hour or any day during the period of reference to be classified as employed. There are also implicit rules in the labour force framework according to which activity status gets priority over inactivity. On the basis of this conceptual framework the unemployment is considered to be an extreme situation of total lack of work.

For making unemployment statistic more reliable and meaningful, it is conventionally reported according to time dimension also, i.e. a person is unemployed since last one year, last one month or last one week prior to the date of survey by the NSSO. This is more relevant issue in a developing economy like India, where large section of labour force gets employment in unorganized sector like agriculture and household industries. Often the employment is seasonal, infrequent and/or on irregular basis. Accordingly, the NSSO collects information for three reference periods, one to capture the employment/ unemployment status for a long period in past one year and calls it the "Principal Usual Status (PUS)". The status prevailing for entire week is known as "Current Weekly Status (CWS)". The "Current Daily Activity Status (CDS)", for a person is determined on the basis of his/her activity status on each day of the reference week. A person is considered employed for the entire day if he/she had worked for at least four hours during the day.

The PUS measures the status of person, which prevailed over a long last period. People belong to this category can be called chronically unemployed. This type of unemployment is, supposedly lowest in a developing economy, because most of unemployed by this definition cannot afford to remain unemployed for longer period. The CWS reduced the reference period to one week. At this juncture it is important to mention that CWS measures the unemployment in a more strict way, i.e., if during the reference week a person is employed even for one hour on any of the seven days of the week, is termed as 'employed' for that week, even though he has been unemployed for rest of the days in the reference week. In order to tackle this tricky issue NSSO, also, collects the statistics on the current activity status on daily (actually half day) basis for all the days of reference week. This gives the information on period of unemployment during the week for a person. In an aggregated form total unemployed person-days can be estimated and when divided by total number of labour force days gives rate of unemployment what is termed as "daily basis". This rate, however, does not give unemployment rate as described by PUS and CWS.

In this chapter, we have discussed first two types of unemployment, i.e., on the PUS and CWS basis to investigate the incidence of unemployment among the States in the NER. Besides these, we have used information on age and sex of all the members of surveyed households along with their social group and consumption levels. This allowed us to look at various aspects of the incidence of unemployment like, youth unemployment, unemployment by the social group and education levels as well as the relationship between poverty and unemployment.

Empirical Findings

In this section we report the incidence of unemployment among the seven States of the NER. We have also, reported for the purpose of comparison, wherever possible, the All India figures with the NER figures.

Table 21.1 : Demographic and Social Group-wise Distribution of Population in the NER States in (1993-94)

States	Rural				Urban				All			
	Females per '000 males	ST*	SC*	Others*	Females per '000 males	ST*	SC*	Others*	Females per '000 males	ST*	SC*	Others*
ARP	914	16.40	0.20	83.39	841	4.13	5.20	90.68	912	16.05	0.34	83.60
ASS	836	14.15	9.23	76.62	910	4.18	7.13	88.69	843	13.14	9.02	77.85
MAN	982	38.96	0.09	60.95	943	8.27	0.52	91.21	966	26.88	0.26	72.86
MEG	957	81.38	0.07	18.55	952	62.64	4.33	33.02	957	78.79	0.66	20.55
MIZ	887	86.28	0.32	13.40	955	98.08	0.63	1.29	908	90.01	0.42	9.57
NAG	902	95.04	0.30	4.76	715	67.39	1.24	31.37	848	87.66	0.33	12.01
TRI	923	12.36	21.99	65.65	982	3.20	15.42	81.38	931	11.14	21.12	67.74
NER	864	20.68	8.81	71.04	917	7.16	5.91	79.50	871	19.93	7.99	72.09
All India	944	10.22	20.12	69.66	904	2.90	12.67	84.43	933	8.40	18.27	73.34

Source: National Sample Survey (NSS) 50th Round (1993-94)

Note: * denotes that the figures are the percentages of the respective social groups out of the total population of the respective States

Population Structure

Table 21.1 reports the gender-wise distribution of population among the seven States and the NER. The females count ratio i.e., number of females per thousand of males. This ratio is higher in Manipur and Meghalaya but lower in the remaining five Sates than All India average. Mizoram, Meghalaya and Manipur have scheduled tribes as dominant population group. In general, all the NER States have higher percentage of scheduled tribes population (higher than All India).

Population distribution between the rural and urban sectors of the region is such that 87.6 per cent population lives in the rural sector. This is much lower (75.2 per cent) at All India level. This is indicative of predominant rural sector with lower degree of urbanization in NER. Within the rural sector of NER, all the seven States have higher population of scheduled tribes population. Tripura is the only State where scheduled castes population is found to be as high as 21.99 per cent whereas Nagaland, Mizoram, Meghalaya, Manipur and Arunachal Pradesh have less than one per cent total rural population belong to scheduled castes group. Similar population distribution holds in the urban sector except that SC population is slightly higher (than one per cent in rural sector) in ARP and MEG.

Labour Force Participation

Recall that labour force is defined as the subset of the population in 15-59 years age group, who are employed, or unemployed and seeking/available for work. Table 21.2 reports the salient features of labour force among the NER states for rural and urban sectors. Table 21.2 details the rate of labour force participation and proportion of population out of labour force, which can be derived conveniently. For example, 55.39 per cent of persons in NER are in labour force; consequently, 44.61 per cent (i.e., 100.00 – 55.39) persons are out of labour force.

Table 21.2 also, suggests that the labour force participation rates for rural male vary in the range of 65-92 per cent and for rural female 16 to 74 per cent. Similarly, in the urban areas, male labour force participation rates vary between 67-80 per cent and for the females, it is 14-40 per cent. The economically active population ratios

Table 21.2 : Labour Force in the North Eastern States in the Age Group of 15-59 in 1993-94

States	Rural			Urban			All		
	Male	**Female**	**Persons**	**Male**	**Female**	**Persons**	**Male**	**Female**	**Persons**
ARP	79.20	64.52	72.14	79.00	16.54	51.13	79.19	63.16	71.50
ASS	84.60	16.12	53.00	78.00	15.31	48.92	83.84	16.03	52.54
MAN	70.71	34.31	52.54	69.00	14.98	41.50	69.94	26.83	48.30
MEG	92.81	74.29	83.76	80.00	30.85	56.12	91.03	68.53	80.05
MIZ	81.57	47.53	65.49	76.00	40.01	57.94	79.70	45.04	63.06
NAG	65.88	18.40	43.56	67.00	15.66	45.25	66.26	17.71	44.01
TRI	82.98	17.49	51.10	79.00	21.45	50.43	82.40	18.05	51.01
NER	83.47	25.83	56.44	76.00	17.82	48.46	82.50	24.77	55.39
All India	88.38	37.35	63.19	83.00	20.05	53.19	86.85	32.92	60.54

Source: As in Table 21.1

Note: The figures spell out labour force as a percentage of the total population in the age group 15-59 years.

are on the higher side in the rural sector in comparison to the corresponding figures for the urban sector of NER. However, compared to national average, proportion of persons belong to labour force in NER is smaller for both males and females. This gap is much higher for females, which shows that relatively a large section of female population does not participate in the economic activities. The male female differential is more striking within the NE States, where, female labour participation is lowest among the States like Assam, Nagaland and Tripura. On the contrary, Meghalaya and Arunachal Pradesh have much higher (68.53 and 63.16 per cent respectively) proportions of female labour forces than All India Average (32.92 per cent).

Status of Unemployment

Table 21.3 reports the incidence of unemployment based on principal usual activity status (PUS) by sex and place of residence. The figures presented in the form of rate of unemployment are based on the concept of usual activity, taking into account the principal status and subsidiary status. It is to be noted that this type of unemployment represents the situation where people remained unemployed for fairly longer period (one year) and called 'chronically' unemployed. This indicates relatively persistent structural unemployment in these States.

The figures shown in Table 21.3 are in terms of rate of unemployment. In fact this rate represents the total number of unemployed persons in a particular group divided by the total number of persons belonging to labour force in the same group in percentage form. For example, 1.49 per cent of rural males are unemployed in Arunachal Pradesh out of the total labour force of the rural male in Arunachal Pradesh. The rates based on the usual status approach would be pointers about the relatively persistent unemployment situation during the reference year, i.e. 1993-94.

First, the incidence of unemployment in the NER at 5.73 per cent is almost double to that at All India level. Gender-wise break-up shows that it is about three times higher among the females in NER. Among the NE States, the unemployment rate is highest (7.91 per cent) in Assam. The degree of unemployment is lowest in Meghalaya (0.4 per cent) and other NE States like Arunachal Pradesh, Manipur

Table 21.3 : Rate of Unemployment (Principal Usual Activities) in the NER States in 1993-94

States	Rural			Urban			All		
	Male	Female	Persons	Male	Female	Persons	Male	Female	Persons
ARP	1.51	0.57	1.11	0.75	5.80	1.48	1.49	0.61	1.12
ASS	6.51	14.56	7.64	6.45	31.80	10.12	6.51	16.43	7.91
MAN	2.17	0.86	1.74	3.60	3.83	3.64	2.71	1.50	2.37
MEG	0.43	0.00	0.25	1.43	3.51	1.98	0.55	0.21	0.41
MIZ	1.76	0.73	1.40	0.43	0.74	0.54	1.37	0.73	1.15
NAG	2.46	0.06	1.98	7.12	7.03	7.10	3.80	1.59	3.39
TRI	1.67	9.32	2.94	6.73	21.06	9.74	2.33	11.29	3.88
NER	5.05	6.94	5.46	5.42	19.26	7.83	5.09	8.12	5.73
All India	2.16	1.50	1.97	4.70	8.81	5.43	2.82	2.64	2.77

Source: As in Table 21.1

Note: The figures denote the proportion of unemployed persons out of the total labour force (15-59 years).

and Mizoram having the rates lower than All India. Nagaland shows the second highest male unemployment rate among the NER States after the Assam. The unemployment rates for rural males vary between 0.5-6.0 per cent and for rural females from 0-15 per cent, similarly, for urban males from 0.5 to 7 per cent and for urban females 0.7-32 per cent for NE States.

General trends that can be highlighted are that the degree of unemployment is significantly higher in urban sectors than rural sector in the NER like at All India level. However, unemployment rate in the rural sector is much higher than at All India level of which the major contribution is coming from female unemployment.

In rural sector of the NER, the percentage of unemployment for females is highest for Assam (14.56 per cent) followed by Tripura (9.32 per cent). But in the remaining five States, there is lesser degree of unemployment for rural females. Higher female unemployment in rural Assam may be because of the division of work in agricultural practices is strictly gender biased in favour of male and against the female labourers whereas this may not be true in the case of other tribal dominated NE states.[1] The female unemployment rates are higher in Assam (31.80 per cent), followed by Tripura (21.06 per cent) comparing to All India average (8.81 per cent).

As noted earlier, the unemployment on weekly basis suggests that a person is called unemployed if he/she remained unemployed on the all the seven days of the referenced week, but was 'seeking and available for work' at the time of survey conducted by the NSSO. This measures the unemployment for relatively shorter period. Table 21.4 reports the incidence of unemployment based on current weekly status (CWS).

It is evident from Table 21.4 that the incidence of unemployment based on CWS is higher than we got on the basis of PUS for both NER as well as for All India level. This result is expected as the CWS reflects under-unemployment also.[2] Unlike the incidence of unemployment reported in Table 21.3, the NER States have lower incidence of unemployment compared to All India. But by the place of residence, the unemployment rate is higher in the NER than All India in the urban sector with a prominent female bias. Within the

Table 21.4 : Rate of Unemployment (Current Weekly Status) in the Labour Force among the NER States in 1993-94

States	Rural			Urban			All		
	Male	Female	Persons	Male	Female	Persons	Male	Female	Persons
ARP	1.94	1.68	1.81	1.91	4.60	3.00	1.94	1.72	1.84
ASS	9.66	9.32	9.51	12.87	13.61	13.20	9.92	9.68	9.82
MAN	3.95	3.96	3.96	4.94	4.61	4.77	4.23	4.15	4.19
MEG	0.53	0.73	0.63	2.90	3.16	3.02	0.70	0.89	0.79
MIZ	2.00	1.86	1.94	0.34	0.50	0.41	1.56	1.48	1.52
NAG	2.47	1.50	2.01	10.15	12.33	11.07	4.36	3.77	4.09
TRI	7.23	7.48	7.35	15.74	18.79	17.26	8.35	9.14	8.72
NER	7.74	7.31	7.55	10.55	11.22	10.86	7.85	7.53	7.70
All India	7.61	7.49	7.55	10.29	9.85	10.08	8.17	7.97	8.07

Source: As in Table 21.1

Note: As in Table 21.1

States in the NER, Assam and Tripura have very high unemployment rates in both rural and the urban sectors. Other Sates have much lower incidence compared to All India.

Youth Unemployment

In recent times, there has been a strong concern expressed by various social scientists, youth organizations and student groups in NER that there is very high incidence of unemployment among youths in almost all the States. To investigate this point, we tabulated the incidence of unemployment in five age groups, 15-23, 24-32, 33-41, 42-50 and 51-59 years based on CWS.

Table 21.5 shows that indeed the incidence of unemployment is highest in the first two age groups among the States in the NER compared to national level. However, it is in the urban sector that male unemployment among the youths is phenomenally higher at over 77 per cent compared to national average of nearly 40 per cent. Further, male unemployment in rural sector is as high as 38.41 per cent in the age group 15-23 years, whereas female unemployment is higher in 24-32 age group. This proportion is significantly higher than All India average. Male unemployment in the age group 15-23, under which most of the youths finish their education and achieve the adulthood, such high youth unemployment is alarming.

This observation motivated us to take up the issue of youth unemployment in more detail. For this purpose state-wise distribution of unemployment within the age group 15-23 years is reported in Table 21.6. The proportion of youth unemployment is in general higher in NER compared to All India levels. But Assam and Tripura are having highest level of youth unemployment. It is significantly high for both males and females in rural sector of Assam.

As mentioned earlier, the youth unemployment is higher in urban sector of NER, but State-wise distribution suggests that Tripura has highest male youth unemployment (17.35 per cent) followed by Assam (14.64 per cent). Female youth unemployment is highest for Nagaland (19.02 per cent) followed by Tripura (17.47 per cent) and Assam (16.92 per cent). Alarmingly higher level of unemployment is given as one of the major explanation for youth unrest, root cause for on

Table 21.5 : Age Group-wise distribution of Unemployment among the States in the NER (in Percent) in 1993-94.

Age- group		15-23	24-32	33-41	42-50	51-59	Total
NER: Rural	Male	38.41	30.45	8.96	12.2	9.99	100
	Female	8.93	28.75	18.05	29.74	14.53	100
	Persons	28.3	29.87	12.08	18.21	11.55	100
All India: Rural	Male	35.96	26.2	15.17	13.72	8.95	100
	Female	33.21	24.16	16.46	17.34	8.83	100
	Persons	34.65	25.23	15.78	15.45	8.89	100
NER: Urban	Male	77.01	11.84	3.61	3.74	3.81	100
	Female	37.02	30.06	8.88	17.11	6.93	100
	Persons	66.99	16.4	4.93	7.09	4.59	100
All India: Urban	Male	39.86	27.5	11.36	12.4	8.88	100
	Female	35.22	21.98	16.17	18.21	8.43	100
	Persons	37.74	24.98	13.56	15.05	8.67	100
NER: All	Male	36.99	26.55	14.15	13.37	8.93	100
	Female	33.71	23.62	16.39	17.56	8.73	100
	Persons	35.45	25.17	15.21	15.34	8.84	100
All India: All	Male	49.74	24.99	7.39	9.71	8.18	100
	Female	14.83	29.03	16.12	27.09	12.93	100
	Persons	38.63	26.27	10.17	15.24	9.69	100

Source: As in Table 21.1.

Table 21.6 : Status of Youth Unemployment (in the Age Group of 15- 23 Years) in NER in 1993-94

States	NER rural			NER urban			State all		
	Male	Female	Persons	Male	Female	Persons	Male	Female	Persons
ARP	2.48	2.13	2.32	3.99	6.83	5.61	2.50	2.23	2.38
ASS	10.85	11.36	11.08	14.64	16.92	15.72	11.13	11.82	11.44
MAN	3.49	3.69	3.59	4.46	6.61	5.58	3.76	4.52	4.15
MEG	0.67	1.04	0.85	5.85	2.09	4.02	0.94	1.09	1.01
MIZ	2.17	2.45	2.29	0.17	0.39	0.28	1.72	1.95	1.83
NAG	1.66	0.82	1.29	5.77	19.02	11.82	2.42	4.28	3.26
TRI	7.08	7.97	7.49	17.35	17.47	17.41	8.19	9.22	8.67
NER	8.63	8.79	8.70	11.71	13.58	12.62	8.88	9.24	9.04
All India	7.92	7.75	7.84	11.78	10.83	11.36	8.74	8.38	8.57

Source: As in Table 1.

going insurgencies and social tensions in these states. This requires an immediate attention of policy makers and planners.

Unemployment and Education

Table 21.7 presents the distribution of unemployed by their level of education. The entire population is divided into four groups, illiterate, literate but below primary, above primary and below secondary and secondary and above. Table 21.7 clearly shows that at All India levels, the majority of unemployed are illiterate. It declines as we go down the column. Thus, the incidence of unemployment declines with the increasing level of education. This trend is more clearly visible for rural India, whereas urban India has highest proportion of unemployed coming from the education level above primary and below secondary level education.

We get a completely different picture in the northeastern States. In the rural sector of NER, the highest proportion of unemployed is not the illiterate. This is indicative of higher literacy rate even in the rural sector both for male and female populations. As pointed out earlier, this is more so, for urban sector of NER, where only 6.65 per cent of unemployed are illiterate and about 50 per cent of unemployed belong to above primary and below secondary level of education. Significantly higher level of unemployed (27.45 per cent) have educational level secondary and above.

This finding suggests that jobs in the urban sector require higher investment in human capital development. The finding that even in the highest education category, there is alarmingly high incidence of unemployment in the NER suggests that the job opportunities in the urban formal sector are almost approaching saturation level.[3] With very little investment going in the manufacturing sector among the States in NER, the employment situation is unlikely to improve in the coming years.

Unemployment and Poverty

In development economics literature, we find a close link between poverty and unemployment. It is suggested that people are poor because they are unemployed. On the contrary, some economists suggested that poor person can not afford to remain unemployed

Table 21.7 : General Educational Standard of Unemployed in 1993-94

Educational standard	NER			All India		
	Rural	**Urban**	**All**	**Rural**	**Urban**	**All**
Illiterate	26.48	6.65	23.87	53.25	25.03	45.95
Literate primary	28.78	16.34	27.14	22.92	23.56	23.08
Above primary but below secondary	31.47	49.56	33.86	18.34	33.66	22.30
Above secondary	13.26	27.45	15.13	5.50	17.75	8.67
Total	100.00	100.00	100.00	100.00	100.00	100.00

Source: As in Table 21.1.

Table 21.8 : Unemployment among the Poor and Non-Poor in 1993-94

Economic group	NER			All India		
	Rural	**Urban**	**All**	**Rural**	**Urban**	**All**
Unemployed among the poor	7.01	4.86	6.95	9.13	10.56	7.44
Unemployed among the non-poor	8.08	11.77	8.65	6.32	9.79	7.10
Total	7.54	10.86	7.86	7.55	10.08	5.99

Source: As in Table21. 1.

for longer period and take up the first available opportunity of unemployment even on lower wage and adverse job conditions. To analyze this aspect we estimated the proportion of unemployed who are living below and above the standard poverty line.

Table 21.8 has the incidence of unemployment among the households divided into two mutually exclusive groups, poor and non-poor for NER and also at All India level for rural and urban sectors separately. Recall that the poor households have been identified using State-wise official poverty line (Planning Commission poverty line) and NSS expenditure distribution of the households for the two sectors separately. The rate of unemployment is based on current weekly status (CWS). At All India level the incidence of unemployment among the poor households is higher than of those who are unemployed and coming from non-poor households in both rural and urban sectors. But this situation is reversed in case of NER. The rate of unemployment is lower among the poor compared to non-poor households. This observation is more pronounced in the urban sector of NER, where proportion of unemployed in the poor households is as low as 4.86 per cent than 11.77 per cent in the non-poor group.

This could imply that at All India level unemployment appears to have a causal link with poverty. This linkage appears more clearly in the rural sector. But in the NER lower incidence of unemployment among the poor implies that the rural workers are willing to take up jobs at prevailing wages. In urban sector, however, the implication could be that those who are in the labour force are willing to take up work that is more rewarding. This could also be due to weaker causal link between poverty and unemployment, especially in the urban sector of NER. However, this result should be taken with a caution because relationship between poverty and unemployment is a complex one. An in depth analysis of this issue is required to unravel the linkages.

Unemployment among Social Groups

Table 21.9 reports the degree of unemployment by social groups for the NER and All India. At All India level, unemployment is higher among the SCs and lowest among the STs. Similar result holds for rural India. In the urban sector also SCs continue to have highest

Table 21.9 : Unemployment among the Social Groups in 1993-94

Social Group	NER			All India		
	Rural	**Urban**	**All**	**Rural**	**Urban**	**All**
Scheduled tribe	4.36	4.20	4.35	5.75	10.72	6.08
Scheduled castes	9.53	7.46	9.39	12.26	14.70	12.60
Others	8.36	12.19	8.78	6.50	9.39	7.20
Total	7.54	10.86	7.86	7.55	10.08	8.08

Source: As in Table 21.1.

incidence of unemployment followed by the STs. The lowest proportion of unemployed is in the group OTH. In the NER too, exactly same pattern holds at the aggregate level as well as in the rural sector. It is in the urban sector where unemployment rate is highest in the OTH group.

It is interesting to note that the rate of unemployment among the STs is least in both the sectors of NER. Most surprising is the highest incidence of unemployment among OTH households. One possible explanation could be that the highest proportion of OTH households is in Assam and could be migrants from neighbouring countries.

The lowest incidence of unemployment among the STs compared to SCs in the NER could be due to the fact that STs have access to land, forest and other common property resources (CPR). The SCs on the other hand are scattered lot and often do not have access to these resources. Other explanation could be that STs have higher education level that could have resulted in better access to public sector jobs. These issues and its relationship with unemployment require detailed investigation.

Conclusion

In this chapter, we investigated the incidence of unemployment among the seven northeastern States of India and compared it with All India figures. We used household level data on employment and unemployment collected by the NSSO for the year 1993-94. The level of unemployment has been estimated considering the principal usual activity and current weekly status of the persons in the working age group of 15-59 years. The incidence of unemployment in NER is in general higher than national average. It is highest for Assam among these States. The data suggests that the common belief that youth unemployment is high in NE States is indeed true. There is an urgent need of all out efforts for a "Job oriented economic growth". Encouraging non-farming activities in the rural areas and enlarging the scope of economic activities in urban areas. It may help in creating additional employment opportunities. The improved intra- and inter-regional trade links coupled with international trade links with neighbouring countries like Myanmar, Bhutan, Bangladesh and Nepal could create additional employment opportunities in the long run. Of course, these linkages might not take shape unless proper infrastructural facilities are created. But how this could materialize is the biggest challenge for the policy makers in the region.

NOTES

1. Sakia (1989) also observed that by and large, women do not go for wage employment in agricultural sector of Assam except when driven by acute economic hardship.
2. Recall that under CWS, a person is classified as unemployed even if he might have been employed in the earlier weeks.
3. In the NER, urban formal sector consists of jobs in the government and other related service sector like education.

REFERENCES

Dantwala, M.L. (1979), "Rural Unemployment: Facts and Issues", *Economic and Political Weekly*, Vol. XIV, No. 25, June 23, Bombay.

Dantwala, M.L. (1981), "Understanding Poverty and Unemployment", *Artha-Jijnasa*, Vol. 1, No. 2, Indian Merchants Chamber, Economic Research and Training Foundation, Bombay, 7-32.

Dubey, A. and O.J. Kharpuri (1999), "Poverty Incidence in North-Eastern States", *Labour and Development*, 4(1), 32-51.

Government of India (1997), *Report of the High Powered Commission for the North East*, Planning Commission, March.

Sakia, A. (1989), "Role of Women in Agriculture in Assam", in Sakia and Phukan (eds.), *Rural Development in North East India*, D.K. Publishing and Distribution (P) Ltd., Delhi, 195-206.

22

CONTRACTUAL EMPLOYMENT IN INDIAN LABOUR MARKET

A Study of Faizabad District

ASHUTOSH N. SINHA

Introduction

Employment of contractual workers has been an age long practice all over the world. Workers have been employed under this arrangement in the different sectors of the economy, viz., agriculture, industry, service. This cuts the size of the firm's inputs and is very much in line with the objective of profit maximization.

However, from the employees' side this may not be a very good arrangement. Though it provides job for the jobless yet these workers are discriminated against and they may not get the same treatment and job conditions as the regular employees get. In the present era of globalization and liberalization things have gone worse for the contract employees as firms facing stiff competition from the domestic and foreign firms are fighting for their survival. They are always keen on cutting production costs and in the process are in search of the technology that offers maximum scope for factor substitutions and employment of cheap inputs. Contractual workers offer the most promising solution under the circumstances and their numbers have increased enormously in India over the last 10 to 15 years.

Contractual employment is a tripartite arrangement between the establishment i.e. the principle employer, the contractor and the worker. The workers are indirect employees as they are hired, supervised and paid by the contractor who in turn is compensated by the principal employer. Under this arrangement workers are exposed to exploitation by the employer and the contractor who often collude to serve their interests.

Table 22.1 gives some information about the contract employment in factories at national Level. Three important things which Table 22.1 reports are (i) the number of registered factories has shown a declining trend; (ii) the employment of contract workers exhibits an increasing trend; and (iii) there are disparities in wages/ salaries between regular and contract workers and the latter are discriminated against in matters of payment. The above is thus indicative of the fact that firms are increasingly substituting relatively cheap contract workers for regular employees. This, information is unable to depict the true picture as it only tells about the formal sector of the contractual labour market. The informal sector for contract workers is considerably big and has grown over the years.

Considering the sensitiveness of the issue it would be imperative to have a closer look at the problem. Faizabad District of the State of Uttar Pradesh has been selected for the purpose. The succeeding

Table 22.1: Trend in Contractual Employment in Factories at National Level

Year	No. of reporting factories	Average daily employment of contract workers	Wage salaries per man day worked (Rs.)	
			All workers	Contract workers
1999-2000	126537	1240238 (19.7)	138.09	81.09
2000-2001	128339	1253468 (20.4)	148.86	90.10
2001-2002	125834	1297458 (21.8)	152.38	90.95
2002-2003	125834	1422155 (23.1)	158.75	96.68
2003-2004	125844	1495671 (24.6)	165.55	100.96

Note: Figures in parenthesis are percentage of total.
Source: Labour Bureau, Government of India.

section discusses about the statutory provisions and regulatory mechanism for the contractual labour market. The third section provides a profile of the study area. The fourth section empirically undertakes a study of the study area. The final section concludes the work.

At present there is proper legislation, set of rules, legislative provisions to regulate the contractual labour market and to check the exploitation of contract labour. But this was not case earlier. Though the poor plight and the vulnerable status of the contract workers was realised and commissions and committees deliberated upon it in both the pre- and post-independence period, nothing concrete could come out.

It was only in 1960 that for the first time judiciary intervened into the matter and in its historic judgement in the case of the Standard Vacuum Refinery company *vs.* their workers the Supreme Court prohibited the employment of contract workers in the work which was of perennial nature, which was incidental to and necessary for the work of the factory; which was sufficient to employ considerable number of full time workers and which was being done in most concerns by regular workers. This was certainly an indirect respite to the workers who were exploited as non-regular employees. However, this was not enough as the exploitation of non-regular employees continued unabated.

The enactment of the Contract Labour (Regulation and Abolition) Act, 1970 and coming into force of the Contract Labour (Regulation and Abolition) Central Rules, 1971, which were finally enforced with effect from 21.03.1974, brought a safeguard mechanism against atrocities committed in the contractual labour market by the employers. It would be appropriate at this juncture to have a look at the salient features of the Act and Rules which are as follows:

Application of Act

The Act applies to every establishment including Government and local authorities and every contractor, which employs 20 or more workers or have employed on any day on the last 12 months. In case of establishments where work is of intermittent nature the Act can only be applicable if work is performed more than 120 days and 60 days in a year, respectively.

Jurisdiction

The definition of 'Appropriate Government' has been used to demarcate the jurisdiction of the Central and State Governments.

The appropriate government would be Central Government if (i) the concerned Central Government company/undertaking is included by name in clause (a) of section 2 of Industrial Disputes Act, or (ii) any industry carried on by or under the authority of Central Government or by a railway company, or (iii) any such controlled industry as may be specified in this behalf by the Central Government. Apart from the above for any other establishment the 'appropriate government' would be the government of the State where the establishment is situated.

Advisory Bodies

The Central and State Advisory Contract Labour Boards are the advisory bodies, which are required to be set up by Central and State governments for administering the Act. The Boards are empowered under the Act to constitute committees if deemed proper.

Registration and Licensing

The establishments under the purview of the Act are required to obtain registration as 'Principal employers' and the contractors are required to obtain licences and to take work from contract workers in accordance with the licence issued which stipulates working hours, fixation of wages and essential facilities for contract worker. If the contractor fails to provide such facilities, it becomes the responsibility of the principal employer to do the same.

Remuneration

Contract workers are to be paid wages by the contractors in presence of the authorized representative of the principal employer. In case the contractor falters then the principal employer is liable to do the same. Under the Act for similar work there should be no difference in the wages of the regular employee and the contract worker. Wages should also not fall below the statutory minimum wages. Provident fund benefits are also applicable to the contract labour.

Welfare Provisions

The contractor is required to ensure the establishment of canteens and rest rooms; sufficient supply of drinking water, toilets, urinals and washing facilities along with first aid facility with a trained staff. In case of failure on part of contractor it becomes the responsibility of the principal employer to ensure the facilities within 30 days.

Enforcement of Act

For Central Government the Central Industrial Relations Machinery (CIRM) has been given the responsibility for enforcing the provisions of Act through Inspectors, Licensing Officers, Registering Officers, other Appellate Authorities. Similar provision exists for the States also.

Exemption

There is a provision of granting exemption by the 'appropriate government' to establishments and contractors from the applicability of Act and related rules under pressing circumstances.

Prohibition

Prohibition powers have been given to the appropriate government, which is to be used for the benefit of contract labour. These are exercised by prohibiting employment of contract workers in different operations/category of jobs in different establishments mainly where there is full justification of employing regular employees.

Penal Provision

For violating the Act and the rules made thereunder penal action may be taken against the principal employer and/or the contractor. The punishment is imprisonment for a maximum period of 3 years and fine up to a maximum limit of Rs. 1000.

From the above we can safely conclude that the existing law is sufficient to take care of the contract workers though penal provisions have to be strengthened and imprisonment period and fine limit need to be raised for better enforcement of the law.

In the wake of economic liberalization and globalisation employers have been advocating for the dilution of the provisions in their favour so that they can be on even terms with their competitors. While Labour Unions hold a diametrically opposite view. In this connection it can be said that if the Act needs to be amended then it should be ensured that there is a proper balance between equity and efficiency considerations.

The district of Faizabad is located in the Avadh region on the eastern border of Uttar Pradesh. It covers an area of 2,015 sq. km. It is divided into 4 tehsils and 9 community blocks and has 1,028 inhabited villages.

The district receives an annual precipitation of 98.3 cm. with many blocks falling in the drought prone zone. Geographically, the district shares the features of the eastern plateau. The district has a forest cover of about 1.25 per cent of the total area.

According to the Census 2001, the population of Faizabad district is 20.88 lakhs constituting 1.26 per cent of the States population and the District ranks 38th in the State. The density of population at 755 per sq. km. is high for the district and the district ranks 31st in this regard.

With a sex ratio of 940, the city ranks 15th in the State and the figures for the district are better than the State figures.

The degree of urbanization is extremely low in the district with 86 per cent of the population living in the rural area. The Per Capita Domestic Product at current prices for 2002-03 is 6,755 which is very low and is suggestive of the relative economic backwardness of the district.

The social backwardness of the area is reflected in the low literacy rates. Here also figures for the females are pathetically low as shown in Table 22.2.

The occupational pattern of the workforce is shown in Table 22.4, which reveals the backward economic structure of the area.

Table 22.2 : Socio-Economic Profile of Faizabad

Sl. No.	Items	Faizabad distt.	U.P.
1.	Area sq.km.	2015	240928
2.	Population	2087914	166052859
3.	Population density per sq. km.	755	689
4.	Literacy rate (per cent)		
	Persons	57.48	57.36
	Males	70.73	70.23
	Females	43.35	42.98
5.	Per capita domestic product at current prices 2002-03	6755	9963

Sources: 1. Census of India 2001,

2. Statistical Diary, U.P. 2005 Statistical Division, State Planning Institute.

3. *Statistical Bulletin*, Faizabad, 2005.

The industrial picture of the District is given in Table 22.3. The industrial profile of Faizabad clearly shows satisfactory but not very promising progress.

Table 22.3 : Industrial Profile of Faizabad

Sl. No.	Items	1998-99	2000-01
1.	Registered factories	80	157
2.	Factories in operation	40	148
3.	No. of average daily labourers & employees	1495	5051
4.	Value of industrial output (thousand Rs.)	1735279	20214253

Source: Statistical Bulletin, Faizabad 2005.

The Table 22.4 informs that over three quarters of the workers are engaged in the primary sector. The proportion of agriculture labourers is also fairly large. Manufacturing activities are conspicuous

Table 22.4 : Workers Classification according to Occupational Categories

Sl. No.	Occupational categories	Faizabad district
1.	Cultivators	59.8
2.	Agricultural labourers	18.1
3.	Livestock, forestry, plantation	0.5
4.	Mining & quarrying	0.0
	Primary sector	78.4
5.	(a) Household industry	1.1
	(b) Non-house industry	2.1
	(c) Total	3.2
6.	Construction	1.5
	Secondary sector	3.7
7.	Trade and commerce	4.4
8.	Transport, storage and communication	0.5
9.	Other services	12.0
	Tertiary sector	15.9
	Total main workers	100.00

Sources: 1. Census of India 2001.

2. *Statistical Bulletin*, Faizabad, 2005.

by their absence with around 5 per cent of workers engaged in secondary sector in Faizabad district. Even household industrial activity is quite rare. In the absence of productive agriculture and flourishing industry the tertiary sector is also poorly developed.

For having a clear assessment of the functioning of the contractual labour market in the study area i.e., Faizabad district responses to following queries were obtained :

(i) To know whether establishments using contract workers are registered and related contractors have obtained licences i.e., to ascertain the relative size of the informal part of the contractual labour market.

(ii) To know whether prohibition powers are properly exercised by the authorities.

(iii) To find out whether contract workers are remunerated as per the provisions of the Act and whether they are provided the essential facilities at the work place.

(iv) To know whether penal provisions are exercised strictly.

Both primary as well as secondary information has been used for analysis. The secondary information obtained from the Office of the Deputy Labour Commissioner, Faizabad. This information was necessary as no other data source is available. This is reported in Table 22.5. Data reveals that there are a very few number of registered firms with very little variation in their numbers in the 10 years period, in the district. The numbers of contractors and contract workers show an increasing trend.

Table 22.5: Contractual Labour Market of Faizabad

Year	No. of registered firms	No. of licensed contractors	No. of contract workers
1998	2	6	200
1999	3	7	375
2000	3	4	120
2001	3	4	135
2002	3	6	233
2003	3	8	340
2004	3	13	734
2005	5	13	790
2006	4	11	640
2007	4	12	525

Source: Labour Department, Faizabad.

Sample Design

The Table 22.5 reports that presently there are 4 registered establishments and hence all 4 have been purposely selected for study.

The size of informal sector was found to be considerably large in the area. However for facilitating comparison between the formal and informal sector only 4 unregistered establishments were randomly selected from the different parts of the district. Information was collected from 10 per cent of the employees from each establishment by interviewing them by a pre-determined questionnaire.

Responses of Employees from Registered Establishments

65 per cent of employees accused the establishments and the authorities for not exercising the prohibition provisions properly, i.e., contract workers were being used where only regular employees were supposed to work.

72 per cent employees reported wage disparities, i.e., differential wages to contract and regular workers for similar work. However, no case of minimum wage norm violation was reported. 82 per cent employees had no problem with the provident fund facility. 18 per cent employees reported loss on this count. Only 44 per cent employees were satisfied with the facilities provided to them at the work place. 95 per cent employees were of the view that law enforcing authorities collude with the employers and the contractors.

No one reported of the exercise of penal provisions of the Act, which means less penal action taken by authorities.

Response of Employers/Contractors

All the employers/their representatives (managers), contractors as expected assertively stated that workers were provided all the facilities under law and no rule was violated.

Responses of Employees from Unregistered Firms

93 per cent of employees were not having proper knowledge of the statutory provisions meant for contract workers, 38 per cent of employees reported of the violation of the minimum wage law and this information was obtained by comparing the wages reported by the employees and the statutory minimum wage. Only 39 per cent of employees were satisfied with the amenities provided at the work place. 99 per cent of workers reported of collusion between Employers/Contractors:

No clear explanation was provided by employers and contractors for non-registration.

Both the primary and the secondary data clearly reveal that law enforcing authorities are not discharging their duties properly. This was evident as majority of the establishments operating in the district and contractors were employing workers (which should have been covered by the Act) without registration and licenses and thus denying the workers the rightful benefits of the Act. Even the workers covered by the Act were not satisfied with their employers and reported that they were not getting what was due to than as per the provisions of the Act.

Conclusion

The study area i.e. the District of Faizabad is relatively a socio-economically backward district where the majority of the labour force is unorganised, very poor and belongs to the informal sector. This is equally true for the contractual labourers also. The statutory provisions meant for the protection of the contract workers are adequate. However they are not successful in checking their exploitation from the employers and contractors. There appears to be a tacit understanding between the law enforcing authorities, principal owners and the contractors, which is working against the interests of the contract workers. This calls for immediate attention and prompt action from the government's side to rectify the ills in the system and to ensure that the workers get what rightfully belongs to them.

REFERENCES

Besley, Timothy and R. Burgess (2002), *Can Labour Regulation Hinder Economic Performance?*, Evidence from India, CEPR Discussion Paper 3260.

Davala, Sarath (Ed.) (1994), *Unprotected Labour in India—Issue and Concerns*, New Delhi: Friedrich Ebert Stiftung.

Dutt, Rudder (Ed.) (1997), *Organising the Unorganised Workers*, New Delhi: Vikas Publishing House.

Fernandes, Walter (1986), "Construction Workers, Powerlessness and Bondage: The Case of the Asian Games", *Social Action*, Vol. 36, No. 3, July-September.

Philip, Sajin (2007), "Economic Growth and Informalization of Labour", *Labour and Development*, Vol. 12, No. 2.

Singh, Darshan (2007), "Working Conditions and Problems of Unorganised Labour", *Labour and Development*, Vol. 13, No. 1.

Statistical Diary, U.P. 2005, State Planning Institute, U.P.

Statistical Bulletin, Faizabad, 2005, State Planning Institute, U.P.

The Contractual Labour (Regulation and Abolition) Act, 1970, Law Publishers Pvt. Ltd.

23

EFFECT OF OUTSOURCING ON MANPOWER REQUIREMENTS

SUNIT KUMAR

It is very true that Indian call center sector is experiencing an unprecedented growth in the past few years. It is an industry that has been at the forefront of global attention. It is an industry that has raised more debates and outcry than any other. It is an industry that has been on democrat candidate John Kerry's agenda in his presidential campaign in the last US elections. Yes, it is the BPO industry, which has not only brought jobs to India but has created a whole new generation of young Indians who service the entire world. The BPO industry has been a pioneer of sorts on many people initiatives. Pickups and drops, office parties, fat paychecks for very young graduates; the BPO was just another great party till things started looking, well, not so rosy.

The charm and glamour started declining and everyone started seeing the flipside of the job—never ending night shifts, health problems, stress and, most importantly, growth. Today, the industry's single-largest problem is attrition.

While factors like odd timings and stressful work are major causes of employee attrition despite high entry-level salaries—often Rs 2 lakh (Rs 200,000) per annum or more—the image of BPO jobs being a short-term career option has only reinforced this phenomenon.

Ironically, the 'fun at work' image that attracted most of the current 416,000 BPO employees has also become the culprit in causing high employee attrition. The attrition rate in BPO firms is also at the highest because of opportunities factor, which encourages its technical pool of human resource for greener pastures.

Expectation of higher salary is other key cause identified for high attrition rate in the BPO industry.

This research work has been done in order to find out the extent of contributions made by the call center industry in providing employment to the young population of India and also to have an insight into the major problem of attrition as reported by and faced by most of the call center organizations.

Annual Increase or Decrease in Manpower Requirements

As the researchers subject area is related to manpower requirements it was very necessary to ascertain the annual increase or decrease in manpower requirements of the organizations as such the data related to that shows that two organizations—Apex communication and Ramantra reported only 50 per cent annual increase or decrease in manpower requirements whereas Apple E. Service and Colwell & Salmon answered 100 per cent increase and decrease followed by 200 per cent in Tirupati world links and Energizer.

Process of Manpower Planning

To make an organization successful the most important asset leaving aside other requirements is the presence and combination of right kind of personnel's which is the main responsibility of HR department and each organization has its own way of manpower planning as such it was very necessary to collect information related to this which is given Fig. 23.1 which depicts that out of 6 organizations 4 (66.67%) carry their manpower planning all round the year whereas only 2 (33.33%) organizations reported their manpower planning business based.

Recruitment Ideology

The accumulated data shows the recruitment ideology of the selected organizations in which 2 (33.33%) organizations emphasized more

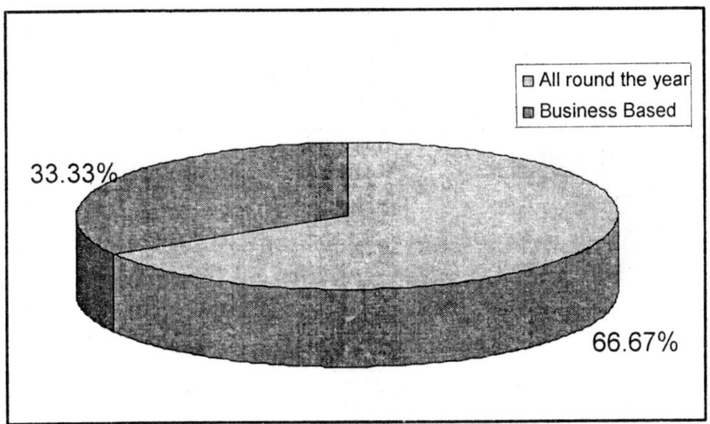

Fig. 23.1 : Manpower Process

on people relations whereas 2 (33.33%) prefer people who have functional experience and equally 2 (33.33%) organization emphasized on presentable and pleasing personality.

Sources of Acquiring Manpower

Acquiring the right kind of talents and dedicated workforce cannot be possible by relying on one single source as such organizations today go in for various means of getting the required workforce. The present data depicts the information related with the same as 3 (50.00%) organizations takes the help of the specialized agencies who particularly deals with recruitment only and 2 (33.33%) organizations adopts agencies, advertising, internal HR department and word of mouth as given in the interview schedule to hire manpower whereas only (16.67 %) organization fulfil their manpower requirements through advertising.

Local Availability of Manpower

Fig. 23.2 given shows the data related to local availability of manpower when asked by the selected organizations 4 (66.67%) organizations responded average availability and another 2 (33.33%) reported good availability thus majority of organizations reported having average availability of manpower resources.

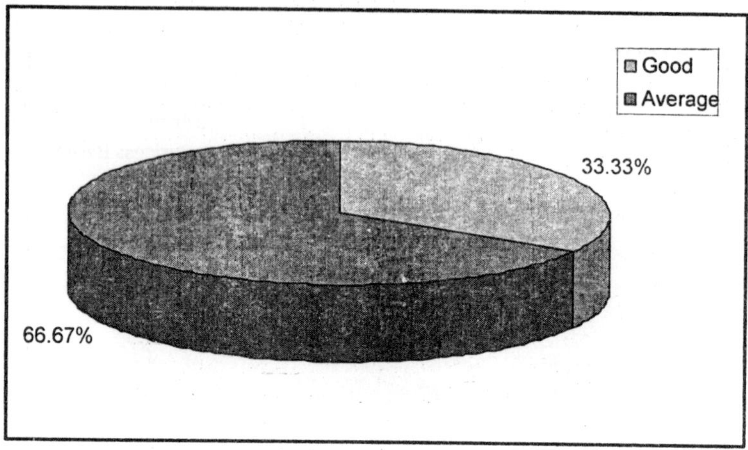

Fig. 23.2 : Local Availability of Candidates

Qualification at Entry Level

The Fig. 23.2 shows the information related to the level of education of the applicants for entry level recruitment in which 3 (50.00%) showed their preference for candidates holding the graduation degree, and remaining 2 (33.33%) preferred professionally qualified candidates while 1(16.67%) preferred undergraduates candidates.

Essential Criteria for Recruitment at Entry Level

Every industry has its particular requirement for selecting a new employee for different positions, at different levels in the organization, the call center industry too have some essential criteria which is required for positions at entry level. The presented data contains the information related to it only which says that out of 6 organizations 4 (66.67%) of the organizations require the presence of all the mentioned requirements (graduates, good command over English and presentable personality) whereas 2 respondent organizations (33.33%) responded in favour of graduates and good command over English each respectively whereas only 1 organization (16.67%) presentable personality as essential criteria for recruitment at entry level positions.

Essential Qualifications for Recruitment at Middle and Higher Level

The Fig. 23.2 is related with essential qualification for recruitment at middle and higher level which avers that more companies prefer candidates having prior experience of BPOs as 3 (50.00%) out of 6 companies replied for the same, followed by 2 (33.33%) organizations who prefer to recruit I.T. professionals and only 1 (16.67%) respondent organization regarded professionals as their choice for recruitment at middle and high level positions.

Ways of Providing Training

After hiring candidates every good organization go for a training programme so that new entrants can learn the required skills for completing a task and to do their job more effectively. Different organizations have different ways of providing training to the new joiners. Out of 6 companies 3 (50.00%) answered in favour of conducting training through specialized agencies whereas 2 (33.33%) respondent companies provide the training with the help of the clients and only 1 (16.67%) respondent company goes for training provided in house as is evident in the given data.

Techniques for Measuring Performance

The presented data is related to information about the techniques used by different organizations for measuring performance of the employees working in the organization. It is evident from the given information that out of 6 respondent companies 4 (66.67%) of them follow regular appraisals by seniors and executives on the shop floor whereas only 2 (33.33%) organizations go for quarterly/half yearly appraisal of their employees.

Average Stay Duration of the Employees

The most predictable thing in today's world is change rest nothing is fixed. Everywhere everything is changing so is the people, their expectations, their likings, their attitude, their personal and professional lives. Today everybody wants to catch hold of the best present opportunities present in the market. With so much attractive and always seem to be better opportunities. Thus, it was very important for the researcher to find out the average stay duration of the employees in the industry, which has been a pioneer in providing employment to lots and lots of Indians. It is evident through the following data that majority of the employees duration of stay in the organization is in between 1-2 as reported by 4 organizations (66-67%) followed by 2-3 replied by 3 organizations (50.00%) and 0-1 (33.33%) answered by 2 of the organization and lastly the average stay duration of employees in between 3-4 years was found to be 16.67 per cent as reported by 1 organization thus it can be estimated that majority of organizations have average stay duration of their employees in the period between 1-2 years.

Rate of Attrition

As it is very difficult to select the right candidate by the organizations equally difficult is to retain the good ones in the organization for a long period. Most of the business process outsourcing companies are faced with the problem of increasing attrition rate as such the data acquired through this research analysis shows that maximum companies 4 (66.67%) out of the selected ones replied high attrition rate whereas only 2 (33.33%) of the organizations rated the attrition rate in their organization as average and none of the selected companies answered their attrition rate as normal. Thus this data given shows the severity of the problem faced by these organizations in terms of retaining manpower.

Means to Control Attrition

If there is a problem there has to be a solution is an accepted fact. It applies to organization facing different problems as they keep themselves always ready to deal with the negative circumstances. When asked about the means to control attrition by the respondent organizations majority of the respondent organization that is 3 (50.00%) out of 6 believed in providing more facilities to the employees who wish to leave the organization whereas only 2 (33.33%) organizations applies the means of increasing the salary of the ones wishing to leave the present organization and only 1 (16.67%)

respondent organization said that their means of dealing with attrition will be based on the specific case. Thus more and more companies believe in providing more facilities to control high attrition rate.

India as Major Destination for Outsourcing

No one than those in the actual situation is in the better condition of experiencing and telling the right information. It was very essential to know the view points of those responsible for hiring manpower in the industry concerned that whether India will remain a major destination for outsourcing business as given presents that more of the respondents believe that India will remain a major player in outsourcing business as 4 (66.67%) out of 6 respondent companies answered in favour followed by 1 (16.67%) respondent each who don't expect any such possibility and 1 (16.67%) who have no clear cut idea. Thus it is clear from the given data that it is assumed that India will remain a major outsourcing destination.

Industries Ability to Generate Employment

With lots of multi nationals doing their business in the country it is very important to ascertain that how people of country think about them or what are the views that people hold about them that whether they would like to be part of that industry and whether the industry is able to generate employment for the deserving ones. The data related to this aspect depicts that there was a mixed response from all the respondent companies as 2 (33.33%) of the companies answered that yes they believe that this industry will be able to attract and employ more and more able and willing workforce followed by 2 (33.33%) of the respondent companies who holds just opposite views and 2 (33.33%) of the respondent companies failed to give any comments. Thus it can be made out that there might be a possibility of both.

Highest Demand of the Level

The basic objective and functions of the organization determines what kind of and for what level the manpower is required. People today have become very calculative, as they know to make their career grow in the best possible way they have to be very clear about the choices they make in their professional lives that is how to grow step by step. It is not necessary that all the organizations have the best opportunities at all levels within the organization or have openings at all level. To ascertain this information researcher enquired about the highest demand of which entry level from the respondent companies which avers that the highest demand in call center industry is for lower level as answered by 3 (50.00%) of the respondent companies whereas 2 (33.33%) out of 6 companies replied in favour of middle level and lastly only 1 (16.67%) respondent organizations believes that the highest demand is for the positions at higher level. It can be concluded that these call center industries have more opening for the fresher or employees joining at the lower level.

Supply and Demand of the Employees

It is very important for every organization to have competent and required workforce present every time within the organization. At times it becomes very difficult to have access to the kind of people or talent been required to finish a task and at times the situation is just the opposite as such the researcher gathered the data related to this context which has been presented which reveals that 4 (66.66%) out of 6 companies say that the supply of adequate number of employees does not equal to demand whereas less number of companies that is 2 (33.33%) companies believe that the demand and supply remain equal. Thus it can be concluded that there is a situation of non-availability as reported by the companies.

Compromises to be Made

At times to fulfil the target and to make things run smoothly it becomes very important for the organization that they are required to make some compromises with the kind of personnel required with the kind of personnel available. This was very important aspect of enquiry for the researcher as such the question was asked from the respondents and same has been presented in Fig. 23.3 which clearly depicts that more of the companies have reported that at times they have to compromise with the kind of talent required and to cope up with the situation they heavily rely on providing training to augment and increase the skills of the new incumbents as was reported by 4 (66.67%) of the organizations, followed by 2 (33.33%) respondent company who reported no problems and no compromises to avail the required and best manpower for accomplishing their targets. Thus this is evident from the above data that most of the times companies do compromise with the quality of manpower required but heavily relies on effective training techniques to get rid of the under skilled and underperformance.

The Quality of Recruits

The birth of these business process outsourcing organizations have been the result of Indian governments policy of liberalization, privatization and globalization and the outcome has been the coming of different kind of opportunities for Indian youths. No other industry than this call center industry has been in limelight for any other than for providing employment to large population of very young educated Indian population. It has been years when these call center industry started doing their business and now almost everybody is aware what this call center industry is all about which was not so few years back as such those employed in call center industries or those wishing to enter, enter with open mind that is they are almost aware about things and know what is required and what they are

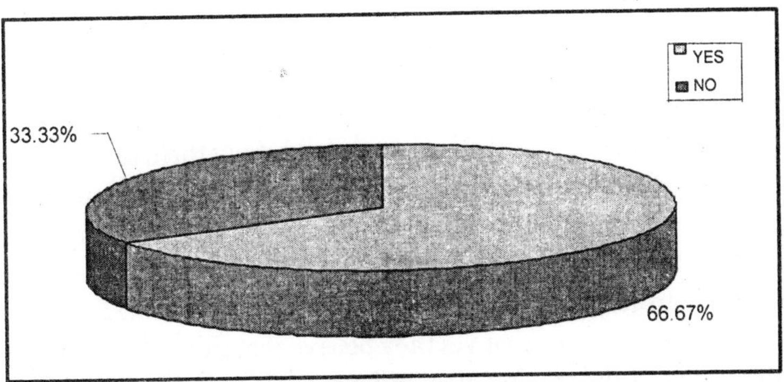

Fig. 23.3: Compromises to be made

supposed to do, thus it was researched by the researcher that whether the quality of recruits was same as it was earlier which has been presented through the following data which avers that the major percentage of companies 4 (66.67%) out of 6 reported that quality of recruits has not remained same whereas 2 organizations (33.33%) still believe that quality of recruits is same as it was earlier. Thus it can be concluded that there has been a decline in quality of recruits as it was earlier.

Availability of Backup Staff

It is very important for any organization to have availability of willing and capable workforce to be utilized in the situation of emergency so that process is not hampered. This is one of the very essential responsibility of the human resource department as their manpower planning process will only be successful if they have required kind of personnel's present at the right time to finish a task and is always ready with those who are there to take up future responsibilities. With this aspect into consideration the researcher tried to collect the information, which is presented in the Fig. 23.3, reveals that 4 (66.66%) of the respondent companies reported that they have to face the problems of non-availability of backup staff whereas 2 (33.33%) other companies reported no problems in availability of backup staff. It is thus very clear that the organizations are facing the problem of non-availability of backup staff.

BPOS to Attract and Employ More

With lots of multi nationals doing their business in the country it is very important to ascertain that how people of country think about them or what are the views that people hold about them that whether they would like to be part of that industry and whether the industry is able to generate employment for the deserving ones. The given data deals with this aspect which depicts that there was a mixed response from all the respondent companies as two (33.33%) of the companies answered that yes they believe that this industry will be able to attract and employ more and more able and willing workforce followed by another two (33.33%) of the respondent companies who holds just opposite views and two of the respondent companies failed to give any comments. Thus it can be made out that there might be a possibility of both.

Highest Demand of the Level

The basic objective and functions of the organization determines what kind of and for what level the manpower is required. People today have become very calculative, as they know to make their career grow in the best possible way they have to be very clear about the choices they make in their professional lives that is how to grow step by step. It is not necessary that all the organizations have the best opportunities at all levels within the organization or have openings at all level. To ascertain this information researcher enquired about the highest demand of which entry level from the respondent companies and the data related to that has been presented in Fig. 23.4 which avers that the highest demand in call center industry is for lower level as answered by 3 (50.00%)of the respondent companies whereas 2 (33.33%) out of 6 companies replied in favour of middle level and lastly only 1(16.67%) respondent organizations believes that the highest demand is for the positions at higher level. It can be concluded that these call center industries have more opening for the fresher or employees joining at the lower level.

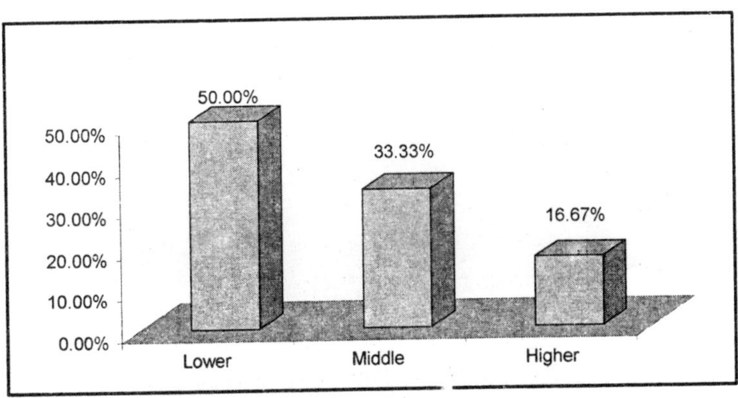

Fig. 23.4 : Highest Demand of the Level

Supply and Demand of Employees

It is very important for every organization to have competent and required workforce present every time within the organization. At times it becomes very difficult to have access to the kind of people or talent been required to finish a task and at times the situation is just the opposite as such the researcher gathered the data related to this context which has been presented in which reveals that 4(66.67%) out of 6 companies say that the supply of adequate number of employees does not equal to demand whereas 2 of companies that is (33.33%) companies believe that the demand and supply remains equal. Thus it can be concluded that there is shortage of candidates as per the demand (see Fig. 23.5).

The recruitment in the Indian call center industry has happened and is still happening on a speed never seen before in any industry. With fortune 500 and other international companies increasing their work to be outsourced, and in some cases even setting their captive units in India, BPO industry's future in India is very bright. The BPO industry has definitely played a role in addressing India's unemployment problems, and would continue to do so even more in the future. India's BPO industry is growing at about 50 per cent annually and currently employs over 3, 50,000 people.

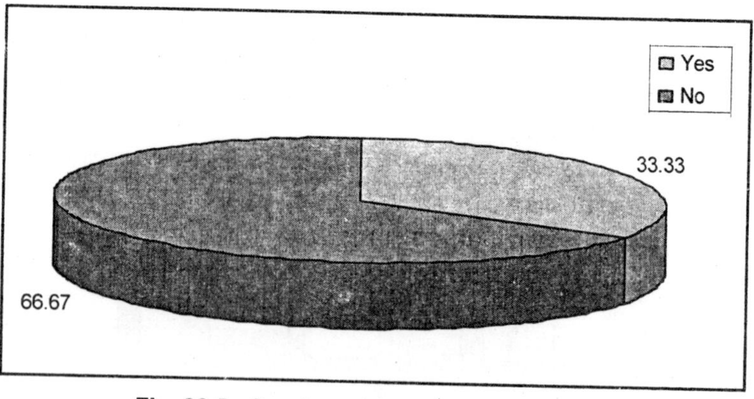

Fig. 23.5 : Supply and Demand of Employees

Main Causes Behind Joining the Call Center

Every individual is always motivated by number of factors, which motivates him to behave and act in a manner it wants. It is proved through various theories of motivation that if one individual is motivated by one factor it is not necessary that the other person also but at times there are some factors which generally is a motivational factor for most. As lots and lots of young generation are or are interested in joining call centers it became very essential to find out the main motive behind joining the call centres and for this reason the researcher collected the data which primarily enquired about the reasons or causes behind joining the call centre which is presented in graph which shows that financial benefits has been a major cause behind joining call centre where 95.83 per cent answered for it, following 49.48 per cent respondents for social prestige, whereas 27.08 per cent stated more job opportunities as their main reason for preferring this industry and only 27.08 per cent joined call centre for self satisfaction.

This it is absolutely clear that financial benefit stands out highest reason of joining the call center by more respondents.

Joining Interest in BPOs

The present era of liberalization, privatization and globalization (LPG) has opened up new vistas and opportunities in order to utilize their fund of knowledge theoretical as well as practical, acquired in the course of their studentship of professional courses available throughout length and breadth of the country. Such passed out professionals find varied modes of joining the various professional organizations. Against this background, it was found important to collect information from the present set of respondents regarding their various modes of joining the concerned organizations. The trend of information revealed in this context depicts, that a greater per cent of respondents indicated that they had the choice of joining the BPOs (63.80%) while (33.86%) of respondents indicated that they joined the BPOs by chance. However, (2.34%) of respondents could not offer any clear-cut response in this context.

Thus it is revealed; a greater percentage of respondents related their choice in order to join BPOs.

Motive Behind the Joining of Call Center Industry

Insuing from the nature of information revealed that there are various motives behind joining the call centres by the present set of respondents. The data this aspect avers that a dominant section i.e., 83.07 per cent among the present set of respondents joined the call centers because of the high salary package; while 55.73 per cent of respondents joined call centre because of higher incentives; followed by 45.83 per cent of the respondents joining the industry because of the motives termed as better facilities in terms of life style available in the concerned industry; 29.95 per cent career oriented in the concerned call centre industry and 26.56 per cent easy entry of the concerned call centre industry.

Thus it is evident from the given data that the high salary package has an assertive motive behind joining the call centre industry, as revealed in the present research.

The Expectation of the Respondents

Accepting the fact that every person has some or other expectations from his job and his organization, thus the information related to the expectations of the respondents with their jobs is an important area of the present study, as such the information related with this context was collected and the same has been presented in the given findings which depicts that the majority of respondents, i.e. 88.54 per cent expected good working culture; followed by 66.67 per cent of the respondents who expected high potential for growth; whereas 63.54 per cent of respondents had expected high salary and recognition; and the lowest of respondents, i.e., 54.43 per cent expected better facilities in their present job.

Thus it is evident that majority of respondents join call centre industry with expectation of good working culture.

Fulfilment of the Required Expectation

People come from different background and different expectations but reality is different from what people expect, this was the interest of the researcher that whether the circumstances are same as assumed by the respondents, in this context findings were made as presented which reveals that larger number of respondents 76.30 per cent were not lucky enough to have their expectations fulfilled whereas lesser number of respondents 21.62 per cent had fulfilled expectations whereas there was no straight reply from 2.08 per cent respondents who had no such thought. Thus, it can be concluded that more respondents had their expectations unfulfilled.

Call Centres have Changed the Lifestyle of Youths

With the coming of liberalization, privatization and globalization almost everywhere in every area, mark change was witnessed. In this context the youths of India also witnessed change in their values, beliefs, attitudes, life styles, expectations and confidence level. The overall impact of being in a call centre industry on the life of Indian youths bears a high importance as such the given graph avers the findings drawn after conducting research on this area which indicates that larger number of respondents 82.55 per cent believed that call centre industry has changed the life style of Indian youths., whereas 14.58 per cent believed that as such Indian youths have not witnessed any such change in their life style and 2.87 per cent of respondents had no opinion in this context.

Thus it can be understood from the above result that Indian youths have taken a new look because of the impact of call centre industry.

Lifestyle Changed after Taking up this Job

When change occurs or when society passes through a changed phase, one-aspect gets more affected whereas some don't. It is not necessary that a change always creates a same impact on everybody and everywhere of its kind. This aspect has its relevance in this research work, as with coming of call center industry and being employed in call centre industry, life does not remain the same as it was. Against this background it was found important to collect from the present set of respondents regarding impact of their job on their life style. The trend revealed through the collected data in this context clearly indicates that more number of respondents (72.92%) had favoured absolute change in their life style after joining call center whereas (25.00%) respondents experienced only slight change in their life style and (2.08%) respondents felts that their life style remained unchanged even after joining call center industry.

Thus it is revealed that after joining call center majority of respondents experienced change in their life style.

Best Part of Working in a Call Centre

Every industry offers different kind of environment, benefits and facilities, etc., to its employee's .The main important determinants of preference call center industry by the new entrants to join a particular industry. Everybody expects best from the organization to which they are part. This contains the data on the aspect which avers that a dominant section among the present set of respondents answered high salary (71.61%) to be the best part of working in a call center, followed by working with young people (59.90%) with slight margin of respondents (58.07%) found good working culture and lowest number (29.17%) found better facilities as the best part of working in a call center. This data reveals that more young Indian youths are joining the call center industry because of the high salary packages being offered in such industry to even young graduates, which if compared from other industries is far too high. Thus it can be concluded that call centers have a lot to offer in terms of money to young educated Indian population.

Impact on Family Life of the Respondents

It has been a common experience that when a person joins any job not only his professional life but his family life also gets affected. This is an established fact that both professional life and personal life affect each other and are affected. Thus, it was very important to find out this aspect of impact of job of respondents on their family life and thus the given graph reveals the information regarding the impact of job on family life .It shows that single largest group of respondents has been formed by those who reported negative impact of their job on family life (46.36%) followed by the respondents who had positive impact of their job on family life (39.32%) with only (14.32%) reported no change in any case.

Thus it is very clear that the industry has lot in offer but somehow it has failed to create a positive impact on the family life of the respondents.

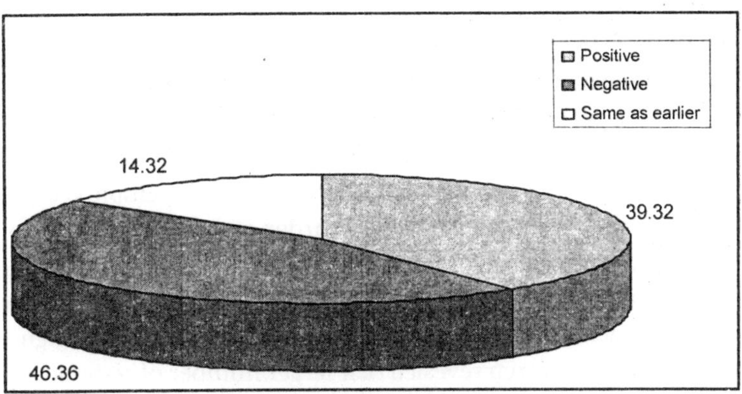

Fig. 23.6 : Impact on Family Life

Various Problems of the Call Center Industry

No industry only offers good things for its employees everywhere if some positive aspects are present, undoubtedly negative also remains with the same. Only difference being there is extent of each. To get an insight into another side of the coin that is the other aspect of the call center, it was very important to study respondents experience of various problems associated with their being in call center. For this purpose, information was gathered, as such the data collected depicts the same which clearly shows that there are number of problems present in call center industry as felt by different respondents, the highest (40.88%), reported for lack of proper growth opportunities, following it another very major problem reported by the respondents was monotonous job nature (38.02%), to problem of late shifts (33.33%) and finally poor policies which accounted for (28.64%) of total respondents were considered as the major problem of the call centre.

By looking at the percentage it is very evident that there is only slight difference between percentage of one problem to another problem which depicts that these problems are felt by all and everyone who work in call centers, but of course the highest percentage of respondents maintained lack of proper growth opportunities as the major problem.

Job Satisfaction

It is an important belief in management thought that happy workers are the most productive workers. Always higher productivity is linked with higher job satisfaction. Organizations today apply all techniques to increase the level of job satisfaction of their employees, as unproductive employee is always a burden rather than an asset for any organization. This was a very important area of interest for the research as such study was carried and questions were asked from the respondents related with their job satisfaction level. The figure acquired after research revealed that larger number of respondents (63.02%) were not satisfied with their jobs, whereas only (29.43%) of respondents were satisfied with their jobs and (7.55%) respondents were not able to answer anything.

The analysis clearly shows that though more and more people are working in call centres but they are not much satisfied with their jobs.

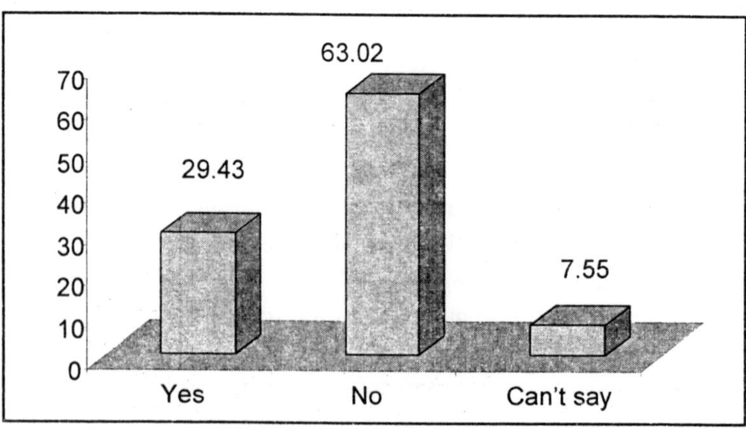

Fig. 23.7 : Job Satisfaction

Planning to Switch Over in Near Future

Today's organizations are not the place where employees want to stay for the rest of their life after joining. Everybody today joins the organization with the motive of gaining experience and then moving in to new one. This has created lot of problems for the organizations, as retaining good employees for longer duration has been a major headache for human resource department of the organization. The data which has been acquired for the purpose of ascertaining their intention of remaining or leaving the present organization revealed that (68.75%) respondents had intention of switching over to new organizations, whereas only (24.22%) wanted to be the part of same organization for longer duration and only (7.03%) respondents had no clear cut idea about staying or leaving.

To conclude it can be said that the duration of stay of the respondents in the same organization is decreasing day-by-day.

Industry is Going to Stay in India for a Long Period

Success and failure of any organization largely depends upon its manner of conducting business and the acceptance of the services provided by the organizations to the society in which it is running. The survival of any organization or industry is dependent upon many factors. It was very important to find this answer from those working in the organization as such the data presented is related with the same as when asked that whether the call center industry is going to stay in India for longer duration, most of the respondents (71.36%) answered in favour of the question and only (19.79%) answer was no and only (8.85%) gave no clear response.

It can be concluded that most respondents believe that call center industry will remain in India for a longer period.

Industry has More Jobs Opportunity for Educated Youths

The progress of any country is dependent upon the number of persons employed; leading a good social and economic life, satisfied citizens, and proper growth opportunities for everyone and this is the reason government keeps on opening up new opportunities of employment for its people. Due to opening of economy and abolition of entry for private players in the growth of Indian economy various types of industries were established in India with different things to offer for the country. The very prominent industry which had proved to be a big player in giving the new shape to Indian economy is call center industry as such it was very important to find out from the respondents that do they believe or are they aware that does this industry has lot of jobs to offer to the educated youths or not. The data related to the same information shows that (76.30%) of respondents believe that the industry has lot to offer for educated youths of India, followed by (19.01%) who had just opposite views and only (4.69%) remained neutral with no reply in favour or against.

Thus it can be inferred that more of the respondents believe that this industry has lot to offer for young educated Indian youths.

Industry to Generate More Employment Offer in Future

It is proved that experience is your best teacher and who else better than those working in call centers can clearly come out with their views about the real situation, the information related to the possibility of call center industry to generate more employment opportunities in times a head was collected from the respondents working in call centers and the same has been presented in which avers that the majority of respondents (74.74%) believe that the call center industry will be offering more employments in coming days, followed by only (21.35%) who believe that this industry will not be able to generate more employment in future ahead whereas (3.91%) gave no reply.

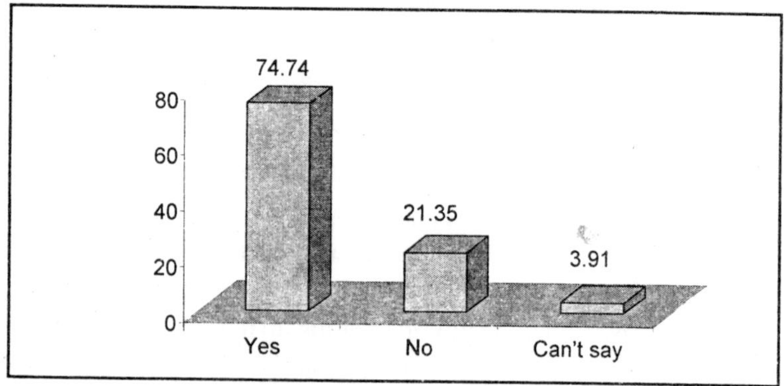

Fig. 23.8 : Industry to Generate More Employment Offer in Future

Thus it can be concluded that more and more people believe that this industry has a lot to offer in future.

Recommend Your Younger Siblings to Join this Industry

With the coming of multinationals and prominence of private enterprises the industry has lot to offer for young Indians who have lot of confidence and zeal to work and to prove their worth and today the mindset of people have also changed as working in private sector was never accepted and recommended over public sector but now people don't have any hassles in working in private sectors because of numerable facilities being offered by this sector, so it was very essential to collect data related to the opinion of those working in call centers that whether they will suggest their younger siblings or friends to join this industry for making their carrier or not. The data reveals that the experiences of majority of respondents (55.73%) had not been very positive the response being not recommending their siblings or friends to make a career in call center industry whereas half of the respondents (26.82%) favoured recommending working in call center industry to their close ones while a considerable section of respondents gave no response.

Thus it is very clear that though people are working themselves in call centers but when recommending the same nature of job to the close ones majority of the respondents answered in negative.

Industry is Able to Fulfil the Required Need

After assessing all the areas of interest and concern of those working in call centres it became very essential to finally assess the major contribution of these call centres in the professional life of those working in. The acquired data relates to the following information which shows that (67.45%) of those working in call centres believe that this industry is able to fulfil their need of high salary and only (32.55%) had credited industry with providing the need of long term career growth.

It can be concluded that more and more people join this industry because of the high salary package being offered.

Conclusion and Suggestions

Manpower Requirement for BPO in India

BPO in India enjoyed the advantage of manpower at a very nominal cost in comparison to the developed nation—the likes of US and in Europe. The trend of Business Process Outsourcing (BPO) flourished in United States to ease the pressure from numerous small business activities. The industry grew larger to spread its feet in low cost countries as India.

BPO industry in India boomed the economy and took many by surprise. Since BPO in India started growing some few years back, the prime necessity felt out of it was lack or say the inadequacy of the skilled manpower for these jobs. Till the time, companies were able to deal with the required manpower resource. But something concrete is required the way BPO industry in India is growing. In this context the Indian Government and business players are making extra efforts to fill this gap. Several forums and seminars are emphasizing this vacuum regularly.

India as the "preferred country over all" for offshore business processing followed by Canada, Brazil, the Philippines, Mexico, Hungary, Ireland, Australia, Russia and China. If the US economy has shown too much faith over the output by the Indian work force there had to be foolproof reason about it.

It's an industry that has been at the forefront of global attention. It's an industry that has raised more debates and outcry than any other. It's an industry that.has been on democrat candidate John Kerry's agenda in his presidential campaign in the last US elections. Yes, it is the BPO industry, which has not only brought jobs to India but has created a whole new generation of young Indians.

Satisfaction, as they say, can be more relative than anything else. The BPO industry has been a pioneer of sorts on many people initiatives. Pickups and drops, office parties, fat paychecks for very young graduates; The BPO was just another great Party till things started looking, well, not so rosy.

The charm and glamour started declining and everyone started seeing the flipside of the job—never ending night shifts, health problems, stress and, most importantly, growth. Today, the industry's single-largest problem is attrition. As BPOs try to get the right pill for their ailments, it is again the time when we put the average employee and HR Managers in the industry under the Lens, tried to find out what it is that satisfies the average young Indian at BPOs.

Present work was carried out in Noida, a city of Uttar Pradesh and the city connected with Delhi. The basic motive behind this research was to study the call center part of business process outsourcing industry in detail and what has been its impact on manpower requirements in India.

Out of 60 call centers presently doing their business in Noida 6 call center companies were selected by the researcher using proportionate stratified random sampling to study the manpower planning process of these call center industries and what are the problems faced by the Human Resource Department especially attrition problem and what all they do to control the situation.

The another part of research focused on those working in these call centers at different level on different positions. There were total 1920 employees working in these call center companies and due to constraints of time, money and of shortage of other resources the researcher was not able to study a large sample as such a representative sample of 20 per cent employees were selected from each call center by using proportionate random sampling method. Thus total number of employees being studied were 384.This study focused on gathering information about those working in the call center companies, their experiences, the working culture, the facilities being provided by these call center organizations and the major problems faced by them while working in these call center organizations.

The main focus of this study is to ascertain the impact of the call center part of business process outsourcing industry on the manpower requirements in India.

Major Findings of Study Carried on Human Resource Department are as Under

- The years of operations of the selected call center organizations were in the period of 1-6 years.
- Majority of the call centers were having their business from U.K followed by U.S. and Australia and few with multiple nations.
- The total strength of the employees working in these calls centers were not less than 120 and not more than 1000.

The Annual Increase or Decrease

- Majority of the organizations 4 out of 6 reported all the year round manpower planning and only two organizations reported business-based manpower planning process.
- The study has found that majority of call center organizations 4 (66.67%) out of 6 takes the help of all given ways (agencies, advertising, internal HR department and word of mouth) whereas 2 (33.33%) takes the help of the specialized agencies for hiring new candidates, followed by 1 (16.67%) organizations who applies advertising, internal HR department and word of mouth each respectively for hiring their manpower. Thus majority (66.67%) of organizations follow all available means for recruitment.
- Equal percentage of organizations reported availability of local manpower as good and average followed by least 16.5 per cent reply as poor availability of local manpower.
- Majority of respondents 4, preferred all the criterias as mentioned in the questionnaire for entry level recruitment and equal respondents that is 1 each preferred graduates and good command over English respectively as their essential criteria for recruitment at entry level.
- Out of six organizations equal responses were given by the companies for entry level recruitment as two selected organizations showed their preference for undergraduates

and two other for candidates holding the graduation degree, while the remaining two preferred postgraduate and professionally qualified candidates each respectively.

- Majority of companies prefer candidates having prior experience of BPOs as three out of six companies replied for the same, followed by two organizations who prefer to recruit people having professional qualifications and only one respondent organization regarded I.T. professionals as their choice for recruitment at middle and high level positions.
- Out of six companies three answered in favour of conducting training through specialized agencies whereas two respondent companies provide the training with the help of the clients and only one respondent company goes for training provided in house.
- Maximum respondent companies (four) of them follow regular appraisals by seniors and executives on the shop floor whereas only two organizations go for quarterly / half yearly appraisal of their employees.
- The respondents had the monthly income in the range of Rs. 15000–30000 (60.68%), followed by the respondents placed in the monthly income range of below Rs. 15000 (28.65%), Rs. 30,000–45,000 (5.47%), Rs.45000–60000 (2.60%), Rs. 60,000–75,000 (1.56%), Rs. 75,000-90,000, Rs. 90,000–1 lac 5 thousand (52%), with mean being in the present context of Rs. 21000.
- Majority of the employees' duration of stay in the organization is in between 1-2 years (66.67%) whereas minimum stay duration accounts only (16.67%) for 3-4 years.
- Maximum companies out of the selected ones replied high attrition rate whereas only two of the organizations rated the attrition rate in their organization as average and none of the selected companies answered their attrition rate as normal.
- Majority of the respondent organization (three out of six)

believed in providing more facilities to the employees who wish to leave the organization whereas only two organizations applies the means of increasing the salary and only one respondent said that their means of dealing with attrition will be based on the specific case.

- Mostly organizations lose their employees to companies with similar business offering better salary and to bigger companies whereas equal response came from the organizations that lose their employees to organizations offering better shift timings.
- More of the respondents (4) believe that India will remain a major player in outsourcing business followed by one respondent each who don't expect any such possibility and one who have no clear cut idea. It is clear from the given data that it is assumed that India will remain a major outsourcing destination.
- Mixed response from all the respondent companies as two of the companies answered that yes they believe that this industry will be able to attract and employ more and more able and willing workforce followed by two of the respondent companies who holds just opposite views and two of the respondent companies failed to give any comments. Thus it can be made out that there might be a possibility of both.
- Highest demand in call center industry is for lower level as answered by three of the respondent companies whereas two out of six companies replied in favour of middle level and lastly only one respondent organization believes that the highest demand is for the positions at higher level. It can be concluded that these call center industries have more opening for the fresher or employees joining at the lower level.
- 4 (66.66%) out of 6 companies say that the supply of adequate number of employees does not equal to demand whereas less number of companies that is 2 (33.33%)

companies believe that the demand and supply remain equal. Thus it can be concluded that there is a situation of non-availability as reported by the companies.

- Majority of the companies have reported that at times they have to compromise with the kind of talent required as was reported by three of the organizations, followed by two respondent company who reported no problems and no compromises to avail the required and best manpower and lastly there was no such clear cut indication of compromises or no compromises reported by only one respondent organization. Thus this is evident from the above data that most of the times companies do compromise with the quality of manpower required but heavily relies on effective training techniques to get rid of the under skilled and underperformance.

24

TRENDS IN BANKING INDUSTRY IN INDIA

1969-2006 and onwards

MUKUL SRIVASTAVA

The Indian Banking Sector is poised for another sea change after March 2009, when the Foreign Banks present in India are scheduled to get the National Treatment. The Indian Banking sector has already entered a phase where it has become the backbone of many sectors for development. But the Indian Banking sector has not become so competitive, so as to face the challenges globally. For this, the Indian Banks will have to expand and grow. Time will come when Indian Banks would also find their names in the list of top 10 Banks globally.

This chapter tries to study the trends in growth of the Banking sector in India especially related to employment issues, the effect of increased business on the productivity, the business per employee, the challenges the industry has to face, and the training and human resource development required to face the upcoming challenges.

Indian banking system has been taking strides to acquire strength, efficiency, and vibrancy necessary to meet global competition. There has been a persistent effort towards adoption of international benchmarks as appropriate to Indian conditions, improvement in management practices and corporate governance. The start of First Generation of Economic reforms led with liberalization, privatization and globalization paved the way for a new regime of Banking in

India. Banking sector reforms got the kick start with the First Narasimham Committee Report on Financial Sector Reforms in 1991, which focused on operational flexibility and functional autonomy for enhancing the efficiency, productivity and profitability of the banking system along with improvement in Human Resource. The Second Narasimham Committee Report in 1998 on Banking Sector Reforms gave emphasis on risk and technology and the necessity for reforms on Human Resource Management. Due to reforms, the old way of doing business gave way to increased emphasis on customers' requirement and shareholder value.

Indian banking system as of today is dominated by Public Sector Banks, which include Nationalised Banks and State Bank group with a share of 75 per cent, followed by new private sector banks. Private banks and foreign banks share the rest. The market share of Foreign Banks in the Commercial Banking System has been around 5-6 per cent in Deposits and Advances, but in case of Off-Balance Sheet Business, their market share is around 70 per cent. The prime reason is that Foreign Banks cater to 'niche clientele'. The share of Foreign Banks would increase drastically from 2009 when Indian Banking sector will be fully opened for Foreign Banks. The Indian Banking industry has already been opened up through unveiling of the roadmap by Reserve Bank of India (RBI) on "Presence of Foreign Banks in India" in 2005, involving two phases for implementation, viz., Phase I – March 2005 – March 2009 and Phase II – April 2009 and onwards. Phase I involves permission to Foreign Banks to establish their presence by way of setting up of wholly owned banking subsidiaries or by conversion of existing branches into holding subsidiaries. Phase II will involve national treatment being extended to wholly owned subsidiaries, dilution of stake and permitting mergers/ acquisitions of any Private Sector Bank in India. This is in tandem with India's commitments under World Trade Organisation (WTO) agreement. Under WTO commitments, which came into effect in 1997-98, RBI's obligation is to permit, to Foreign Banks, only 12 licenses per year, including both the new entrants and existing banks.

The year 2009 would unfold many challenges for the Indian Banking Sector and real competitive era would begin, wherein the

Indian Banking would see few mega mergers and general banking would give way to segment-specific banking. This would result in increase in banking for the public in general and would require specialized personnel, catering to tailor made products and services. This would also result in a very stiff competition from the finest global banks such as UB World, Bank of Scotland, Credit Suisse, GE etc. besides the foreign banks which are already operating in India such as, Standard Chartered, Citi Group, HSBC, ABN Amro, Barclays and Deutsche Bank. The areas of competition in the banking industry are based on price, product, service, technology, skill, location and targeted market segment. The competition is demand driven rather than supply driven. The major characteristic of competition in the banking industry is the presence of large number of users and providers of banking services and none is able to influence the price and the product in a significant manner—almost a near perfect competition stage.

The Indian Banks would have to face one more challenge from 2008 onwards due to implementation of BASEL II norms. Commercial Banks in India are expected to start implementation of BASEL-II norms with effect from March 2008. BASEL II is based on three mutually reinforcing pillars—minimum capital requirements, supervisory review, and market discipline. RBI has already started strengthening the Indian Banks by empowering the banks with autonomy, strengthening of bank boards with more powers and infusion of whole-time directors on the board. The managerial autonomy package was unveiled in February 2005 for giving more freedom to the banks. Indian banks will have to raise their efficiency levels to come up in meeting the emerging challenges. The Public Sector Banks have the advantage of understanding of the rural markets, systems of lending in rural areas, have large manpower, adaptability to changing scenarios of the reformist phase, particularly the deregulated regime, providing customer service to stratified clients, but the efficiency and productivity levels in these banks will have to go up in a dramatic manner. With the disadvantages, which the public sector banks have, they will have to be strategically segregated and focused for solutions, through better-integrated planning, adoption of new business and operating models and synchronizing them with skilled manpower.

Past 30 Years Trends (1969-1999)

Due to focus on mass banking by the Government, the Indian Banking sector witnessed a growth in number of Commercial Banks over the periods, started with 89 in the year of Bank's nationalization (1969) to 303 (1999) over a period of 30 years. The number of Scheduled Commercial Banks increased from 73 to 302 during the same period. The Aggregate Deposits of the Scheduled Commercial Banks increased from Rs. 4,646 crore to Rs. 7, 22,203 crore over the period 1969 to 1999. The Credit of Scheduled Commercial Banks also increased from Rs. 3,599 crore to Rs. 3,68,837 crore over the same period. The employment offered by the Indian Banking Sector also increased to 10,17,490 in the year 1999.

Like any other sector, the Banking Sector also saw an increase in banking during this phase, especially an increase in rural banking; mass banking became the focal point of banking with emphasis on priority sector advances.

Trends During the Period 1999-2000 to 2005-2006

From 1999, the number of Scheduled Commercial Banks has been reduced to 218 in 2005-2006, but the Total Business (Deposits + Advances) of the Scheduled Commercial Banks has increased from Rs. 10,91,040 crore to Rs 36,16,126 crore. The total employment offered by the Scheduled Commercial Banks decreased from 10,17,490 in 1999 to 9,00,124 in 2005-06, resulting in an increase in Business per Employee from Rs. 1.07 crore to Rs.4.02 crore during the same period.

The Business of the Scheduled Commercial Banks grew with a Compound Annual Growth Rate (CAGR) of 18.67 per cent from 1998–1999 to 2005 – 2006, the total employment decreased with a CAGR of 1.74 per cent but Business per Employee increased with a CAGR of 20.77 per cent during the same period.

No doubt this increase has been due to technological upgradation of the systems and procedures, but the raw untrained manpower also became trained during the course of work.

Table 24.1 captures the growth of business and the growth rate of employment over the periods 1969 to 2006.

Bank Group-wise (Private/Public Sector Banks) Trends (2002-03 to 2006-07)

The number of branches of Public Sector Banks increased from 47,963 to 51,392 with a growth rate of 7 per cent, while the branches of Private Sector Banks grew from 5,592 to 7,363 showing a growth rate of 32 per cent. As majority of Indian population is still under banked, the Business of all the groups of the Banks grew by a CAGR of more than 20 per cent. The Business per Employee of all Private Sector Banks grew by a CAGR of 4.58 per cent while that of all Public Sector Banks grew by a CAGR of 21.65 per cent over the period 2002-03 to 2006-07, thereby showing that with increased usage of technology, the productivity of Public Sector Banks grew at a much faster pace than the private sector. The performance of Public Sector Banks and the Private Sector Banks are converging with competition.

The total employment offered by the banking sector has reduced over the periods, but the employment offered by the private sector banks has increased at the cost of public sector banks due to migration of staff from public sector banks to private sector banks. It is said that public sector banks are a good rearing ground for the untrained staff. The raw talent is nurtured/groomed in public sector banks but the fruits are reaped by the private banks. The public sector banks fail to retain the talent because of their fixed pay norms.

The Employee per Branch of All Private Sector Banks increased with a CAGR of 3.34 per cent while that of All Public Sector Banks decreased with a CAGR of 2.34 per cent.

Contractual Employment in the Indian Banking

The employment in banking had been mostly a full time job. All the jobs of the Banking are bound by the 'terms of contract', where it is clearly defined about the 'job conditions' and 'notice under which job can be terminated'. Since, the employment in banking sector in India was dominated by Public Sector Banks, whose 'terms of contract' were bound by negotiations with unions and bi-partite treaties; the job insecurity for Bank personnel was very less.

'Indian Banks Association', the apex organization provides support to Banking Industry in India, it co-ordinates and negotiates with other organizations' for and on behalf of the banks, helps in developing policies beneficial for the business prospects of the banks.

The jobs before the first generation of economic reforms were on 'contract basis for a fixed term' in banking, predominated by low-paid jobs related to data-entry, cyclostyle and menial jobs, but off late the trend has changed and high end jobs like law experts, economist, chartered accountants and marketing professionals are also being offered on 'contract basis for a short term'.

The conversion of hard money (cash based) into soft money (electronic form) will pave the way for new and large number of contractual banking jobs in India. The jobs will include data analysis and processing, voice based customer service, financial advising, loan appraisal and recovery follow-ups. With India providing Business Process Outsourcing solutions to the Global Banking giants, the contractual employment in the Indian Industry has increased. Business Process Outsourcing jobs includes the job of Knowledge Process Outsourcing, thus the outsourcing of the jobs from developed countries to India incorporates both low end jobs as well as high end jobs. The plight remains same for the personnel employed on contract for a term, whether for high end job or low end job, there are no unions who can give a good deal by bilateral negotiations. Although, the job market for high end job in this category is supply driven, but the working conditions are more or less same, due to lack of group buying power. As the private sector Banks have more operational freedom, they employ a number of staff for a fixed term with fixed salary for a specified work. Once that particular work is done, the services of the workers are terminated, of course with a notice. The trend has started where Bankers also have to sign "bonds" of employment contract. The "bonds" may be taken over/paid by another Bank due to shortage of trained manpower in the specified area of work. The employee may not only have to sign a contract at the time of joining the Bank, but would also have to sign an exit contract, whereby the employee agrees (i) not to disclose the confidential information, (ii) not to work with the business partners/ associates/clients of the Bank for a certain specified period.

Due to specific jobs and industry-specific skills, which cannot be transferred in the short to medium term, the plight of Contractual employees is weak. With Indian Banking going global, the trend in employment will change and more employees will be recruited 'on contract basis for a fixed term'. In days to come, Universal Banking will take over general banking, experts in the fields of merchant banking, underwriting, mutual funds, corporate financing, mergers and acquisition will get an edge and they would have rental value due to specialized nature of job which cannot be transferred in the short run.

Challenges 2009 : Are the Indian Banks Ready

India's largest and the second largest Bank, viz SBI and ICICI are no match for the world's finest Bank such as Citigroup, HSBC or the UBS. These Banks lack in size, products offered and human resource that the global giants have. The Citi Group has an asset base of more than Rs.55 lac crore and employs more than 3 lac employees, while 'All scheduled Commercial Banks' in India have an asset base of Rs. 17 lac crore and employ around 10 lac workforce. It is not that in India, we are wasting our workforce, but we are underutilizing the untrained staff. With Indian Banking going Global, Human Resource will play a big role in transformation of the Banking Industry in India. It is the quality of human resource and the skills in human capital that will give competitive advantage to the business of the Banks by skillful alignment of the HR with technology. Specialization of work and specialized workforce will rule and show the door to general banking. Reskilling of existing staff and recruitment of skilled persons from abroad will have to be undertaken. The easy way to learn the best global practices of banking is either by exporting or importing i.e. either Indian Banker should send their staff to foreign countries to learn the best banking practices or hire top class management from abroad so that our staff members have some exposure of global financial markets. One more way is that the Indian Banks may acquire banks abroad to learn best practice, earn substantial profits, hire top class management, raise money on global financial markets and grow. Presence of foreign competition is one of the ways to improve performance. Bank employees will have to navigate through the steep learning curve and upgrade their skills and knowledge to meet the emerging challenges in the global financial super-highway. The total employment of the Banking Industry will expand and not shrink as the business is bound to increase.

The Banks needs to upgrade their HRD skills and resources. The search and retention of talent should occupy the minds of the top management. The issue is of 'getting right people' encompassing everything from finding the right talent to retaining, nurturing and growing it. Focus should be on areas of talent acquisition, talent management and retention. The industry should think of creating a pool of 'employable' workforce. The Banks should benchmark their quality of workforce with that of the Best in the industry. There is dire need for induction of high quality people at entry levels and through lateral recruitments. The need of the hour is skill development so as to adopt the new generation banking techniques; synchronization and harmonization of planning process with various business and operating models; keeping technology as the base and upgrade the skills of the manpower. The requirement for the Banking Industry is for setting up Institutes catering to the specialized needs of the banking sector with trained staff. The arduous path for the Indian Banks can be traversed with high educational skill endowment.

25

WOMEN EMPOWERMENT AND IT'S REFLECTION ON SOCIETY

SHALINI TIWARI AND ANKITA GUPTA

This chapter attempts to deal with socio-economic aspects of women empowerment. This chapter is divided into 4 sections. In section I we discuss the dimensions of women empowerment, causes and constraints, including the political and legal empowerment of women in India. Section II deals with the social empowerment of women with the help of three indicators; education, health and nutrition. In section III we discuss the economic empowerment with the help of three indicators; women in workforce, micro-financing and land ownership. Finally, in the last section we give the findings, conclusions and suggestion. In this paper we have employed secondary data from various Government sources to show the indicators of empowerment and the same have been depicted through various charts.

I. WOMEN EMPOWERMENT

Women empowerment has several dimensions, the process involves both social, economic forces and political will power. It encompasses women's multiple interests and addresses the inter-relationship between them. Women Empowerment has several dimensions :

1. Understanding of the causes due to which women are not empowered.

2. Enhancing self-esteem and altering self-image.
3. Increased access to social, financial and intellectual resources.
4. Acquiring the confidence, knowledge, information and skills to understanding in social, economic and political structures and process.
5. Increasing participation in, and control of, decision- making process in the family and community.
6. Moving into new roles and spaces, which were hitherto seen as exclusive male domains.
7. Coming together to question, challenge and change unjust and iniquitous practices, which lead to gender inequality.

The process of woman empowerment challenges the basic assumptions of social institutions, systems and values. It is, therefore, inevitable that it should encourage resistance from the existing power structure. It is easier for women collectively, rather than individuals, to take the process of empowerment forward.

Development efforts over the years have by and large not addressed women's subordination and have, therefore, failed to impact gender inequality in the required way. Most mainstream approaches[1] to women development have not been the base of the overall reality of women's lives, but have focused either on their roles as housewives or as economic agents. Several underlying reasons may be cited for this underdevelopment; a few of them are enumerated below :

- Continuation of excess domestic responsibilities;
- Low motivation, aspiration, and low self- esteem;
- Greater participation in care economy through the assumption of domestic responsibilities in early life; and
- Dependence upon their male counterparts for social recognition and economic access to ownership of land and assets.

The whole process of empowerment of women can be classified into four broad categories; that is, political, legal, social and economic empowerment out of which the political empowerment holds the key for Women Empowerment.

Political Empowerment

Political process is the shaping, sharing and exercise of power. Involvement in politics is directed towards influencing power channels and elite for protecting one's rights and self-interests and giving legitimacy to political elite and their decisions. It ensures that such people are able to take part in deciding the common goals of the society and the best way of achieving it. It is a global experience that in any political system, right from the developed to the developing countries, women's presence in the political process is marginal and low. Women fall mainly into the group of those who are apathetic to politics because of their low status and adverse political environment. Women comprise a very small percentage in the total number of contestants, and their presence in the Lok-Sabha is small. The gap between male and female is very wide. Till 2003, while women were only 9 per cent in Lok Sabha, which was highest during last fifty years, but in present Lok Sabha it is 7 per cent.[2]

The participation of women in political affairs is better after the implementation of 73rd Amendment. This initiative by the GOI is expected to narrow down the gender inequality and solve some of the problems of women in the coming decades. Also they are increasingly becoming more politically aware and conscious about the programmes and schemes available for their development and they are utilizing their power to take benefit of such programmes and improving their conditions. Though it adds additional responsibility on the part of women, it, however, may adversely affect their family responsibilities as a wife and mother in the household, to which many may not adjust.

Earlier, women were unable to protest against violence and undesirable habits of their husbands. The local women panchyats members have tackled this effectively and they have been able to mitigate the common male dominance. Women had no say in exercising their economic power in activities. After political participation, they do check the discrimination against women. In a case-study[3] in Rampur Gram Panchayat in Birbhum District, West

Bengal, it was seen that they could get sanctioned funds available for some of the welfare programmes, such as loans for manufacturing cane-basket and agro based business like fried rice, selling vegetables and rope making etc. This is a significant achievement by Women Panchayat members, which is a step forward in resolving some of the traditional gender inequalities in the erstwhile male dominated.

Rural society. Though these are some of the achievements, there is some change in the attitude of men regarding women as equal partners in the social, political and administrative spheres. Gender inequality is inextricably bound with power relations. The empowerment of women has to be the goal of efforts to reduce such inequality.

Empowerment involves understanding and challenging the existing socio-political environment so that those with power start thinking about shifting in favour of the powerless and deprived and make it feasible through some negotiation as a strategy of socio-economic reform. Reservation is one such strategy or instrument, which at first helps the hitherto, deprived women to at least understand properly the reasons behind their powerlessness. Second, political empowerment ultimately seeks to change the distribution of social power in favour of women, both in interpersonal relations and in social institutions. Third, once empowered, the powerless not only share the fruits of development, but they ultimately become the agents of their own development. Lastly, political empowerment generates awareness and self confidence in the minds of the exploited to fight the resistance of the powerful. Moreover, it initiates a process of collective action, which will finally end in social change or transformation. Therefore, political empowerment enables women to be the spokesperson of their own rights and hence reservation serves as starting point.

Legal Empowerment

Violence against women is not the issue of any particular region or group, it is an ugly, fact crossing the frontiers of ideology, social class and ethnic identity. At the individual level, violence disrupts the lives of women, limits their options undermines their confidence and self esteem and impairs their health, psychologically as well as physically.

Violence against women deprives society of the full participation of women in all aspects of development, not just in terms of hours of labour missed due to violence but also in terms of the cost of services to the victims. It also has serious consequences for the mental and physical health of dependent children.

Women are given some rights like non-discrimination, right to be a child, right to education, right to protection from economic exploitation, right to protection from sexual exploitation, right to social security, etc., through legal empowerment. The first exercise of legal empowerment of women is to improve their status to destroy the "invisible barrier"[4] of traditional thinking. Family court accessible to women with women members should be set up to deal with family problems and disputes in conciliatory manner. In addition "legal literacy" among both rural and urban and especially urban women should be promoted. So that they in turn, can help promote it in the rural areas. Legislation should be reviewed from time to time to ensure that it keeps in tune with changing male and female roles and responsibilities and safeguards not only men's but also women's rights.

Some women empowerment institutions like ANANDI'[5] entry point have been to help women to organize around their immediate personal and local level. In many cases, but by no means all, a key organizational focus has been women groups, which provide women with an opportunity for coming together regularly for exchanging information and discussing issues for action.

Once the organizational set-up has been established and immediate perceived needs develop a more permanent identity and women start to discuss and learn how they can also carry it forward, success on one issue gives them the confidence to address other problems which had always been there but which they have not felt they could address. This learning can help in focused and strategic collection of information in order to be able to argue their case at lower level in community, village meetings, training and cluster meetings, and to reflect on their positive and negative experiences and develop collective action plan for a way out.

II. SOCIAL EMPOWERMENT

The social position of Indian women is seen to be very difficult. Traditionally, women in Indian society suffer from various social and cultural handicaps and it is felt that unless the women are sufficiently empowered, the social development may not reach the desired target of literacy, health, nutrition etc. Centuries old social practices, beliefs, attitudes and biases against the women may be difficult to overcome in a short period of time.

When we see the social status of women in India, it is clear that gender disparity manifests itself in various forms, the most obvious being the trend of continuously declining Sex Ratio in the population since independence as the census enumeration from 1951-2001 shows in Table 25.1.

Table 25.1: Sex-ratio 1951-2001: Female per 1000 Male

Year	1951	1961	1971	1981	1991	2001
Sex-ratio	946	941	930	933	927	933

Source: Census of India, 2001.

The disappointing factor in 2001 census is that the ratio of girl child in the age group of 0-6 years has decreased, as seen from Table 25.2.

Table 25.2: Sex-Ratio in the Age-group 0-6 Years (Female per 1000 Male)

Year	1961	1971	1981	1991	2001
Sex-ratio	976	964	968	945	927

Source: Census of India, 2001.

This is not a healthy trend. The sex ratio should be 1 : 1, otherwise the equilibrium of the society will not be maintained, and discrimination against women begins even before birth. The reason for declining sex ratio is definitely the cruel practice of female infanticide and the other reason lies in our patriarchal society. In India a majority of the females do not survive due to sheer negligence of food, nutrition, medicine and care and due to low social status accorded to a female child. In the early stage of our society, female employment was thought to be against the pride of the family and society. Not only that, they had to be dependent throughout their whole life on their male counterpart as in their early life they were dependent on their father, in their married life they were taken care of by their husbands and in their old age they were to be looked after by their sons. This led to the preference for male child over female child that later took the form of even rampant female infanticide.

The social empowerment of women begins when she becomes aware of social injustice that is in every sphere of her life. It starts as and when she becomes fully aware of her positive self-image, self-esteem, positive rights and duties of her capabilities. Eradication of illiteracy, gender sensitive educational system, increase in enrollment and retention rates for girls, imparting of professional skill and expertise, positive approach to women's health including nutrition and health services at all stages of life cycle are the few measures that are aimed at enhancing social empowerment.

The main indicators selected for measuring the social empowerment of Women are: Education, Health, and Nutrition.

Education

Education is the vehicle through which systematic and meaningful instruction can be imparted for improving the mental facilities and latent wisdom in a young mind, literacy can be viewed as the first major step for attaining the spread of education in society, literacy helps in enlarging the capabilities of a person and it serves as the first defense in the struggle towards existence. In India, especially after independence, importance of female education alongside that of men began to be socially recognized. "When you educate a man you educate an individual, but when you educate a woman you educate a generation." The first contact, which a newborn has, is with the mother, which forms a bond between them, this bond helps the baby in the learning process. As the baby becomes older it is the mother or elder sister or aunts who take over some of the teaching responsibilities from the mother, thus we can say that a child in its formative years learns a lot from females. If these females are literate/ educated then their contribution towards the learning process attains a significant importance as compared to illiterate/uneducated females. A glimpse of this can be seen in the literacy rates for female in India from the Table 25.3 which clearly reflects the facts that apart from other causes, an increase in female literacy rates is accompanied by an increase in male and as well as overall literacy rates and reducing the gender gap specially after 1981.

Table 25.3: Literacy Rates in India 1951-2001 (*in percentage*)

Year	Total	Male	Female	Gender gap
1951	18.33	27.16	8.86	18.3
1961	28.3	40.4	15.35	25.05
1971	34.45	45.96	21.97	23.98
1981	43.57	56.38	29.76	26.62
1991	52.21	64.13	39.29	24.84
2001	64.84	75.85	54.16	21.69

Source: Economic Survey 2003-04, Government of India, Planning Commission.

Both male and female literacy increased at faster rates in 1990's compared to the preceding decade, but female literacy increased faster than male literacy by 15 per cent points, reducing the gender gap to some extent. Literacy for males increased from 56.38 per cent in 1981 to 75.85 per cent in 2001, the corresponding change in female literacy has been from 29.76 per cent to 54.16 per cent. The gender gap peaked in 1981 at 26.6 per cent points but came down to 21.7 per cent in 2001 because during this period the female literacy is growing with consistent rate but for male it is inconsistent, as is evident from chart 25.1.

If we assume that literacy rates are increasing with the same rate till 2011, then where do we go? We find that if this situation happens we would not able to reach the 100 per cent literacy target according to NPP 2000 till 2010. The projections for 2011 indicate that TLR,

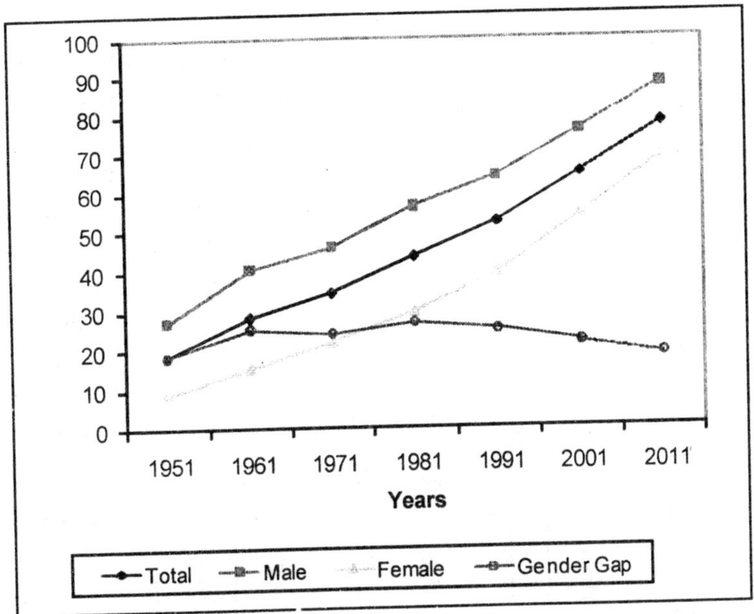

*Note: Dotted lines are projected.

Chart 25.1 : Literacy Rates in India 1951-2001

MLR, FLR and the gender gap would be about approximately 75.8 per cent, 88.8 per cent, 67.2 per cent and 16.7 per cent respectively. Literacy rates are much better in urban area in comparison to rural areas. We found major gender gap in education attainment in rural and urban areas. This trend is clearly shown in Table 25.4.

In Table 25.4, literacy rates are very low in rural areas in various years in comparison to urban areas, and also the gap between the genders is high. During the period of 1971-2001 the increase in rural male literacy is 22.8 per cent points and rural female literacy is 31.2 per centpoints and corresponding to urban area male and female literacy is respectively 16.9 per cent points and 24.4 per cent points. During the period of 1991 to 2001 growth of rural male and female literacy is 13.5 per cent points and 16.1 per cent points and in the urban area this is 6 per cent points and 9.2 per cent points. So it is clear from the table that in rural area efforts are going on and this is shown in growth of male and female literacy rate from chart 25.2.

Table 25.4 : Gender Difference in Education Attainment in India, 1971 – 2001.

Year	Rural			Urban			Total		
	Male	**Female**	**Gap**	**Male**	**Female**	**Gap**	**Male**	**Female**	**Gap**
1971	48.6	15.5	33.1	69.8	48.8	21	45.96	21.97	23.19
1981	49.6	21.7	27.9	76.7	56.3	20.4	56.38	29.76	26.62
1991	57.9	30.6	27.3	81.1	64	17.1	64.13	39.29	24.84
2001	71.4	46.7	24.7	86.7	73.2	13.5	75.85	54.16	21.69

Source: Census of India, 2001.

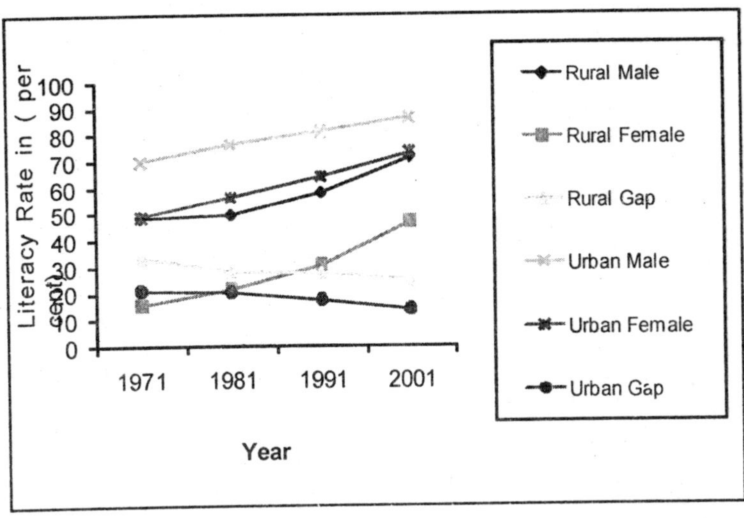

Chart 25.2 : Gender Differences in Education Attainments in India

While literacy rates are growing faster in rural areas but it still lower than urban areas. The decline in gender gap is very slow in rural area but in urban area it is much better so we can say that after empowerment decade 1975-85 empowerment efforts are very much visible in urban areas, though this did not percolate in the rural areas. Here we need to reduce the gender gap in rural areas because female literacy is the most important component for increasing the level of society. Low literacy rates in rural area especially in woman are the main reason of lack of awareness about their health and nutrition.

Female literacy has always lagged behind male literacy in India. But the difference between the two has been narrowing. In Table 25.5 we discuss sex-wise school level enrolment by stages like primary middle and High School/High School Secondary. We found in all stages school level enrolment is increasing and boys enrolment is higher than girls, and in primary level enrolment is much higher.

After 1990-91 the girl enrolment is growing faster than boys at all levels. Such as in primary stage where boys enrolment increased 7.1 per cent points but in girl this is 9.1 per cent points and in middle stage it is respectively 3.8 per cent points and 4.4 per cent points and

Table 25.5 : Sex-wise School Level Enrolment by Stages in India (in percentage) 1960-2000

Year	**Primary**		**Middle**		**High school/ Higher Secondary**	
	Boys	Girls	Boys	Girls	Boys	Girls
1960-61	23.6	11.4	5.1	1.6	2.7	0.7
1970-71	35.7	21.3	9.4	3.9	5.7	1.9
1980-81	45.3	28.5	13.9	6.8	7.6	3.4
1990-91	57	40.4	21.5	12.5	12.8	6.3
1999-2000	64.1	49.5	25.1	16.9	17.2	10.9

Source: Census of India, 2001.

in high school / higher secondary stage it is 4.4 per cent points and 4.6 per cent points. So we can say that after the women decade 1975-85 the performance of empowerment programmes of woman showed high growth and girls education attainment are increasing.

High enrolment rates may mean little if high percentage of students discontinue going to school for some reason. Dropout rate tell us the percentage of student who dropout or discontinue a class during a given year. Dropout rate is as per the given formula.

$$\text{Dropout rate} = \frac{\text{No. of Students dropping out from grade 'g' in year 't'}}{\text{Total no. of Students in grade 'g' in year 't'}} \times 100$$

$$(d)_g^t = \frac{D_g^t}{E_g^t} \times 100$$

Though this percentage has been declining, it is still unacceptably high. Here in the next Table 25.6 we discuss about the drop out rates in India during 1970-71 to 2000-01.

Table 25.6 : Dropout Rates in India by Gender and Stages 1970-71 to 2000-01

	Primary level [Class I - V]			Middle level [Class I - VIII]		
Year	Boys	Girls	Gap	Boys	Girls	Gap
1970-71	64.5	70.9	6.4	74.6	83.4	8.8
1980-81	56.2	62.5	6.3	68	79.4	11.4
1990-91	40.1	46	5.9	59.8	65.1	5.3
2000-01	39.7	41.9	2.2	50.3	57.7	7.4

Source: DWCD, MHRD, GOI, Annual Report 2002-2003, page 63.

In the above Table 25.6 it is clear that DOR for boys are always lower in comparison to girls between 1970-71 and 2000-01. It is because girls are always treated as a second preference regarding education in comparison to boys. During 1970-71, DOR is much higher in both levels of education. It may be because more children of both sex are engaged with some kind of income generating work or may be more girls are taking care of home based responsibilities.

During 1970-70 to 1980-81, DOR declined in both the levels, but at primary level decline in DOR is faster than middle level. It shows that more children are going to schools at primary level rather than middle level or more children are getting enrolled in primary level rather than middle level, therefore, the base of DOR formula is increasing and because of this DOR is declining. At primary level boys DOR declined by 8.3 per cent points and girls DOR declined by 8.4 per cent points which is almost the same, therefore, gender gap in DOR is almost constant [6.4 *vs.* 6.3] during this period. This is shown in Chart 25.3. At middle level, boys DOR declined by 6.6 per cent points and girls DOR declined by 4.0 per cent points, here girls DOR declined slower than boys, therefore, gender gap increased [8.8 *vs.* 11.4] during 1970-71 to 1980-81.

During 1980-81 to 1990-91 decline in DOR is faster in both levels. Here one thing is striking that at primary level boys DOR declined faster than girls [16.1 per cent points *vs.* 12.5 per cent points] but at the middle level reverse thing happened, here girls DOR declined faster than boys [14.3 per cent points *vs.* 8.2 per cent points], therefore, during this period gender gap is narrowing fast at middle level [11.4 *vs.* 5.3] and primary level gender gap declined with slow rate [6.3 *vs.* 5.9]. This shows that during this period more people are getting aware about the value of education and they send their children to school, especially girls. It may be because 1975-1985 decade was women empowerment decade and government gave various incentives to those people who sent their children to school especially girl child.

During 1990-91 to 2000-01 decline in DOR is getting slower at primary level especially for boys [0.4 per cent points for boys and 4.1 per cent points for girls], but at middle level DOR declined almost constantly for boys 9.5 per cent points and for girls DOR declined by 7.4 per cent points which is slower as compared to previous decade [shown in chart 25.4], therefore, gender gap has grown at middle level as compared to primary level [7.4 *vs.* 2.2] till 2000-01. Here in primary level decline in gender DOR especially for boys is

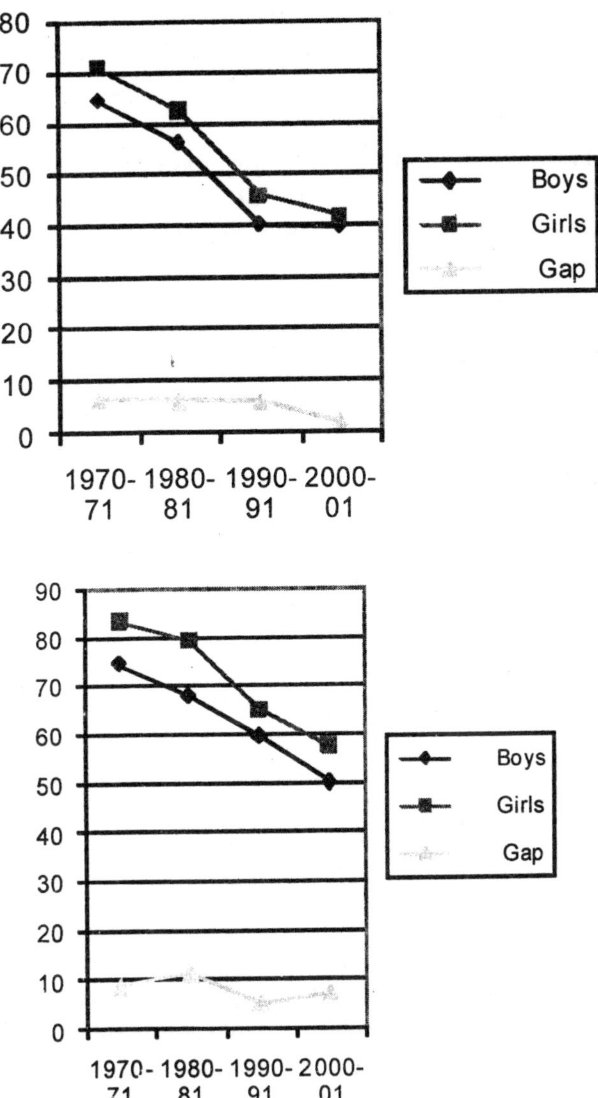

Chart 25.3 : Primary Level DOR in per cent Middle Level DOR in per cent

alarming situation and further studies are required as to why this decline in DOR for boys in the primary level has almost become constant especially since the growth rate for girls in primary level also shows a declining trend after 1990-91 and the fear is that, this DOR may also flatten out beyond 2000-01.

The stagnation in the DOR for boys primary level between 1990-91 to 2000-01 is indicative of the fact that the growth in enrollment rates has been neutralized by the DOR growth apart from the fact that the increase in the enrollment rates by 7.1 per cent points is defiantly smaller than the increase of 11.7 per cent points between 1990-91 to 1999-00 and 1980-81, 1990-91 respectively. This also leads us to feel that the various efforts undertaken with regard to enrollment of boys at the primary level have lost steam and hence it becomes necessary to reexamine the effectiveness of these efforts in further increasing the enrollment growth rates of boys at the primary level. Even though the DOR for girls still shows a decline although at a falling rate, this also needs to be addressed in the context of the various efforts for reducing female DOR.

It is well known that mere provision of enrollment in the school is not enough for achieving the goal of education for all. These should be coupled with suitable measures to ensure that children stay in the school to complete the full cycle of education. Through most States of India have done well in enrolling more and more children in the school through various programmes, lack of capacity of the school to retain the children in the school has been a serious problem. Efforts have been made for last several decades to ensure that children do not drop out from the school after initial enrollment.

The internal benefits of female literacy are in terms of reduced infant mortality, higher work participation of women and bolstering women's agency to be strongly patriarchal. A number of factors like adult literacy, free, education among girls and financial incentives, etc., may have contributed to this change of heart. Many State governments have been providing added incentives like in U.P. [*Kanya Vidya Dhan Yojana*] towards girl's education.

The age at marriage is going up, and girls themselves are keen to get educated, often much more so than their brothers. However, higher education need not necessarily get translated into easing the process of labour market entry. In some communities, sending their unmarried girls for paid work is yet not acceptable, although there may not be such a strong taboo on sending the wife for work because of the extra money brought in. In some other communities, however, especially in urban and semi-urban areas, young girls are getting into paid work of all varieties and some degree of education is needed for getting the job.

All in all, the mindset of girls appears to be undergoing a transformation, even in the traditional Hindi speaking North Indian States, but the extent to which it is translated into true employment is a different issue altogether, because it needs micro level changes (thinking, behaviour, etc.). In many cases the same families who are willing to see their daughters go through college education, may react violently if they decide to choose their marriage partners or to challenge set norms of feminine behaviours. So the links between female literacy and empowerment are not as simple and uncomplicated as it is sometimes believed.

Health

India is a country where women and men have nearly the same life expectancy at birth [Table 25.8] in spite of the fact that there are systematic problems regarding women's health. The health of Indian women is linked to their status in society. Poor health has repercussions not only for women but also for their families. Women in poor health are more likely to give birth to low-weight infants.[6] They also are less able to provide food and adequate care for their children. Finally, a women's health affects the household economic well-being, as woman in poor health will be less productive in the workforce. Thus poor health leads to all round decay in their contribution towards society and economy. Therefore, special attention should be given to the health needs of women and girls at all stages of the life cycle. The reduction of infant morality and maternal mortality, which are sensitive indicators of human development, is a priority concern. Women should have access to comprehensive, affordable, and quality health care. Measures should be adopted that take into account their vulnerability to health problems together with endemic infections and communicable diseases such as malaria, T.B., and waterborne diseases as well as hypertension and cardio-pulmonary diseases. The social and health consequences of HIV/AIDS and other sexually transmitted diseases have to be tackled from a gender perspective. Health profile of India is shown by some health indicators in Table 25.7.

Table 25.7 : Selected Health Indications in India

Parameters	1951	1981	1991	2002	NPP 2000 target for 2010
CBR (Per 1000 pop)	40.8	33.9	29.5	25.0	–
CDR (Per 1000 pop)	25.1	12.5	9.8	8.1	–
TFR (Per women)	6.0	4.5	3.6	3.2	2.1
MMR (Per 1000 live births)	–	–	437	407	100
IMR (Per 1000 children)	146	110	80	64	30
CPR [in %]	10.4	22.8	44.1	48.2	
CPR [in %]	57.3	41.2	26.5	19.5	–
Life expectancy at birth (in years)					
Male	63.9	37.2	54.1	59.7	–
Female	36.2	54.7	60.9	66.9	–

Source: Economic Survey, 2003-04, GOI. Planning Commission.

In Table 25.7, there has been steady decline in the CBR during the 1990s in spite of the fact that the rise in the CPR in the same period has been very slow. CBR is declining during 1951 - 2002 because TFR is also declining in this period from 6.0 to 3.2. It shows that after 1991 family size is getting smaller and women had less pressure about their family size and home base responsibilities like taking care of her children etc. So she is able to take care of her health and nutritional habit and her children too, then her health status is improves and her working capacity is increasing and she is able to give performance more efficiently regarding her family and society as well. For the same period CPR increased from 10.4 per cent in 1951 to 48.2 per cent in 2002 but during the last decade during 1991 to 2002 it increased from 44.1 per cent to 48.2 per cent which is very slow, so here awareness about benefits of increasing CPR needed more which also reflects the family size and health status of female. Samething we found regarding MMR which declined from 437-407 during 1991-2002 and regarding CDR it declined from 25.1-8.1 during 1951-2002, IMR showed declining rate during 1951 to 2002 from 146 to 64 and CMR declined rate for the same period from 57.3 to 19.5. Here one thing is striking that during last decade 1991-2002 regarding all health profile indicators (except life expectancy) rate is getting slower, but more attention and efforts are needed to improve the health profile of India and then we can achieve the

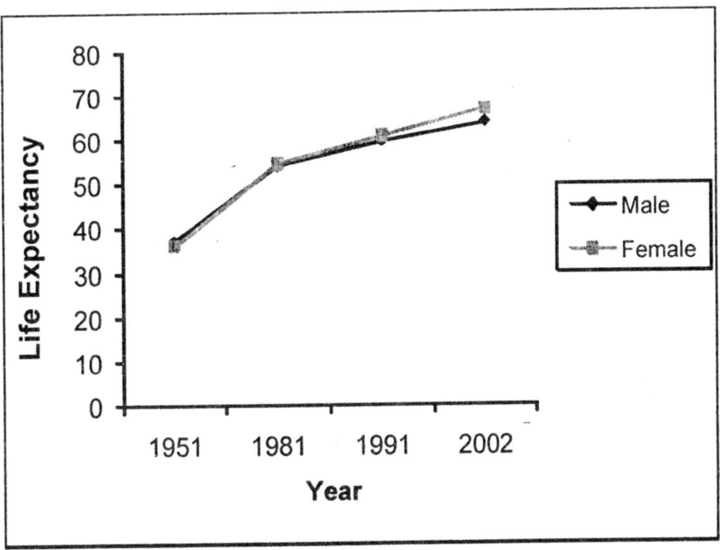

Chart 25.4 : Life Expectancy at Birth for Male and Female in India 1951-2002

target of NPP 2000 which is shown in table-8. Through empowerment, women are able to know about the health related technological advancement and they may provide help to give extension in the health care infrastructure network. This is shown in increasing life expectancy of female in Chart 25.4.

From this chart we find that improving health awareness and positive growth in health indicators are helping more to increasing women life expectancy. During 1951 to 2002 for male it increased from 37.2 to 63.9 and for females it increased from 36.2 to 66.9. In earlier years female life expectancy is less than male but approximately in 1970s it is getting higher than male and after 1991 female life expectancy increase faster than male so the gap between male and female life expectancy is growing, it is shown in chart 25.4. IMR and CMR is one of those indicators, which plays important role to increase life expectancy. IMR in India over the years have declined area and gender-wise IMR are shown in Table 25.9.

Table 25.8: Infant Mortality Rates in India by Gender and Area (1982 – 2002)

Year	Total			Rural			Urban		
	T	M	F	T	M	F	T	M	F
1982-84	105	106	104	114	114	114	66	69	63
1985-87	96	96	97	105	104	106	61	61	60
1988-90	88	89	88	95	96	96	57	58	55
1991-93	78	78	78	85	84	86	50	51	49
1994-96	73	73	73	79	77	80	49	48	45
1997-99	71	70	72	76	76	78	45	45	44
2000-02	66	64	67	72	70	74	42	42	42

Source: Office of the Registrar General of India, Compendium of Fertility and Mortality Indicators 1971 -1997, and SRS Statistical Reports 1998, 1999, 2000 and SRS Bulletin April 2004.

Table 25.9 presents that IMR of India was reduced from 105 to 66 during 1982 - 2002. In early 1980s the male IMR was slightly higher than the females (160 as against 104) and which was reversed towards the end of the twentieth century (64 as against 67 in 2000-2002). The rural urban differences were wider [114 *vs.* 66] showing gradual convergence over the years [72 *vs.* 42] and also the level of male IMR which was higher over the years in urban areas than their females counterparts [69 *vs.* 63 in 1982-84] has come down to the same level [of 42 in 2000 - 2002]. It is reverse in case of rural areas where both IMR for male and female were equal [114 in 1982 - 84] but male IMR has declined faster than female IMR to 70 compared to 74, one reason may be because health care service is increasing faster in urban area and in rural areas lack of awareness about health care and traditional thinking leads people to depend more on superstition, witch doctors and quacks for curative remedies. Generally females are more prone to believe in such remedies and it is also true that they initiate decisions regarding family health care. The decline in Infant mortality rate is much faster in rural areas from 114 to 85 up to 1991-95.

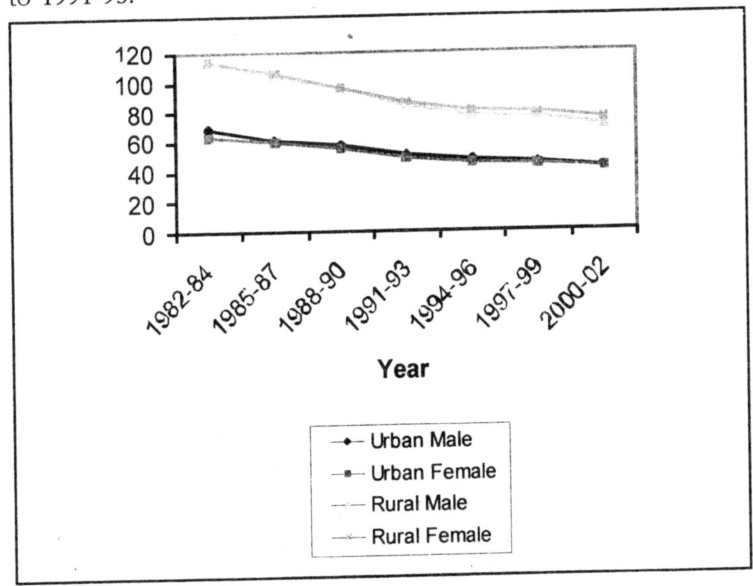

Chart 25.5 : IMR in India by Gender and Area during 1982-2002

In Chart 25.5 the IMR in urban areas shows a gradual consistent decline unlike the trend in rural areas where there was a steeper decline in these rates during 1982 - 96. In 1991 onwards the decline in urban areas IMR appears to be almost linear reflecting a constant rate of decline unlike the urban female growth rates which shows a decline till 1994, which appears to have tapered off gradually between 1994 - 2002, as the decline is very slow. Decline in rural areas IMR regarding both for male and female during 1994 - 99 is getting slower and after this period the decline in male IMR in rural areas is faster than females, therefore, in rural areas gender gap in IMR is getting large, but in urban area during 2000 - 2002 the male and female IMR reached the same level.

One thing is also shown in this chart that the higher level of IMR in Urban area during 1982 - 84 is 69 for male and 63 for female, and in rural areas it was 114 both for male and female, but after 20 years during 2000-02 urban IMR is reached the level of 42 both for male and female but in rural areas IMR is 70 for male and 74 for female. So it is clear from this chart that IMR in rural areas even could not reach the higher level of IMR in urban areas, therefore, more efforts will be needed regarding decline in rural IMR both for males and females, special attention will be needed regarding female. Over the

Table 25.9 : Child Mortality Rates of India by Gender and Area during 1981- 2000

Years	Rural			Urban		
	Total	Male	Female	Total	Male	Female
1981	46	43	48	20	20	21
1986	41	39	43	21	20	22
1991	29	28	30	16	15	17
1996	26	24	28	14	14	15
2000	22	21	23	12	11	12

Source: Office of the Registrar General of India, 1997 and SRS Statistical Reports 2000.

years, male IMR in both areas declined faster than female because male child gets more preference about their health and nutrition and female infanticide is also the main cause for this, we have to change this attitude and for this micro level efforts will be needed.

We found same situation in the context of Child Mortality Rates (CMR). The decline of CMR is shown in Table 25.9, where we discuss area and gender wise CMR between 1981-2000.

Table 25.9 shows that in rural areas decline in CMR is faster than urban areas, within 20 years during 1981 - 2000. In Rural areas decline in male CMR is 43 to 21 per 1000 and for female it is 48 to 23 per 1000, for urban area male CMR declined from 20-11 and it is for female 21 to 12 per 1000. This is because in rural areas many efforts are made by the government to improve their health and nutritional status and these programmes are able to generate awareness among the people, therefore, in initial years where CMR in rural area is very high but over the years gender differences in CMR in both rural and urban area is narrowing, this is shown in Chart 25.6.

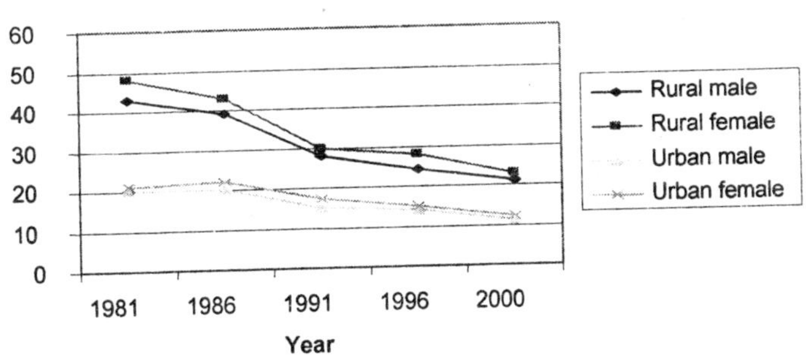

Chart 25.6 : Child Mortality Rates in India by Gender and Area during 1981-2000

Chart 25.6 shows that female CMR are higher than male CMR in both rural as well as urban areas. The declining trend in rural CMR regarding both for male and female during 1981 - 1986 is approximately the same regarding gender gap, but from 1986 - 1991 female CMR declined faster than male CMR but after that declining trend continues although the female rates have slowed down so that gender gap appears to be maximum in 1996, after that male CMR shows gradual decline while female CMR shows a very rapid decline leading to a fast reduction in gender differential. The declining trend in urban CMR between 1981-86 both for males and females appears flats and after that during 1986-91 both show rapid decline at almost the same rate of change, between 1991-96 the decline has slowed down for both and specially male rates declined slower than female, so that gender differential are reduced and during 1999-2000 both rates again show rapid decline at almost constant rates and gender gap also appears to be constant.

An important observation can be made that rural India is about 20 years behind the urban India so far as CMR are concerned. This is so because in urban India in 1981 the male and female CMR were 20 and 21 respectively while in rural India in 2000 they are 21 and 23 respectively and, therefore, it will take a long time to bring down the rural CMR to the levels achieved in Urban CMR in 2000 unless drastic and immediate measures are taken.

Increase in literacy level helps them in taking care about their health and make them aware about the problems, which exist, through high level of IMR and CMR. In Chart 25.7 and 25.8 we clearly understand the link between literacy and IMR and CMR for both rural and urban females.

Chart 25.7 and 25.8 clearly express that when female literacy rates are increasing then IMR and CMR are declining. In rural areas growth of literacy rates is faster than urban areas, therefore, the declining trend of IMR and CMR is also more in rural area in comparison to urban area, as in clear from chart 25.7 and chart 25.8, where CMR [during 1981-1986] and IMR [during 1982-1990] decline with constant rate, but during this period IMR curve is steeper than CMR, this shows that decline in IMR is faster than CMR. During this period literacy rates for females in rural India is also increasing but after 1991 it is increased faster so that after 1991 literacy curve in rural area is much steeper. For the same period CMR declined faster than IMR. In urban area female literacy is increasing approximately at the same rate during same period but regarding IMR it is declining for the same period. After 1986 decline in CMR and IMR increased and this trend continue till 1991 for CMR and 1996 for IMR and

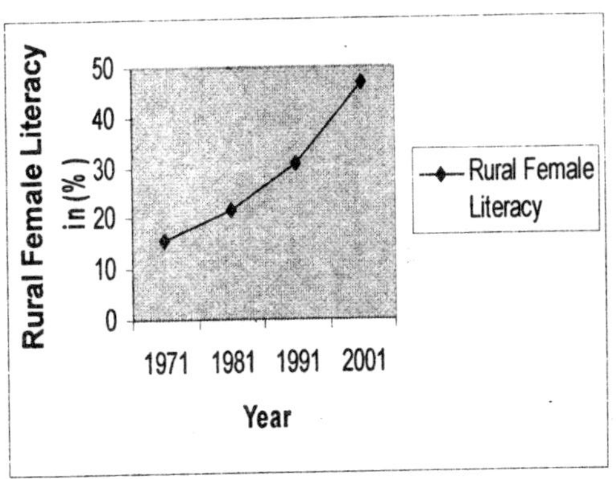

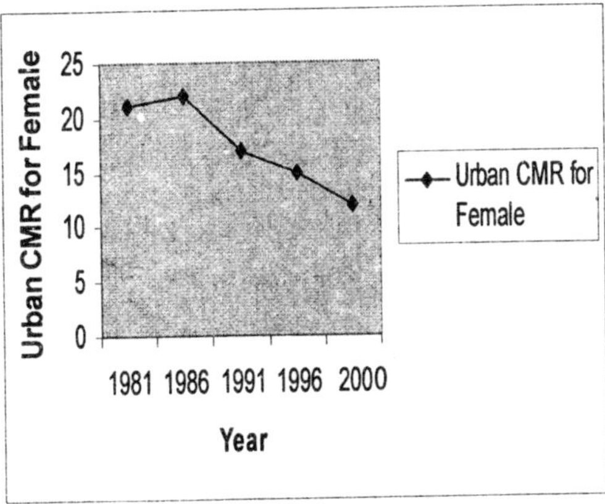

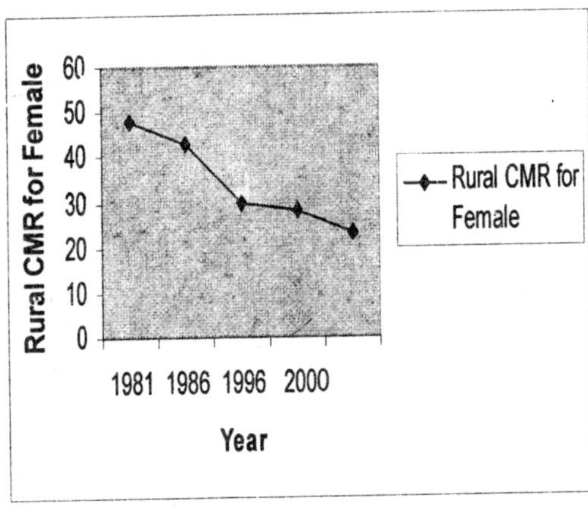

Chart 25.7 : CMR and Literacy

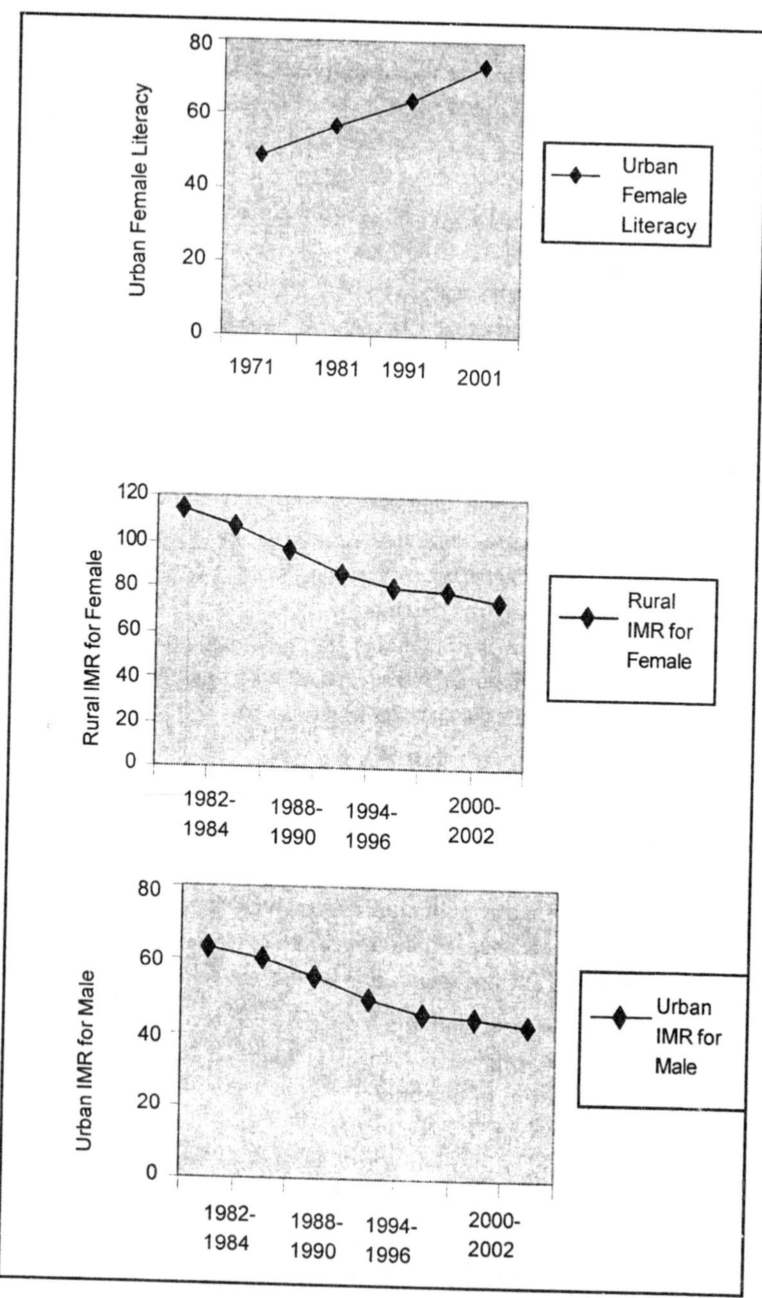

Chart 25.8 : IMR and Literacy

after that once again CMR declined slower till 1996 and after that it declined faster, and for female IMR after 1994 it declined with slow rate, like in rural area.

Here one question shows that when literacy rates are improving faster, then why IMR and CMR not decline as fast as compared to literacy increase. It may be because literacy is not at all the only factor which effect the IMR and CMR, here other factors like traditional beliefs regarding male child preferences, health care services, traditional social and health patterns also affect the IMR and CMR trends. The total government expenditure on family welfare increased from Rs. 4.9 billion in Fifth Plan (1974-79) to Rs. 271.25 billion in the Tenth Plan (2002-07), but still it is just 1.8 per cent of the total plan outlay.[7] Consequent to the adoption of NPP 2000, the village panchayats have become important and motivational measures are to reward the Panchayats and the Zila Parishad for exemplary performance. Panchayats can play an important role in the universalisation of the small family norm and thereby achieving the target of reduction in IMR (30/1000), TFR (2.1), CBR (21), MMR from (100 per lac) and CPR (meets 100 per cent needs) and promoting literacy for completing of primary school for achieving the goal of health for all by 2010.

Nutrition

It is ironic that women should suffer from poor health because they have the responsibility of feeding others in the family. They are the food gatherers and food providers. When it comes to the woman herself, culture ordains that she eats last in the family and poverty constraints that she eats last. This complex web of patriarchy and poverty reflects on the nutritional status of woman.

High prevalence of low birth weight, high morbidity and mortality in children and poor maternal nutrition continue to be major nutritional concerns in India. One-third of babies born in India are of low birth weight (<2.5 kg) and this continues to be the major public health problem. In India poor foetal growth has been attributed to widespread maternal under nutrition.[8] Dietary intakes of energy and protein of rural Indian mothers are known to be low and they are often engaged in high level of physical activity. Now for understanding the nutritional status of Indian women, we have the data related to height in U.P. State in India, which is one of the BIMARU States. The data has shown in Table 25.10, shows strikingly the impact of factors such as education, residence and standard of living in nutritional status with regard to average height of women in different categories.

Table 25.10 : Nutritional Status of Women in U.P. (2001)

Factor	Mean height (cm)	% below 145 cm
Residence		
Urban	151.6	12
Rural	151.1	13.6
Education		
Illiterate	150.6	15.4
Middle school complete	152	9.8
H.S. completed and above	152.9	7.7
Standard of living		
Low	150	17.7
Middle	151.3	12.5
High	153	7.5
India	151.2	13.2

Source: NFHS (1998-99), IIPS (2001).

The height of an adult depends among other factors on consumption during childhood and adolescence. Mothers who are short are more likely to have low birth weight babies. Mothers whose height is below the range of 140-145 cm. are considered nutritionally at risk. The mean height of women in the country is just around 151 cm. but that is only the average. There is large number of women in rural areas (13.6 per cent) who are below 145 cm. in height and in urban area it is only 12 per cent.

In fact women from poor households are twice as likely to suffer from chronic energy deficiency compared to women from better household. It is shown in Table 25.11 where 17.7 per cent women are below 145 cm. height and their standard of living is low, but in high standard of living just only 7.5 per cent females are below 145 cm. and in middle standard of living 12.5 per cent females are below 145 cm. Widespread education should be made to address the issue of intra household imbalance in nutrition as is clear from the Table 25.11 where large percentage of illiterate female (15.4 per cent) are below 145 cm. and those are completed middle school is just 9.8 per cent and those who are below 145 cm height and educated upto High School level are just 7.7 per cent. So it is clear that education positively affects the health status of women.

It is clear from the Table 25.11 that intra-household discrimination in nutritional matter for girls and women are affected from level of education and standard of living, so here we need to improve the standard of living of women through economic empowerment.

III. ECONOMIC EMPOWERMENT

Economic empowerment is usually interpreted as creation of income earning opportunities for women either through intervention or through the operation of market forces. The concept of economics empowerment is a process in which women are enabled to become their own autonomous agents, settling their own agendas, exercising informed choice and gaining greater control of yet to be rooted in programme and sub-programme process.

In the past decade, the number of women living in poverty has increased disproportionately to the number of men, particularly in the developing countries.[9] The,Feminization of poverty has also recently become a significant problem in economic in transition as a short-term consequence of the process of political, economies and social transformation. In addition to economic factors, the rigidity of socially ascribed gender rates and women's limited access to power, education, training and productive resource as well as other emerging factors that may lead to insecurity for families are also responsible. The failure to adequately mainstream a gender perspective in all economic analysis and planning and to address the structural cause of poverty is also a contributing factor.

Women contribute to the economy and to combating poverty through both remunerated and unremunerated work at home, in the community and in the work place. It would not be out of place to mention that the domestic contribution of women is not reflected in National Income Accounting. The economic empowerment of the women is a critical factor in the eradication of poverty. In developing countries the productive capacity of women should be increased through the access to capital, resource, credit, land, technology, information, technical assistance and training so as to raise their income and improve nutrition, education, health care and status within the households.

Three indicators measure the present status of women's economic empowerment.

(a) Women in workforce,

(b) Micro credit facilities, and

(c) Landownership.

Women in Workforce

Women contribute a significant proportion of the labour force. Women participate in the workforce, however, varies across rural and urban areas. Table 25.12 provides the occupational distribution of male and female workers in 1983 to 2004, which is obtained from various rounds of NSSO survey.

It can be seen from Table 25.11 that the direction of change in the occupational distribution of the workforce has been almost identical for genders between 1983 to 2004, although the rate of change have varied considerably. The rural male participation in the primary sector is declining during 1983-2004 from 77.5 per cent to 65.9 per cent as well as for female from offset by this person going either in secondary or in tertiary sector. In rural area secondary sector male workforce increased from 10 per cent to 16 per cent and for female it is from 7.4 per cent to 9.4 per cent. In tertiary sector it increased 87.5 per cent to 84.1 per cent. So in primary sector decline in female work participation is very slow. In comparison to male work participation here we have to understand that these person going either in secondary or in tertiary sector offsets this decline. In rural area secondary sector male work force increased from 10 per cent to 16 per cent and for female it is from 7.4 per cent to 9.4 per cent. In tertiary sector it increased for male from 12.2 per cent to 18 per cent and for female it is increased from 4.8 per cent to 6.5 per cent .So the occupation change in rural area during the period of 1983-04. For male is a shift from primary to tertiary and for female is a shift from primary to secondary sector. It is because in rural areas the attitudes change in society is very slow and growth in the secondary sector due to infusion of agro based activities, therefore, women employment status is affected and many of them are allowed to do work within limited conditions.

Table 25.11 : Percentage Change in the Occupational Distribution of Workers in India 1983 to 2004

Round/ year	Male			Female		
	Primary	Secondary	Tertiary	Primary	Secondary	Tertiary
			Rural area			
38th (1983)	77.5	10	12.2	87.5	7.4	4.8
49th (1993)	75	10.9	14.1	87.2	7.4	5.4
55th (2000)	71.4	12.6	16	85.4	8.9	5.7
60th (2004)	65.9	16	18	84.1	9.4	6.5
			Urban area			
38th (1983)	10.3	34.2	55	31	30.6	37.6
49th (1993)	10.2	34.4	55.4	25.8	30.6	43.6
55th (2000)	6.6	32.8	60.6	17.7	29.3	52.9
60th (2004)	6.3	34.7	59	16.1	30.9	53

Source: Report No. 506: Employment and Unemployment Situation in India, January-June - 2004. 60th Round NSSO Survey.

In urban areas during the period of 1983-04, primary sector occupation males declined from 10.3 per cent to 6.3 per cent and from female it declined from 31 per cent to 16 per cent. Here in urban area female occupation fell in primary sector much faster as compared to their male counterparts. In secondary sector, occupation marginal increased from 34.2 per cent to 34.7 per cent for males and for females from 30.6 per cent to 30.9 per cent, which is also almost same. So there is not a big change in this sector. In tertiary sector for males it increased from 55.0 per cent to 59.0 per cent and for females it increased from 37.6 per cent to 53 per cent, which shows that female work participation in tertiary sector in urban areas increased faster than males this is also shown in charts 25.9 and 25.10.

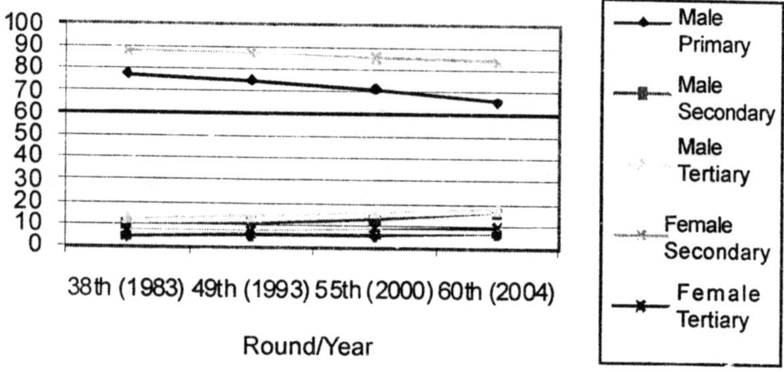

Chart 25.9 : Percentage Change in Occupation in Rural Area by Gender in India 1983-2004

Chart 25.9 shows that during 38th to 49th round NSSO survey rural work participation rate [WPR] in secondary and tertiary sector has increased at almost the same rate except for male WPR in tertiary sector which is slightly better as compared to female WPR in this sector, and for primary sector during this period, male WPR decline faster than females and males shifted from primary to secondary and tertiary sector. This trend continues till 60th round. During 38th to 60th round female WPR decline is very slow in primary sector and so the gender gap is increasing in this sector at very fast rate.

During 49th to 55th round, all WPR increased with consistent rate. Rural female WPR in secondary sector increased faster than that in tertiary sector. After 55th round in rural areas tertiary sector male WPR increased faster than female's, therefore, in this area gender gap has also increased during this period. In secondary sector, male WPR also increased faster than female. Here, one thing is clear that in primary sector change in female WPR is not much expressive as compared to male WPR and another thing is that male shifted more from primary to tertiary sector but after 55th round, male WPR shifted from primary to secondary sector expressively. As far as female WPR is concerned, there is a slow shifting process from primary to secondary sector and in tertiary sector this shift increased consistently but at a slower rate.

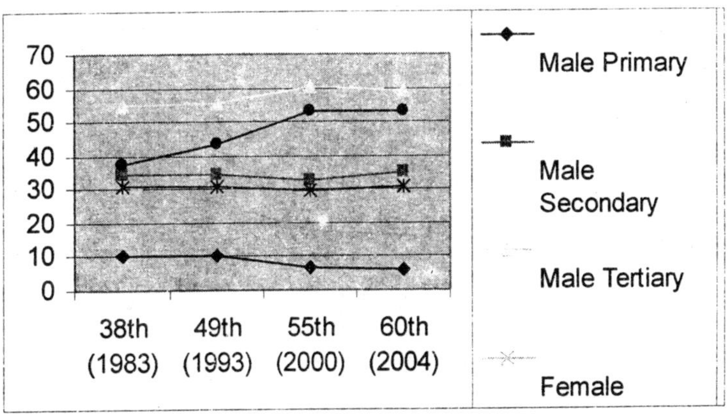

Chart 25.10 : Percentage Change in Occupation in Urban Area by Gender in India 1983-2004

Gender occupational change in urban area is shown in the chart 25.10, where from 38th to 49th round survey of NSSO result show that in this period male WPR in all three sectors shifted with almost the same rate, but for females it is declining and shifted from primary to tertiary sector, because during this period, in tertiary sector females WPR increased but in secondary sector it is almost constant. In tertiary sector WPR increased for females resulting in the decline in gender gap in this area. Also the decline in primary sector female WPR also resulted in the decline in the gender gap in primary sector. During 49th to 55th round survey results same thing is happening but with faster rate, except for secondary sector WPR for both male and female which slightly declined with consistent rate and during 55th to 60th round results the increase in male and female WPR in tertiary sector is slow because in this period the decline in primary sector is also shown and apart from this during this period secondary sector WPR also increased in comparison to past result. In urban area WPR for both male and female has shifted from primary to tertiary sector but this trend is happening more in favour of females. It is because in urban area society is relatively developed in comparison to rural area, therefore, female occupation for this area shifted from primary sector to tertiary sector. In the context of males, there is a significant change according to development, but for females it is higher because female

Table 25.12 : Percentage Change in the Distribution of Labour Status [ps +ss] Categories in India 1983-2004

Area round/year	Male			Female		
Rural area	**Self-employed**	**Regular wage/ salaried**	**Casual**	**Self-employed**	**Regular wage/ salaried**	**Casual**
38th (1983)	60.5	10.3	29.2	61.9	2.8	35.3
55th (2000)	55	8.8	36.2	57.3	3.1	39.6
60th (2004)	57.2	9.3	33.5	61.5	3.8	34.7
Urban area						
38th (1983)	40.9	43.7	15.4	45.8	25.8	28.4
55th (2000)	41.5	41.7	16.8	45.3	33.3	21.4
60th (2004)	44.1	40.6	15.3	44.6	36.2	19.2

Source: Report no.506, Employment and Unemployment situation in India 2004, 60th round NSSO survey.

literacy and opportunity of employment is going up and they are more successful to utilize it. One thing also shown in Table 25.12 is that gender gaps in occupational distribution are closing more quickly in urban area, but in rural area the gap if anything has been increasing although the direction. of occupation change may have been similarly i.e. increasing. In terms of labour categories the scenario is as follows in Table 25.12.

Table 25.12 shows that percentage change in the distribution of labour status categories for all (PS + SS), the direction of change during 1983 to 2004 has been nearly similar for men and women in rural areas, where during 1983-2000 self employment for males declined from 60.5 per cent to 55 per cent and female self employment declined from 61.9 per cent to 57.3 per cent, here both declined at approximately by the same level respectively 4.5 per cent and 4.6 per cent. For the same time period male regular employed also declined from 10.3 per cent to 8.8 per cent but at the same time female regular employed increase from 2.8 per cent to 3.1 per cent which is very small, but it is expressive because this shows that more women are looking for regular employment indicating her sincerity and ability of work, but at the same time percentage of casual labour in rural areas also increased at faster rate. For males it increased from 29.2 per cent to 36.2 per cent and for females it increased from 35.3 per cent to 39.6 per cent. So more women are casualised then men till 2000. One special thing happened during 1983-2000 that in rural areas, the male shifted from self employed and regular employment to casual employment but for females this shift is from self-employment to regular and casual employment.

Table 25.13 : Performance of SEWA Bank (in thousands)

Year	No. of share-holders	Depos-itions	Deposits (Rs.)	Profit (Rs.)
1975 - 76	6.6	10.5	950	30
1985 - 86	9.8	22.2	11279	222
1995 - 96	17.5	44.8	72165	1001

Source: SEWA Report, 1997.

After that during 2000-2004, percentage of self-employment increased for both male and female which are respectively 55.0 per cent to 57.2 per cent and 57.3 per cent to 61.5 per cent and regular employment also increased for both male and female respectively 8.8 per cent to 9.8 per cent and 3.1 per cent to 3.8 per cent. During this period, change in regular employment for both male and female is the same (0.7%) and decline in casual employment for male is from 36.2 per cent to 33.5 per cent and for female is from 39.6 per cent to 34.7 per cent. In rural area gender gap in casual employment is narrowing till 2004. Labour is getting regular or self employed which shows the positive change in the distribution of labour status categories in rural area.

In urban area during 1983-2004 male self-employed have increased but for female it is almost the same and regular employment for male has consistently declined and for female it increased consistently and apart from that casual employment is almost same for male but it declines for female, during 1983-2000 the direction of change in distribution of labour status categories for male self employment increased from 40.9 per cent to 41.5 per cent and for female it declined from 45.8 per cent to 45.3 per cent but here one thing is clear that percentage of self employed female is more than men. This gap is narrowing during 2000-2004, where male self-employment increases from 41.5 per cent to 44.1 per cent while female self-employment continuously declined from 45.3 per cent to 44.6 per cent. But inverse thing happened regarding regular employment where during 1983-2000 male declined from 43.7 per cent to 41.7 per cent and female increased from 25.8 per cent to 33.3 per cent and this trend continued till 2004 where declined in male regular employment is from 41.7 per cent to 40.6 per cent and increase in female regular employment is from 33.3 per cent to 36.2 per cent. Here we need to understand why this thing is happening. It may be because females have become more conscious and serious about employment in comparison to males. Also, the unemployability of females increasing when compared to males since they are literate and educated while there is increasing tendency for illiterate literates among males or it may be because regular employment has fixed demand (regarding time, punctuality, work efficiency and responsibilities) and females are more comfortable with regular routine so they also want the regular employment.

The increasing in unemployability and diminishing opportunities force a shift among males to get self employed Casual employment declined for both male and female but it declined more regarding female which is during 1983-2000 from 28.4 per cent to 21.4 per cent and during 2000-2004 from 21.4 per cent to 19.2 per cent but regarding male during 1983-2000 it is just increase from 15.4 per cent to 16.8 per cent and after that during 2000-04, it again declined from 16.8 per cent to 15.3 per cent for males. Overall in urban area, casual employment declined for female and more female are getting self employment than men in percentage-wise and more men are getting regular employment in percentage-wise than females. But increase in regular employment is more in female than the reduction in males. Thereby bringing the female distribution closer to the distribution for the urban males as is clear from the fact that the percentage of males was 43.7 per cent and 25.8 per cent for female during 38th round, but in the 60th round males were 40.6 per cent compared to 36.2 per cent for females. There is a little evident to suggest that on average things have changed substantially for the better in this area after the movement of women empowerment.

Micro Credit Facilities

In India the poor, particularly women have not received adequate institutional credit. During the past 50 years the government has tried to increase institutional credit to the poor by strengthening the cooperative credit structure through the commercial bank and through regional rural banks. Despite scheme of differential interest rates and 'Finance against Poverty'[10] appears to defy solution.

A few voluntary agencies have taken up the challenge of financing the poor and have achieved noteworthy success. The self-employed women's association (SEWA) is one such agency. According to SEWA[11] all workers who does not have a regular salaried job are self-employed. On this basis, SEWA consider about 93 per cent of all workers in India to be self-employed. A majority of the women workers are self-employed. Self-employed workers generally have only assurance of employment and low income; they have limited capital and assets. Because of the lack of direct access to mainstream markets and limited institutional support, their productivity tend to be low and they suffer high level of poverty and vulnerability. For long financial institution did not reach them.

When the SEWA bank was established poor self-employed women had been facing two major financial problems, lack of working capital and non-ownership of assets, which can be used as collateral for credit. As a result, a large portion of their incomes went towards the payment of interest on working capital and rent for trade equipment. A possible solution to free SEWA members from this vicious circle was to link them with registered banks. In 1973, SEWA made arrangement with some nationalized banks to provide loans to self-employment women with SEWA acting as an intermediary.

Initially, the SEWA bank concentrated on mobilizing self-employed women to deposit their savings and acted as an intermediary to enable depositions to secure loans from nationalized banks. Later, the Bank began advancing money from its own funds to its depositors and since then it has developed into a viable financial unit. As given in Table 25.13, the SEWA bank has grown slowly but steadily over the years with a spurt in growth after the liberalization policies.

The SEWA bank started as an urban bank, but in recent years it has extended its operations to the rural areas, serving the growing rural population of self employed women. As mentioned earlier along with saving, credit, financial services and financial counselling the SEWA bank looks after deposit linked work insurance schemes and housing services.

The women did not have any banking track record on the basis of which financial decision was absent because on account books were maintained by them. Since most women were illiterate, different links of mechanisms like door-to-door service and simpler procedures were required. Of course, the lending risk was high because of the financial vulnerability of the poor women and their group.

The SEWA bank evolved creative solutions to these problems and developed its own blueprint of lending to the poor. The solutions involved assessing their creditability with respect to financial behaviour rather than collateral or security. The emphasis was on group pressure of the trade group. Extension service was made an integral part of all loans.

The challenge was to create banks own track record of women's banking and to design simple and suitable procedure. Linking loans with other much needed support services like insurance, health care, childcare, legal aid and training helped to reduce women's vulnerability. Table 25.14 shows credit has expanded rapidly between 1975-76 to 1995-96 and the repayment rate has been excellent. Every year the members have repaid about 50 per cent of the funds advanced and they become eligible for further advances and most loans have to be repaid in 36 monthly installment. Technical assistance is provided to borrowers when needed to enable them to use their credit productivity by identifying direct sources of purchase of raw materials and equipment links with the market for their goods and services. The bank also helps them acquire skill to make a new products and identify work opportunities. Close monitoring of loans ensures that they are used for economic activities. It facilitates repayments. The facts that loans are advanced to members of the SEWA union, and that SEWA encourages and assists its members to become economically viable, has a significant bearing on their repayment. The rural group itself decides about loans to its members. It also decides about the interest rates. This helps the group to capitalize and manage their own growing funds.

Table 25.14 : Advances and Repayment of SEWA Banks Funds

Year	Women	Advances	Repayment	Repay ment
	Numbers	(Rs.)	(Rs.)	Rate
1975-76	5	680	—	—
1980-81	163	248,975	262,738	96%
1985-86	3366	4,312,237	3,492,911	93%
1990-91	9132	20,015,000	9,324,070	95%
1995-96	11,522	23,020,000	15.525,000	96%

Source: SEWA Report, 1997.

Perhaps the most important indicator of sustainability is the repayment rate, which has been between 93 per cent and 96 per cent. It could be achieved because the credit advanced by the bank led to a real growth of economic enterprise and to higher incomes and ownership of assets. The improved economic conditions translated in to high repayment also because of close monitoring by the bank. The link between the group leader and borrowers and constant contact between the SEWA bank, the cooperative and other villages group.

From the view point of the sustainability of the micro credit programme itself, if the people own the institution and participate in its management, the benefit of the small group guarantee approach will extent to all the operations. From the point of view of the women themselves, their involvement in, and ownership of a successful institution enhances the collective strength and empowerment that comes with organization. Poverty is characterized by not only the lack of finance but also vulnerability, powerlessness and dependence. Collective organization and ownership of wealth helps overcome the psychological consequences of poverty and help challenge the wider structure of society.

Land Ownership

"How can we say we own the land ? How can we own something that will outlive us ? Truly it is not we who own land, rather it is the land which own us."[12] Land rights, particularly in the context of developing countries, are inextricable linked with the right to food, the right to work and a host of other human rights. In many instances, the right to land is bound up with a Community's Identity, its livelihood and thus its very survival. Rural women in many developing and transitional countries are among those with no or very insecure rights to land. Increasing number of women in rural areas bear primary responsibilities for agricultural production. Studies[13] by RDI underline the importance of women's secure access to land, with its relationship to gains in agricultural productivity, family welfare (particularly child nutrition) and women's empowerment.

In rural areas married women have access to land for farming through their husbands, but in the event of a divorce or widowhood, they may continue to use the land but will not inherit control of the land. Most women go back to their villages where they are dependent on a male kin for access to land. Special attention should be paid to the right of women to land. In many societies women are excluded from owning property, including land or they do not enjoy the same rights as the men. In marriage and family relations women's right to property is often subject to the authority of the husband or father. Ensuring equal rights to property translated into economic empowerment and has a direct bearing on the status of women. Lack of rights and security regarding land is one of the most serious obstacles to increasing the agricultural food production and income of rural women. For the past few years Food and Agricultural organization of the United Nations (FAO's) Gender and Development service[14] has addressed the issue of land tenure and women's right in various ways. An important task has be advising governments around the world on how to make agrarian reform programmes more gender sensitive, government needs to recognize women as farmers and landowners, and this is important when land tenure reforms are initiated.

The first task is to create awareness within organization, other development agencies and governments, about the importance of recognizing women's right to land. Here we needs to incorporate the gender aspect in all activities regarding agriculture and land tenure, both when working with governments and in the villages women also needs to be included in the training meetings and extension services. If women are not present in the meetings where the right to land and other resources is discussed and decisions taken, how will they know their rights.

Here in Table 25.15, we discuss about the Indian female status regarding land-ownership. In this Table we found that in total land holding women shares are just only around 10 per cent which is very low and 5,457 women land owners have land below 0.5 (hac.) land area and these owners are 11.34 per cent of the total number, this area ownership by women is highest among the others like 9.16 per cent, 8.78 per cent etc. so we can say that in India this issue could not get widely considered. There is need to raise this issues because women wants as such a kind of security which encourage them to be decision-

Table 25.15 : Distribution of Number and Area of Operational Holdings by Gender in India, 1995–96

Sl. No.	Holding size (ha.)	Sex	Number	% holding	Area	Average area per ha.
1	Below 0.5	Male	42578		10247	0.24
		Female	5457	11.34%	1151	0.21
		Total	48127		11414	0.24
2	0.5-1.0	Male	20911		14152	0.72
		Female	2112	9.16%	1533	0.73
		Total	23052		16707	0.72
3	1.0-2.0	Male	19713		27991	1.42
		Female	1900	8.78%	2688	1.41
		Total	21643		30722	1.42
4	2.0-3.0	Male	8873		21291	2.4
		Female	739	7.68%	1759	2.38
		Total	9628		23090	2.4
5	3.0-4.0	Male	4308		14751	3.42
		Female	316	6.80%	1081	3.42
		Total	4633		15863	3.42
6	4.0-5.0	Male	2627		11632	4.43
		Female	176	6.27%	777	4.43
		Total	2809		12438	4.43
7	10.0-20.0	Male	1079		14251	13.21
		Female	55	4.80%	742	13.14
		Total	1142		15089	13.21
8	20.0 and above	Male	244		7709	31.6
		Female	9	3.40%	331	37.49
		Total	262		9074	34.58
9	All sizes	Male	104354		150219	1.44
		Female	11012	9.53%	11715	1.06
		Total	11580		163357	1.41

Source: All India Agricultural Census 1995-96,GOI, Publication Year 2004.

makers and avoid many hurdles which exist in their way. In India the distribution of number and area of operational holdings is not very much of gender sensitive, for this purpose we use the given Table 25.15.

In situations of restricted mobility, leading to restricted choices, as in large parts of northern India, women may prefer to abide by the rules and regulations of marriage, as survival and protection is better assured by doing so. They often prefer stability to autonomy. Women in Rajasthan for example, prefer to forego their land claims keeping in mind the considerably lower status and power their husbands would then enjoy in their natal villages relatives to their own.[15] In north-west India it was found that though dependent on their relations with men for control over lands rather than feeling excluded, women continued to see land as a joint resource, with their contribution leading to male prestige and in turn their own. Perhaps this is also related to the fact that women are more vulnerable to poverty in the absence of a fit adult male than men are in the absence of a fit adult female.

It is the socially nature of land within kinship and marriage system its strong association within culture identity and symbolism that makes it different from other aspects of gender inequality whether violence, sexual harassment, poorer literacy or health status and also different from other resources. The area of land rights becomes more ambiguous. Yet more significant increasing land scarcity, combined with diversified livelihood systems as well as the broader understanding of food security, land alone cannot give women work and income, improve their status or even ensure household food security. This has to be integrated with other opportunities as well as conscious attempts in the rural economy and consequently the gendered valuations of work and worth.

IV. FINDINGS

The study of women empowerment in its social, economic and political dimensions leads us to the following findings and conclusions:

1. After 73rd amendment women are becoming politically, conscious and try to take advantage of power to solve their problems. Many women are now taking part increasingly in

local development activities and also involved in decision-making process, as is evident from the case study cited.

2. Revamping of legal procedure to ensure gender quality is viewed as equivalent to policy and restructuring for providing a better status of womanhood. Thus to reduce labour hours lost and also reduce expenditure on violence victims along with the emotional, mental and physical status of women and children, enhancement of legal empowerment becomes imperative.
3. So far as social empowerment is concerned, literacy rates in India since independence have been increasing while the gender gap has started falling since 1981 and the tremendous increase by almost six times in female literacy has been the main factor towards increasing the male literacy, and reducing gender gap. It was also found that between 1971-2001, growth in literacy rates in the rural areas have shown a greater increase compared to the urban areas. Female literacy is also increasing faster than male during 1971-2001 as is evident from Table 25.4, and because of this gender gap is reducing. Here one thing we found that gender gap is reducing faster in rural areas as compared to urban areas, it is because female literacy increased faster in rural areas as compared to urban area whereas it increased with steady growth as it is evident from chart 25.2.
4. Female dropout declined faster than male because girl enrollment is increasing more than boys; it is evident from chart 25.4 and Table 25.7. This is because of growing awareness through empowerment.
5. Improving health facilities and declining trend in CBR, CDR, TFR, MMR, CMR, IMR are helping to increase life expectancy in India and especially after 1981 female life expectancy increased faster than males it is evident from Table 25.8 and chart 25.4. These are the effect of female consciousness regarding health, which is essential for them.

6. Decline in IMR and CMR is faster in rural areas as compared to urban areas. It is because rural literacy rates increased faster in rural area as compared to urban area but only literacy is not influencing the health status; It is evident from Chart 25.7 and 25.8 where after 1991 literacy rates increase with fast rate but decline in IMR and CMR is not as fast as increase in literacy rates, this shows that apart from literacy there are other factors like health care facilities, nutrition standard of living etc. which also affect them as is evident from Table 25.11.

7. As far as economic empowerment is concerned, in urban areas society is relatively developed in comparison to rural areas, therefore, female occupation shift from primary to tertiary in urban areas, due to increase in literacy and awareness and opportunities. But in rural area it shifts from primary to secondary due to orthodox attitude in the family and also may be because of infusion of agro based activities. It is evident from Chart 25.9 and 25.10.

8. We also found that female is getting regular employment faster than men. The increasing unemployability and diminishing opportunities force a shift among males to get self-employed as is evident from Table 25.13.

9. Micro credit facilities are able to improve the status of women as is evident from Table 25.13 and 25.14 where SEWA Bank is doing good job to the women, by the women, and for the women.

10. Lastly, we found that land ownership is essential for womanhood because ensuring equal right to property is translated into economic empowerment, as this increases self esteem and status and endows a sense of financial independent among the females. Unfortunately, in India, this ownership issue is highly based in favour of males and hence assumes greater importance as a step towards the empowerment of women.

Conclusion

If women receive greater education and training, they will earn more, which they can use for the education and health of their children, as opposed to men, who often spend it on undesirable things. As a result of this, as women rise in economic status, they will gain greater social standing in the household and the area; and will have greater voice. When women gain confidence and consciousness, they will make stronger claims to their entitlements—gaining further training, better access to credit and higher incomes and command attention of authorities need arises.

Again as women's economic power grows it will be easier to overcome the tradition of "son preference" and thus put an end to the evil of female infanticide. As a result of this, son preference declines and acceptance of violence declines, families will be more likely to educate their daughters, and age at marriage will rise. When women are better nourished and marry later, they will be healthier, more productive and will give birth to healthier, more productive and will give birth to healthier babies. Only through action to remedy discrimination against women, we can have the vision of India's independence—an India where all people have the chance to live healthily and productive lives be realized.

Thus it is obvious from the analysis of the measures taken for empowerment of women that due to the social upsurge and change in attitudes manifesting themselves into various forms and ways and partly due to the accompanying social economic political and legal measures, the women in India has started acquiring a better status in the society, with the march of time and progress the women has gradually come to acquire considerable emancipation from the complexities and ills with which she has been suffering for long. Today's women has better acceptability and respectability, better status of equalities with men, better rights and privileges, better opportunities and avenues in all spheres of national life.

Suggestions

In the light of the above facts, it is necessary to discuss some strategies required for improving the status of Indian women, some of them are :

- Every educational institution should take up active programmes for women's development. All teachers and instructors to be trained as agents of women's empowerment.
- Gender sensitization programmes should be developed for poverty alleviation. In this aspect last year (2005) government had taken a step in the form of national Rural Employment Guarantee Act, where guaranteed employment to an individual ensures Rs. 6,000 per annum entitlement. A majority of labourers employed under this is likely to be women, because more percentage of females is employed in primary sector (see Table 25.12). On the other hand, if the guarantee is limited to "100 days per household" it is possible that women will be marginalised. If individual entitlements are replaced with household entitlements, there may be a case of introducing a reservation for women of at least 50 per cent of all labourers employed in every block.
- In order to create a grater confidence and to motivate rural parents to send girls to schools without fear of sexual harassment preference should be given to recruitment and appointment of women teachers in the rural schools. Preferably from rural background like Anganwadi, Asha's and programmes by government, for creating awareness about health and education.
- Maternal nutrition intervention programmes need to examine the role of micro nutrient rich foods to improve preconception maternal nutritional status of rural young girls may be more beneficial than those during pregnancy.
- Most problems related to IMR and CMR will need awareness regarding mothers milk feeding, as supplementation cannot be proper and permanent solution.
- While it may be difficult to increase age at marriage in rural areas, postponement of first pregnancy appears to be a feasible, and achievable goal to ensure better reproductive health.

- Policy of free education for girls has long-term health benefits, apart from other benefits, as it will prompt delay in the age at marriage and conception.

It cannot be denied that formulating appropriate programmes and strategies are essential but effective implementation is the key to success. Efforts are necessary for exploring the utility education and employment, nutritional and health awareness among young girls especially in the rural areas, to ensure a better quality of life for the next generation.

Lastly we can say that empowerment is a process and not a product. The outcome of empowerment would then be a redistribution of power. Therefore, the empowerment process is one where women find "time and space" of their own for their own and begin to reexamine their lives critically and collectively for a better tomorrow.

ACKNOWLEDGEMENTS

We owe sincere thanks to Dr. S.K. Sashi Kumar and Dr. M.M. Rehman, Senior fellows, V.V.G. N.L.I. Noida for their guidance in preparation of this paper.

NOTES

1. See for example, Jha V.S., Mehta A., Menon L., *Status of Indian Women: Crises and Conflicts in Gender Issues*, Vol. 1, Kanishka Publication, New Delhi, 1998, and De, U.K., Ghosh B.N., *Issues on Empowerment of Women*, 2004, Mohit Publication, New Delhi.
2. Report of Election Commission 2004.
3. Ghosh, B.N,. (2002), *Rural Women Leadership*, Mohit Publication, New Delhi.
4. Bhattacharya, M., *Empowerment and Development, Confusing Association Perspective in Political Science*, Academic Staff College, University of Burdwan [1997] pp. 3-10.
5. Area Networking and Development Initiatives, Google.Com
6. Velkaff, A., Adlakha, A., *Women's Health in India*, U.S. Deptt. of Commerce Bureau of the Census 1998.
7. Health Information of India 2003, p. 93.
8. Gopalan, C., 1994, Low Birth Weight : Significant and Implications. Nutrition in Children, Developing Countries Concerns, New Delhi.

9. Sharma, U., (1980), Women Work and Poverty in Northwest India, Tavistock Publication, London.
10. De, U.K., Ghosh, B.N., 2004, *Issues on Empowerment of Women*, Mohit Publication, New Delhi.
11. Dantawala, M.L., Visaria, P., 1998, *Social Change Through Voluntary Action*, Sage Publication, New Delhi.
12. Paraphrasing Macling Dulag, *Tribal Chieftan of the Kalings*, the Cordillira Mountains, and Philippines.
13. Rao, N., 2005, "Gender Equality, Land Rights and Household Food Security," *EPW*, Jan. 18, Vol. XL, No. 25, A Sameeksha Trust Publication. *http://In web18, world bank.org/sar/sa.nsffo. 22/01/06.*
14. Sjoblom, D., 1999, *Land Matters: Social Relation and Livelihoods in a Bhil Community in Rajasthan, India*, University of East Anglia, Norwich.
15. Dreze, J., Sen, A., 1995, *India : Economic Development and Social Opportunity*, Oxford University Press, New Delhi.

REFERENCES

Bhattacharya, M. (1997), *Empowerment and Development: Confusing Association Perspective in Political Science*, Academic Staff College, University of Burdwan, pp. 3-11.

Behar, A., Aiyar, Y. (2003), "Networks of Panchayat Women", *Economic and Political Weekly*, Nov. 22, p.4936, Vol. XXXVIII, No. 47, A Sameeksha Trust Publication.

Chatterjee, M. and Vyas, J., (2002), "Organizing Insurance for Women Workers in the Unorganized Sector" *Work Security and Social Protection*, Editors: Renana J. Subrahmanyam, R.K.A., p.74.

Clots, F.I. (2005), *Are Female Leaders Good for Education: Evidence from India*, Deptt. of Economics, London School of Economics.

Dantawala, M.L.; Sethi, H. and Visaria, P. (1998), *Social Change Through Voluntary Action*, Sage Publication, New Delhi /Thousand Oaks/London, p. 146.

De, U.K. and Ghosh, B.N. (2004), *Issues on Empowerment of Women*, Mohit Publication, New Delhi.

Dreze, J., and Sen, A. (1995), *India: Economic Development and Social Opportunity*, Oxford University Press, New Delhi.

Dreze, J.; Deaton A., (2002), "Poverty and Inequality in India", *Economic and Political Weekly*, Sep. 7, 2002, p. 3729.

Dreze, J. (1990), *Windows in Rural India*, DERP No. 26, London School of Economics, London.

Ghosh, B.N., (2002), *Rural Women Leadership*, Mohit Publication, New Delhi.

Gopalan, C. (1994), "Low Birth Weight: Significant and Implications", *Nutrition in Children, Developing Countries Concerns*, New Delhi.

Health Information of India, 2003.

Indianngos.com. (Statistics related to education), 4/1/2006.

Inweb18.worldbank.org, 22/01/2006.

Jha, V.S.; Mehta A. and Menon, L. (1998), *Status of Indian Women: Crises and Conflicts in Gender Issues*, Vol. 1, Kanishka Publication, New Delhi.

Kishwar, M. (1997), "Yes to Sita, No to Ram: The Continuing Hold of Sita on Popular Imagination", *Manushi Issues* 98.

Mehta, A.C., (2005), "Drop-out Rates at Primary Level: A Note Based on Dise 2003-04 and 2004-05 Data", National Institute of Educational Planning and Administration, 17-B, Shri Aurobindo Marg, New Delhi.

Ministry of Agriculture, Agricultural Census 1995-1996, GoI, 2004.

Ministry of Finance, *Economic Survey*, Various Years (during 2001-2004).

Ministry of Human Resource Development, *Annual Reports* of Various Years, Deptt. of Education.

Ministry of Human Resource Development, *Annual Report 2002-2003*, Deptt. of Women and Child Development, , GoI.

Mukhopadhyay, S. (2003), *Status of Women Under Economic Reform : The Indian Case*, IDRC Publication.

National Council of Educational Research and Training (1999), *Sixth All India Educational Survey*.

National Human Development Report, 2001, Planning Commission, Government of India.

National Family Health Survey-2 Data during 1998-1999.

National Policy for the Empowerment of Women, 2001.

National Sample Survey Organisation (NSSO), Various Rounds Survey.

Panda, S. "Infant and Child Mortality in India, A Comparative Study in Three Selected States", 2004-05, IIPS.

Planning Commission, *Tenth Five-Year Plan Document of India, 2005.*

Rao, N. (2005), "Gender Equality Land Rights and Household Food Security", *Economic and Political Weekly*, June 18, Vol. XL, No. 25, A Sameeksha Trust Publication.

Rao, S. (2001), *Nutritional Status of Indian Population*, J. Biosci, Vol. 26, No. 4, Indian Academy of Sciences, pp. 481-489.

Registrar General of India, *Census of India, 2001.*

Registrar General of India, SRS, *Various Years Data*, New Delhi.

Report of Election Commission, 2004.

Sharma, U. (1980), *Women Work and Poverty in North West India*, Tavistok Publication London.

Sjoblom, D. (1999), *Land Matters: Social Relations and Livelihoods in a Bhil Community in Rajasthan*, India, University of East Anglia, Norwich.

Solutions@maps of India.com, 18/01/2006.

Srivastava, N. (2004), *And Promises to Keep : The Challenges of Gender Disparities in India's Economic Development.*

Velkoff, A.V. (1998), *Women's Education in India*, U.S. Deptt. of Commerce, Bureau of the Census.

Velkaff, A. and Adalakha, A. (1998), *Women's Health in India*, U.S. Deptt. of Commerce, Bureau of the Census.

World Bank (2001), *World Development Report 2000-2001*, "Attacking Poverty", Oxford University Press, New York.

www.education.nic.in (For Educational Statistics Compiled by IAMR), 4/01/2006.

www.ncert.nic.in (Main outcomes of 6th All India Educational survey), 17/01/2006.

www.india budget.nic.in, 18/01/2006.

www.*idrc.ca/en/ev*-58035-201-1-DOtopic.html, 22/01/2006.

www.manushi_india.e.org, 18/02/2006.

www.globalissues.org/Human Rights/Women Rights. asp, 19/02/2006.

INDEX